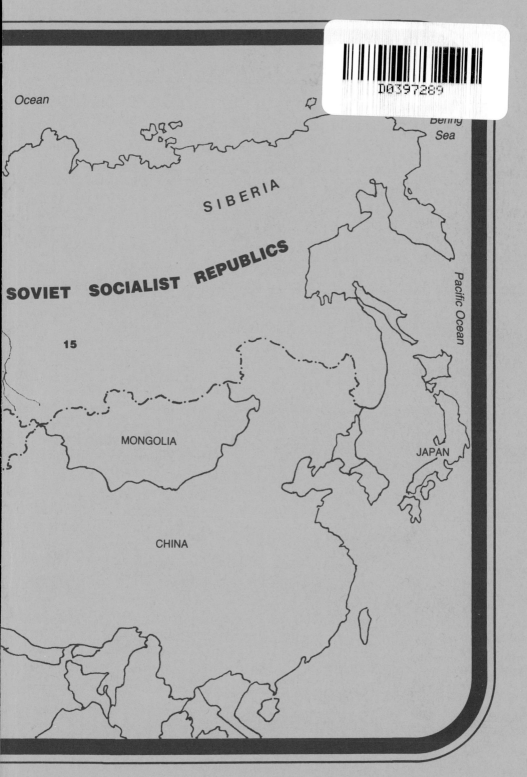

5500

Ocean

Bering
Sea

SIBERIA

SOVIET SOCIALIST REPUBLICS

15

Pacific Ocean

MONGOLIA

JAPAN

CHINA

The Fall of the Russian Empire

THE FALL
of the
RUSSIAN
EMPIRE

Donald James

G. P. PUTNAM'S SONS   NEW YORK

Published simultaneously in Canada by
General Publishing Co. Limited, Toronto

Library of Congress Cataloging in Publication Data

James, Donald
    The fall of the Russian Empire.

    I. Title.
PR6060.A453F3   1982   823′.914   81-21175
ISBN 0-399-12689-9   AACR2

Printed in the United States of America

Contents

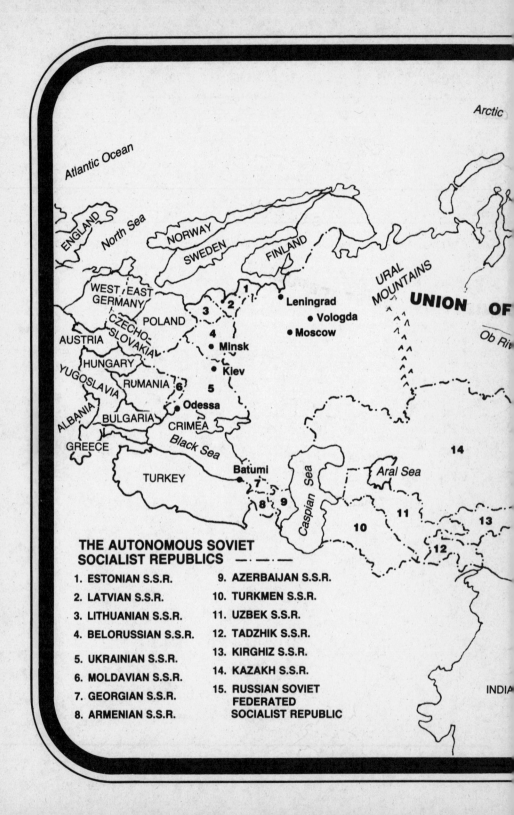

THE AUTONOMOUS SOVIET
SOCIALIST REPUBLICS — - —

1. ESTONIAN S.S.R.

2. LATVIAN S.S.R.

3. LITHUANIAN S.S.R.

4. BELORUSSIAN S.S.R.

5. UKRAINIAN S.S.R.

6. MOLDAVIAN S.S.R.

7. GEORGIAN S.S.R.

8. ARMENIAN S.S.R.

9. AZERBAIJAN S.S.R.

10. TURKMEN S.S.R.

11. UZBEK S.S.R.

12. TADZHIK S.S.R.

13. KIRGHIZ S.S.R.

14. KAZAKH S.S.R.

15. RUSSIAN SOVIET
FEDERATED
SOCIALIST REPUBLIC

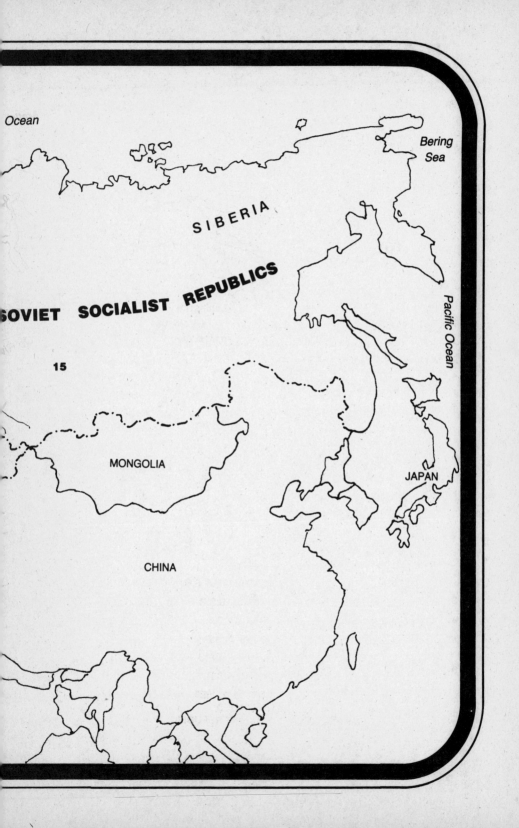

Ocean

SIBERIA

Bering
Sea

SOVIET SOCIALIST REPUBLICS

Pacific Ocean

15

MONGOLIA

JAPAN

CHINA

For Robert Frank Wheal

Prologue

The château stood above the village, a cluster of turrets and square *pigeonniers*. A pair of white doves circled it, brilliant in the sunshine. I drove under the clock tower and stopped the car in the cobbled courtyard. On both sides arched openings in stone barns gave into a darkness where cattle stirred.

As I got out of the car a man descended the stone staircase ahead. He was in his sixties, slightly built. I crossed the courtyard towards him. "Monsieur le Marquis de Nerval?"

"Yes." He inclined his head with grave politeness.

"I wrote to you to ask if I might come and see you," I said. "My name is Georges de Nerval."

We shook hands.

"Georges de Nerval," he shook his head, smiling now. "Yet you are not French?"

"No," I said, "I'm Russian. I was born in Moscow during the events of the nineteen eighties. *That* much I know."

"And you've come here in the hope of discovering more."

"If possible."

"Come in and take an *apéritif*," he said. "It just may be that I have something for you."

We entered the cool flagged hallway. I looked curiously at the faded elegance around me. No far-off bell tolled in my memory, no distant

11

mirror glinted a sunlit shaft of childhood. The portraits on the walls were of small men with fair hair and light eyes. There was no trace of my dark complexion, my height, my Slavonic features.

Like so many of Russia's children I have never known who my parents were. Born amidst the cataclysmic events of the nineteen eighties in the former Soviet Union, I spent my childhood in refugee camps and orphanages. I have a name which I have no reason to believe is my own; I have an education provided by an anonymous refugee trust. But I am not alone in needing roots.

I turned from my examination of the portraits on the walls. Monsieur de Nerval was smiling wryly. "We bear the same name Monsieur," he said, "but . . ." he looked from me to the portraits . . ."no, I see no help there."

We walked out onto the terrace and sat down.

"When I received your letter," he said, "I was naturally curious. I believe myself to be the last of the de Nerval line."

He looked out across the rolling hills. "But Moscow is far away, the de Nervals have been small country gentlemen for centuries. I can find no evidence that we were great travelers." He paused. "So one thinks of military service. There was, it's true, a de Nerval in the army of Napoleon. But he died at Iena, before the Emperor's Russian campaign."

I felt my disappointment acutely. And strangely enough I could detect, too, a certain sadness in the Marquis.

"You're saying, Monsieur, that the de Nerval family has no Russian connections whatsoever."

He pursed his lips. "There is one curious item. A fact which led me to encourage you to come here today."

I sat forward in my seat.

"Upstairs in the attic," he said, "I have an old traveling trunk. It was sent here many years ago by a firm of German lawyers on the death of an old lady who, it appears, used the name de Nerval. The accompanying letter from the lawyers has been lost."

"An old lady?"

"Too old to be your mother."

"And the trunk—what connections might that have with me?"

"The trunk is full of documents. I am unable to tell what connection it might have with you," he smiled. "I am after all unable to read its contents, Monsieur. They are all in Russian."

I could have shouted with joy. A trunkful of Russian documents in a house in central France, a house that bore the name I bore.

A few minutes later we sat in an enormous beamed attic. Sunlight pierced the gaps in the roof tiles and fell on dusty tables stacked high with old books, frameless portraits and chipped crockery. The empty case of a grandfather clock stood between huge walnut cupboards of a century earlier. Delicate, gold-leafed chairs with broken legs leaned against each other for support.

The Marquis opened the shutter on a mansard window and led me across the flood of sunlight to a table on which an old traveling trunk lay. Its curved top was covered in frayed dark-blue leather and carried a no longer recognizable emblem, once stamped in gold.

I opened the trunk. Inside were packets of letters tied with string, stained typescripts of what looked like interviews conducted God knows how long ago—memoirs, diaries and old Soviet official documents.

I stayed two days at the château de Nerval reading through the bundles of papers in the old blue-leather traveling trunk. At the end of my time at the château I had decided to write this book.

The diaries, interviews and typescript memoirs on which the following account is based were assembled by a survivor of the great events of the 1980s which finally swept away the Soviet Union. For me the story must have a particular poignancy. In the course of reading the documents in that battered trunk I discovered who I was.

One strange, almost flinching fragment among the documents can be said with certainty to be written by the original collector, by the woman I now believe to have been my mother. I have let it stand as the introduction to this book:

Believe me, Brothers, I am a nobody. But I have brought these documents together as an act of homage to a man who was never my husband but who was the father of my child. It is the only way I can conceive of doing homage to *all* men who lived through the Sovietschina, the long days of the Soviet Union.

Some say the Russian cold has shaped the history of our land. Napoleon, they instance, or Hitler's summer-clad armies. But the truth goes deeper—to the bone. O *Rodina,* O Mother Russia, your role is sacrifice. No land like ours has been called upon by history—no land like ours has the deep will to respond.

Believe me, Brothers.

On the Eve

Chapter One

THIS IS A book that can start at any one of a hundred points in the history
of Russia. It could begin over a thousand years ago when Rurik of
Novgorod founded the first Russian dynasty. Or nearly a millennium later
with the dying Lenin's prophetic denunciation of Joseph Stalin. But for no
other reason than that the papers in the traveling trunk start it here, let it
begin on an April evening in Leningrad in 1986 with a young girl walking
along the embankment of the River Neva.

Her name is Zoya Densky. At the time her account of these events
begins she is seventeen, a tall, pretty Leningrad teenager who has just
started her first year in pre-medical school. With her blond hair and fine
features it is not difficult to imagine an ancestry which orginated with
Leningrad's Scandinavian neighbors. Follow her now as, arms linked with
her friend as Russian girls do, she walks along the Winter Palace
embankment. Spring, moving north across the European continent, has
barely touched Leningrad. A light fall of snow sparkles in the lamplight on
the Kirovsky Bridge, militiamen still wear long winter overcoats and high
fur *shapkas*. But for the last week the ice has been melting on the River
Neva and Zoya Densky is already thinking of warm evenings and student
dances in University Square. She has no reason to imagine that, for her,
tonight will put an end to all such dreams.

How could I? [she asks in her account of that evening] I knew nothing of politics. I was a patriot, proud of my city above all things, proud of its past as the capital of old Russia, the birthplace of the October Revolution and the site of the Great Siege in the Patriotic War against Fascism. I was interested in the things that interest any girl of my age—a pair of Western jeans, music, boys . . .

I no longer remember where we were going that night, my friend and I. To the Poet's Café, I suppose, which is where we usually spent our Saturday nights, ogling the boys, and blushingly contemptuous if they dared make an approach.

I know we had passed the Admiralty before we were aware of people bustling past us, talking in high voices. By the time we drew level with the monument some people were running, slipping in the snow, supporting each other, but hurrying on. Because it was the Soviet Union in the mid-eighties we immediately thought some shop had received a consignment of Hungarian shoes, or Czech dresses. We began to run, too, infected by the excitement in the air. Whatever it was, was happening in St. Isaac's Square.

So we came to the Blue Bridge where the crowd had gathered. And as we joined them, breathless, laughing, we were aware of a change of mood. People turned angrily and told us to be quiet, to show respect.

I lost touch with my friend as I pushed and eased my way forward. There was no laughter here. I was among silent figures, some of them, I noticed, with tears running down their cheeks.

"What is it?" I asked the people around me. "What's happening?"

"A workers' demonstration," someone said as I pushed closer. Over the heads of the watching crowd I could see forty, perhaps fifty men on the Blue Bridge itself, pacing in a wide circle, their hands behind their backs, a placard round each man's neck. And on each placard a price—a hundred rubles, eighty, ten . . .

"In the old days before the Revolution," a voice whispered next to me, "the Blue Bridge was the main serf market in the city."

Did I understand that these men were saying that they were the serfs of our own Soviet system? Did I understand that they were saying that the *vlasti,* the men of power and importance, were still a race apart with their corrupt and privileged existence, and that the workers were their serfs?

I think I only really understood the silent sadness of the men on the bridge. Part of the crowd behind me had begun to sing quietly, an old haunting song that perhaps I'd heard somewhere in childhood. It touched me deeply and I was moved to tears as I watched the slow pacing of the demonstrators.

Then from the far side of the circle of demonstrators a man stepped out of line and walked toward a rough podium of wooden crates which had been placed in the middle of the Blue Bridge. To this day I can remember the shock of recognition as that short, broad-shouldered figure climbed onto the wooden crates. As the crowd fell silent, it was my father who prepared to address them.

"Citizens of Leningrad," he began, "Comrade citizens of this Hero City, our protest tonight is on behalf of all who are suffering at the hands of the distant bureaucrats who run our lives. It is on behalf of the women who spend hours of every day of their lives standing in line for such *luxuries* as a light bulb or a packet of washing powder. It is on behalf of their husbands unable, for fear, to raise their voices against the corruption of official trade union leaders with their dachas, their whores and their Western clothes. It is on behalf of the young people of Leningrad for whom there is no future unless they are prepared to join the very ranks of the corrupt bureaucrats themselves. But most of all this protest, the first I promise you of many, is on behalf of the men, our worker comrades, illegally exiled or enslaved for claiming those very rights that are guaranteed to us by the Soviet Constitution . . ."

My attention was so riveted by what my father was saying that I hardly felt the insistent nudging of the old man next to me.

"Get along home, girl," he said urgently. "There's going to be trouble." He was looking toward the cathedral as he spoke. I turned my head quickly in the same direction. A line of men in helmets and long green overcoats was moving across the square. Behind them a second line of KGB guards was emerging from the cathedral shadows.

With what seemed a single fearful intake of breath, the crowd drew back. My father continued to speak as people turned away and began to surge past me.

I fought against the flow of the crowd, glimpsing between swiftly moving heads the two lines of KGB guards moving toward the demonstrators. Thrusting people aside, I clawed my way forward shouting my empty warnings to my father.

Of course the men had seen the guards. But they stood their ground as the crowd streamed back toward the river.

Then the guards struck. With silent determined fury they fell on the demonstrators, clubbing them around the head and shoulders with long black batons. I ran forward slipping, screaming as my father was pulled down, but I was thrown back by other guards who had now formed a double line between us and the grunts and shouts and bloodied snow on the bridge. Between the green greatcoats I caught snatches of a brutality which will live with me forever. I saw my father clubbed where he lay. I saw a workmate of his whom I recognized, kicked to the ground by a ring of guards as he tried again and again to scramble to his feet. I saw their loose-chained dogs tearing at fallen men.

When the trucks came I watched helplessly as the guards loaded the broken men. Hardly one of the demonstrators could stand unaided after five violent minutes.

I barely remember the other guards marching away. I found myself sitting on a worn carriage stone at the entrance to the cathedral yard with the old man patting my shoulder and advising me to go home. It was vital, he kept saying, to tell my mother as soon as possible. Demonstrators' wives and families should go in force to the militia station. It was the only hope for some of the men.

Well, the long and the short of it is that that evening I grew up. For most girls maturity begins when they lose their virginity. Not for me—that seemed a very small thing compared with telling my mother what had happened. And then going down with her, morning and evening, day after day, to the gray-stone militia station on Praskoye Street. And worst of all, being greeted with no information whatsoever. They could neither confirm, they said, nor deny, that my father was under arrest. They had no details of an anti-Soviet demonstration on the Blue Bridge and no record of arrests.

Fifty men simply vanished. Fifty men might never be seen again. But in those awful days of contemptuous denials at the militia station, I became a different person. For the authorities I conceived a festering hatred. As I said, I grew up.

Water dripped from the walls of the old brick tunnels and swirled around the high rubber boots of the inspection team as they waded forward among the bobbing segments of black ice. The beam of Engineer Ovsenko's flashlight probed the arched vaults ahead. Where a crack in the brickwork was revealed, the inspection team's rough timber raft, piled with sand and cement, was hauled forward and made fast to an iron ring. In the light of the kerosene lamps attached to the corner posts of the raft, men mixed the mortar and carried it in wooden hods, wading across to where ladders had been set up against the weeping brickwork.

In Leningrad the first week of the thaw is traditionally the time to repair the ravages of the winter's ice. Stone bastions of the countless bridges and the vaulted foundations of palaces along the River Neva are all examined for the damage that only spring reveals. The damage can show itself in long dark splits in the ancient brickwork, or whole blocks of stone thrust out of position by the winter's buildup of ice.

Among the cavernous foundations of the Peter Paul Fortress, knee-deep in the still freezing water, Engineer Anton Ovsenko's twelve-man inspection team cemented the crumbling brickwork and levered stone blocks back into position. Sweat poured from their faces, though their legs remained numb with cold. They had worked without stopping since the early morning, and by three o'clock in the afternoon they had already fulfilled their day's norm. The three tunnels allocated to them had been inspected and the ice damage repaired.

On Anton Ovsenko's signal the team shouldered their dripping workbags and began to haul the raft back along the dark tunnel.

In the great central vault, above the waterline, five or six other inspection teams had already gathered. A fire was burning in an iron brazier set on the brick floor. In its flickering light men passed quart bottles of vodka among them and chewed bread and sausage. As each new inspection team joined them a faint ironic cheer was raised.

When the last team arrived there were almost a hundred men gathered around the brazier. Cigarettes were lit, men talked in low voices. Others shuffled from group to group, exchanging a few words, glancing expectantly at anyone who raised his voice.

"What's it to be then, comrades," a voice said finally from beyond the firelight. "Do we go on, or give in?"

"We go on," voices from the darkness muttered.

"If we go on, we know what to expect from the authorities," a man squatting beside the fire said.

Engineer Ovsenko's youthful face glowed in the light of the brazier. "They can't imprison every worker in Leningrad," he said.

The man squatting beside the fire gulped vodka and wiped his lips. "We don't have every worker in Leningrad backing us, comrade," he said. "Not yet we don't."

"Let's be practical," another man said, "our task is to get Joseph Densky and the others released. Our first step is to elect a delegate to the Release Committee. Agreed?"

The men around the brazier looked down, scuffing their heavy rubber boots against the damp brickwork.

"No volunteers?" the man by the fire laughed harshly. "Nobody looking for ten years in a labor camp?"

"Some of us have children to think of," another man said. "What future is there for them if their father's in a camp somewhere in Siberia?"

Anton Ovsenko shouldered his way forward. He stood well above the height of most men around him. He had removed his work helmet and sweat plastered strands of blond hair to his forehead.

"I'll go to the meeting," he said. "I don't have a wife or children."

Men pressed forward silently to look at him. For a few moments no one spoke. Then the man squatting by the fireside stood up. "Those in favor of Engineer Ovsenko as delegate?"

The raised hands showed as black shadows on the encircling walls.

"So be it," the speaker said. "Engineer Ovsenko is our delegate to the Release Committee. We in turn bind ourselves to act as that committee decides. Is that so, comrades? Yes or no?"

The hands rose more slowly this time, in ones and twos, or in clusters as friends and workmates voted together. But in the end every hand was raised.

"Speak for us then, Anton," the man by the fire said, shaking Ovsenko's hand. "And speak for Joseph Densky and the other Blue Bridge prisoners."

Still a hundred yards or more from where the workers stood around the fire, deep in a long tunnel which led to the central vault, thirty uniformed men waded silently forward, the sodden skirts of their greatcoats trailing in the black water. They moved slowly, their eyes on the outline of the man ahead, his dark back silhouetted against the glimmering light of the kerosene lamps at the far end of the tunnel. The militia officer in the lead took his riot pistol from his holster. He could hear voices clearly now and even make out the shadowy figures of the men in the central vault. Straining his ears, he could almost hear what they were saying. But for just too long the effort absorbed his concentration. His boot, feeling forward, came down on a piece of fallen masonry. As he slipped, he shouted involuntarily, his arms flying as he fell forward into the still water.

In the vault the shout echoed and reechoed like a gunshot from the mouth of the tunnel. From other tunnels police whistles brayed.

Seized with near-panic, the men of the inspection teams plunged into the water and splashed along those waterways which seemed farthest from the approaching militia.

To men who had worked the tunnels all their lives the few seconds' warning was invaluable. Like sewer rats they slithered into crevasses known only to them, or crouched in conduits with the water at the level of their chins. Others collided with militia units in the blackness, kicking and punching as they fought their way past. From time to time the beam of a flashlight would pick out a face, as a man rose, water cascading over his shoulders, to hurl a militiaman aside.

Within less than an hour the militia units were regrouping in the great vault. Their overcoats steamed in the heat from the still burning brazier. Some limped, others held soaking handkerchiefs to cut eyes and swollen lips. Among the six full militia sections involved, no one could claim a single prisoner.

Yet for the commander of the operation there was perhaps one small scrap of hope. The informer who had revealed the meeting to the militia claimed that during the fighting in the tunnels he had been able to identify, in a flashlight beam, a certain Engineer Ovsenko.

It was almost a week since Joseph Densky's arrest. Every day, morning and evening, Zoya had queued at the militia headquarters for information, each time to be met with that cold and complete denial that the Blue Bridge demonstration had ever taken place.

Twice a day [Zoya Densky recounts] I would pass from anger to fear and from fear to despair. My mother's courage astonished me, as had my father's a week ago.

I suppose it's some essential part of growing up to see, as if through some other eyes, your own parents as courageous or cowardly, attractive or ugly, stubborn or pliable. As people, in fact, and not simply as parents.

In this week I learned a great deal about them both. I learned of my father's agitation for better working conditions and I learned of the attempts by the authorities to buy him off with promotions and offers of a larger apartment. Most of all I learned, often simply from the quiet pride in my mother's voice, that my father was rapidly becoming a force for the local authorities to reckon with.

It was some five or six days after the arrests that we arrived back home one evening to find that my mother had a visitor. In our minute apartment she took him into the kitchen and for ten minutes they spoke in lowered voices. Then when the visitor had gone she had begun to prepare some bread and sausage, all the time looking at me in a way I found strangely disturbing.

After a few moments she sat down opposite me at the kitchen table.

"What is it?" I asked her anxiously. "Did that man bring news?"

"Of your father? No, Zoyushka," she shook her head. "Other news." She was rolling the bread and sausage in a white cloth. She placed a half-quart of vodka next to it on the table. "There is a man," she said, "who has been trying to help your father. Tonight he needs *our* help. The militia are watching his apartment. He has had to go into hiding." She nodded to the things on the table. "Will you take these to him?"

I felt, of course, immensely proud of having been asked. Although half an hour later as I picked my way in the half-dark across a vast demolition site on Vasilyevsky Island my pride quickly gave way to alarm.

The wind rattled the thin metal lampstandards along the shoreline, driving inland scattered rags of sea mist so that it hung like battle smoke around half-demolished buildings. Small fires burned among the debris and groups of ragged men sat around them passing the vodka bottle. Known ironically as Vasilyevsky Park, it was a place of beggars and outcasts. All those who lived outside the system lived here, men without city residence permits, aging whores, professional beggars. The vast broken area functioned as the thieves' quarter might have in other cities, in other times.

I turned down an alley between wrecked warehouses [Zoya continues] and found myself facing the archway I was looking for. I tapped on the door in the pattern I had been told to and waited. After a few moments the door opened and I stepped inside a single, candlelit room. As I turned I found my heart thumping madly. I had of course expected that the man I was to bring the food to would be old, that's to say my father's age, in his fifties perhaps. But the tall, slender figure in Western jeans looking down at me was no more than twenty-three or four.

"Please sit down," he said, pulling a crate closer to the small fire. "I didn't expect a girl, I mean someone like you."

"I didn't expect someone like you," I blurted out. And felt covered with embarrassment.

He stood holding the half-quart in his hand. "You must be Zoya, Joseph Densky's daughter."

"Yes."

"My name is Anton."

"Anton," I repeated stupidly.

I looked around at the crumbling walls and tattered blankets hanging over the window. "What will you do?" I asked him. "You can't live like this."

"Many people do, Zoya," he said. "You've seen them out there, people that the Soviet system has used, broken and tossed aside. And they're the ones who are still free."

"You're against the Soviet system then?" I said with awe.

"As long as it continues to put the good life for the few above justice for the many, I'm against it in the same way your father is."

Of course I had heard my father talking over the years, but I think he must have been careful to hide from me the full extent of his opposition. I had continued to believe that dissenters were Moscow intellectuals with strong Western links, poets and writers who made money from running down their own country in the books they sold abroad. It seemed to shatter everything I had believed in to see my father and someone like Anton in the same light.

"My father loves Russia," I said. "I've often heard him say he would never live anywhere else." I was speaking desperately, with images of the flailing police batons on the Blue Bridge and the cold denials from the militia fresh in my mind.

He put a warm brown hand on my arm. "Zoya," he said, "Surely a man can love Russia and despise the Soviet system."

I suppose I must have looked as stunned as I felt. Was it really possible that those two thoughts could exist together?

Perhaps he saw the shock I had suffered. He reached for the half-quart. "Will you have some of this?" He lifted the bottle. "There are no glasses I'm afraid."

I had never drunk vodka in my life, but I had no intention of losing the opportunity of drinking from a bottle *his* lips had touched.

"You first," I said.

He drank and passed the bottle to me. I raised it to my lips. Lost in my reverie I was completely unprepared for the rush of fire that entered my mouth and coursed down my throat.

He saved the bottle from crashing to the floor by snatching it from my hand. I gasped, spluttered. Vodka snorted from my nostrils and streamed from the corners of my mouth.

He was laughing. "My God, he said. "You looked so much older."

Mortification overwhelmed any conceivable fear as I made my way back across Vasilyevsky Park that night. How can we suffer the blasts of two contrary emotions? Desperate to see him again, it was at the same time the last thing in the world I felt I could bear.

Chapter Two

THE DEATH OF Leonid Brezhnev after so long an illness could not have been expected to have had the impact which a sudden collapse might have had.

Much of the credit for the easy transfer of power must undoubtedly go to the octogenarian Mikhail Romanovsky who had become, effectively, leader of the Soviet Union from the time of Brezhnev's first unpublicized hospitalization and was sworn in as President of the Soviet Union on the morning of Brezhnev's death.

The world and the Russian dominions had no doubt that President Romanovsky was a caretaker president. He was, to begin with, even older than Brezhnev. In the mid-eighties he was, however, still a solid, impressive figure, well able to stand upright in driving snow while welcoming foreign dignitaries, or to endure the interminable speeches of the Palace of Congresses.

He had been a close friend of President Brezhnev since their childhood in the Czarist steel town of Kamenskoye where they were both born. Over three-quarters of a century stood between the unpaved streets, the dugout cottages, the huddled buildings of the Tailors' Synagogue of their youth together, and the moving funeral oration Romanovsky delivered at his friend's death. It was three-quarters of a century in which Romanovsky, always in the background, had absorbed the Brezhnev style and the Brezhnev approach to Party and international affairs. When he became President, Mikhail Romanovsky simply and deliberately extended the Brezhnev years.

Then, after less than three years of power, the new Soviet leader, on a visit to Oslo, collapsed on the steps of the presidential aircraft and pitched forward onto the runway.

Before Soviet security men jerked the cameras away, Romanovsky was shown gasping for breath, trying to raise himself on one hand.

He was flown immediately back to Moscow and a Tass report described the incident as an accident due to oil on the runway.

In the West, hours of television time were taken over by the incident. Hundreds of newspaper articles explained that President Romanovsky had not reached the runway when he fell, that doctors rerunning the film saw that his legs had buckled under him, that it was not a simple slip, but much more a collapse of the muscular system indicating the possibility of a heart attack. The few feet of film as he lay on the runway was equally examined. It was pointed out that he was levering himself up on his right hand only. Did this suggest a stroke? Everybody agreed that there was a certain contortion of the features. But might not this be simply the pain of the fall? The West waited impatiently. From Moscow there came no word.

Nobody now doubts that for the Soviet Union and the world, 1980 to 1985 were the fateful years.

At the root of its looming problems was the simple fact that the Soviet Union was an empire comprising fifteen totally different nations, one hundred languages, a racial spectrum from Slav to Mongol, a half dozen different residual religions.

At the center of the empire stood the Russia of the Czars, proud, patriotic, the first among equals. But as the 1980s began it was not necessary to be a Ukrainian, an Estonian, an Armenian or an Uzbek to be aware that Soviet triumphs were now ringing from a cracked bell.

In so many ways it was the Soviet Army in which many of these nationalist stresses were concentrated. Not surprisingly, people in the West reading of the vast defense budgets announced by the Kremlin, thought of the Soviet army as a highly trained and integrated force.

Yet the truth was far from that. The truth was that the Army was the point at which all those promises to the Soviet Union's non-Russian peoples ended. Every training camp for conscripts might well have had a sign over the gate reading: *Local Languages and Cultures Stop Here.*

The truth was that the Soviet Army was one vast school for the Russification of the Union's one hundred different nationalities.

In the 1970s a typical conscript might leave his home in the grazing lands of Uzbekistan in southern central Asia. He would be just over eighteen years old, literate in his own language but barely able to speak Russian. The northwest of the Soviet Union, the lands of the Slavs, would have been totally unknown to him. Yet he would be entering a *Russian* army where Russian was the only language, where almost every senior officer was Russian or at least Ukrainian, where the need for technical expertise had directed the Slavs into aviation, armor and artillery and the less highly educated Asiatics into pioneer and construction battalions. Some young men from the Soviet Asiatic Republics claimed they did not know their nations were colonies until they entered the Red Army.

It was an old struggle. When the October Revolution threw the Czarist Empire into confusion, breaking the bonds which held the colonized nationalities to the center, national armies had begun to appear to defend the newly independent status of their peoples. Lenin immediately decreed the integration of the national armies into the Red Army wherever it was militarily possible to do so—whether the nationalists liked it or not.

But as the revolution exploded into Civil War, the Bolsheviks were forced to cut their coats according to their cloth. Large national armies in the Ukraine, Georgia, Armenia and the Asiatic nations could not be forced into the Red Army. Attempts to do so led to new national uprisings in Central Asia in the 1920s, suppressed only after years of bloody fighting. Yet slowly, at immense cost, the Russian Empire was reformed in these years before World War II as one after another the national armies were browbeaten into submission.

In 1941, war was once again the modifier of theory. As the German armies advanced there was no time to force conscript soldiers to become Russians. Instead divisions and army corps of Kazaks and Azerbaijanians were raised, whole units speaking their own national language, officered by their own nationals and necessarily developing an esprit de corps rooted in their own cultures.

Again, with peace, the inevitable began to happen. The bonds lashing the nationalities to the elder brother, Russia, began to snap. Two years of bloody civil war (1945–47) in the Ukraine were hardly noticed in the West. A small nation, the Crimean Tatars, were simply deported into Siberia as revenge for their uncertain loyalty to the Soviet Union. Once again, painfully and bloodily, the Russian Army became the sole army of the Soviet Union. Some claim that it was only in 1967 with the new military service law that the Red Army was fully reconstituted.

So as the severe stresses of the 1980s began to develop within the Soviet Union, what appeared to the West as a loyally monolithic force was in fact a unity less than twenty years old; a unity devoted to forcing the Russian language, culture and customs on peoples who demanded their own national expression. It was also a unity which had yet to have its cohesion and common purpose tested by fire.

The secret was kept astonishingly well, but by the early 1980s all but the first rank of Soviet Army divisions were riddled with racial tensions.

In the light of later events the consequences for the Soviet Union cannot be exaggerated. In their thousands soldiers were sent to penal brigades for using their national language in the barrack block. But in the company of fifty brother Uzbeks a man was not going to speak haltingly in Russian.

A whole penal system had evolved to enforce the Russification program. Separate from the corrective labor camps, military prisoners were organized into penal brigades. Their camps were situated in the same harsh areas of the country as the civilian camps, frequently indeed standing side by side.

There was brutality enough, of course, in the civilian labor camps, but in the camps that housed the penal brigades an even harsher tradition evolved. Because the members of the penal brigades were overwhelmingly from the Central Soviet Asian republics, their Slav guards came to treat the penals as subhumans, *Untermenschen*. Throughout the seventies and into the eighties ugly stories of Slav brutality filtered back to the southern republics. In the Soviet Union, it began to be said, the penal brigade was the price a young man paid to remain true to his own national language and culture.

These were the deep fissures in the Soviet Union. But the system itself contributed massively to increasing unrest, as much in the Baltic and Slav republics as in the Asiatic republics of the south and southeast.

In these years foreign reporters began to comment on the lack of vitality in Soviet life. And on the marked growth of alcoholism. Every township by 1980 had its own drunk-tank.

Poles rioted and struggled for liberal institutions. Georgians, Tajiks and Latvians demanded more autonomy. Burdened with a huge military budget, Brezhnev and his Politburo colleagues struggled to distribute oil and foreign currency reserves to satellite nations demanding more connections with, and more loans from, the West.

As the first half decade of the 1980s wore on, the slumbrous apathy of the Soviet peoples was seen, by some observers, to be changing. In the dark wooden lanes of Moscow's Red Presnya district it was no longer unusual to see militiamen assaulted. Graffiti, previously rare, now adorned the walls of apartment blocks, bus stations and government offices. From a call for improved food supplies in the city the scrawled messages began to carry political or nationalistic themes.

In a very literal sense, as 1985 drew near, for the men within the great Kremlin gates the writing was on the wall.

Yet for some the lights still shone brightly. Igor Bukansky, editor of the Soviet cultural magazine *Novaya Literatura*, was particularly well placed to enjoy the benefits of life in Moscow in the 1980s.

Outside the government itself Bukansky was one of the best-known figures in the capital. His vast bulk, well over six foot tall and barrel-chested, contributed, with his reputation for high living, to his notoriety. His magazine was unique in its coverage of fashion, theater, literature and painting. It was clear to most people in the Arts that *Novaya Literatura*, or Igor Bukansky himself, enjoyed a special dispensation from the government. The sheer glossiness of the magazine made it sought after as was no other publication in Moscow. Its Soviet fashion pages came intriguingly close to the softest of soft porn; its reproductions of modern painting strayed a long way from the officially approved Soviet realism; and its poetry and serialization of novels could be thought to reflect the uncertain liberation of the age of Khrushchev rather than the hardening present.

In his youth a poet of some talent himself, Igor Bukansky knew exactly the compromises he had made. At this time he began to record a series of memoirs on tape:

For some of us it was the life of the old pre-Revolution aristos [Bukansky recorded]. People might have said that we'd forgotten nothing and learned nothing. I can understand it when they looked at the life of a senior Party member and committeeman of the Writers' Union like myself.

Take living conditions. Apartments in Moscow are strictly allocated by square feet. Most families have a small place to themselves, one or two rooms, no more. And the new tower blocks are as grim and uninviting as the old slums, but without the friendliness. Yet where do we live, we the *vlasti*, the powers that be?

First, of course, we all have apartments in the city, often in the older buildings where the rooms are spacious and light. In addition there is the dacha, the country house, a long-established tradition for the rich and powerful that goes back deep into Czarist times.

So we have the little village of Zhukova, 20 miles from Moscow, nothing much to look at if you're passing through. A few comfortable clapboard village houses, that's all. But in the woods behind, my friends, and on the bosky bluffs overlooking the river, are some of the finest dachas in the country. Khrushchev lived here in a fine mansion with marble steps down to his private jetty. Brezhnev and Molotov had places here, grand beyond imagining for most Soviet citizens. Scientists, academics, writers—they all live here. Yes, this little village in the Moscow *oblast* doesn't look like much from the road . . . there are other villages too, such as Peredelkino where I have a dacha.

To Russians, this is the way of the world. Of course a lot of people thought it would all change with the Revolution; good, honest people. But it didn't. For myself, I like the story about Leonid Brezhnev. Muscovites love a story, especially one aimed at the *vlasti*. It appears Brezhnev's old mother came up from the Ukraine on her first visit to Moscow just before she died. Her son, not unnaturally perhaps, set out to show her how well he was doing. He took her to his apartment on Kutuzov Prospekt. Standing in the wide entry foyer the old lady looked baffled. "But where are the beds, Leonid? Where do you sleep?"

"This, Mama," he said, "is just the entrance hall. We have separate bedrooms, six of them, a separate kitchen, a television room . . ."

The old lady shook her head. Far from being impressed she looked slightly worried.

This was not good enough for Brezhnev. He called for a limousine and rushed her out of Moscow to his great mansion at Zhukova. Here he showed her the grounds, the dozens of rooms, the tapestries, the helicopter apron with his own private helicopter standing by.

Still the old lady looked more concerned than impressed.

Finally Brezhnev could take it no more. "What is it, Mama?" he asked. "Don't you find all this just a little bit impressive?"

"Leonid, Leonid . . ." the old woman is supposed to have answered. "Impressive? Of course I find it impressive. But what worries me is this: What, I ask myself, will happen if the Reds come back?"

Well, it's a story. Muscovites like it. I tell it because it could happen to me if my mother, God rest her, were alive today.

Perhaps the old don't understand. Our only hope is that the young do.

They seem to. They seem to take their fistful of privilege as easily as we older ones. Lydia Petrovna, my little secretary, is a case in point. Well, little she isn't. A nice tall, well-made girl from Sverdlovsk. A working family. But Lydia has made a very sharp estimate of her talents. She's a good secretary; quick, neat, knows how to cover for a chief like me who likes his bottle.

It didn't take her long to let me know that she was available. A few hints about a pair of Western shoes on my next visit to Munich or Rome. A slight raising of the eyebrows when I mentioned a party I was planning at Peredelkino.

Sometime around 1980 she became my mistress. I'm not pretending she was the only one, and I never pretended to her. It was an arrangement.

She wanted to dress like a Westerner, live among the *vlasti*, and I liked a pretty girl around.

Strangely enough it was through Lydia that I first heard about Kuletsyn. It's odd to think that this may well go down in literary history as my claim to fame, me, Igor Alexandrovich Bukansky.

How did it happen now? There had been a big party at the dacha the night before. Some foreign correspondents, one or two of the younger general staff, a few provincial Party people. When I say we drank a lot I don't exaggerate. The party started on Friday evening and went on the whole weekend. New people arrived, others left.

Saturday morning, I think it was, I was lying in bed. Lydia had first got up to get me what the American correspondents christened a Morning Glory, a half-pint of lemon vodka heated with sliced lemon and a twist of paprika. My own creation for the morning after.

She came back with a tall glass in one hand and a thick typescript balanced on the palm of the other.

"Igor Alexandrovich," she said diffidently. She was standing there, near naked by the side of the bed, "I have tried not to take advantage of our friendship."

I took the Morning Glory from her.

"It's true you've given me a great deal, clothes, parties like this, holidays . . ."

I gulped the lemon vodka. It lifted my head pleasantly.

"But perhaps you don't know how difficult it can be to be the secretary to an important man."

"Get into bed and tell me," I said like some capitalist mogul from a Hollywood movie.

She sat on the side of the bed. "People ask me constantly to put their work before you. I have never done it."

She paused, holding the typescript in both hands.

"I have an uncle. My mother's brother. His name is Kuletsyn, Valentin Sergeivich Kuletsyn. My mother begged me to give this to you."

She was almost in tears. She thrust the dog-eared manuscript forward.

"Forgive me, Igor Alexandrovich, I would do this for no one else."

She knew which side her bread was buttered. Why ask favors for others when you can ask them for yourself? But I didn't blame her. She was an honest enough gold digger.

I took the manuscript. It was entitled: *To Be Preserved Forever*.

"To Be Preserved Forever," I should explain, is the stamp placed by the KGB on the dossiers of all dissenters.

The irony appealed to me.

Lydia went to take a bath. I sipped my Morning Glory and started to read. After twenty pages I could feel that excitement rising in the throat. It was, of course, quite unpublishable, But by the time she came back I knew that the manuscript of Valentin Kuletsyn was an authentic work of genius.

Chapter Three

WHO WERE THEY, this group of old people waiting in the lobby of the Kalasty Clinic so late at night? With the exception of the one woman among them, they were mostly approaching seventy, some a few years more, and one or two, sitting gray-faced in the vinyl armchairs, were clearly into their eighties. Were they perhaps a group of old folk long forgotten by the hospital authorities, waiting deferentially for X-ray results or news of a sick relative? Some were without ties, their shirt collars buttoned above shapeless dark suits. Others were sunk deep in their overcoat collars. Nobody spoke. From time to time an old man yawned out a mouthful of cigarette smoke. Old eyelids closed and opened with a guilty start. It was 1:45 A.M., Moscow time, and the Politburo of the Soviet Union were waiting for the doctors' announcement on the condition of their President, Mikhail Romanovsky.

It was the legacy of the Soviet system of government that even after years of working together they were still unable to guess the direction of each other's thoughts. Who did old Brostov, the "kingmaker," favor to succeed the ailing, perhaps at this very moment dying, President? Who did dour ex-Foreign Secretary Gromyko incline towards? A noncandidate himself because of his lack of a power base in the Party, the military or the bureaucracy, his goodwill, if any had ever existed behind the dark eyebrows and set mouth, would be vitally important to any contender for the leadership. And who were the challengers for this, along with the Presidency of the United States the most powerful position in the world?

Nobody in the drab waiting room of the Kalasty Clinic that night doubted the claim of KGB General Semyon Kuba, Head of the

Committee for State Security. President Romanovsky's downstairs neighbor in the apartment block on Kutuzov Prospekt, Kuba, at sixty-four, was one of the youngest members of the Politburo.

Some claimed for the mind of Semyon Trofimovich Kuba the same inscrutably evil workings as that of his predecessor, Stalin's hangman, Lavrenti Beria. Certainly as the internal problems of the Soviet state increased in severity during the first years of the eighties, Kuba's solutions had seemed never to extend beyond the concentration camp and the psychiatric asylum.

He was popular though, with Brostov the kingmaker and the aging majority of the Politburo from the simple fact that he saw all the Soviet Union's problems in terms of maintaining the status quo. The Communist Party must remain utterly supreme. The Russian Federal Republic must continue its "elder Brother" domination of the rest of the Union's other fourteen autonomous republics. Above all the Soviet Union must, he stated again and again in those years, continue to maintain the status quo in the peoples' democracies of Hungary, Czechoslovakia, Rumania . . .

Yet the short Romanovsky years had seen the emergence of another figure who in the early eighties had been virtually unknown to anyone but a few Kremlin-watchers in the West.

The one woman who sat among the men in the Kalasty Clinic, chain-smoking a pack of Belomors cigarettes, had occupied, since the death of Leonid Brezhnev, one of the most powerful positions in the Party—the Chairmanship of the Russian Socialist Federal Republic, that huge segment of the Soviet Union which stretched from Leningrad to the Pacific.

Fifty-eight years old, imposingly built, Natalya Roginova still retained some traces of the attractiveness of her youth. Perhaps in the last few years she had deliberately sought a more severe image. Certainly now the dark-blue skirt and jacket and the almost flat-heeled shoes had become her hallmark. Her thick blond hair had been allowed to fade and she now wore it drawn back severely to the nape of her neck.

Until 1982 she had not been a candidate member of the Politburo, but as a deputy minister of Defense, she had shared Dimitry Ustinov's close connection with the military, without being directly responsible for its shortcomings in Afghanistan. She was also a creature of the Party and had served as first secretary in a wide range of *oblasts* before reaching minor republic level in the seventies. She was a Russian, born twenty miles east of Moscow. An engineer technocrat of MGU, Moscow University, she had negotiated technological exchanges with the United States and not only spoke English well but had achieved a reputation for considerable experience in foreign affairs.

As the Politburo waited at the Kalasty Clinic that night, possibly only KGB General Semyon Kuba did not underrate her as a contender for the leadership of the Soviet Union.

From along the hall beyond the waiting room the sound of approaching footsteps held the attention of the waiting Politburo. Suslov rose with difficulty from his chair. General Semyon Kuba moved closer to the door. Natalya Roginova watched from the back of the room.

The door opened and three white-coated doctors entered. For a moment they stood, uncertain whom to address. Brostov cleared his throat and gestured for them to begin.

"Distinguished comrade members of the Politburo," the senior doctor said, "President Romanovsky is comfortable under light sedation. While it is possible that he suffered a very mild coronary infarction, a heart attack, in Oslo, our tests give no positive confirmation."

General Kuba looked angrily at the doctors. "You mean the President just slipped at Oslo?" he said unbelievingly.

"It's the most likely explanation, Comrade General," the senior doctor said nervously.

Kuba turned to the other members of the Politburo. "You see what these fools have done," his small eyes glittered with fury, "by bringing the President back to Moscow? They've set the West alight with speculation!"

"It was a heavy fall, Comrade General," the senior doctor protested feebly. "At the time there was no way of knowing . . ."

Kuba silenced him with a dismissive gesture. He turned to the other Politburo members. "The decision should be investigated," he said.

"Consider . . ." Natalya Roginova said as she came forward into the middle of the room until she was facing Kuba. "Consider the possibility that the President was in fact suffering from a serious illness, Semyon Trofimovich. Could we entertain for one moment the idea of a President of the Soviet Union being treated in the West? I move that the Politburo publicly commend the doctors' decision. Any investigation by the Bureau of State Security will make doctors less decisive should the situation arise again with any Politburo member traveling abroad."

It was an open challenge, the first Natalya Roginova had ever issued to the leading contender. In the complex chess game which was the struggle for power in the Soviet Union, Roginova had made her first move. Was it dangerously rash or supremely confident? The old men around her looked down at the floor. Nobody was prepared to offer Kuba support at this moment. Too many calculations had still to be made.

Thickset, Stalin-like in build, Semyon Kuba looked up at the tall woman facing him. Like the others in the room he recognized the challenge. But he knew this was no issue to fight on. "I agree," he said to

Roginova. "It is policy that no senior figure in Soviet government should be treated by Western doctors. That principle must of course be upheld."

By his retreat he had defused the moment. But in that moment Natalya Roginova had established herself as a leading contender for the succession.

Igor Bukansky leaned over the bed. He could make out the line of his secretary's bare shoulder but her face and blond hair were pillowed in darkness. He reached downward for her shoulder. Taking it harder than he intended he shook her.

"Wake up, little dove," he said.

"I'm too tired to talk, Igor Alexandrovich," she protested.

"This is important," he said. "You must get dressed."

Full of vodka he sat down heavily on the side of the bed. She was awake now.

"Come to bed," she said. "You drink too much when you sit up alone."

He switched on the bedside light, suffusing her in a pale pink glow. Twenty, twenty-one was she? Youth was an invisible wand. The moment it ceased to touch you strange things happened. Your boringness became boring. Your crumpled waking look became sad. That long line between your breasts compressed in sleep would take all morning to disappear. Or never.

Some morning the wand would no longer touch Lydia Petrovna. The tousled hair, the crumpled face of sleep would lose its charm.

Not yet.

He reached out and stroked her arm. "You must go, Lydia. I have a visitor arriving."

She licked her lips and passed her hand across them.

"A woman?" she said.

"A visitor. Important. You must go, my dove."

With a girlish grumpiness she got up and dressed. He had already called his chauffeur. The big black car was waiting outside the dacha.

"Sleep late tomorrow morning," Bukansky said, knowing she wouldn't.

She nodded and climbed into the back of the car.

"It may be that my visitor will have something to say about your uncle's manuscript," he said.

She lay full length on the back seat as he slammed the door shut. The driver flicked on the headlights, the engine kicked and the car pulled away along the gravel drive.

Bukansky watched the taillights disappear as the car turned onto the Peredelkino road which led to the Moscow highway, then walked back toward the house. The dark surrounding woods with their thick summer leaves seemed to sing on one throbbing note. Yet there were guards in these woods, discreet, silent men. Every dacha in the village had them.

He passed through the hall and into the long timbered modern room. Even in summer he kept the fire burning. An empty liter stood on the smoked-glass coffee table. He opened another bottle and sat down. The news of President Romanovsky's collapse in Oslo had not of course been broadcast on television, but Bukansky was among the privileged recipients of *White Tass,* the *vlastis'* own news service. He knew that at this moment the Soviet Union might be about to choose a new leader.

When he heard the car arrive he went to the door. Natalya Roginova hurried past him as he opened it.

"Did you get rid of your little friend?" she asked over her shoulder.

"I dragged her out of bed and kicked her protesting into the car. She's halfway to Moscow by now. To what do I owe this visit? The sudden stirrings of irrepressible memory?"

Years ago they had been lovers.

"You old fool," she said. "Do you have coffee?"

"I have vodka."

She hesitated then nodded and he found her a glass.

"You've just come from the Kalasty Clinic?"

"The Politburo has just been told that President Romanovsky will live," she said, sitting down.

"All good Russians will rejoice."

"You have a dangerous tongue when you're drunk, Igor. And that's most of the time now."

"Yes," he agreed. "So the Comrade President will recover?"

"The doctors think there was probably nothing to recover from."

"No heart attack?"

"Probably not."

"And yet?"

She shrugged.

He stood, swaying slightly, the vodka bottle in his hand. "Think if we'd never met, Natalya. I would probably, even now, be living in the country. A simple thatched cottage, a hunting bag behind the door, children, a comfortable wife . . ."

"Fat," she said. "With a hare lip and evil armpits."

"Perhaps." He drank from the bottle in his hand. "Why do you visit me in the dead of night, Natalya? What do you want from me?" He slapped his belly. "My body? You want my body?"

"Are you too drunk to talk seriously to an old friend?" she said sharply.

"God forbid," he put the vodka bottle aside.

"After the rest of the Politburo left, I spoke to the doctors alone. They owed me a small favor. I think they repaid it with the truth. President Romanovsky is a very old man. You understand?"

He sat heavily on the arm of the sofa. "Semyon Kuba will block your way."

"He'll try," she said.

"And what then?"

"Then you and all my friends will go down, too. Perhaps you especially."

"Is this a warning?"

"Why not? I loved you once, as far I suppose as I'm capable. Let me arrange for you now to take some post in the West for a few months."

He shook his head.

"If I fail, you'll be the first to go, Igor. The past is all on Kuba's files."

"I can't leave Russia," he said.

"You could take your little secretary with you. Or find others in the West."

"I can't leave Russia," he repeated. "And who knows, some day I might even be of help to you."

She stood up. "The President's doctors give him until the end of the year. At the most." She put her arm round his waist as they walked to the door.

"The manuscript I sent you . . ."

"By your little secretary's uncle, Valentin Kuletsyn."

"Did you read it?"

"Yes, I read it."

"A remarkable novel."

She stood at the door, shaking her head. "Publication at a time like this? You're mad, my little bear. Publish Kuletsyn's novel in your magazine and I will have you arrested an hour after it's issued." She prodded him in the stomach. "Much as I love you."

Chapter Four

THE BLUE BRIDGE had not seen its last demonstration. During the week after the arrest of Joseph Densky factory workers in plants and enterprises

in and around Leningrad held meetings. Some, like the meeting in the
tunnels below the ancient buildings on the River Neva, were informed
upon and broken up by the militia. Others, perhaps many others, went
undetected. Certainly the authorities were aware that a committee had
been formed to obtain the release of the Blue Bridge demonstrators, but it
was unlikely that they guessed the extent and intensity of the Release
Committee's backing.

At that time the police commander in Leningrad was Lieutenant
General Stefan Dora. Aged seventy-four (the retirement age for KGB
generals was flexible), Dora had assisted in most of the extremities of
Stalinism. As an assistant first to Yezhov and then to Lavrenti Beria,
Stalin's murderous chiefs of secret police, killing and enslavement had
been part of Dora's life for half a century. As a junior leader in the
collectivization program before the war against Hitler, he had ordered
machine gunners to fire on starving peasants. As commanding Soviet
police officer in the Katyn area of Poland in 1940 he had carried out, on
Stalin's direct orders, the Katyn forest massacre of the officer corps of the
Polish Army. He was one of those murderous functionaries that total-
itarian systems breed, honor and reward. Sometimes they, too, disappear
into the night, but General Dora's time had not yet come.

Florid-faced, overweight and with a senile confidence in the power of
sheer repression, Dora was certain that the steps he had taken in the Blue
Bridge affair would effectively prevent any recurrence. Thus it was that
when in his ornate office in Peter the Great's Admiralty Building on the
Nevsky Prospekt he was shown the first reports of the factory meetings, he
was inclined to attach little importance to them. To a subordinate officer
he assigned the task of identifying and arresting any worker who had
attended a meeting. Again, the Blue Bridge technique would be applied.
There would be no acknowledgment of the worker's arrest. No relative's
questions would be answered. All knowledge of the prisoner's whereabouts or fate would be denied.

But before the KGB could strike, the workers made their move. A
week after the first demonstration three hundred men assembled quietly
on the Blue Bridge. They wore their caps and fur hats pulled down over
their eyes. Scarves were wrapped round the lower part of their faces.
Their placards demanded the release of their fifty comrades. On the wide
bridge, in the bitter, keening wind, they stood silently in six long columns,
black figures hunched against the driven snow.

Laryssa Navratovna, a prostitute in her early thirties, could see
everything from her third-floor window:

I won't disguise from anyone what my profession was at the time. Nor will I make excuses. I was born in the last days of Stalin and both my parents died in a camp. There were thousands of us street kids at that time, roaming free to starve in the streets of Leningrad, the children of the millions the system had shipped off to Siberia. We lived like young wolves, in packs. We ate scraps, stole, sold what we could. Before I was fourteen I had discovered what *I* could sell: big blue eyes, a plump figure and a submissive willingness to do whatever the old goats wanted.

Frankly, for me it was a good life, at least as soon as I learned to choose my clients, because, dealing with foreign customers and Party members as I began to, the shortages didn't much affect me. Of course all the days of reduced heating that winter had been bad for people, but again I had my own methods of keeping the place warm. What I'm saying is that I was lucky: a nice 350-square-foot apartment all to myself (and no question about how I got it) and the best of everything from the foreign currency shops or the Party seniors' special store.

I was expecting a client that night or I would have been out on the Nevsky Prospekt, not streetwalking, of course, but sipping tea or coffee in one of the restaurants or hotels, the Kravkazky or the Progress Café on the corner of Suvorovsky Prospekt. They were the ones I favored.

My apartment looks right across the Blue Bridge and I could swear that by seven-thirty all was normal because several times I had been to the window to see if I could see the car of Committee Chairman Z—no names even now—draw up. The moment that happened I would race down six flights of stairs and let him in. He didn't like to be kept hanging around outside. In those days he was quite a well-known face—or liked to think he was.

So I remember looking down at about seven-thirty and noticing that two or three men were standing on the bridge unrolling what looked like placards from under their jackets. I looked down, fascinated, and suddenly these few men were joined by others, six or seven at a time slipping quietly out of the shadows around the cathedral and forming up on the bridge until there must have been over three or four hundred of them. Then, of course, as luck would have it, my bell rang, four or five times, impatiently. I'd completely forgotten my fat little Committeeman.

Well, I raced down the stairs and let him in and by the time we got up to my apartment again we were *both* too exhausted to talk so I dragged him to the window and just pointed. Straightaway he got on the phone. To whom I don't know, and I certainly didn't ask. He shouted at me to get a glass of vodka and I rushed into the kitchen as he talked. By the time I was back with the glasses, he had finished phoning. But he didn't feel like relaxing. Standing at the window, glass in hand, he glared down at the bridge.

I suppose we had been watching the demonstration for about ten minutes when I saw the police cars screech to a halt downstairs.

"Get down and let them in," my Committee chairman shouted at me. So down I raced again and I didn't need any telling who it was waiting at the door with about a dozen guards all round him. Everybody in Leningrad knew Dora, and I doubt there was anyone who wasn't terrified out of their wits at the thought of him. But then again that can't be true. The demonstrators on the bridge weren't afraid, obviously.

Up in the apartment the two fat men seemed to forget I was there for a moment. The one thing I remember before they noticed me and told me to clear out (of my own apartment!) is that Dora told Chairman Z that they had received a warning from something called the Release Committee of Leningrad Free Trade Union Movement: If the men on the bridge were arrested that night they would be replaced by double that number the next night, and so on and so on until half of Leningrad was in prison. Chairman Z said it was a bluff, but I could tell that Dora wasn't at all sure. Then they bawled at me to get out . . .

The night of the second Blue Bridge demonstration is cut scalpel-sharp in my memory, Zoya wrote long afterward, mostly because I was on my way to see Anton again. As I had left the shoreline and started along the wrecked streets of Vasilyevsky Park I had seen a militia car, like some scavenger dog, nosing its way along the gutters toward me.

I turned quickly off the street, taking cover under the half-demolished walls of an old factory building. The thick spring mists clung like ivy to the old walls. I was sure they had not seen me, yet the car, creeping slowly forward, stopped almost opposite the place where I pressed myself back into the darkness. I could hear the music from their radio and from time to time the voices and laughter of the militiamen inside the car.

Perhaps half an hour passed. Perhaps more. Long enough certainly for me to feel for the first time in my life all the sensations of a hunted animal.

When the car at last moved away I crawled out of my hiding place savoring the feeling of triumph that I had something, some experience of my own, to recount to Anton Ovsenko when I arrived.

The alley between the warehouses was not far off. Beyond looming walls I could see the glow of firelight through the mist and the reeling figures of the drunks. Snatches of song began and ended abruptly. Women cackled and swore. But the militia car had disappeared.

I stood in the archway waiting for Anton to open the door. After a few moments I knocked again. This time the split timbers of the unlocked door swung away from my hand. In the room the ends of two candles still guttered in their empty vodka bottles. But there was no sign of Anton.

I was shaking with fear for myself and concern for him. I dropped the bag of food on the floor and unscrewed the top of the liter I had brought with me. This time I drank more slowly, taking the hot spirit into my mouth and swallowing carefully. Perhaps in all I drank four or five mouthfuls and when I stepped through the archway again I seemed already to be trembling less.

It was on the crowded trolley bus back to the Nevsky Prospekt that I first heard that the workers were demonstrating again at the Blue Bridge. As we crossed the Dvortsovy I could see the embankment was lined with militia trucks. The trolley bus itself was allowed to go no further. Militiamen ordered the passengers out. The area directly west of the Nevsky Prospekt (and this would include the Blue Bridge) was under curfew, they claimed. The nearest available Metro was the Chernyshevskaya station.

It was another hour before I arrived home. My mother was sitting unusually tense in the kitchen. When I told her that Anton had gone, she nodded. "He's that sort of young man," she said. "The Release Committee strongly advised him not to go to the Blue Bridge tonight."

"You mean he's at the demonstration."

"He must be."

"If he's recognized by the militia he'll be arrested immediately."

"Of course. But then he knew that."

I stood up. "We must go, too," I said.

I saw the look of astonishment come over my mother's face. "But you just said the militia have cordoned the area."

"Then we'll go and shout and scream and spit at them," I said. "So that they know the women of Leningrad feel the same as their men."

My mother was smiling at me as she got her coat. At the door she suddenly put her arm round me and kissed me. "What happened to the little girl I knew last week?" she said, hugging me.

Our fickle northern spring had retreated again. It was a bitterly cold night as we left the metro station and made for the Nevsky Prospekt. But we soon realized that we were not alone. Along the Nevsky Prospekt hundreds, thousands, of people, mostly women, were facing the line of militia. Of course we couldn't see what was happening at the Blue Bridge itself, but in front of us women were openly jeering at the militiamen who stood behind their fixed bayonets with drawn, frightened faces.

The hours we stayed there, singing, shouting, taunting the militiamen! And all the time it seemed as if the crowds around us were getting thicker and thicker.

There was no violence, nothing harder than insults were hurled at the militiamen, but there was in the crowd a curious sense that somehow we were winning. Most of all it was obvious that the militia had no power to break up a crowd of this size unless they resorted to guns and tear gas.

And whoever was in command clearly hesitated to take that step.

Then, perhaps about three o'clock in the morning, we heard a tremendous burst of cheering coming from the direction of the Blue Bridge. Our vast crowd answered it jubilantly. And before our astonished eyes we saw the lines of armed militia facing us begin to pull back. We surged forward and suddenly the gleaming bayonets were no longer pointing at us. Slinking away toward their armored vehicles the all-powerful Leningrad militia left the way open to the Blue Bridge.

We heard afterward what had happened. The confrontation at the Blue Bridge was even more tense than our own. The demonstrators with their placards detailing factory after factory throughout the Leningrad *oblast* had stood their ground before the lines of KGB guards with their riot guns, their long batons and their snarling dogs.

Of course everybody, guards and demonstrators, were thinking only of the week before. But however much the men in the long green topcoats and the polished black helmets itched to release the dogs and charge into the unarmed workers, hour after hour throughout that night the order still had not come.

Then, when dawn was only an hour or two away, a heavily escorted convoy of three black sedans had pushed its way through the crowd and driven forward to the Blue Bridge. It is said that when General Dora climbed out of the leading car he approached the demonstrators with all the joviality of a fat snake. A fuss about nothing, he insisted. One or two of his subordinates had overstepped the mark last week. They were already being brought up before their superiors, charged with excessive and un-Soviet zeal. The demonstrators cheered the phrase.

And the fifty men arrested last week?

Already on their way back home, Dora assured them. Except a few that still required hospitalization. There had been a lot of confusion last week, men slipping and sliding on the ice. There were a few broken limbs, but nothing serious. And for good measure, Dora added, he could assure the demonstrators that the Party was entirely on their side. The supply system of the whole Leningrad *oblast* was going to be radically overhauled. In a country as rich as ours, he insisted, it was nothing short of criminal that some of the outlying suburbs had seen no meat deliveries for weeks.

"Off you go home," Dora said genially, "and drink a liter for me. It's been a good night's work."

Cheering, laughing, arms round each other, the men left the Blue Bridge and marched toward the women surging forward from the Nevsky Prospekt.

For me, for all the cold and keening wind it was a night of sweetest triumph. My father would be home soon. And I would see Anton Ovsenko again.

Two days later we held a celebration in our own tiny apartment. My father had returned, his face yellow with bruises but not seriously hurt. Perhaps forty or fifty people crowded our two rooms and spilled out onto the landing. Somebody played an accordion and Anton Ovsenko asked me to dance. Wives of the imprisoned men cried with happiness as the vodka flowed. Neighbors joined us from downstairs apartments bringing offerings of sausage and vodka. Toasts were drunk to my father and to the Blue Bridge. To a rhythmic stomping on the floor, the guests chanted, "Joseph Densky . . . Joseph Densky . . ."

My father stood on a chair, his head almost touching the ceiling. Anton stood beside me, his arm round my waist.

I looked at my father's face and suddenly the happiness seemed to drain from me. This, he said somberly, was the beginning, not the end. Leningrad had a responsibility to the rest of Russia. Leningrad, he said, wiping beads of vodka from his gray mustache, must pay its dues.

Chapter Five

BUT THE LOOMING problems of the Soviet Union in the mid-eighties were by no means confined to the Russian heartland. Of all the subject nationalities within the Russian Empire the Ukrainians were the most populous, their land the richest and most strategically vulnerable, and their recent history the most rebellious. It is true that under the constitution of the U.S.S.R. they enjoyed an apparent, virtually complete autonomy, and that the Ukraine even sat as a separate seat in the United Nations. But even while arguing for that U.N. seat, Stalin had been bloodily suppressing a full-scale uprising in the Ukraine itself. And even though the Ukrainian National Army had been defeated, so resilient was Ukrainian national feeling that there remained no nightmare for Soviet leaders comparable to the idea of an uprising in the Ukraine.

But the nationalist movement did not exist solely in small military cells in Kiev or Kharkov or Poltava. There were organizations abroad in the United States, Australia, Britain and France where several million Ukrainians nurtured a persistent hatred for the Soviet Union and fostered national movements in the Ukrainian homeland itself. It was to this problem that General Semyon Kuba now secretly applied himself.

In that same spring of the Blue Bridge demonstrations, on an April morning twelve hundred miles to the southeast in the city of Paris, an American woman wandered alone across the Pont Neuf, among the wheeling flocks of pigeons, the blue-shirted policemen and the drifting groups of tourists on the Île de la Cité. The next day Carole Yates would deny that she had been openly looking for sexual adventure. She had simply met the man in a small restaurant-bar on the Île St. Louis where, after seeing the old prisons of Paris in the Conciergerie, she had gone for lunch.

She knew immediately that he was Russian. She herself had had a Russian mother. His accent as he struggled to speak to the French barman was an obvious giveaway. When she offered, in Russian, her help, he had in turn smilingly recognized her American accent. His English was, he said, thank God, better than his French. From then on they had spoken English together.

He had told her that he was an agronomist, in France for a month to study viticulture. She had no reason to be other than frank with him. Her husband, she responded in turn, worked for the State Department at the American Embassy in Dublin. On their first day's holiday in Paris he had been called back for a meeting. If you were married to a diplomat it happened all the time.

He had asked a little about her husband's work, where they had been posted in the past, if they were able to travel a great deal . . . no more than an interested Westerner would ask.

On her side there had been questions, too. He had answered, she thought, frankly, sometimes showing just the edge of an infectious sense of humor. On neutral ground, France and the French, they had laughed a great deal, especially as they drank more.

They had sat past four o'clock over coffee and two or three glasses of Marc de Bourgogne each. She had found it easy to like him. He had a flattering ability to listen without interruption and then, when she felt she was running on too long, to encourage or reassure her with yet another question. He had, too, a range of mannerisms, a frown before he laughed, a way of stroking his bottom lip which offered some instant, familiar warmth.

After lunch they had walked the corridors of the Louvre and had drunk beer on the Champs-Élysées and in the evening strolled through the Beaubourg quarter and eaten *merguèz,* the hot sausages of North Africa, in a workman's café on the rue Rembutin. And drunk wine. A bottle, almost two, between them. And afterward they had gone back to her hotel room.

She had sat on the edge of the bed unbuttoning her dress while he stood by the window, a glass of whisky in his hand.

"How did we get here?" she said as the dress opened across her legs.

"We swam," he said, rattling the ice cubes in his glass.

She ran her hand through her blond curls. Her head was spinning. "I'm a married woman. I guess I told you that."

"Yes," he said gravely.

"We'll never meet again, will we?"

"No."

"I suppose that makes it all right, then." She frowned at the inadequacy of her own logic.

He put his whisky aside and began to take off his shirt. She watched him undress until he stood naked before her.

"No phone calls tomorrow, nothing," she said. "Agreed?"

"Nothing. I promise you."

She stretched out a hand to him.

The insistent buzz of the bedside phone had awoken her at nine o'clock the next morning. When the receptionist said the police wished to speak to her she had thought immediately that something had happened in Dublin to her husband, Tom.

That was the first awful moment of that awful day. She had climbed out of bed and found her robe. The mirror showed all too clearly the ravages of sex and drink. She brushed her hair quickly and wondered if she had time to order coffee.

On the phone the police inspector had assured her no accident had befallen Tom. She sat on the bed too tired to speculate. Her hand ran across the sheets automatically smoothing the creases. Her eyes rested on two stains in the center of the undersheet. The bed was too far gone, she decided, ever again to look respectable. She pulled up the top sheet halfway and went into the bathroom to get herself a glass of water. As she turned the tap there was a knock on the outer door.

The Inspector from the Brigade Criminelle was polite but distant. "When I was a young man patrolling the rich suburb of Le Vesinet," he said in answer to her question, "it's what my chief used to call a delicate matter."

"It's to do with my husband?"

"That's not for me to say, Mrs. Yates," the Inspector shrugged. "Not when I've come to talk to you about the man you had up here in your room last night."

Involuntarily she glanced down at the crumpled bed sheets.

"*This* man, I believe." He handed her a photograph. Taken at an airport it showed a tall, fair-haired man carrying a canvas airline bag across the concourse. Even from the twenty- or thirty-yard distance it was taken from, there was no doubt that it was he.

Later in his office at the prefecture the inspector had been more sympathetic.

"The American authorities will have to be told, you know that?"

She shrugged bitterly.

"This Russian, Alex, you say was the name he gave you?"

"Just Alex."

"No patronymic? No surname?"

"Just Alex."

"He picked you up at the Bar St. Louis?"

"He didn't pick me up, we met."

"You went there by chance?"

"Not entirely. I knew it was a Russian restaurant. My mother used to go there when she first came to Paris after the war."

"A Russian restaurant?"

"Yes."

"Not completely accurate, Mrs. Yates. There are many old Russian restaurants in Paris. This one, however, is Ukrainian."

"So?"

"Did you hear Ukrainian spoken in the restaurant?"

"The little I can understand, yes. A few men in the corner greeting each other with 'Dobri Dyen' . . . saying ne instead of nyet, tuk rather than da. Yes, I knew they were Ukrainian."

"And your friend, Alex?"

"Of course he knew."

"I'm sorry," the Inspector said. "I myself am not a Slavonic linguist." He paused. "So Alex was there before you?"

"He was sitting at the bar trying to get a table for lunch."

"He entered into conversation with you?"

"No. I with him. He was having some difficulty understanding the barman."

"This agronomist studying French viticulture could not speak French?"

"I assume for this work the Soviet embassy supplied an interpreter."

"Possibly."

"Inspector," Carole Yates said deliberately, "unless you're prepared to tell me what this is about, I'm going to get up and walk out of here."

"Just one more question. What time did this man leave your room last night?"

He had left while she was still asleep. He had told her he would.

"He left when it got light," she said.

"You mean you don't know exactly?"

"Five. Five-thirty perhaps."

The Inspector's eyes wandered around the office. It was newly decorated in a pale gray. The furnishings, also new, might have been chosen by an interior designer. It was like no precinct office she had ever been in in the United States.

Completing their leisurely tour of the room the Inspector's eyes came back to rest on her.

"Were you still asleep, Mrs. Yates, when Alex left?"

Resenting it, she said firmly, "Five, five-thirty."

The Inspector nodded slowly.

"No more questions," she said. "Unless you're prepared to tell me what this is about."

"Yes," he said. "I'm prepared to tell you that. When you see this morning's papers you'll know anyway. Are you familiar with the Ukrainian Nationalist movement, Mrs. Yates?"

"I know that there are many Ukrainians living in the West who are opposed to the Soviet Union."

"That's all?"

"Their leader—Bandera was it?—was assassinated in Munich ten or so years ago."

"Assassinated by the KGB."

"The Russians claimed it was some sort of Ukrainian internecine struggle."

"They would, of course. Did you know, Mrs. Yates, that the Ukrainian émigrés were meeting in Paris this week?"

"No."

"Did your friend Alex mention such a meeting?"

"No."

"Émigrés from England, France, Denmark, Holland, Australia, the United States?"

"I knew nothing about it."

"They have problems, these Ukrainians, differing views on how the Ukraine might become independent of the Soviets."

"I told you I know nothing about it."

"This week at the conference a leader emerged. Stepan X. We don't yet know his name. There was a chance that he would be able to unite all the various Ukrainian ambitions."

"There *was* a chance?"

"Until he was assassinated."

"Assassinated?"

The Inspector nodded, his eyes never leaving her face.

"When?"

"I think you have guessed, Mrs. Yates. Here in Paris. Between five and five-thirty this morning. We think your friend Alex left your bed, walked three blocks to the Ukrainian's hotel—and shot Stepan X in the back of the head."

Her husband arrived from Dublin later that morning. His instructions were to take her back to Dublin to be interviewed by the Embassy security staff. It had already been made clear to him that his promising future with the State Department depended on her cooperation.

Tom Foster Yates had tried to behave with cold dignity, but every attempt to speak was prefaced by a faint trembling of the lower lip. As they drove across Paris to Charles de Gaulle Airport the question he had been trying to ask exploded from him. "Why, for Christ's sake? Why just pick up a stranger and sleep with him?"

How could she explain yesterday? How could she explain a day that was already half a lifetime distant? Paris in the spring? A cliché, but significant. The three French boys in the rue de Rivoli with their outrageous compliments and explicit invitations? That was important, too. And it was her thirtieth birthday. But most of all, perhaps, it was Alex himself, and the excitement she had felt in their night of lovemaking.

"Was this some kind of experiment, then?" her husband said.

"Something like that."

"I appreciate the effort to help me understand."

"I don't understand it myself, Tom."

A fine rain patterned the windscreen. Northeast of the city the car swooped through underpasses and over concrete ramps. She knew he was driving too fast. As they came up behind a slow-moving truck Tom Yates braked overhard, jerking her forward, then released the brakes and gunned the accelerator, throwing her back against the headrest. She glanced at him but his set face proclaimed clearly that she had forfeited all rights to complain. "I've got to ask you . . ." he said . . .

"You've got to ask me, was it the first time?"

"I think I have the right to know if there have been others."

Quite unreasonably she had hoped he would not ask.

"No," she said truthfully, "it was the first time, Tom."

But she knew as she said it that it would not be the last.

The shock wave from the assassination of Stepan X did not take long to reach the Ukraine. A dozen underground newspapers condemned Semyon Kuba's KGB.

In a bitterly argued Politburo meeting Natalya Roginova accused Kuba of doing more for the recruitment of the clandestine Ukrainian National Army than Stepan X could have done himself. Discipline and loyalty to Moscow were already under attack in other parts of the Soviet Union, Kuba responded. In Minsk there had been food riots; in most of the southern republics student movements promoted breakaway nationalist ideas in the guise of rediscovering the national past. In Leningrad itself unwise concessions had been made to the workers on Roginova's insistence. Perhaps none of this was a danger yet. But unless such opposition were rooted out now, the Soviet Union would suffer. In short, he stood by his decision to order the assassination of Stepan X.

Vainly trying to maintain some balance between Kuba and Natalya Roginova, the frail President Romanovsky decided sometimes in favor of Kuba's recommendations, sometimes for Roginova. While he lived, the other members of the Politburo were absolved from the responsibility of choosing between the two. But nobody attending the meeting in the smoke-filled room at Romanovsky's dacha had any doubt that the choice loomed closer with every passing week.

Chapter Six

IN THE SPRING and summer months of that year the policy of the Leningrad authorities became clear. The vegetable supply improved dramatically in the stores. At the Finland Station a new meat market was opened, supplied by Finnish farmers who were encouraged to cross the border for the weekend. Their compensation for the low ruble exchange was rumored to be nights of girls and vodka in the special hotels reserved for them.

But there was another side to the coin. No child of any of the identified demonstrators at the Blue Bridge was accepted as a Komsomol candidate, a candidate for the youth wing of the Party. In terms of jobs and preferments it could be a serious blow. Zoya Densky was one of many who was dismissed from the University at the end of the semester, "for inadequate achievement." She was unable to find employment except as a road sweeper:

I think my father suffered more than I did. I didn't object so much to the work because I was young and I got on well with those elderly women who were now my colleagues. I learned a few things about life, too, from them. They had the most cheerfully dirty minds I ever came across, before or since. But they really had hard lives. War widows most of them, from all over Russia, with tales to tell about what it had been like in the countryside under the glorious Stalin that made your stomach turn.

I saw Anton Ovsenko only once that summer. It had been a bitter, if fairly temporary, blow, to my seventeen-year-old ego to discover that he was already engaged to be married. Of course I dreamed of him leaving his fiancée and suddenly appearing at our apartment asking for me. I would be wearing my best dress and German shoes or sometimes even a wedding dress, about to leave that very moment for the wedding office to be married to a fat bureaucrat only to be saved by Anton. But life isn't like that. In fact, when I did see him next, I was in heavy overalls and work gloves, shoveling a pile of rubbish into the back of a truck as he approached along the embankment. It was a hot summer day and my hair was thick with dust and sweat. And instead of that romantic meeting on the doorstep of our apartment, I dodged round the back of the truck and let him pass without seeing me.

I stuck to the street work because I had to. But I kept my contacts with the University because a lot of the students there were beginning to think differently about things. That summer a number of us started an underground magazine. *Cat and Mouse* we called it for obvious reasons. The idea was to print anything that Leningrad *Pravda* ("Truth" it means in Russian!) wouldn't print. And in that summer, that was plenty.

I can't really explain to you how in those days we all seemed to be waiting for something. Certainly we waited for winter, because we knew food would become short again and the power cuts would begin to have an effect. But also we knew the authorities were waiting—or if we didn't know we certainly felt it. In our bones somehow we felt that they weren't satisfied with the outcome of the spring's Blue Bridge affair. It wasn't their way, unless they'd changed a lot, to be content with banning a few students when people like my father were still free.

So we waited and worked at spreading the truth about the way the Party sucked the country dry. In the meantime people like my father were making plans, but by some sort of agreement we never told each other exactly what we were up to.

As I say, throughout that short Leningrad summer, we waited.

For the authorities, the Leningrad summer was passing quietly. Natalya Roginova, of course, claimed it was the result of the Blue Bridge concessions. But for Semyon Kuba the task ahead was to restore the respect for authority which had been dangerously diminished there in the spring.

By early September he had reinforced Lieutenant General Dora's combined militia and KGB command with five thousand border guards now barracked at key points in the city. Lists were drawn up and the leading man on each list was followed for a period of two weeks to establish his likely whereabouts on a particular night in late September. It had been agreed by the KGB planning staff that all principals must be arrested on the same night, even if mopping-up operations continued with less important figures during the next day.

Early in September Joseph Densky became aware that he was being followed. Two days later Anton Ovsenko reported that he, too, was being watched and within the week a dozen or more other demonstrators believed that they had identified a permanent KGB tail.

On September 15 all were arrested.

But Joseph Densky had already made his preparations. Two days later the first of a series of statements signed by him began to circulate in illegal typescript, *samizdat,* throughout Leningrad. Within a week of his arrest it was published in the Western press and broadcast into the Soviet Union by the BBC Overseas Service:

Open Letter
to
International Opinion

We are Soviet citizens from various towns of the Soviet Union—united in bitterness.

Our comrade workers, who bear surnames, forenames and have children who bear their patronyms—*they are suffering.* They are undeservedly insulted, beaten, thrown into prison and psychiatric hospitals.

A dog would not bear the kind of humiliation and derision we have suffered.

It has been claimed that we are represented by Trade Unions of workers. Would we be in prison today if that were true?

At home we have been denied justice by the very State organ which is charged under the Soviet Constitution to see that justice is done, the Procurator's Office of the U.S.S.R. For all these reasons we have been forced to proclaim the existence of, and our membership in, a Free Trade Union Movement of the U.S.S.R. A fish, the peasants say, rots from the head.

Fellow workers, we ask your support.

Signed: Joseph Densky
Worker

Consciousness for Joseph Densky was the sensation of the cold concrete floor against his cheek. His body, hunched somewhere behind him, seemed to be enveloped in a numbed sleep. But the rasp of the concrete was real. He opened his eyes. One seemed to be full, sticky, the eyelid hardly moving. The other, closer to the floor, focused on a concrete gully an inch or two away. Blood from his hand or arm dripped into the white disinfectant fluid that swirled along the gully. He could smell the disinfectant now, sharp in his nostrils. The dripping blood creamed into milky whiteness.

His body was returning from the depths. He was crouched, like a wounded animal, head down. He rolled over, his hip thumping hard against the concrete.

He sat up slowly easing himself back to rest against the wall. His arms moved where he directed them. There were no sharp pains. He turned and with his thumbnail scratched a mark in the slime below the leaking windows. He had just survived his fifteenth night of interrogation.

Joseph Densky brushed the bloodied graying sandy hair across his forehead. He rose to his feet unsteadily. With his fingers he eased open his left eyelid. All was well. Dried blood crackled on the eyelashes, but he could see.

He leaned back against the wall to take stock. The room was a not untypical examination room. Concrete floor. Washout gully. Small barred windows six or eight feet above his head. Steel door with spy-hole.

The spy-hole slid back. Densky watched the eye watching him. A moment later bolts were drawn back and the door opened.

"Where to now, my friend?" Densky said to the young militiaman who stood holding the door open.

The militiaman leaned forward.

"Only the bathhouse," he whispered in a country accent. "There's someone coming from Moscow to interrogate you." Then as Densky stumbled into the corridor, the man raised his voice: "Hands behind the back! March!"

Chapter Seven

IT WAS A soft gray Leningrad morning. The sun had not yet risen above the rooftops. The streetlamps in the square were still on, feeble now in the growing daylight.

Outside the air terminal building passengers were alighting from the airport bus. The tall, fair-haired man in a light Western raincoat who detached himself from the group of minor officials off the Moscow flight, set out briskly along the Nevsky Prospekt, street map in hand. From time to time he stopped and consulted his map, tucking his briefcase up under his arm. There were few people on the streets. A militiaman passed without a glance. Two drunks reeled from side to side, crashing into each other and falling on their knees in helpless laughter. A group of office cleaners, their head-scarves wrapped tightly round their necks, the pails on their arms full of cloths and scrubbing brushes, hurried toward the Lenfilm Studios. For Alex Letsukov it still seemed as if he were embarking on an ordinary day's work.

Captain Zhubov at Police Station 16 had been briskly cooperative on the telephone. Yes, he understood perfectly why the Trade Union Department of the Nationalities Ministry might be interested in the Prisoner Densky. Yes, he had received an official Ministry request for specialist Letsukov to examine the prisoner. Yes, Prisoner Densky would be made available to him if Ministry Specialist Letsukov would present himself at Leningrad 16 at 7:30 A.M. on the morning of June 25th. He apologized for the early hour, but the station routine started early in the day. This was traditional.

The light over the main door flicked off as Letsukov began to mount the steps. It was exactly 7:30 A.M. Captain Zhubov welcomed him warmly with an offer of a bacon and sausage breakfast at the station cafeteria, the best in Leningrad, he claimed.

Letsukov declined and accepted instead tea in the Captain's office while they discussed the preliminaries.

"Since the day of the arrest," the Captain offered with some pride, "Densky has become an important figure. I have received no less than five separate requests for interviews by representatives of the highest authorities."

Letsukov found it difficult to dislike this vainglorious young man who seemed to feel personally responsible for the growth of official interest in his new prisoner.

Zhubov handed him the file. It carried Densky's name, Internal Passport number and the KGB stamp: *To Be Preserved Forever*.

"How long has Densky been a prisoner?" Letsukov opened the file.

"Three weeks."

"What charges have been brought?"

"All charges are pending."

Letsukov nodded and read quickly through the file. It seemed to contain little that was new to him. Densky's part in the Blue Bridge demonstrations was already familiar. What Letsukov himself had been sent to ascertain was whether or not there was any evidence of dissident worker links between say, Leningrad and Tashkent, or Leningrad and the Ukrainian worker-dissidents in Kiev. He was himself inclined to believe there was none, that these shop-floor dissidents were mostly concerned with the price of vegetables and the scarcity of meat. Then he turned the page in the Densky dossier and began to read the appeal to international opinion. It was the first time Letsukov heard the title Free Trade Union Movement.

They had finished their tea and Zhubov rose to lead the way down to the examination room beside the basement cells. The steps were bare concrete, the walls white tiles decorated with a black diamond pattern. The stench of disinfectant rose to meet them.

Zhubov led the way to a room about ten feet by ten. A table and three chairs stood in the middle. The concrete floor was badly cracked and a large patch of damp spread around the crazed area. An ancient German steel helmet, upturned for use as an ashtray, rocked in the corner as Letsukov took a seat.

"Where is Comrade Densky being held, Captain?" Letsukov said.

"*Citizen* Densky," the Captain corrected him sternly. "We do not accord the fraternal form of address to a prisoner."

"I see."

"Citizen Densky has been informed only that he will be presented for questioning this morning. Not by whom. You're therefore free to assume whatever role is most convenient. With some prisoners it is helpful to create the illusion that you are a defense lawyer. This, however, is unlikely to work in Densky's case."

He checked his watch. "He should be brought in here any time now."

"Captain, I wonder if my ministry made my technique clear. You are aware that I always examine prisoners alone."

"The ministry did request that facility, yes."

"Good. One more question. Physically, is Joseph Densky in good condition?"

"Powerful as a bull, Comrade."

Outside Letsukov heard the stamp of boots . . . shouts . . . chains. And Joseph Densky stood in the doorway flanked by guards. Each wrist was chained to the corresponding ankle. One eyebrow was split by a partially healed scar. "Good morning, Comrade," he said to Letsukov. "Where shall I sit?" He bustled forward, chains rattling. "I can't tell you how much I look forward to these discussions. Now, shall it be here opposite you, so that you can catch the evasive gleam in my eye? Yes, just under the light? That's where I'd certainly put you if the roles were reversed." He grinned at Letsukov. "Which God forbid!"

Zhubov struggled vainly to assert his authority. "You will sit where and when directed, Prisoner Densky," he bawled. Then fell silent. He knew he had made himself ridiculous.

The guards knew it, too. One of them stepped forward and struck Densky a blow across the kidneys with his short baton. "Listen to what the Captain tells you," he snarled.

There was no mistaking the pain on Densky's face. He arched his back and straightened slowly. "Ah, my friend," he said, with a smile of pure menace, "come the Revolution!"

When they were seated and the door had closed behind Zhubov, Letsukov took a notepad from his briefcase, and placed it on the table in front of him. "You are Citizen Joseph Petrovitch Densky, worker, born Leningrad, nineteen twenty-six. Married. One child."

"Correct," Densky said. "Except for the designation, *Citizen*. Citizenship surely implies rights. I have none. I would prefer us to be accurate from the beginning."

Letsukov nodded warily.

"I am First Assistant Secretary Letsukov."

"A bureaucrat, then. Not a policeman."

"Not a policeman."

"And how can I be of help to you, First Assistant Secretary Letsukov?"

Again Letsukov was struck by Densky's ability to surmount his chains, his split eyebrow, the squalor of this room . . .

"Your open letter to so-called international opinion mentions an anti-Soviet organization which goes under the cover name of the Free Trade Union Movement."

"Except for the bias of your terminology, agreed."

"When did this movement begin?"

"It's been rising in the hearts of Soviet workers for over a decade, Comrade."

"And you have been associated with it for how long?"

"Five years at least."

"You admit to five years?"

"With pride."

"You also admit that its objectives are anti-Soviet?"

"Its objectives are fair and free representation of workers in enterprises throughout the U.S.S.R. Its objectives are the strict enforcement of the Constitution of 1977 and of the guarantees to workers and citizens contained within the Labor Code. I will admit that those objectives are anti-Soviet if you will, First Assistant Secretary Letsukov."

Letsukov held his pen suspended above the notebook. He found he had nothing to write.

"What is your view of the size of the membership of your movement?" he said at length.

"I am unable to answer you with any certainty," Densky said. "There are obvious constraints on communication. But I have reason to believe that our objectives are widely shared by Soviet workers."

Letsukov took out a packet of Belomors cigarettes. He hesitated, then gave one to Densky and took another for himself.

"Are your activities confined to the Russian Federated Republic?" He got up and crossed the room. Picking up the rusting German helmet, he carried it back, placed it on the table between them and lit both cigarettes.

"Justice at work is a problem that affects the whole Soviet Union," Densky said.

"Do you have direct contact with the autonomous Republics?"

"Yes."

"Please specify them."

"The movement in Leningrad has received pledges of support from workers and enterprises in the Caucasian Republics, in the Central Asia Republics, in the Slav Republics of Ukraine and Belorussia and from the Baltic Republics."

"You admit this?"

"I *claim* it, comrade. Furthermore, the agents who ransacked my apartment would have all the original documents in their possession today if the fools had not maliciously burned before my wife's eyes two packets of what they imagined were my wartime love letters to her from the front." He smiled.

Letsukov noted the incident, the German steel helmet rocking as he wrote.

He lifted his head. "In the past," he said, "bourgeois nationalist decadence has been associated with other forms of self-seeking dissident activity."

"Let me answer you in *simple* Russian," Denský said. "You may be right, comrade."

"I'm asking you whether your movement, to the extent it exists, encourages this anti-Soviet nationalism in the autonomous republics and regions."

"Comrade, I can see you are an intelligent man. I don't have to tell you that national aspirations need no encouragement in the Soviet Union today. I have worked with Ukrainians, Estonians, Latvians, Uzbeks . . . each and all of them sing the same song. They are not Russians, they never will be."

"Nobody expects them to be Russians," Letsukov said. "They are all Soviet citizens."

"With the undoubted rights of Soviet citizens. Except in their case they are losing today not only their rights to true citizenship but their rights to nationhood also. This is their belief when they are forced to speak Russian, to leave their homelands to work in alien parts, to serve as cooks and cleaners in the army for true-bred Russian soldiers." He spread his hands in a gesture of mock innocence and pulled taut his chains. "I have no comment to make on these anti-Soviet attitudes, of course. I merely repeat them to you, safe in the knowledge that here I am free to do so." He rattled his chains.

"The equality of the republics and autonomous regions is a recognized principle of Soviet constitutional practice," Letsukov said.

"We are equals, Comrade First Assistant Secretary, but we are not free. During the war when I was a young soldier advancing through the ruins of a Jewish ghetto in a Polish town, I saw this slogan scrawled by Jews upon the burned walls: 'We are all equal—we are marked to die.'"

Letsukov sat watching him silently.

"I believe you to be a decent man, Comrade Letsukov. You will therefore understand what those Jews knew in nineteen forty-four. Equality is the opium of the people."

Letsukov stood up. Densky bent his head forward to scratch the sandy hair at his temple with the knuckle of his thumb.

When Letsukov hammered on the steel door, the guards appeared within seconds.

Leaving the militia station, Letsukov walked slowly along the Nevsky Prospekt. The queues here, he saw, were if anything worse than in Moscow. But standing in line was no part of his life. In Moscow he had the Ministry Club and its commissariat. At a favorable price, and with marked politeness from the assistants, he could buy any home-produced goods and a limited range of foreign goods, too. Next year with his expected grade promotion, he would be eligible to shop in the Club on Sverdlov

Square where prices were even lower and the range of Western goods considerably greater.

And Joseph Densky was in prison. Well, he had put himself beyond the law. Letsukov bumped into a stocky woman carrying two bags of vegetables. Recoiling without apologies they continued on their separate ways. What law had Joseph Densky transgressed? Section this, subsection that, he had a photocopy in his briefcase. But what law had Densky really broken? He had disobeyed not the open published dictates of the State, but the secret well-understood clauses. And in Paris that spring he, Alexei Letsukov, had obeyed the law. Not, of course, its open proclamations of national autonomy. But its secret intent to stifle all national feelings.

Later that morning, before a huge concrete apartment block, Letsukov got out of a taxi. The gray wall was cracking down 20 yards of its length. The narrow balconies sagged dangerously. A plaque proclaimed that the Kirov Apartment Building had been completed in record time on January 1, 1981, by the 171st Shock Construction Worker Brigade.

The two plainclothesmen approached him as he crossed the bald grass. Before they had a chance to speak, Letsukov drew his Ministry card from his pocket and handed it to them. They both wore the short car coats and brogue shoes available in KGB commissariats.

"I'm going to interview the prisoner Densky's wife. Is she in the apartment?"

"She's in, Comrade Letsukov. Do you want us to accompany you?"

Letsukov shook his head. "Has she had many visitors since her husband's arrest?"

The short Bureau man with the bald spot on the back of his head glanced toward the apartment entrance as if someone might be trying to slip in behind his back. "No Comrade," he said, turning back to Letsukov. "In the first few days there were dozens, but we had a full squad on then, we turned them all away, of course. Now you get one or two trying to call, mostly after dark, but we pull them up quickly enough, that's what we're here for after all."

"They usually pretend they're lost," the other man laughed. "We take their names all the same."

Letsukov left the two men and entered the apartment building. The flat was on the sixth floor and the lift was out of order. A staircase like a medieval spiral led him upward. The concrete walls were chalked with obscenities, faded expressions of support for the Soviet Olympic soccer team and new whitewashed slogans of praise for Joseph Densky.

At the sixth floor he rang the bell of apartment 28. A woman answered almost immediately.

"I've come to speak to the wife of Joseph Densky," Letsukov said.

"Then you've come to speak to me." She was a tall, slender woman, somewhere in her early fifties.

"May I come in?"

"If Kuba's gentlemen downstairs have allowed you to pass, how can I refuse?"

She held the door open and he walked past her into a two-room apartment. A kitchen door stood between two rough-timber empty bookshelves.

"My name is Letsukov," he said. "I am an official of the Nationalities Ministry, Trade Union Section."

"My name is Densky," she parodied. "I am the wife of a prisoner of the Militia, KGB Section."

"Please tell me your forename and patronymic," he said.

She gestured for him to sit down. "I am Leonida Donsova Densky."

"Thank you. I saw your husband this morning," he said.

"Is he . . ."

"Well? Yes. Even aggressively so. He has a scar over one eyebrow which is now healing. Apart from that he shows some physical signs of having been beaten. But most certainly no other signs."

She frowned, already finding his openness disturbing. "I thought that beatings were agreed to be illegal."

"Of course. But we all know they happen."

"It's not something I would expect you to admit."

He took out a packet of Belomors and offered her one. She shook her head.

"May I?"

She laughed. "Smoke, Comrade Letsukov? The men downstairs have allowed you up. You can do as you please, obviously."

He put away the packet of cigarettes.

"Is your husband's movement widespread?"

"I hope so."

"But you don't know."

"I know nothing. I am a chattel, the woman of a monstrous wife-beating bigot, whom I happen to love to distraction," she was laughing at him.

He smiled. "I don't see you as a chattel, Leonida Donsova. I don't see Joseph Densky as a man who would keep a chattel."

"Smoke your cigarette, Comrade Letsukov," she said lightheartedly. "Give me one, too. I see you've come here to be subtle with me. Well, why not?"

She got up and produced a liter and two glasses from a corner cupboard. "It's seldom I have the chance to entertain one of Semyon

Kuba's gentlemen. But one should take what opportunities are presented. After all, you are playing host to my husband. I'm sure he's eating adequately in his squalid prison cell."

Letsukov took out the cigarettes. He watched her pour the vodka. She took a cigarette and sat down again.

"I need not have come here today," he said.

"Or any day."

"I mean that I have come here under cover of official business. My department is concerned with any . . . unorthodox trade union activity. So I have the excuse ready-made."

"Why should you think of it as an excuse?" She inhaled her cigarette inexpertly.

"I came here because, after speaking to your husband, I felt I wanted to know more about his movement. For my own purposes, not for official reasons," he said clumsily.

"Comrade, my daughter and I have been questioned at least twenty times since my husband's arrest. I have nothing to say about my husband's activities."

"Can you believe I have come as a friend?"

"No."

They were, he thought, an indomitable couple, Joseph Densky and his wife.

"Your husband is not the only one who has doubts about the exercise of Soviet power."

"Most people would be shocked to hear you say so," she said, her eyes sparkling.

"I am one such, Leonida Donsova," he said.

"A member of the Party?"

"Yes."

"Then this is serious," she drank her vodka in one gulp with a rapid movement of the wrist and smiled at him. "Very serious."

"Leonida Donsova, I can understand your fears about me. I come to your house under the umbrella of the men who have imprisoned your husband. But I ask you to listen to me. After that you can decide whether or not it is safe for you to have more to do with me."

She put out her cigarette and sat back in her chair. Her fingers locked in her lap.

"Like your husband," he began . . .

"I had the impression you were to talk about yourself, Comrade Letsukov. Not my husband."

"Very well," he said. "I did not come here to make a confession. But I see that circumstances force it upon me. You wish me to speak of myself. I am a senior official in a Union Ministry. I no longer believe in all that the

Ministry or indeed the Soviet government stands for. There, I've spoken openly."

"Perhaps." Her eyes were fixed on his.

"Like your husband I now see flaws in the Communist ideal."

"My husband is a Communist. Do you understand that, Comrade?"

"I think I do."

"Do you believe it?"

"If you say so, yes."

"What else is there to be after all?" She opened her arms wide. "Are you then *not* a Communist, Comrade Letsukov?"

"I have been all my life."

"That is an ambiguous answer."

"Yes, it is. Communism was good to me, Leonida Donsova. I prospered. I was happy."

"Until?"

"I found the path was not straight and strewn with flowers as I had imagined." He hesitated. "I was asked to go to Paris to kill a man."

She looked at him for a moment, her lower lip tucked pensively under her teeth. She was not shocked. "The KGB asked you?" she said.

"Yes."

"You refused."

"No. Without giving you all the details, I agreed."

Perhaps she was shocked now.

"Why are you telling me this?"

"I am telling you because I know no other way of persuading you that I am your husband's friend."

"Go on."

"It was a political murder."

"But you don't think of yourself as a murderer."

"More and more," he said.

"You did it for someone else?"

"Perhaps. Leonida Donsova . . ." Letsukov leaned forward in his chair. "I no longer know whether I am a Communist. Most certainly I am not one of those who dotes on Western ways. In any case I am convinced that Russia must find her own way through the dark wood."

She smiled. "My husband reads Dante, too. Through *his* Inferno Joseph Stalin lights the way, holding high the glowing severed head of Kirov."

"And yet your husband calls himself a Communist."

"He *is* a Communist," she insisted. "He believes that Communism expresses a deep truth about human nature. What confuses and depresses him is that it has always exalted the power of the lie."

"More than Western capitalism?"

"Far, far more, Joseph says. Capitalist lies are of course more subtle, but the system still allows for their rejection. Our system depends for its existence on the lie. Mendacity is the foundation stone, far more than terror has ever been."

"The Free Trade Union Movement then is a Communist movement?"

"Yes."

"It is one I would like to join," Letsukov said.

"But how can we trust you?"

"I am an official, a reasonably highly placed official. I travel throughout the Union. I have a certain freedom, like now, to investigate so-called anti-trade union movements. For your communications you need some-one like me."

"That may or may not be true, Comrade Letsukov. For all your past, you seem a decent man. But if the KGB were worried, as they are, about the growth of free trade unionism among the nationalities, then surely you are just the man they would send to just this house."

"That is so."

"Can you offer no proof that you are really a friend?"

"None that I can think of."

She stood up. "It's a long road through the dark wood, Comrade." She held out her hand. "We owe it to others to beware the beckoning of false lanterns."

Chapter Eight

YELENDA OVSENKO HAD been at the plow all day. Or more accurately harnessed to the plow all day. With five other women she had "borrowed" an iron plow from the collective and in one long day from before dawn to just before dusk had turned over the earth in all six of their private allotments.

For most of the village women the achievement had been enough to call for a celebration. But Yelenda had other things on her mind. As yet she had said nothing of her troubles to her friends in the village, but word, she knew, would get round. It always did.

Yet before the gossiping began she wanted to talk to the Farm Chairman Pavel Rodontov. He was a good man and knew about these things.

Yelenda had lived all her life in the village of Morisa, 30 miles west of Moscow. In her youth, Moscow, though only an hour or two away by train, had been some unknown but glittering center of the world, and trains themselves on the few occasions she had seen one, had terrified her with their snorting smoke and great flashing central eye.

Now, of course, Moscow was a familiar city, the market she went to once a week to sell the produce of her private plot. But even so she remained in all ways a peasant. She retained a terror of lightning which she still somehow believed was a divine punishment, although she no longer believed in God. She considered it necessary to speak with caution to goatherds and tailors because they were invariably the source of malicious gossip. And she kept, sewn into the lining of her boot, a gold ruble from the Czar's days, which was destined to pay for her funeral.

She had married late, after half a lifetime of looking after her aged mother. Her husband, finally retired from the army after twenty years' service, had returned to his village in search of a wife. But in the Moscow *oblast* where all the young girls received internal passports at sixteen, there were no young women left. So he had married the forty-year-old Yelenda and had a son by her the next year. In the remaining twelve years of his life he had been a good father to Anton, teaching him about other peoples he had seen as a soldier, making him study and even securing a place for him in the school at Noginsk.

When he had died he left Yelenda a set of medals and a gold ruble. And a boy who was no longer a peasant's son.

But Yelenda had loved her son. And he had loved her. Even when, as a University student, he would laugh at her superstitions he could still admire the crafty peasant intelligence of her market transactions.

She had dressed in her best winter coat to see the Farm Chairman and waiting now in the bare concrete room, she felt hot and anxious. Like all the other women workers on the Morisa Kolkhoz she was respectful of the Collective Chairman, Pavel Rodontov. Over many years she knew him to be just in his dealings with the peasants and for that reason perhaps there was less pilfering at Morisa than at any of the other collective farms in the region.

The door opened and Pavel Ivanovich invited her into his office. She admired the strong concrete walls and the metal window frames. It was all very fitting for a man of Pavel Ivanovich's importance.

"Sit down, Yelenda," Rodontov said.

She took a chair in front of his desk. It was the first time she had been into his office, but of course she had met him many times out in the fields.

"I am sorry to take up your valuable time, Comrade Chairman," she muttered.

Rodontov seated himself behind the desk. "It's about your son, Anton," he said.

"You've heard about it already?" She was amazed that news could travel from Moscow that fast.

"The verdict of every trial is sent to the birthplace of the defendant," Rodontov said. "Naturally, no one else will know about it, if that's your wish. Was it that, that was troubling you?"

Hot in her winter coat, she hesitated. "Partly that, Comrade Chairman. But mostly I came to ask what can be done. Seven years in a camp, Comrade. He'll be a grown man long before he is released."

"Seven years is a severe sentence," Rodontov agreed.

"And at the trial they told lies, Comrade."

"Ah . . ."

"So can he not appeal to have the sentence removed?"

"Yelenda, he appealed within the seven days allowed under Soviet law. It was determined, also under Soviet law, that he had been justly convicted and sentenced."

"Justly?"

"According to Soviet law, yes."

"But in the court the prosecutor told lies."

"You're sure of that?"

"In his evidence, Anton said so. I was there."

Rodontov rubbed the edge of his nose with a pencil. He knew this was going to be a difficult interview. "Yelenda," he said patiently, "courts are not like normal life. Among friends, in the village, if an egg is bad you don't try to sell it to your neighbor."

"No, she'd beat me with a broom handle."

"But Yelenda, in the market in Moscow, that would be different."

"Perhaps," she conceded.

"You see it's not so much lies, Yelenda, as different sides of the truth."

She frowned. "I have money, Comrade Chairman, I can tell you this in confidence. A gold ruble, from the old Czar's days. Who do I give it to?"

"Give it to?"

"Someone at the court. A gold ruble's always a gold ruble."

"Yelenda," Rodontov said carefully, "I'm sure this is difficult to understand. But not even Soviet lawmakers have always been as wise as Solomon."

"Was Joseph Stalin not as wise as Solomon, Comrade Chairman?"

Rodontov paled. "I think," he rose to conclude the interview, "we can safely say that he was not always as wise as Marx or Lenin."

Yelenda left the office and walked back through the village. Electric lights shone brightly in the windows of the sturdy log houses. In every kitchen was a tap, turn it and water would flow into the bucket. These were things that Joseph Stalin had brought the village. And when the Germans came with the great tanks with the black crosses on them, it was Joseph Stalin who had driven them out.

Yelenda mounted the wooden steps of her izba and let herself in the door. She crossed to the three-legged table by the stove and, taking matches from her pocket, lit the brass ikon-lamp. The guttering flame rose beside the ikon, illuminating the fatherly smile on the face of Joseph Stalin, pasted over the figure of some long-forgotten saint.

"Seven years!" She was weeping. "It would never have happened in your day!"

Less than ten miles from Yelenda's village high wooded bluffs looked down on a wide marshy expanse contained within a great bend of the river. Streams wound through the area, thin brown brackish trickles among the clumps of reed and marsh grass, or broad, shallow rivulets winding between clumps of alders.

The whole wide area had once been the preserve of reed cutters and here and there it was still possible to come across a wooden shack, collapsing now on its timber stilts, with a sunken mud-filled punt in the stream beside it.

But as men had abandoned the marsh, the snipe and waterfowl had taken it for their own. It was now one of the prime shooting areas within easy reach of Moscow.

Count Franz von Boden considered it a rare privilege to be asked to shoot over this land. On any autumn visit to Moscow he was sure of an invitation from Igor Bukansky, the editor of *Novaya Literatura,* and he eagerly took it up.

Not that today had been a good day for him. The snipe were plentiful. The peasant loaders were efficient enough. But somehow it was still not a good day.

Behind him the wings whirred. In swift zigzag flight the snipe passed the clump of alders. He fired, wide again, then heard Bukansky or the American Hal Bashford's shot from beyond the peat bank.

Ruefully he looked down at his empty hunting bag. Bukansky, huge as a bear, appeared over the bank, black mud up to his thighs. His dog, Bob, held the snipe.

"You Germans," Bukansky roared, slithering down the bank with Hal Bashford behind. "You didn't miss when you had a Russian in your sights!"

The three men splashed through shallow streams toward the crumbling reed cutter's hut where the loaders had set up lunch.

"Watch your footing," Bukansky warned. "One rotten board and you go straight down into the water."

It was a single-room shack with a split and rickety table in the middle, but it was piled with bottles of vodka, fruit, cheese and bread. A huge soup bowl steamed in the middle of the table and the three men ladled soup into pottery bowls while the two peasants stood by attentively.

"Help yourselves," Bukansky waved an arm at the peasants. "Here . . ." He ladled out a bowl of soup and handed it to one of them, "you've got your feet as wet as ours. Give that to Vanya. Take this one. How's that fish coming on, Vanya?" he shouted to the peasant turning the spit over the fire. He took his own bowl of soup across to examine the salmon roasting on the spit and turned back to pour vodka into five glasses.

"That young secretary of yours, Igor," Hal Bashford said. "She likes Western clothes."

"She does."

"Do you think it'd be a good idea if I brought her back something from New York next month?"

"A good idea, brother. But it won't get you what you want. She's spoken for."

The two foreigners laughed. "Now listen, friends," Bukansky said, "all this talk of sport and women is good enough in its place. But I have more important things to discuss with you publishing gentlemen."

"Kuletsyn's novel, *To Be Preserved Forever*," Bashford said. "I've already told you I agree."

"Our translation will be completed this month," the German said. "But from what I've already read, there's no doubt in my mind either."

"Speed, speed is what counts now," Bukansky said urgently. "My ragged-arsed genius sends me weekly messages demanding to know what I'm doing. So?"

"I've already organized the serialization you want in the States and Britain. It could be serialized in December and published in the New Year," Bashford said.

"In Germany we'll be less than a month behind you."

Bukansky lifted his vodka glass. "You gentlemen will earn a fortune."

"And you?" Bashford said.

"And I will publish a great Russian novel. Albeit by proxy."

Chapter Nine

As THE COLD returned sharply to western Russia that year it was announced to a stunned Leningrad that the annual November 7th parade to celebrate the October Revolution would not take place. A brief line in Leningrad *Pravda* mentioned the absence of army units on important maneuvers in the German Democratic Republic. Perhaps in the West only an announcement that Christmas would not be celebrated that year would produce an equivalent sense of shock and disbelief.

So totally exceptional a cancellation in the birthplace of the Revolution immediately prompted the State Department in Washington to ask that a senior official from the Moscow Embassy be sent to Leningrad to evaluate the position. It was assumed that the recent rash of small strikes and demonstrations by students had forced the authorities to cancel the parade. It normally attracted, after Moscow's own parade, more tourists than any other event in the Soviet year.

Then on the day the cancellation was announced, a message from the imprisoned Joseph Densky to the workers of Leningrad began to circulate. It called on all workers, united in bitterness, to stage a massive march through the city on the night of November 7th.

Tom Foster Yates, arriving from the Moscow Embassy with his wife, Carole, on the morning of the cancelled parade, had every reason to feel pleased with himself. In his early forties, his previously overthin frame had filled out pleasingly and his dark hair was now flecked with gray at the temples. Carole, of course, had always attracted attention, especially the attention of men. For a moment, Tom Yates' feeling of well-being receded as the memory of that incident in Paris last spring thrust itself into his mind. He pushed it aside resolutely. It had in any case made no difference to his expected promotion to the Moscow Embassy. His present mission indicated strongly the confidence his ambassador placed in him.

For Carole Yates the fact that she was in Leningrad was in itself a source of satisfaction. In two months she had seen most of what she wanted to see in Moscow; Leningrad, by all accounts, would offer a pleasant contrast to the brute-modern skyscrapers that increasingly dominated the capital.

*　　*　　*

I think we were already crossing the concourse [Carole wrote] when it happened. I could never have imagined before the terrifying violence of an explosion like that. Talons of black-red flame reached out toward us and a rush of hot air threw me to the ground. Perhaps I was deafened for a few moments or perhaps in their terror the people in the concourse were themselves struck dumb. Then suddenly everyone seemed to scream at once. Men howled in anguish, women shrieked their panic as they dragged themselves on broken limbs away from the point of the explosion. Glass from the roof was clattering down in great sheets; sections of splintered timber and whole panels of plastic arced slowly down on us.

In the screaming confusion I looked round for Tom. He was about five yards away, on his feet, but with a look of open-mouthed bewilderment on his face. A child of about five, his hair singed black, his clothes in tatters, collided with Tom's legs, and ran on past him. I'm not sure that Tom even noticed.

The singing in my ears from the explosion suddenly stopped. I realized I was sitting among blood and glass, gaping like Tom, at the pain and horror all around me.

I got to my feet. My head ached unbearably. Tom suddenly was at my side.

"Are you all right, Carole?" He seemed to be shouting.

I nodded dumbly.

"Then let's get out of here," he said savagely. "It was a bomb. There could be another."

I allowed him to drag me away, past the burned bodies, past men and women sobbing with their arms round each other, past even the children running in terror-stricken circles . . .

By midday all Leningrad knew of the incident. Word passed around that it was a student, himself killed when the bomb exploded prematurely. It was said that the airport had been chosen because it was now the main gateway into Leningrad for all those immigrant workers from the Central Asian Republics of the U.S.S.R. It was a point which escaped Western commentators, but it had not escaped students like Zoya Densky. To her the Leningrad airport atrocity marked the resurfacing of an old but ugly form of purely Russian nationalism.

No one in that uncertain summer [Zoya recounts] was more divided than the Leningrad student body, among whom in spirit I still counted myself. Night after night political meetings were held all over the University campus. Student rooms meant for two or three would have thirty crushed in, standing against the walls or squatting on the floor. It was chaos.

On one side there were the people like myself (my father's influence, I suppose) who believed that the Soviet Union had become one vast bureaucracy, a pork barrel for any member of the Party, an easy ride if you were the son or daughter of a General or Collective Farm Chairman or toe-the-line writer or musician. We all knew how well they lived, the *vlasti*. After all, there were plenty of their offspring at the University in their Western jeans, cooking chicken and fillet steaks in their rooms every night. We used to call them the golden boys, although that normally means a homosexual to Russians.

My group, if you like, believed that if we could get rid of the Party bureaucracy we could establish a decent life for all. A place you could speak your mind and where your parents wouldn't be in constant danger of arrest. We had slogans—"No collective guilt," "Smash the Party bureaucracy." You'll smile now when I tell you but we really believed a brave new democratic world was possible.

Then there was the other group. The Rodinists they began to call themselves from the Russian word *Rodina,* Motherland. They were the poets and music players, young men with eyes often as dark and smoldering as their nationalist passions.

They believed in Russia. Not the Soviet Union, not the vast empire that the Czars had bequeathed us, but in the Russian peasant and his infinite capacity to suffer. While we were drawn toward the West they were repelled by it. You never saw them in jeans or T-shirts. They wore felt boots and coarse trousers, with a loose belted blouse on top. Boys and girls. Their view was that the Communist Party was a Western conspiracy. Marx was a cosmopolitan German Jew, a known Slav-hater. Lenin had lived most of his adult life outside Russia and had even been brought back to ferment revolution by the Germans. Most of the big figures from the revolutionary days had disguised their un-Russianness with false names: Trotsky (Bronstein), Zinoviev (Apfelbaum), Kamenev (Rosenfeld). I hardly need to say that the Rodinists were to a man, or girl, violently anti-Semitic. And violently opposed to the other republics in the Soviet Empire.

They had a curious view of Stalin, who was, of course, a Georgian, but they seemed prepared to accept him as an adopted Russian. After all, he had forced the Cyrillic alphabet on the Russian dominions and had led the Motherland through the great Patriotic War. Their struggle with the present was with the vast agricultural and industrialization plans which they saw as only necessary to feed Kazaks and Uzbeks and Poles and Hungarians and Cubans and Ethiopians. If Holy Mother Russia (and they meant *Holy,* too) only slammed its front and back doors tight, the Russian soul—Russian culture, arts and crafts—would flourish in a Slav Utopia divorced from the world.

They believed it. Some of them even lived it. They hated the Party setup in the *oblasts* as much as in Moscow itself. And as that winter began they decided the time had come once again (it was an old Russian tradition) to defend the Russian soul with the bomb. Leningrad Airport was the first step.

Within an hour of the Leningrad Airport bombing the authorities had made an urgent request to Soviet Army Northwest Headquarters for reinforcement.

Reacting to the near panic of the authorities, the Soviet Command had issued orders to the four Field Police Battalions available in neighboring Estonia. Of the four units heading northeast along the Gulf road to Leningrad that afternoon, three were predominantly Slav battalions with a high standard of training and experience. The fourth, No. 29 Field Provost Battalion, was a recently raised unit indistinguishable from the others in equipment. But in one important sense it epitomized much that was wrong with the Soviet Army in the seventies and eighties. Officered entirely by Slavs, its four hundred enlisted men were mostly drawn from the Soviet Central Asian republics.

As a unit its disciplinary record was bad. Only a month earlier a whole company had been sentenced to five years in a penal brigade for a violent assault on their own company officers. In the court martial hearings nobody had seen fit to mention a clash between repressed Asiatics and dominant Slavs.

By early afternoon, with the weather closing in from the Gulf of Finland, the 29th Field Provost was already lagging far behind the other units. Every 30 miles a truck or armored personnel carrier, poorly maintained or badly driven in the thickening fall of snow, would block the road. Each time, Major Sudorov, aware of his unit's reputation, would race back in his command vehicle and curse and exhort men working in the unfamiliar cold, men who could in any case barely understand his instructions.

Throughout that freezing afternoon tension among the Provost soldiers increased hourly. Officers, fearful for their own careers, kicked and struck at men trying to drag the broken-down vehicles into the ditch. There were accidents, a broken leg, a crushed arm. As it began to get dark the wind rose. Driving wet snow clogged headlights. In a chaos of skidding vehicles the 29th Field Provost Battalion crept toward Leningrad.

Bubo Musa was a recent recruit to the 29th Field Provost. Unusually tall for a member of the Tatar race, his close-shaved head showed the sharp outline of a narrow skull. He had learned to trade on the menace of his slanting eyes and the Tatar reputation, to defend himself in this unit of desperate, violent men. He was in his early thirties, old to be a new recruit, and had deliberately done nothing to contradict the general belief among his fellow soldiers that his late conscription into the army was due to the delay caused by a seven-year prison sentence for murder. He *had* in fact served seven years in a labor camp. But the sentence was not for murder. Bubo Musa, a former tailor from Bratsk in Siberia, was a victim of the Stalin past and the Soviet Union's unrelenting present.

When his parents were born, some three hundred thousand members of the Muslim Tatar race lived in the soft climate of the Crimean peninsula of European Russia. They were a people bound closely by ties of religion and national consciousness. They were thus a people who, on both counts, failed to fit the Russian imperialist dreams of the Georgian, Joseph Stalin.

It was the Hitler war which, at first, had threatened the very fabric of the new Russian Empire and, in victory, had presented Stalin with his greatest opportunity to recreate the Czarist Empire. The early years of defeat and occupation by the German armies had revealed the extent of nationalist feeling. Among every occupied nation-republic, anti-Soviet or anti-Russian movements came into existence.

But as the German armies retreated and nationalist sentiments exploded into new life, Stalin struck. In the middle of the greatest war in history he still found time for vengeance. Six small nations were collectively, every man, woman and child, accused of treason. They were torn from their native lands and deported in endless lines of cattle trucks to Siberia. A million people were uprooted and denied every right under the Soviet Constitution. But among all the lost nations it is the story of the Crimean Tatars that best reveals the chilling lengths to which the Russians have been prepared to go to maintain their dominion in the south of the Soviet Union.

During the Brezhnev years it was unusual to hear in the West anything of the continuing struggle of the Tatar people. But they had not given up. From their exile in Siberia and Uzbekistan, Tatars began to return illegally to the Crimea.

For this crime Bubo Musa was arraigned and sentenced to seven years in a labor camp.

Even the Soviet prosecutor had recognized that no violence had been involved. But the violence practiced against Bubo Musa during his seven-year imprisonment had left its mark. Resistant to hating his fellow men, even when they were Russians, Bubo had already begun to focus his hatred on the city of Moscow itself. He would talk, dangerously, not of the Soviet Union, but of the Muscovite Empire. Never having been to Moscow, he nevertheless saw the city, in its past and present, as the

capital of an unchanging Russian Empire relentless in its determination to
impose Russian uniformity throughout its vast dominions.

On the afternoon of November 7th, Bubo Musa had been one of the
victims of a BR7 Armored sliding on the snow-covered roads. Unable to
fling himself clear, his boot had been momentarily trapped by a wheel,
and the heavy vehicle, sliding forward, struck his knee. Ordered by an
officer to ignore the accident, Bubo had limped on throughout that
dreadful afternoon. He had as a result limped on for the rest of his short
life.

In the Hero City itself, unknown of course to Bubo and the members of
his Field Provost unit, tension had been mounting throughout the day.
Before dark fell the militia had contributed to the growing sense that
something was about to happen by touring the streets in search of foreign
visitors. All tourists were instructed to return to their hotels and remain
there until daybreak. At Pulkovo Airport incoming tourists were, without
explanation, taken in buses to hotels well outside the city; some were
immediately placed on return flights to the West; others found their
Leningrad flights mysteriously diverted to Moscow. Again, no explanations were offered.

For Russians no curfew had as yet been declared. But nobody could
escape the presence of militia on the streets. At major intersections and
every bridge over the Neva and the canals, militia trucks and armored
vehicles were stationed in force. No one was allowed to approach the Blue
Bridge itself.

Sometime in the late evening events began to develop in four separate
corners of the city. From the direction of the Baltic station, from
Vasilyevsky Island, from across the Neva at Okhtinsky Bridge and from
the southern metropolitan area around Pulkovo, in response to Joseph
Densky's call, groups of men formed and began to march toward the
Nevsky Prospekt. Their destination was the Winter Palace where in 1917
the marching workers had been ridden and gunned down by the Czar's
cossack troops.

It seems clear now that several attempts were made to disperse the
workers marching on the Winter Palace. But each time the column would
scatter and reassemble at a point closer to the center of the city. By the
time the militia loudspeaker vans began to tour the central area
instructing people to go home, the crowds drifting down the Nevsky
Prospekt were in no mood to comply.

Carole Yates was with her husband in the Dzerzhinsky Restaurant on
the Nevsky Prospekt itself. Against the advice of the Leningrad U.S.
Consular officials they had driven into the city center on what Tom Yates
saw as part of his fact-finding tour. Twice they had narrowly avoided being

escorted back to the consulate by militiamen picking up foreigners on the street. Now, from a table in the Dzerzhinsky, they were able to watch the crowds outside on the Prospekt ignoring the calls of the loudspeaker vans to return to their homes.

It's near impossible to describe the atmosphere in the city that night, Carole Yates recorded. Perhaps if I say that everybody (with the exception of the militia, of course) seemed drunk on either excitement or vodka, or both, it might come close. In the Dzerzhinsky Restaurant the waiters no longer made any attempt to serve the customers. Every one seemed to have a quart of vodka in his hand. Between great gulps from the neck of the bottle the waiters were talking and gesticulating among themselves or at the tables of still unserved customers. I remember the name of Joseph Densky seemed to come up frequently.

What was happening? Well of course they all pretended to know. Some said that it was outright revolution, others that the army was already arresting KGB units in the suburbs as part of a military coup. Yet others said that student bombing teams were planning to attack militia stations throughout the city.

Then from somewhere north or south of the twisting River Neva came the first burst of shooting—No. 29 Field Provost had finally arrived in Leningrad. Assigned a key position at that part of the Nevsky Prospekt closest to the river, their orders were to use minimum force to clear the crowd from the bottom of the Prospekt and to block any approach march by workers along the embankment from the east.

But no unit was less capable of minimum force at that moment. Before them were civilian crowds of Slavs. All the desperate hatred they felt for their Slav officers boiled over. Fixing bayonets on order they drove the crowds before them, jabbing fiercely at men and women alike. Screaming women, blood streaming from hands and faces, fled along the Nevsky Prospekt. Some men fought back with their bare hands. Then at that moment the first workers' column approached along the embankment.

To oppose them effectively the Field Police Battalion would have had to disengage at least two companies from the crowd and turn to face the approaching workers. In fact the discipline and training needed to execute the maneuver simply did not exist. Officers roared orders at men who either didn't understand or refused to obey the Russian commands. In the confusion the workers' column was upon them.

Attacked as they now saw it, from the rear, the Field Police began to fire blindly. Unable to maintain any semblance of a military formation, the soldiers fell back in small clusters pointing their rifles indiscriminately at workers or the crowd.

For minutes the advancing workers were paralyzed with shock. Before them was a unit of the Soviet Army, not militia, not KGB guards, but their own army—and it was shooting down unarmed civilians.

Then the workers surged forward, ducking the crack and whine of bullets, and threw themselves upon the soldiers. Workers fell and were trampled on by fellow workers. Rifles were torn from the soldiers' hands and used to bayonet and club the uniformed figures to the ground.

At such close quarters numbers often proved more effective than weapons. Not more than a few sections of Field Police succeeded in retreating, still firing their automatics into the crowd, to the Kirovsky Bridge where a disciplined KGB guard unit rescued them.

As the firing began, Carole Yates and her husband had left the restaurant and emerged onto the Nevsky Prospekt.

Of course it was a foolish thing to do [Carole admitted in her account of that night]. Almost immediately we were swept along the Prospekt toward the shooting near the embankment. I saw men and women falling silently or in screaming pain. I saw Soviet Army soldiers struck down with pieces of paving stone, rough batons of timber, anything that came to hand.

In one day I had seen more blood and violence than I had experienced in my whole life. Perhaps the vision of the morning's airport bombing combined with the horrors I saw before me now. I'm sure they did for my husband. He was shouting and screaming like a madman, dragging me by the arm through the crowd with no idea where safety might lie. I know I was screaming at him to stop, but he had totally lost control. Blundering and crashing through the crowd we suddenly emerged into a side street off the Nevsky Prospekt. Breathless, sobbing even, he released my arm and fell back against a brick wall. Surfacing above my terror at what I had just seen was a sudden moment of insight. I was of a generation of women who had not felt it relevant to ask if physical courage was an important ingredient in the makeup of the men we were with. But tonight's events had presented me with an image I could never again avoid. I now saw differently his actions at the airport this morning. My husband's blind panic filled me with overwhelming disgust.

Ten thousand incidents were cameoed in Leningrad that night. The disarming and arrest by KGB guards of Bubo Musa, the onetime tailor from Bratsk, was to lead him to a northern labor camp (he was considered too politically unstable for a Penal Brigade which was the fate of the other surviving members of his Field Provost unit). Joseph Densky's wife, her groin lanced by a bayonet, was to drag herself halfway home before dying of loss of blood on an empty pavement in a Leningrad suburb. Laryssa Navratovna, the prostitute with the apartment overlooking the Blue

Bridge, was arrested for seditious activity on the Nevsky Prospekt. None of her influential friends were prepared to support her when she claimed she was simply plying her (illegal) trade in her favorite Prospekt cafés when the events of that night had overtaken her.

For Zoya Densky, still unaware of her mother's death and of the death of so many others at the hands of the Field Police, the night had at first seemed a triumph.

As the 29th Field Provost Battalion had been taking up their positions on the Nevsky Prospekt she had been heading with a group of fellow students for the area of the Baltic Station on the far side of the city. Their object was twofold, first, to demonstrate that the nonviolent wing of the student movement could achieve more popular support with open defiance of the authorities than the Rodinists could with the morning's carnage at Pulkovo Airport. And second, to create a diversion which would occupy substantial numbers of militia while the workers were marching to the center of the city for the mass demonstration Zoya's father had called for.

Untroubled by the militia in the quiet outer area of the city, over a thousand students now converged on an anonymous gray building near the Baltic Station. The assault was well prepared. A student was detailed to hammer on the chipped green door. When it was finally opened on a chain, six students carrying eight feet of telephone pole hurled themselves up the steps. As the battering ram burst the mounting of the door chain, dozens of students, hidden in the shadows, poured through the gaping door.

I had heard [Zoya wrote] about the existence of such places, but of course as a worker's daughter I had never seen the inside of one.

It was a Western fairyland. Within that dingy exterior with the blacked-out windows, were stacked on floor after floor, color television sets, crates of German leather shoes, rack after rack of jeans and T-shirts, furniture, light bulbs, windshield wipers, cheeses, Italian sausage, Western rock records—the *vlastis'* rewards for loyal and silent service to the almighty robber state.

Students, pouring up the staircase, running from room to room, would stop in wonder at racks of sweaters or crates of Japanese recording equipment. The guards, overwhelmed by the flood of young people, were bundled into small office rooms.

We worked quickly. The boys had already burst the windows long before the first militia sirens were heard in the distance. A crowd was already beginning to gather from the apartment buildings nearby as the first items began to rain down. Careless of the damage, we hurled television sets and smoked hams, crates of amplifiers and bundles of dresses down onto the pavement below. Then we drove the guards downstairs and fired the building.

By the time the first militia units arrived, Zoya and her friends had slipped away into the side streets. So indeed had much of the crowd, carrying with it armfuls of Western dresses, crates of shoes or canned tuna fish, whole hams or frozen sides of beef. And the once anonymous building on Balskaya Street now blazed as proof that the students of Leningrad could expose the system without the loss of a single life. Before she knew the toll throughout the city, and learned that her mother was among the dead, this was the measure of Zoya's triumph.

The next morning Carole Yates walked the length of a battered Nevsky Prospekt. Windows were smashed, ripped-up paving stones made the street impassable to traffic, militia patrolled everywhere and a line of burned-out cars spread the reek of rubber over the whole area. But eighty workers had been killed or badly injured and an unknown number were under arrest.

In the West the riot flared briefly as a front-page news story and died away. The next day every official factory committee in Leningrad issued a statement condemning the march.

Somehow, from prison, Joseph Densky smuggled out a brief message:

Workers, we must learn our lesson. Our only weapon is the *General Strike*. Leningrad or Moscow or Odessa or Minsk cannot demonstrate alone! We all suffer the same oppressions. United in bitterness, unity is strength.

J. Densky,
Soviet State Prisoner

So November 7th passed in Leningrad and the immediate sum of its events was death, bitterness and defeat. Yet concealed in this calculation was an item of overwhelming importance for the future. At a secret meeting of the younger Soviet generals in Riga that month it was decided that only in the most exceptional circumstances and only after the fullest investigation should the Soviet Army allow itself to be called upon for internal security duties of the kind the Field Police Units had undertaken in Leningrad. The unpopularity of the system (and many of the younger senior officers were prepared to recognize this as a fact) must never be allowed to engulf the Soviet Army. Marshals of the Soviet Union whose view of the uncertain future was colored by the Stalinist past must be persuaded that the Army's first duty was to *itself*.

*   *   *

In Moscow itself, to those who could interpret the tortuous hiero-glyphics of Soviet power, new, more explosive events were presaged. A visit by the Soviet leadership to Bulgaria was abruptly canceled on December 1st. The reception of the American Presidential envoy on disarmament was attended by no one more elevated (at that time) than Deputy Premier Ustinov, General Kuba and Natalya Roginova.

President Romanovsky, it was recalled by every Western newspaper, had not been seen in public since the November 7th celebration of the anniversary of the Revolution. Photographs were again studied in detail. Some Western doctors read the grainy prints and yet again proclaimed that he was a dying man.

The announcement of President Romanovsky's death was made to the foreign press from the Kalasty Hospital at 7:25 A.M. on December 3rd. Within an hour, radio and television stations were informing the world.

The peoples of the Soviet Empire—Russians, Ukrainians, Balts, Kazaks, Tatars, Georgians, Armenians, Azerbaijanians—were left in ignorance until midday central Soviet time when a brief Tass announcement was carried on television. It concluded:

"The death of the General Secretary of the Party cannot, in the nature of the system, indicate a change in policy.

"The Collective Leadership appeals confidently to Soviet citizens to recognize that at this great juncture in Soviet history, the principles of Marxist-Leninist-Brezhnevist Socialism must be pursued relentlessly.

"The efforts of Western imperialists to sow discord in the collective leadership are doomed to failure by the Socialist awareness of the Soviet people."

With no more reassurance than this, Soviet citizens listened to somber tributes to Mikhail Romanovsky and to funereal music broadcast from blank television screens; and waited, on the eve.

The Funeral

Chapter Ten

THE DAY OF the funeral brought the third fall of snow. To Muscovites this is the real beginning of winter. The first snows, they say, melt and turn to slush within days. Only the third fall can be relied upon.

Yet as dawn broke the street sweepers watched the sky with contempt. Thin, icy droplets whirled through the city, circling the domes of the Kremlin and driving across the open spaces of the University. The dead grayness of the Moskva River absorbed the meager flakes and the cracked timbers of the benches in Sverdlov Square were veined with white. Down Gogolesky Boulevard and the Kalinina Prospekt the powdery snow rolled like gunsmoke before the gusts of wind. In the old wooden lanes of the city it rattled icily against the makeshift plastic double-glazing nailed across the window frames of the single-story izbas.

For four days now Moscow had lived in the grip of silence. In the crowded apartment blocks of the *novye raione,* the new worker districts, children were hushed at play, arguments between husband and wife were cut short and radios turned to a low whisper. Television ran film, hour after hour, of the life and achievements of President Romanovsky. Somber music played over scenes of visits to memorials of the Great Patriotic War. All but food shops were closed and traffic reduced itself, seemingly voluntarily, to a minimum.

Yet it was the future, not the past, which was on the minds of millions of Soviet citizens. Stunned, apprehensive people murmured apologies on the subway as if no one knew what tomorrow would bring in power and influence to his neighbor.

Some were hopeful. They saw an improvement in the conditions of the ordinary workers' lives, an increase in freedom to criticize and write. But they were few. Most Russians, if not most Soviet citizens, felt immediately the withdrawal of that warm, harsh authority which they had grown to live with.

The cult of personality in Russia and her dominions has been no accident. Nor was it, even in the days of Joseph Stalin, conjured by the leader alone. To a great extent it was condoned, encouraged, even required by the Russian people. Monarchist at heart, even today, the Russians require an emperor to venerate. Hardest for them is the interregnum. In the days of the Old Empire primogeniture solved the problem: "The Czar is dead, long live the Czar." But in the days of the new Soviet Empire the leader's death meant doubt, struggle, uncertain allegiance, a people deprived of a personal authority. At these times the deep anarchy in the Russian nature comes to the surface.

The men in the Kremlin knew this well.

As old Yelenda, Anton Ovsenko's mother, stumbled with a blood-stained sack on her shoulder toward the Cheremushki free market that morning, she had other reasons for remembering that day.

The militia guard at the market had been surprised to see the old woman struggling toward him.

"Now come on," he said as she swung the heavy sack down onto the pavement, "you know the market's closed. You know what today is."

"I know," she said. "Don't I remember Stalin's funeral?"

Befuddled by vodka and the numbing cold, he peered down at the bloody sack. "That's meat you've got there."

The frozen blood crackled the hessian fibers as she peeled open the mouth of the sack. "The best part of the bullock," she said, and reaching into the sack, dragged out by the ear the bloodied animal's head.

"Thirty-five pounds." She scooped the grinning object into her arms, letting the sack fall to the ground. "Plenty of meat on the chops and the tongue left in, though that's carrying generosity a bit far. An hour in salt water and there's enough on the tongue alone to feed a family of eight."

The militiaman frowned. "The market's closed, old woman. You know that. Because of the funeral. All your honored foreigners, your gospodin, will be in Red Square for the parade. In any case, you can't see them buying a bullock's head. They're used to a juicier cut than that."

The old woman bundled the huge brown head back into the sack. "I didn't travel forty miles to sell good meat to foreigners," she said. "The bullock's head is for you."

"Now wait a minute," the militiaman slammed his black-gloved hands together. "I can't afford your prices. If I want meat it has to be queued for in the shops. The free market's not for the likes of me."

"Your daughter gets married on Sunday."

The guard shrugged in his heavy, overlarge coat and adjusted his *shapka*.

"So you need meat."

"The neighbors have promised sausages," the man said defensively.

"Sausages! Breadsticks for your *dochka*'s wedding! What sort of father are you, Pavel Alexandrovich? What sort of provider will her new husband's family think you are?"

The snow raced across the pavement between them.

Again he slapped his gloved palms together. It was a militiaman's gesture, not so much of authority as of some Olympian unconcern. "Go back to your village, old woman," he said, "the market's closed."

"Forty miles I've traveled. In a boxcar since before dawn. Then humped this fine head all the way from the Finland Station."

"So go and sell it on Gorky Street, though if you're caught you'll be hauled up for speculation."

The old woman swung the sack toward him. "I'm not selling," she said. "It's yours. If you want it, it's yours."

The heavy bone thumped down at his feet. He ignored it, looking instead into the old woman's wrinkled face.

"What is it you want from me?" he asked suspiciously.

She took a pint bottle from her pocket and unscrewed the cap. Tipping the neck of the bottle to her lips, she swallowed a mouthful of the white spirit.

"Homemade," she cackled, screwing back the cap. "Plenty more where that came from."

"What is it you want from me?" he said again.

The sky was lightening behind the market building. A convoy of military trucks, their headlights blazing, rumbled past on their way to Red Square.

"Last week you told me about your brother," she said. "The one who's been posted to the labor camp at Panaka."

The militiaman watched her sly smile. He hated peasants with their black-grained hands and well-fed wrinkled faces. Do nothing but complain about life in the villages, and yet can buy and sell most Muscovites, he felt sure of that.

"You need my brother to do you a service?"

She took from inside the folds of her gray cloth coat a small linen purse and tipped the contents into her hand.

"You said your brother goes by airplane to Krasibirsk. He'll be at Panaka tonight."

He stared down at the gold coin nestling in the fat grimy palm.

"A gold ruble of the Czar Nicholas," she said. "My husband's grandfather kept it through the Revolution, the Civil War, the famine, the Patriotic War against Fascism, everything."

The militiaman extended his forefinger and rubbed on the surface of the coin as if expecting the dull yellow gleam to wear away.

"Worth a good two hundred rubles now," she said, snapping closed her hand. "Will your brother take it for me?"

"To Panaka? To the labor camp?"

"He's to be promoted detachment guard, you said. He can take in what he wants."

"Take in the coin?"

"To my son," she said shortly. "He's a *zek* there. Seven years he got."

The militiaman barely hesitated before bending down to pick up the sack. "What's your boy's name?" he said. "And number. I'll make sure he gets the ruble."

The bullock's head poked from the opening in the sack, a great hole between the eyes where the metal point had broken through the skull.

"Yes," Yelenda said, "you make sure he gets the ruble." She jerked her thumb at the bullock's head. "Pole-axed it myself," she told him. "Then took a chopper to the neck. Do the same to you in the name of Holy Mother Russia if my boy doesn't get that ruble."

For Yelenda it had been a successful trip. Finishing the half-liter she had in her pocket and buying another half at a shop on October Street, she decided to go down to Red Square to see this great man's funeral.

In the new American Embassy building George Gotz, the Head of Chancery, had been up until the early hours working out allocations of personnel for the funeral. It was the usual problem. The Moscow government departmental overlap was such that on all major occasions the Embassy would be bombarded with invitations. Each invitation would need to be carefully sifted to avoid slighting a minister or an important head of a department. But allocation of the twenty-five principals, from the Ambassador himself down, was a delicate matter. By dawn on the morning of the funeral, he sat back pleased with what he felt was the subtlety of some of his decisions.

At a breakfast meeting that morning he handed out the assignments. To Tom Yates he allocated the buffet lunch at the new Ministry of the

Nationalities, a showpiece department formed in 1982 and consisting mostly of tame Kazaks, White Russians, Georgians, et cetera, who had developed a taste for Moscow living standards and had no objection to writing Soviet exhortatory articles for the folks back home. As a ministry, of course, it was run by Russians. Tom Yates' specific assignment that day was to "sound out the representatives of the nationalities on their preference among the possible leadership candidates." It was expected that his wife, Carole, would accompany him.

Even amid the now thickening fall of snow the tall shambling figure attracted the glances of passersby. It was partly of course the heavy felt peasant boots, their patterns long since faded. Partly, too, the knee-length, ripped sheepskin jacket with the number painted on the back. But mostly the soft khaki cavalry helmet dating from the Patriotic War. With only one earflap hanging down it gave Valentin Kuletsyn a strange, lopsided appearance. It was deliberate. It announced his contempt for the world of Levi jeans and rock bands and high-rise worker flats. With the boots and sheepskin coat it proclaimed his membership in that soldier peasantry that he believed to be the incorruptible heart of Russia.

Kuletsyn turned onto Granovsky Street and stopped opposite the shabby yellowstone Bureau of Passes. As ever, the black government Volga sedans were parked in line outside, their MOC registration a casual giveaway for any Muscovite familiar with Central Committee staff license plates. He watched for a moment while chauffeurs and well-dressed women laden with parcels emerged from under the carriage gate which led to the courtyard entrance at the rear. Only when the militiaman on duty began to cross the road toward him did he turn away and enter the building opposite.

The offices of the magazine *Novaya Literatura* were a showpiece. A fountain played in the marble hall; chromium and hide benches were set around smoked-glass coffee tables piled with the latest copy of the Soviet Union's most prestigious and lavishly produced literary magazine. Members of Soviet legations abroad like to be "surprised" reading a copy of *Novaya Literatura* with its combination of fashionable Moscow photo-gossip and liberal leading articles. It bore above all the stamp of one man, the editor Igor Bukansky.

The doorman approached Kuletsyn cautiously. He was used to the odd fish the editor got to write for the magazine. "You have business with the magazine, comrade?"

"I'm not in Moscow for the sights," Kuletsyn jerked his thumb toward the Bureau of Passes opposite. "I've called to see the editor."

The man's voice, the doorman decided, had that menacing edge of

authority. "We have six editors, comrade—history, poetry, general
literature, comment . . ."

"*The* editor," Kuletsyn cut him short. "Igor Alexandrovich."

"Comrade Bukansky is not available today. Naturally he's attending the
funeral."

"Tell him Kuletsyn is here to see him. Tell him now."

The doorman inclined his head. He rang the editor's secretary. She
knew Bukansky's moods, she could deal with it.

Kuletsyn had wandered off to the glass door. Legs apart, hands behind
his back he stared out across the road.

The doorman peered at the numbers stenciled on the back of his coat.
An ex-prisoner, a *zek*. The doorman shivered. He had long heard rumors
that Igor Bukansky liked to sail close to the wind.

The lift whined, groaned to a halt, and the doors slid open. As the girl
stepped out the doorman nodded toward Kuletsyn's back, then leaned on
his desk to admire her gliding long-legged walk. Western shoes, Western
skirt, too. The editor saw to that.

"Uncle Valentin," she said, "what are you doing here?"

"I came to see Editor Bukansky," Kuletsyn said, turning to face her.

"But it's the funeral today."

"So?"

Her face showed her distress. "Igor Alexandrovich has agreed to see
you for a few minutes only. He has been invited to the Head of State
reception. You know what that means."

They were walking toward the lift.

"No," Kuletsyn said without interest.

"It's the main reception at the Kremlin."

Kuletsyn pursed his lips.

They entered the lift.

In his office on the fourth floor Bukansky poured himself a glass of
vodka. He would have to leave for the funeral in less than an hour, but he
was curious to meet Kuletsyn. Lydia had told him her uncle was a strange
man. From his manuscript Bukansky could have told her a great deal
more about him.

The door opened and Kuletsyn entered. Bukansky waved his glass in
greeting. Taller even than Kuletsyn and twenty-five pounds heavier, he
threw one arm round the writer's thin shoulders.

"Valentin Sergeivich, what a time you choose to call! The funeral, man
. . . even you must have heard that today's the funeral."

Kuletsyn drew away from the other man and removed his odd cavalry
cap. "Have you read the manuscript?"

"I have." Bukansky refilled his glass and turned to face Kuletsyn.

"And?"

"I think it's a work of genius."

Kuletsyn nodded. "Yes," he said, standing cap in hand. "When will you publish it?"

"Publish it?" Bukansky said. "God in Heaven, that's another matter."

Kuletsyn's eyes squinted angrily. "I have a right to publication," he said stiffly.

Bukansky swept his free arm around Kuletsyn's shoulders. "My dear, difficult friend," he said. "May I call you a friend? Well I will anyway, like it or not. I'm a friend of yours, Valentin Sergeivich, whatever you feel about me."

He drained his glass. Pushing Kuletsyn aside he stood swaying in the middle of the room. "You're not like me. You don't drink vodka, you don't ride young girls, you don't boast or curse or dress up your vanity in Western clothes." He chuckled deep in his huge chest. "But a man can be a simple fool, too. Understand me, Uncle," he reverted to his Northern peasant accent. "I loved you from the first moment I read your book," he said. "I loved your belief in Russia. In *Russia,* not in this mishmash of nationalities we've surrounded ourselves with. In Russia and the Russian peasant. But I know something about peasants, more than you know, my bourgeois Uncle. I grew up in a village."

Kuletsyn's face was tense. "Igor Alexandrovich, you haven't answered me. Are you prepared to publish?"

"In my bloated, long-winded fashion I'm answering you. I'm telling you about peasants. I'm also telling you about publishing in Moscow."

"You recognize the value of the work. Isn't that enough?"

"No. Listen, forty years ago, a half century almost, just at the end of the Great Patriotic War against the Hitlerites, I wrote a short story. I was a soldier. A boy-soldier, like you. I wrote a story about Napoleon. A childish piece. About the invasion of Russia. The enemy at the gates, you know the stuff. But in my naiveté I coined a phrase: *The strategic counteroffensive.* I tell you what it meant. It meant that every single step in that war against Napoleon was planned by *us.* It meant that when we retreated to Moscow we were simply drawing the enemy on. It meant that when the weather broke we'd planned that, too. It meant that when we fought him at Borodino it was a calculated battle of attrition. It meant the final victory was known and planned and inevitable from the *beginning.*"

Bukansky lurched across the room waving his arms, spilling vodka across his Alexandrine desk. "I was a simple soldier-boy. But without knowing it I'd provided the complete explanation for every *apparent* failure of Stalin's leadership. How, if the leader was so all-knowing, so far-seeing, had the Hitlerites reached the gates of Moscow? Strategic counteroffensive! How was it the Hitlerites took the Crimea in nineteen forty-two? Strategic counteroffensive! Even while we lost battles, you see, we were out-thinking the enemy. The godhead in the Kremlin needed a formula. And the simple soldier-boy provided him with one. So Academician Tarle was forced to recant. I, Bukansky, engineer with the 131st Siberians, had got it right. And when the victories came, Stalingrad and the great Zhukov offensives, it was based on our leader's foresight. Strategic counteroffensive had made him right—even when he was wrong."

"You still haven't told me when you will publish," Kuletsyn said.

"Interest yourself in other people," Bukansky chided. "I was telling you about my rise to literary eminence."

"I have traveled all the way from Rostropin. I am more interested in the fate of my novel."

Bukansky smiled. "I very much doubt if I control that. It's the greatest book I've read in a decade. My blood bubbles with envy."

"If you like the book that much . . ."

"Like it? No. But it's Russian. It's written from your own Russian gut. It's not a political compromise masquerading as literature. Trust me, Valentin Sergeivich, I will do my best to publish it. But we have a leader now staring from his open coffin. We have no way of knowing who comes next." He swayed across the room and rang the desk bell.

"Come back this evening, Comrade. I want to talk to you."

"I am returning to my village this afternoon."

"Get off that high horse, Kuletsyn. I've got things to show you. Be here this evening, early. Forget your village, it won't run away."

When his secretary entered he smiled at her. "Show out this gifted author, Lydia," he said. "Then come back here and prepare me for the funeral."

Chapter Eleven

ON THE DAY of the death of President Romanovsky, a short tense meeting of the Politburo had taken place. It was fully accepted that on this day there could be no jostling for position among the leading contenders for power. The black armbands of the members and the black dress of Natalya Roginova guaranteed that.

This discussion solely concerned security for the funeral. Not only had the whole length of the route to be protected against demonstrators; at the same time the greatest assembly of Heads of State ever was due to arrive in Moscow with wives, husbands, staffs, all of whom had to be accommodated, protected and conducted safely to the funeral.

It was Natalya Roginova who suggested that the principal planning and security function would be most sensibly controlled by one organization, the KGB.

General Kuba was evidently, and pleasantly, surprised. He saw the planning of the parade as a challenge and an opportunity. Natalya Roginova saw it as a challenge, too, but one she believed Semyon Kuba would find difficult to meet.

Thus, unanimously, the meeting decided that the basic blueprint for the funeral and ceremony should be drawn up at Bureau Headquarters on Dzerzhinsky Square, and that security for the mass parade and the ceremony in Red Square was to be the responsibility of no less than Bureau Chairman Kuba himself.

The broad plan devised by two of his senior officers was calculated to remove any predictable elements which might be capitalized on by terrorists or demonstrators. The pattern of so many past May Day parades was therefore abandoned from the beginning.

The parade itself was to begin from two separate forming-up points and would take three separate routes to Red Square. The first, and by far the largest of the forming-up points, was the 1,000-acre Gorky Park which lies between the Lenin Prospekt and the Moskva River almost due south of the Kremlin. The north part of the park is bisected by the broad Krimsky Val along which the tanks and armored vehicles could form up in line of march. Infantry units, hospital representatives and workers' shock brigades could assemble in the vast open areas to the south of Krimsky Val. The park itself would of course be forbidden to the public, its famous amusement area and restaurants closed. Kuba's lieutenants had allocated a full 5,000-man regiment of KGB border guards to secure the perimeter of the park alone.

The second part of the parade was to form up in the much smaller Plevna Monument gardens and march from there by the most direct route along the Razina Ulitza, past the north face of the giant Rossiya Hotel and into Red Square at St. Basil's Cathedral. Ten thousand border guards were allocated to the route and a further 5,000 would be on duty in Red Square itself, which would of course be sealed from all but officially invited guests and those units of the parade which were scheduled to take part in the funeral ceremony. The key moment in the whole blueprint was to remain a secret to everybody but senior planning officers until the very last: not more than fifty people were to be informed how, where and when the embalmed body of the leader was to be introduced into the vast parade.

Along the routes themselves militia and Bureau agents drafted in from surrounding *oblasts* were to occupy official buildings and apartment blocks to secure all windows overlooking the route. In the Rossiya Hotel alone, a vast complex capable of accommodating over 5,000 guests, it was calculated that something like 2,000 windows overlooked, north and west, the parade routes.

When Bureau Chairman Semyon Trofimovich Kuba arose as usual at six-thirty that morning and stood at the bedroom window of his apartment on Kutuzov Prospekt, he knew that the greatest single internal security operation in Soviet history was about to begin.

The KGB security blueprint was handed to Senior Organizing Parade Marshal General N.V. Berisov four days before the funeral. A tall, alarmingly thin officer of nearly seventy, Berisov wore his gray hair short-cropped, accentuating his great fleshy, jug-like ears. He was a soldier, a general who had never seen a shot fired in anger. Indeed, he had hardly seen a shot fired at all that wasn't a fusillade or a salute. He was the regime's processional organizer, a man who had planned innumerable May Days, Olympic Parades and Workers' Production Week celebrations. His permanent staff consisted of over a thousand administrators who on the appointed day would don the white cap-covers and armbands of Parade Marshals.

Yet for all his vast experience General Berisov had only once before organized a similar occasion, on the death of Stalin in 1953. And in those days the world had been different, or at least the Soviet world had. Nobody then expected the demonstrations that the KGB feared today.

On the morning of the funeral Berisov left his command caravan in Gorky Park at 8:00 A.M. Already units of five tank battalions, a total of one hundred T-72s, stood in line along the Krimsky Val, dark masses of steel against the lightening sky. Columns of men were marching across the Krimsky Bridge from the west of the city and white-capped Parade Marshals were directing them into forming-up areas designated by colored tapes. In each reception area smoking field kitchens would serve hot soup to each unit as it arrived. Along the riverbank a line of coaches was already drawn up, each one carrying on its flank details of the factory or *oblast* from which the workers, now sleeping inside, had been drawn.

Berisov completed his tour and returned to the command caravan to take the eight-thirty radio report from the smaller reception area at the Plevna Gardens. All, so far, was to his satisfaction.

Considerably less satisfied was the KGB Commander of the Kuntsevo District of factories and workers' apartment blocks west of the city center. In days before the location of factories in this area, Stalin had had his favorite dacha here, and in this country house as it was then, he had died in 1953. Now in the grim featureless apartment blocks a new generation of Soviet citizens had grown up, less servile than the last, more demanding of a better standard of life than their parents knew.

It was mostly a young community whose relatively high earnings did no more than emphasize the fact that there was little in the drab local shops to spend their rubles on. With one of the highest divorce rates in the Moscow *oblast* and an abnormally high turnover in jobs, the population of Kuntsevo was rootless, shifting and frequently given to ferocious bouts of vodka drinking on weekends and holidays. And for the young of the Kuntsevo District this was a holiday.

The drinking had begun the night before, mostly in apartments and work canteen clubs that remained open until late evening. Patrolling militia were called in during the night to an unprecedented number of minor incidents, wife-beatings and petty affrays which they seldom pursued past a warning. Usually by the early hours the local militia station would begin to see a sharp drop in reports and another night would have passed in the Kuntsevo District.

But this night was different. First in the number of incidents and then, as the night wore on, in the fact that it was becoming obvious that the parties were continuing. Still the KGB District Office was not too alarmed. They were several miles from tomorrow's parade route and the vodka was certain to run out before dawn broke.

Only very slowly did it become apparent that the vodka was not running out. Or at least was running out much more slowly than the militia had calculated.

By dawn a few parties had spilled onto the streets. Undeterred by a biting wind and squalls of snow, sharp as grit, groups of men wandered waving bottles and singing among the scarred stilts of the tower blocks, laughing, fighting, joking when they met up with other wandering parties.

Within a short time bonfires were built on the bald hard patches of trampled earth that visionary architects had seen as greenswards separating block from block. A few militiamen who tried to douse the fires quickly withdrew before the naked hostility of the workers. Sausages were brought out by some of the women and huge frying pans. And more vodka was produced from somewhere by the men.

The crowds grew. In a haphazard, disorganized way they grouped themselves round fires that grew bigger as fences were broken and thrown onto the blazing pyres.

The militia now turned out in greater force, assembling in groups of a dozen men, about 30 or 40 yards from the biggest fires.

Some of the workers claimed afterward that if they had been left to get on with it they would have all trailed off home within an hour or two. But it didn't happen that way. The militia moved in, on an order from the KGB District. With the aid of the Fire Services they began to douse the fires. The workers protested, then began to resist. From the grimy concrete blocks other men poured. The militia were punched and pushed aside. Then one of them used his gun.

Within minutes the militia and Fire Services were overwhelmed by a flood of angry workers. Uniformed men were hurled to the ground and kicked unconscious as they struggled to undo their holsters. The thin crack of small arms mingled with the crackle of the fires. The suppressed violence of decades surged through the workmen. Militia vehicles were overturned or pushed into the middle of the fires. Individual militiamen were surrounded and their guns torn from them. More than one of them followed a vehicle into the fire.

The mood now was dangerously exultant. The remaining militiamen had fled. The crowd flowed back and forth among blazing police vehicles, some of the workers firing their captured pistols in the air.

In the way that crowds have they began to drift—toward the square where the Committee offices were located and the few shops the district could boast.

At Lubyanka KGB Headquarters the riot in the Kuntsevo District was the first of many reported that day from the new districts, the workers' suburbs around Moscow's center. It is doubtful whether there was any organization involved, doubtful even that word spread much from one to another. Unlike the Leningrad riots of the early spring, in Moscow there were no leaders, no political demands, but simply an inchoate frustration among the inhabitants of the industrial deserts of the city.

Throughout the morning the Lubyanka received reports of new outbreaks. Some would last for an hour or two only or would be suppressed almost immediately. Foreigners in Moscow on that day reported rising columns of smoke from different parts of the city's suburbs. We shall never know the full extent of the outbreaks.

In the Kuntsevo District we have details. By nine or nine-thirty a large crowd had gathered outside the Committee offices and shops. Windows were smashed and fires soon broke out. The shops were rapidly looted at first of alcohol and then of literally everything they contained. By the time the militia had reassembled and returned with armored vehicles one whole side of the square was blazing.

The militia orders were obvious from the first. A burst of automatic fire scattered the crowd. Those men with pistols fired back. It was an unequal contest. Hounded through the side streets and among the tower blocks by the bouncing armored personnel carriers, men were run down as they fled. Bent on revenge, the militia shot down men and women as they scrambled across gates and fences or cowered in doorways.

The local hospital administrator recorded 62 dead and 119 injured. Among the militia 18 men were killed.

As morning wore on the reports of rioting in the Moscow suburbs began to reach Senior Parade Marshal General Berisov from Lubyanka. They were, of course, no responsibility of his, but nevertheless the possibility of a serious disturbance on the parade route added a new tension to the morning hours.

In terms of organization everything at Gorky and the Plevna Gardens was going smoothly. He had already driven twice along the route and the Border Guards in their distinctive green-piped uniforms were already in position. Throughout the morning a hundred women swept and reswept the vast oblong space of Red Square, out of bounds to all but official cars since the night before. Dozens of plainclothes Bureau experts had already searched every nook and niche in the old Kremlin wall while others had spent hours in the Museum Church of St. Basil and had even ordered the lifting of some of the loaf-shaped paving stones where the possibility of an explosive device was suspected.

Chapter Twelve

IN THE HOUR before midday the limousines of the world's presidents and prime ministers, kings and princes rolled across Alexander Gardens and through the west Kremlin Gate at the fifteenth-century Trinity Tower. Passing the brash glass and concrete of the Palace of Congresses they were directed right past the gilded domes of the Cathedral of the Assumption into Cathedral Square itself and thence to the State Entrance of the Great Kremlin Palace where the reception for heads of state was to be held.

Though by far the most important reception, this was in fact only one of many being held within the Kremlin Walls that morning. In the sixty-foot-high Sverdlov Hall in the eighteenth-century Senate building, senior officers of the Soviet forces were assembled. In the Armory Palace four separate trade ministries had combined to hold a reception in the Gold and Silver Room. In the orange-painted Poteshny Palace where Stalin once had his private apartments, the Ministry of the Nationalities' reception had already begun.

Even from a distance, while the language is still indistinguishable from any other, the sound of Russian official parties has a unique intonation, a rolling, somber cadence quite unlike a gathering of French or Germans or Dutchmen. As they mounted the wide gray carpeted staircase, Carole Yates grimaced at her husband.

"Just for once," she said, "I'd love to be going to a party where I could say what I liked, to whomever I liked, and if I felt like it get stoned out of my mind—on something other than vodka and Russian champagne. How about you?"

He frowned. "What for?"

"For the hell of it, Tom," she said as they reached the balustraded landing and the great open doors, "just for the hell of it."

"It may be as well to remember this is not a celebration," he said shortly, handing his invitation to the doorman in KGB business suit. "It's a State occasion."

They passed through the doors.

There were about 300 people in the long blue and white hall. Huge crystal chandeliers hung from the painted wooden beams, the light sparkling on the portraits of past Czars and present Politburo members unselfconsciously ranged together along the walls.

The usual enormous buffet had been placed at the far end of the hall, an arrangement of white-clothed tables loaded with caviar, smoked sturgeon, vodka and Georgian champagne. White-coated waiters circulated filling glasses.

The guests included a reasonable sprinkling of foreigners among Soviet citizens from the Writers' Union, the ballet, the press and, of course, the bureaucracy. A more important ministry, Foreign Affairs for example, would have more foreigners at a somewhat higher level. Today, when the foreign contingent was stretched thin by the sheer number of invitations, an unglamorous ministry, like Mines or Electric Power, might be able to claim none at all. In these Soviet gatherings Westerners were used like starlets at a Hollywood pool party, to reflect glamour and status on the hosts.

"Two or three times. He's like me, darling, second team. You wouldn't have come across him on your normal circuit."

"What does he do?"

"He's a reasonably senior man in the Nationalities Ministry. Traveled to the West a couple of times I believe, on what sort of business I'm not quite sure."

"He's not an agronomist?"

"No darling, he's not an agronomist. He's very definitely political. The whole Nationalities Ministry is. Can't tell you much more. Not married, if that's of interest."

"Do you know him well enough to organize an introduction? Something casual?"

"Diplomatic?" he smiled.

"Yes. And David, as friends, I don't want *le tout Moscou* to know about this one."

"My word on it," he said seriously. "But look, Carole, if you're feeling frisky, you'd be far safer, and Tom would too, if you chose someone at your embassy. Or even ours, dearest," he added with a grotesque invitatory roll of the eyes.

She took his arm. "Let's see how diplomatic you can be."

They moved from group to group, Butler carefully keeping each exchange down to a few words. Then almost before she realized it she found herself moving through a press of people—and she was standing next to him while Butler made sympathetic noises about the sad occasion and the shock it had been, despite the President's advanced age. And then he had turned, apologizing, and introduced them.

"Mrs. Yates speaks excellent Russian," Butler said. "Indeed, she's half-Russian herself."

"Half-Ukrainian," Carole said. "Since we're at the Ministry of Nationalities we should be accurate."

Letsukov looked at her and smiled slowly. "We have many nationalities in the Soviet Union," he said. "Each with their own story to tell."

"And even more individuals, each with their own story."

He nodded gravely.

Butler frowned. "I have the sense of being present at an unutterably obscure play," he murmured.

"How long have you been in the Soviet Union?" Letsukov asked her.

Did he know the answer already? "Since the summer," she said. "My husband is at the embassy here. Before that he was in Dublin."

"I see."

David Butler looked from one to the other. "Will you excuse me," he said, "I'd like a word with one of my colleagues who's just arrived."

"Of course."

"I'll see you later, David."

Butler inclined his head and dived into the thickening crowd. For a moment or two they stood together like newly acquainted guests at a cocktail party with little to say to each other.

"You didn't tell him you knew me," Letsukov said after a moment.

"No."

"I saw you across the room," he said. "I was looking for an opportunity to talk to you."

She nodded. "We have some things to talk about."

"Yes," he said.

"You're not an agronomist. You therefore weren't in France to study viticulture."

"No, I was not."

"Why were you there?"

Like two self-orbiting moons they circled each other while people drifted back and forth around them.

"I can't explain it to you now," he said, breaking the tension between them. "I was in Paris for my Ministry. I was involved in investigating the Ukrainian Congress taking place there. We fear disunion, too."

"Too?"

"Today many states have their extreme minority nationalists. Governments are forced to take them seriously. The Soviet government is no different."

"Very different. A man was assassinated in Paris."

"These groups struggle among themselves more violently than they do against the mother state."

"That's your explanation?"

"For what?"

"For what happened in Paris. For what you were doing there."

"I wouldn't have thought Americans would find anything objectionable in what I was doing there."

She felt sure he was lying. Her expression communicated it.

"We must talk," he said.

"Why?"

"You don't believe me."

"No, I don't."

"Before you make any decision, will you meet me?"

"You mean before I tell anyone that you were the man in Paris?"

"Yes, that's what I mean."

"I can meet," she said shortly. "But not before next week."

"Monday?"

"My husband has a conference at the embassy all that evening."

"At six o'clock then. On the embankment just below the Moskvoretsky Bridge." He paused. "Try not to look too Western."

Chapter Thirteen

IN GORKY PARK the Parade Marshals were ranging the columns of infantry behind the sixty T-72 tanks of the Tumanchky Guards Division.

The requirements of a Soviet parade were precise. Not only would the infantry wear the special long brown coat and belt of the normal parade uniform, but officers' tabs and shoulder boards were those for a Hero-City parade. The fur caps with raised flaps and the red star at the forehead were of course common to all.

The tanks, too, had been prepared for the occasion with fresh coats of dark-green paint and newly stenciled bright divisional signs. The long, powerful 122-mm. guns of the low T-72 models were draped in streamers of black crepe. Only the Commander, standing in the flat turret, was visible among the crew members.

By midday the order of march was assembled. For the two southern columns it would be the T-72s of the Tumanchky Guards, followed by 800 infantry of the newly formed Russian Federation Division. Behind them a civilian block of medical staff from Moscow Hospital would precede 200 Airborne BMP troop carriers, ranged six abreast and flying red pennants at half mast.

Behind them again came the first of the factory shock brigades, then young Komsomols and 400 teenage pioneers, their red neckerchiefs fluttering in the bitter wind. Then again the military with a contingent from the naval base at Kronstadt, dark blue and gold predominating. And after them, stretching back along the river bank, assembled columns of more workers, KGB special troops, Donbas miners and motor-rifle battalions in their BTR-60s, their 16 infantrymen sitting sternly upright under their polished Russian helmets.

At twelve thirty-five, over the loudspeaker system in the trees beside the Krimsky Val, Parade Marshal Berisov personally set his two alarm stopwatches for ten minutes hence, when the radio order to move would be given to the Plevna Gardens contingents. Then he sat back. Outside he could hear the squeak and rumble of the T-72s, the high singing voices of the young pioneers and the steady tramp of Russian boots. He was deeply happy. He had not thought of those KGB riot reports for a full hour.

At Moscow's Finland Station the train drew in, its locomotive decked with red flags, its carriages crowded with young workers from selected enterprises throughout the *oblast*.

On the platform factory groups lined up under their trade union organizers and group passes were shown to the militiamen at the gate. Among 70 workers from Gorky G.A.Z., the military automobile factory, Zoya Densky moved forward, her eyes on the militiamen counting them through:

On the gate one militiaman had probably been counting factory groups through since the early hours and I could see by his tired eyes that he was no longer counting too accurately. By the time he reached the end of the column from G.A.Z. I think he'd lost count anyway and given up, so I entered Moscow without a city pass with no difficulty.

Not knowing Moscow it took me some time to get to the University, but the ground had been well prepared. They were expecting me, and I must say they gave me a hero's welcome. More important they gave me the grenade and showed me how it worked . . .

Seated in place in the red-draped timber stand which had been constructed the length of the east side of the square, Carole Yates had the curious impression that she was about to watch some northern bullfight. Beside her Jack Bennerman obviously had a similar idea. He leaned toward her.

"You want to see the program," he said. "We open with the polar bear fight. You, as the prettiest woman here, get the right to give the thumbs down to the loser."

"What comes next?"

"After the bears we have a one-to-one gladiatorial combat—Bureau Chairman Semyon Kuba with trident and net against Party Secretary Roginova with short sword and back-stabbing knife. That should be a winner."

"For whom, the world asks anxiously."

He groaned. "Must you always remind me of work, light of my life?"

She settled back, wondering whether or not to smoke. On her left her husband Tom was talking intently to Harriet Bennerman. He certainly would not approve of her smoking here.

"I want a cigarette," she whispered to Jack Bennerman.

"Then have a cigarette," he said. She leaned forward. Nobody else along the lines of heavily muffled guests was smoking. She shrugged and took out her cigarettes. There was still a half-hour to go. The great square between them and the crenellated Kremlin wall with the enormous block of red porphyry which was the Lenin monument was empty except for the women sweepers. As the snow scampered across the open space, they wheeled and turned in line, like a parade themselves, sweeping the errant flakes toward the blackened piles of snow against the great wall.

"Don't you think it's about time those old ladies were given a rest?" Carole said, as the long line of bundled, head-scarved figures began yet another drive across the square.

"They can't let up," Bennerman said.

"Why not?"

"Have you never seen a May Day Parade on TV?"

"Sure."

"Have you never wondered how the hell columns of marching men, sometimes twenty abreast, maintain precise position?"

"No."

"Well, Carole, you're an unmilitary dumb broad."

"Thank you, Jack."

"Because that sort of formation marching is impossible without marked lines."

"Is that so?"

"That is so." He pointed. "See those very faint parallel lines, one pace apart across the parade route?"

She saw for the first time a faint yellow grid painted on the cobbles down the center of the square.

"I see them."

"Right. So those old ladies have to keep sweeping right up to the last moment or the Soviet Army's reputation falls straight on its ass."

"That could be the healthiest outcome of the whole damn day."

He grunted.

She turned toward her husband and felt a surge of guilt as she thought of Letsukov and the meeting she had agreed to. Guilt not because she was secretly meeting another man, but because what she was doing involved Tom's career. Why didn't she tell him now, before it was too late?

"Carole," he said, "you shouldn't be smoking here, you know."

The moment passed. She crushed out the cigarette on the planking underfoot. No, she had not believed Alex Letsukov capable of murder in Paris. She didn't believe it now. She would meet him as he asked.

On the Ulitza Razina, opposite the Rossiya Hotel, Zoya joined the thickening crowd. It had been decided at the student meeting that they would operate in pairs, neither knowing the identity of the other. Zoya's comrade was a tall, bespectacled boy named Andrei. When the pairs had been chosen from the hat she had watched with misgiving this lanky, clearly nervous Muscovite smiling shyly across the room at her. He had crossed and sat down on the floor next to her, offering a long-fingered clammy hand. But at least he was a Muscovite and would know the back streets they would have to take when they made their getaway.

There were eight of us in the room [Zoya wrote later] and four grenades. You do understand they were only percussion grenades, not intended and I was assured incapable, of hurting anyone. But we were determined, and it was of course the object of my being in Moscow, not to let the hearse pass into Red Square without showing what we students thought of the so-called achievements of the past few years and of the man who had been responsible for them.

Our leader was a young MGU student named Volodya. He had worked out the positions of the four groups so that by whichever route the hearse entered Red Square there would be at least two loud, ugly explosions to see the body on its way. And there were so many foreigners in the stands along the Kremlin wall and opposite, backing onto the GUM store, that the incident was bound to be widely reported in the West.

Don't ask me now what good it would all do. We were fervent, but we were still young . . .

Andrei, Zoya's companion, had pointed out the exact spot on Razina Street which Volodya, the student leader, had selected for their team. Somewhere opposite, another pair of students were threading their way toward the front of the crowd. Between the Alarm Tower and the Kremlin Embankment two more pairs were moving into position.

On Razina Street the crowd shoved and shouldered with that lack of good humor for which the public face of the people of Moscow is all too well known. Laboriously, with Andrei a pace behind her, she worked her way forward to the front. The contents of her pocket weighed like lead, seemingly impossible to conceal as she eased her way between the close-packed Muscovite crowd.

On Parade Marshal Berisov's radioed order the bands of the Soviet Air Force, drumming a slow, funereal pace on their black-clad drums, had led off from the forming-up point in the Plevna Gardens. Behind them came five squadrons of cossack cavalry, the men in black fur caps and long dark-gray riding coats sitting imperiously on their small, shaggy-maned horses. As the bridles jingled and the hooves clattered into Nogina Square they were followed by a broad column of marching civilians.

In the parade an honored place had been awarded to the old comrades of the leader. Not, of course, his senior colleagues who had grown with him through the Party, but those dull pedestrian murderers who had done his bidding as they had earlier done that of Stalin and Beria. "An assemblage of infamy unknown since the SS was wiped from the face of the earth," one young Russian described them.

And of course he was right. These old men in their bemedaled civilian topcoats, their fur caps pulled down over their ears, had been the shock troops of socialism in the starving thirties and war-torn forties, the whip-guards of the Gulags in the fifties and the servile committeemen of the sixties. Now they buried their old comrades with vodka and honors and lived on the well-earned privileges of a dutiful past. They are the men any nation must learn to do without, the men all nations have in abundant and plentiful supply.

Behind the old comrades a gap of about 80 yards had been allowed before the next contingents entered the square, a KGB battalion in light BMP troop carriers, followed by broad columns of marching infantry, their rifles taut across their chests, their red flags lowered to brush the icy surface of the road. Then a contingent of children—girls in black dresses and small, unsmiling boys in black breeches—resembling nothing so much as the massed progeny of a Czarist past. Then columns of workers, militia, sportsmen and culturalists moving forward at the slow, deliberate pace of the funeral drums. And behind them again, bringing up the rear of this vast column, the armored units of the border guards, the internal symbol of Soviet power.

Along Razina Street the crowds were thickly sown. The tea and coffee hawkers, banned from Red Square itself, sold five kopecks' worth of stained hot water in a leaking funnel of grease-proof paper. At the slow crash of boots on cobbles, at the somber muffled beat of the drums, at the thin slogan-chanting voices of the children, the crowds stood watching silently.

We had taken our place [Zoya said] on the Ulitza Razina at that point just past St. Barbara's where you have an uninterrupted view down to the Moskvoretsky Bridge and Great Ordinka Street beyond. From where I stood I could see another enormous column of marching men, at least twelve abreast, about to cross the bridge. Dozens of white-capped parade marshals stood by to coordinate their linking with the column flowing along Razina Street from the bend at the Monument of the Sign. It made me sad for a moment, I remember, to think that my quite natural pride in this vast Russian parade had to be stifled.

Yet the man who, in death, this great parade was meant to honor, was one of those who had brought us young Russians to this dilemma. Above me, past the great multi-colored spirals of the bulbous domes of St. Basil's, the Kremlin wall rose through the light snow. Lermontov, 150 years ago, had described "the dark passages of the Kremlin." None of us students, at least from Westernized Leningrad, had any doubt that he was really describing the dark passages of the Russian mind . . .

Yet still the central feature of the parade was missing. It had been announced that the ceremony in Red Square would see the placing of the embalmed body in the porphyry mausoleum next to that of Lenin himself. Yet nowhere in the parade as it approached the great square was there a hearse, a gun-carriage drawn by black horses, or a missile-launcher shrouded in black. The great crowds lining the routes of the procession had come in the most primordial sense to register their fear and hope at the passing of a leader. But the focal point of the whole great parade was missing.

Then, as the Parade Marshals in their white-topped caps expertly directed the two marching columns on either side of St. Basil's and into Red Square, a sound like distant thunder was heard across the rooftops and a flight of helicopters, dark against the snowclouds, swept round the rising tower of the Rossiya Hotel.

From where she stood it was difficult at first for Zoya to make out the shape of the formation, then as it hovered above the marching columns in Razina Street, she could see that 12 smaller helicopters were ranged around a 13th, larger, black-painted, the aerial hearse of the embalmed leader of the Soviet people.

As the helicopters chattered slowly forward, the hearse no more than 50 feet above Razina Street, maintaining perfect position above the procession, the tears poured down Zoya's cheeks.

What good was a puny percussion grenade against a helicopter 50 feet above her head?

Now, along the length of Razina Street, through cutout perspex sections in the helicopter's bodywork, the crowd was able to see the ornate, brightly lit coffin. The helicopter hearse was Semyon Kuba's own conception, worthy he thought of Stalin himself in its combination of the spectacular and the safe.

And now as the helicopter division approached Red Square the black machine dropped lower to a height of no more than 20 feet above the wide surface of Razina Street. Blasted by the rush of air from the rotor blades, spectators and KGB guards alike screwed their eyes to peer at the illuminated flying hearse.

In her pocket, Zoya's hand grasped the percussion grenade. In blind frustration she dragged it out and pulled the pin, hurling the grenade in an underarm movement up toward the approaching helicopter. She knew it must fall far short, but she had not counted on its percussive force. With a bright yellow flash and a deafening roar, the grenade exploded ten feet below the nose of the helicopter. The pilot recoiling in alarm, momentarily lost control. At 20 feet, the helicopter seemed to rear like a horse. Its rotor blade struck the road below churning out a huge slice of asphalt and propelling the machine forward in a slow, spinning skid. As the helicopter came to rest before them the crowd could see within the brilliantly lit perspex dome, that the coffin of President Romanovsky had tumbled from its plinth.

The surging movements of the crowd, first in alarm as the helicopter crashed and skidded in the road in front of them, then in awed curiosity as the KGB surrounded the machine, had offered Zoya protection. She was no longer standing among the same people who must have seen her throw the grenade.

For a moment longer she decided she would wait and gloat as the KGB troops struggled to open the perspex doors of the helicopter. But the crash had distorted the bodywork and jammed tight the locks. There seemed no alternative but to cut open the bodywork with oxyacetylene burners to retrieve the President's body.

In the meantime the great and famous of the Soviet Union, and of the world, were waiting in Red Square.

The great parade moved beneath the Kremlin wall to the hypnotic beat of the drums. From where she sat Carole Yates could see the figures of the Politburo and their distinguished foreign guests looking down from the platform of the Lenin Mausoleum. Kuba, in fur hat and civilian topcoat, Ustinov in uniform, and the tall figure of Natalya Roginova stood a few paces in front of the others. The scene was already set for the struggles to come.

Before her the columns were now wheeling and turning to form an enclosed square. Along the western end, two lines of T-72 tanks, their tracks squealing on the cobbles, slewed round to face inward. A hundred yards opposite them twelve-deep columns of infantry stood, their rifles at the short trail. Long lines of armored troop carriers formed the other two sides of the square. Then, as the drumbeat ceased, the helicopters came over the Byzantine domes of St. Basil's and, the escorts hovering, a huge black machine descended gently to rest before the mausoleum as the Soviet and world leaders looked on.

All around them bands played somber music as 12 Soviet officers, hatless in the flurrying snow, marched to the center of the square.

From where she sat Carole Yates could see the coffin sliding smoothly onto the shoulders of the officers. Then the music changed abruptly to the strains of the Soviet National Anthem.

The spectators rose in their seats. A single voice cried out an order. Ten thousand rifles moved up into the present. The long rows of tanks before St. Basil's dipped their black guns. As the music swelled the coffin was carried across the square to its resting place in the great porphyry vault of the Lenin Mausoleum.

Of the thousands of guests and officials watching the ceremony in Red Square, only the leadership, at that time, were aware that the coffin was empty.

In December darkness falls early. Some days, like this, it hardly seems that the sun rose at all behind the lowering gray skies. But to Zoya the half-light was welcome as she made her way back to the students' apartments of Moscow University. She could see the great wedding-cake tower rising before her now. Lights gleamed at the innumerable windows. She cut quickly across the asphalt soccer fields and reached the main avenue. There were a good number of students about. She felt protection from them, anonymous among so many young people of her own age.

She had deliberately stayed on at Razina Street until the crowds began to drift away. There was no sign of Andrei.

Some instinct told her to linger on the journey back to the University. The men were already posting up the public copies of the evening paper, *Izvestia*. Casually she stood reading the planning details of the great parade and the lengthy speeches of Kuba and Roginova in praise of the dead leader.

At the entrance to Student Hall 4 she paused. Three men in civilian clothes stood in front of the elevators, checking the cards of students as they entered. Without a Moscow stamp on her internal passport she would be in immediate trouble. She was about to turn away when her arms were caught and twisted behind her. Two more plainclothesmen bent her forward and ran her toward a car, the back door of which was already swinging open.

During the short journey to KGB headquarters at Lubyanka her bag was searched and her internal passport quickly examined. One of the men sitting next to her in the back gave a quick nod to his colleague on the other side of her.

In the Lubyanka courtyard she was pulled from the car and pushed toward a small green door.

Once inside she was led through endless corridors brightly lit with overhead lights, the walls pale green, the many doors painted cream.

They descended a stone stairway to a line of cells. Outside one she was dragged to a stop. The door was unlocked. In the corner of the brightly lit room a bloodied mess of rags stirred.

"Yes or no?" a plainclothesman said.

The rags stirred again and a face lifted. From it came a croak of confirmation. She knew it had to be, but could not recognize, the face of Andrei.

Chapter Fourteen

SEVEN HUNDRED MILES northeast of Moscow Anton Ovsenko looked back at the line of men on the rope and gave the signal to haul the great log up the incline. Like them he leaned forward into his leather harness, his feet sliding and slipping on the churned frozen snow, his breath snorting from his nostrils, his back aching from the effort in the bitter cold.

The log, a heavy center post for the new camp's administrative building, inched forward up the slope and stopped. Three or four of the older men were leaning forward into their harness, too exhausted to contribute more than their weight to the task.

"Heave . . ." Anton tore the words from his throat. "Heave . . ."

The log began to move again, slowly at first, then faster as the slope evened off and the men scrambled forward in their harness scenting victory and the promise of rest.

As the log slid and bumped forward to the half-completed administrative building, the guard put his whistle to his mouth and blew three short blasts. It was the end of another workday at Panaka Five.

All over the new campsite men were stamping the circulation back into their feet, clapping their hands together to generate some warmth or easing themselves out of the logging harness in which they had spent the daylight hours.

In response to the guards' shouts they formed up in a long column, four abreast, dark bent figures against the deep drifts of snow. Hands behind their backs, the new *zeks* of the 1980s trudged off behind the swaying lanterns held on poles by the men at the head of the column.

By the mid-decade Western specialists were calculating the Soviet prison population at something in the region of four million, or closing fast on the estimated figure at the end of Stalin's reign. The vast number of Soviet prisoners, almost one in 50 of the population, was KGB General

Kuba's response to industrial and agricultural unrest in the early eighties. Fifteen years earlier, Solzhenitzyn had made the term *Gulag* for the camp administration and *zek* for the unhappy prisoner known throughout the Western world. Attempts by groups such as Amnesty International to monitor the Soviet treatment of prisoners were contemptuously rejected by the Soviets. Their claim was that prisoners in the *Gulag* system had been rightfully convicted under the Soviet Constitution and both the tradition of Soviet penology and the practice over the years showed the treatment of all categories to be firm but just. It was a blank wall against which Western complaints shattered harmlessly.

Behind the wall the picture was grimly different. The camps spread throughout the Soviet Union with a marked concentration in the north and mid-Siberia. Prisoners' reports show clearly that treatment varied greatly with the personality of the commandant and the remoteness of the location as the determinants. From the women's camps accounts of rape, forced concubinage and sexual abuse were common. Probably the easiest camps were mixed. Some of the men's camps on the dreaded Kolyma peninsula were as harsh, even bestial, as the Stalinist *Gulag* had produced.

In their new millions they passed into the camps. Many of course were sentenced for crimes which would have attracted imprisonment in any civilized society. But from 1984 onward an increasing proportion of *zeks* were again there for political crimes—they were the leaders of, or participants in, large or small strike actions from Alma-Ata in Kazakhstan to Minsk in White Russia or Odessa in the southern Ukraine.

Among these politicals there is no doubt that a large proportion were nationalists. In these years people in Kiev began to talk of the Ukrainian camps at Kolyma or the Caucasian camps in the dreaded lead mining complex on Cape Deschnev, the farthest northeasterly point of Soviet Siberia.

Careless of the brutalized creatures they were breeding in these arctic wastes, the Soviet penal system continued to believe that they were safer caged together, in Siberian lumber camps, or living a troglodyte life in the deadly lead mines of the East Cape. It is clear from KGB reports, that it occurred to no one in the government that they were sitting on a powder keg.

Panaka Five was the latest of a group of new camps being built by the *zeks* of Panaka One. Deep in the limitless birchwoods the Panaka complex had grown rapidly since its founding in 1982. From a small free logging camp it had acquired first annexes of long wooden huts and then full-sized sister camps with their own medical and administration buildings, their own high barbed-wire fences, dirt roads and mess halls. The rumor was, and strangely these rumors were seldom totally wrong, that

Panaka Five was to be reserved for a full penal brigade of Asiatics.

At Panaka Anton Ovsenko had lived through his first northern summer, had survived the backbreaking work in the drenching autumn rains and was beginning now on the first of seven long winters to which he had been sentenced. He was twenty-four years old, strongly built. He counted it good fortune that he had been assigned to the only mixed camp in the Panaka complex.

In the light of later events [Anton wrote], it is important to try to describe the feelings of many of my fellow *zeks*. First for the newly arrived prisoner there was the most frightening sense of lonely desolation. This had of course begun back at the railhead at Krasibirsk where the prisoners left the cattle trucks which had brought them from what passes in the Soviet Union for civilization. From the railhead to Panaka was a hundred-kilometer march. Some marched in summer, some in winter snows. All, in their trudging columns, were attended by the whip-guards of the prison service. And here that sense of desolation, of abandonment, gripped a man, as he marched day after day, further from the railhead, as the very road turned first to a track through the birch forests and then seemed barely to exist at all. Russia can swallow a man, can swallow his soul. Perhaps our national character is more based on the dread of isolation than on anything else, the fear of the limitless snowfields or the unwalked summer forest.

Once at Panaka all but the strongest are lost. Tremblingly they question the older *zeks*. There are no published rules. It is the prisoners responsibility to discover his duties and perform them. As a new arrival he is cheated of his bread ration, assigned to the duties of other *zeks,* forced to struggle for a position in the pecking order even of us, the lowest of the low. For we are not kind to each other.

Later there are friendships, it is true, slender relationships that moderate the desolation. But for most prisoners the sentence is not to the hard labor of this hard land, but to suffer its awful emptiness, to endure this cosmic sense of abandonment.

With it, grows quickly inside you a bitter hatred of all those who are not suffering as you are. Not of the guards so much, as of the people you knew in Moscow or Omsk or Odessa, of the warmth and comfort of their lives. We, the *zeks* of Panaka, and of a hundred other camps, worse and better, are the price paid for your years of silence . . .

Anton realized that Saturday, December 7th, was not a day like any other.

I think it's true to say that we had hardly marched through the gates of

Panaka One that night when we sensed the electric air of excitement in the camp. Groups of *zeks* stood in the doorways of the huts waiting, it seemed to us, for our roll call to be completed. When we were dismissed they hurried across toward us. This hour after the return from labor was the most free of our camp life. Normally food would be collected from the kitchens and section leaders would be busy filing their day's report. One hour later we would be back in our hutches, locked in for the night, but for the moment we could talk with *zeks* from other huts, exchange details seen or heard with the ever-present object of trying to fathom new plans or projects of the authorities.

On this night the news was of some massive event in Moscow. No one had real information. A woman prisoner who cleaned the office of the camp commander was said to have overheard him on the phone. Her version was that the leadership had been overthrown by an anti-Party group. Others said that a helicopter transport of new guards who had arrived that afternoon had brought news of an assassination at the highest possible level. The two stories were not mutually exclusive, of course, but they were the only two I can remember among ten or fifteen wild rumors, each of which implied, of course, an amnesty for all political *zeks* wrongfully imprisoned by the past regime.

Bubo, my Tatar friend of the last week or two, a tall, limping tailor from Bratsk, walked with me back to the hut. Like me, he believed none of the stories but agreed that perhaps somewhere a few grains of truth inspired them.

"You may have a chance to find out, Anton," he said as we stepped into the dimly lit hut. "One of the guards who arrived from Krasibirsk by helicopter this evening came over here asking for you."

"Me? What would he want with me?"

"He's from Moscow. He says he's got a message from your mother."

I burst out laughing in love and admiration and sheer wonder. My mother is an ignorant peasant woman. Until she was thirty she couldn't write her name. But she could bribe and bully a guard to bring me a letter. For a while the whole absurd idea lifted that sense of isolation we all suffered . . .

It was another hour before Anton was able to make contact with the new guard. The man had not been disposed to talk. He had reached into his pocket and taken out the gold ruble. Anton was stunned.

I looked at the ruble lying in the palm of my hand. This dull, glinting piece of metal with the heavy milled edge and the double eagle insignia of the old Russia, could, in this place, buy me a month's good food, vodka for the whole hut, or even, a wild, ever-present idea, the basis of an escape. I thanked the man and he turned quickly away. Before he disappeared into the guard's compound I ran to catch up with him.

"One more kindness. What exactly is happening in Moscow?"

"You mean the funeral?"

"There's been a funeral?" I was deeply disappointed.

"Not *a* funeral," the man said. "The Soviet President is dead. His State Funeral took place today."

The President. My hopes lifted again.

"An assassination?" I asked cautiously.

"Of course not. Age mostly. Overwork I expect."

A new leader with new ideas. Perhaps gentler ideas. Hope should never be allowed within a prison gate. That night we talked and dreamed.

At eight-thirty on the evening of the funeral the emergency meeting of the Politburo was convened in what had once been the anteroom to Stalin's Kremlin offices. The old leather sofas had long since been removed, the walls repainted and the portraits changed. Only the big dark-red Turkish carpet remained from other days.

And now another leader was dead, and around the oval table the thirteen members of the Politburo were to chart the future's course.

We have an account of this meeting from one of the best-placed witnesses to the atmosphere in the Politburo that evening. Peter Rinsky was an administrative secretary of the Politburo staff:

Of course we never knew anything at the time it happened. The doors would be closed before the December Chairman, I think it was Defense Minister Ustinov that month, would open the proceedings. Yet even so it is astonishing how much can penetrate a closed door. No sounds, no overheard voices. But the few lines left jotted on a scratch-pad, the few words spoken as they left. Somehow we administrative secretaries developed a sixth sense.

First there was no agenda. Thirteen sealed copies of the agenda were normally placed on the oval table immediately before the meeting. No agenda meant that they were discussing a single subject, and usually one of immediate and overriding concern. During the Polish crisis I remember we had meeting after meeting without agenda.

So it was the guess of all administrative secretaries to the members (my responsibility was to Natalya Roginova) that the issue that night was the outbreak of unrest, arson and looting in the suburbs. In fact I had been in Roginova's office while she was taking a telephone call earlier in the evening and it was quite clear from the conversation that the disturbances had not been limited to Moscow alone. Kiev, Minsk and Tbilisi were mentioned. In the national capitals it seemed the local Central Committee headquarters was the invariable target.

But what struck me as strange was that at the end of that telephone call Natalya Roginova was looking definitely quite pleased. Of course in the light of later events one can see why. Her rival, Bureau Chairman Kuba, was in charge of internal security. There could be no better time from Roginova's point of view for him to be seen to be losing his grip. He marched into the meeting, his face like a thundercloud, while Roginova walked in smiling to everyone like the uncrowned queen a lot of us thought she already was.

Naturally the meeting was a long one. And tense for us outside as well. The point was that we knew perfectly well that whatever the subject under discussion, the actual decision that was taking place was quite simply who was to rule over one-sixth of the earth's surface in the years to come.

Now I should make it clear that none of us secretaries expected an announcement that evening. That is not the way things were done in the Soviet Union. Indeed, on the day President Romanovsky's death was announced the principle of collective leadership had been emphasized in a special Tass statement. But at least we in the Kremlin knew exactly how that was to be taken. It meant the struggle was continuing; neither side had yet won. But every meeting, every issue discussed from now on, would be part of that struggle.

As far as that particular evening goes we can now see that it was decided to hold back the militia for a few hours. The forecast was for a particularly cold night, with blizzards reaching the Moscow area shortly after midnight. The thinking was, I've no doubt, that the weather would drive the majority off the streets by the early hours. And at that point the militia would move in and order would be restored. I can see the hand of Natalya Roginova behind all this. It suited her perfectly to underline even a temporary breakdown in Bureau Chairman Kuba's apparatus.

The meeting broke up shortly after midnight. Although supposedly a totally informal occasion, we waiting secretaries could see the members holding back to let Kuba and Roginova leave first. They passed through the door together as they had entered, one smiling, the other looking grim. But we all knew we had a long way to go yet before the shape of the Soviet future became clearer.

Chapter Fifteen

WEST OF MOSCOW, in the rolling hills near Zhukova, the dachas of the great and powerful of the Soviet Union stood each in their extensive grounds behind high railings and stone gate-posts like exclusive golf clubs in Connecticut or Vermont. The ever-present guards were housed discreetly in charmingly antique gatehouses packed with modern electronic anti-intruder equipment. Here were not only the dachas of powerful individuals but of the high institutions of Communism as well: trade union dachas which no ordinary worker would ever see the inside of, the College of Soviet Surgeons' dacha, the dachas of the scientific establishment, of the senior officers of the Army, Navy and Air Force, and one of the most luxurious of these country clubs of high privilege, the dacha allocated to the senior staff journalists of the Soviet daily, *Pravda*.

Igor Bukansky was a frequent visitor. Although as editor of the nation's most important literary magazine his own club was the Writers' Union dacha at Borodino, he used, as was his privilege, the *Pravda* club because it lay on his way home to the new Swedish-designed house which he had just been allowed to buy.

It is not difficult to reconstruct the scene at Zhukova on the evening of the funeral. Too many journalists in later years described it in articles and memoirs. Most of them make the point that when Bukansky entered the long bar with the weird, shabby figure of Kuletsyn in tow, the writer's air of surprise, shock even, was evident for all to see. It seems that on the car journey out to the dacha, Bukansky had said nothing about their destination. In this long elegant room (it had been built by the architect Megelev in 1721) with the elaborate stucco walls and the decorated ceiling, Kuletsyn had stood, his head jerking from side to side, glaring at the group of journalists at the cold meats table, at the trim, short-skirted waitresses or the group of high-heeled club girls at the bar.

Standing there in the middle of the room [Bukansky wrote in his memoir], he looked like the wrath of God. He turned on me, those long spindly fingers grabbing my coat. "How dare you bring me to your whorehouse!" he bawled in my face.

Just the reaction I expected. I knocked his hands down easily enough. "Come and drink, Valentin Sergeivich," I told him. "You've jumped the first hurdle, but I've got a lot more in store for you."

The frown lines across his forehead were like sand ribs left by the receding tide. He didn't know what to make of it.

I walked to the bar and the girls twittered around, all excited at the prospect of trouble. But Kuletsyn followed me like a lamb.

Of course everything's free: drinks, food, girls—a room for the night. I sat Kuletsyn down with a big plate of smoked sturgeon and a half-liter of iced Starka. This man needed a talking to . . .

Kuletsyn's view of what followed appears in a scene from his Publication Notes to his novel *To Be Preserved Forever:*

Amidst these dim red lights, whorishly inappropriate to the grace and delicacy of architect Megelev's salon, Igor Bukansky hunched his great shoulders toward me. "All this, Valentin Sergeivich," he said, "could be yours. This is what I've brought you here to show you."

How could I tell him that I rejected utterly this sybaritic life of the corrupt scribblers I saw all around me? How could I tell him of the nauseous contempt with which I viewed his friends and colleagues as they poured Starka down their ever open gullets, as they munched the food of the Russian people and pawed at the skirts of the painted prostitutes provided for their pleasures?

Bukansky's message to me was clear. I could write a different novel, a Soviet novel. By which he meant a sycophantic, lying panegyric to the system. By which he meant a betrayal of that Russia deep inside every honest Russian. By which he meant a novel that would buy me, Valentin Kuletsyn, the entrée to this scarlet life of guiltless repose.

I would have nothing of it. I admired Bukansky for his early front-line poetry. I despised him for the compromise he had made. I saw sitting beside me a once great, now addled genius. And I saw the direction in which his fat, beringed finger was pointing.

The food and drink I left untouched. I feared even the corruption of my boots' contact with the thick carpet as I strode from the whorehouse . . .

Not surprisingly, in the light of later events, Bukansky had a different view of what happened.

Well, I did my best. I had brought him to the club and showed him the life of ease that was his for the taking—*if he wrote a Soviet novel.* I talked of the cars, houses, dachas, first-class medical care, holidays, access to foreign literature, travel, everything that could be his if he reached out those thin bony fingers to grasp it.

I remember the expression on his face as I talked. I thought then, as I have so often thought since, that this man knew little or nothing about the labyrinthine paths of Soviet administration. He had spent a lifetime of suffering in labor camps and he imagined that I, as a powerfully placed figure in the literary bureaucracy, could decide to publish his book or not, as I chose. I looked around me as we sat there and saw across the room my old friend Dr. Jacob Felperin. I called him over and introduced Kuletsyn. "This author," I said, "has written a great book. A great Russian book. He believes that if I, Bukansky, decide to publish it, it will be published."

Felperin smiled. "Ah, then your friend Kuletsyn has lived a long life in the woods, I'm afraid."

"Truer than you can possibly know," Kuletsyn snarled.

"Tell him," I said to Felperin, "about your statistics."

"I have no interest in statistics," Kuletsyn said. "I am a writer. I deal not in masses but in individuals."

"I am a doctor," Felperin said. "I, too, try to deal in individuals."

"Listen carefully, Kuletsyn," I insisted. "This could be your first lesson in Soviet reality."

"You will not be unaware that alcoholism and related disease is a massive problem in our society," Felperin said, speaking directly to Kuletsyn. "But tell me, do you know what percentage of our hospital admissions are due to alcohol-related problems?

"This, as doctors, is our problem: In its wisdom the Health Ministry has decided that no more than ten percent of admissions can be for alcoholism. Consider, Mr. Kuletsyn, no larger percentage would be acceptable in Soviet society. Yet the figure *is* larger, by how much nobody knows because a doctor is forced, in order to obey the directive, to misrepresent the nature of an admission once the magic ten percent has been reached in his hospital. Thus our alcoholism statistics are made useless by decree. But not only the statistics on alcoholism, because consider also that every time a doctor misrepresents a patient's problem as thyroid, industrial accident, bronchitis, emphysema or whatever, those statistics *also* become inaccurate. This then is a burden of Soviet life. Practice must be straitjacketed by theory. There is nothing I can do, senior consultant that I am at Moscow Hospital, to make those statistics conform to life. The figures have already been determined far above my head, long before some derelict Soviet citizen collapses drunk and dies of hypothermia on a freezing sidewalk. Or industrial accident as perhaps I'm forced to record it."

Felperin left us with a smile for Kuletsyn and rejoined his group of friends.

I turned back to my author. "What can be published, Valentin Sergeivich, is what is determined on high."

"Yes, yes," he said impatiently, "but we must break through these false constraints."

"Neither Dr. Felperin nor myself have the power, or perhaps the courage, to ensure that the truth is accurately represented."

He sat there glowering at me. "So, Igor Alexandrovich, you refuse to publish my book."

"I cannot publish your book. Not in Russia."

He got up slowly, I remember, and thanked me. I told him again that I thought the book a masterpiece. He nodded and looked around as if to say good-bye to this life he had known only in these brief minutes.

"I can never change the book, Igor Alexandrovich," he said.

"I would have wept if you'd agreed," I told him. "But I had to show you clearly what you are missing."

"It will be no loss," Kuletsyn said. He stretched out his hand to me. "Thank you, Igor Alexandrovich," he said, "for showing me all this," he swept his tattered sleeve around to encompass the whole room. "I shall go underground. I shall immediately start arrangements for a *samizdat* circulation of my book."

I walked with him to the door. "I have already made arrangements to publish your novel in the West," I said. "To be well known, famous even, *there* is your only protection against the KGB."

"It is a Russian book," he said, "written for *Russians* to read."

"They'll read it, Valentin Sergeivich," I said. "It'll be passed from hand to hand in battered, ill-typed *samizdat,* it'll be copied and pored over in secret. Ten million Russians will read it. Twenty million. But you will be safe. It will be already published in the West."

He shrugged his indifference.

"Allow me, at least, to do this for you, and for my conscience."

For a moment he paused. "You have my authority," he said finally.

I walked back to the clubroom. There was, of course, one other possibility that I had not mentioned to my shabbily dressed genius. And that was that our new leaders, whoever they were to be, would welcome Kuletsyn's novel as a denunciation of the past, as part of a new, more liberal course they determined to take toward a freer Russia. A possibility I had not even mentioned to Valentin Kuletsyn for the simple reason that it was too remote to waste my breath on.

"Gather ye rosebuds while ye may," the Englishman Herrick had sung. For myself and the others in the *Pravda* dacha that night, there was no knowing what the next day or next week might bring. Any of us could be replaced without notice, flung back into the thick ooze of Soviet society, deprived of all that made tolerable the daily postures, half-truths and bare-faced lies.

That night, while sporadic fires twinkled and leapt in the Moscow suburbs a few miles away, news had reached some of the other nearby dachas that *this* was the place to be. Members of my own Writers' Union came in a group of about twenty hacks. The *Izvestia* people brought a dozen secretaries with them. There were even a few senior Army officers with a bunch of pretty, uniformed girl lieutenants.

I said a party, but it rapidly became an orgy. Crates of Starka were dragged in from the ice-compound in the garden. The kitchens brought up roasted suckling pigs and great pots of jugged hare. The record player blasted Western rock music across the room. By midnight everybody was dancing, shouting, arguing, laughing. Men and girls rolled in the corners of the room. Stripped down to their underclothes and polished boots the pretty lieutenants were forced, not against their will, to dance on the bar top. Vodka bottles were spilt and gurgled spirit across the floor. Men laughed and sputtered and gorged on suckling pig.

The whole night through we sang and danced and drank. And beyond the windows of our world, across the white snowscapes, the distant fires of Moscow glowed like unheeded beacons, warning of an uncertain future . . .

The Legacy

Chapter Sixteen

AT THE BRIDGE she got out and paid off the cab. A flight of stone steps descended toward the embankment walk. Her high heels clicking, she descended the steps and stood in the darkness below. Pools of light were thrown every 50 yards or so by the street lamps mounted on top of the granite balustrade. It was no longer snowing and the wind had dropped. Below her the river flowed slowly past, dark and glistening.

She knew she had been a fool. In the excitement of getting ready in the apartment in the Foreign Compound, in the even greater excitement of the casually delivered lie to her husband about her plans to visit with a girl friend that evening, she had not thought of the danger she might be in.

But in the darkness of the embankment and with the slow, sinister flow of the Moskva waters below her, she knew she was taking an enormous risk. One scurrying rush from the darkness around her and she could be hurled over the embankment and into those freezing waters below. And there would be reason to do it if Letsukov *had* killed the Ukrainian Stepan X. Because if he had killed the Ukrainian she was the only Westerner who could identify him, the only one who could pin the guilt for the assassination on the KGB.

What a fool she'd been to come here! Across the river the lights of the Rossiya Hotel glittered warmth and the security of other foreigners. She turned quickly away from the river and headed for the stone steps leading up to the bridge. There was a light there at the top. Two uniformed militiamen paused underneath it. She had never believed she would see those uniforms as a symbol of safety but now she hurried toward the steps. A man approaching from across the bridge was stopped for his papers by the two policemen. The lamplight fell on his bare head. Unusual for a Muscovite not to be wearing a hat or fur cap in this temperature. She reached the stone steps. She could see Letsukov clearly now handing his identity papers to the militiamen. She still had a choice. If she hurried up the steps she would reach the level of the brightly lit bridge before Letsukov was released. Or she could wait where she was, on the granite steps, clutching the cast iron rail embossed with the double-headed eagle of the past, here in the half-darkness.

Within a few moments she saw him receive back his papers and turn away from under the light. Footsteps now, the sharp ring of leather on granite. Then he appeared at the bend of the stairway, hesitated, and came down into the darkness.

It was something in the quality of the man that he offered no word of greeting. Instead he took her arm and led her back down onto the level of the embankment. No apology for being late, no conventional doubt that she would in fact come at all.

But it was almost a whole year ago, she reminded herself. In Paris, not here in Moscow. And in any case it had been one short night, nothing more.

"In this weather," she said, "I get a terrible headache without a hat."

He nodded. "I don't."

They passed under a light, walking slowly. Again it was snowing, fat flakes now, floating through the lamplight. A barge, a bright neon-red star at its bow, churned along the river. Lights shone from its net-curtained cabin windows. A dog raced back and forth along the deck barking furiously.

"As I confessed to you," Letsukov said without preamble, "I was not in Paris as an agronomist. I was there as an investigator for the Ministry of Nationalities."

"A spy."

"You wouldn't call a football manager a spy if he went to watch the opposing team play."

"Too glib," she said shortly.

"Perhaps. Let me just say then that my task was the same sort of information gathering as I'm sure your husband has done a thousand times. My Minister wished to know what was discussed at the Ukrainian Conference. I was sent to find out."

"A man was killed. Assassinated."

"Yes." He remained silent.

"You're telling me you had nothing to do with that."

"That is correct," he said stiffly.

"But you left for Moscow that very morning. Long before the first announcement of the killing was carried on French radio. I don't believe your leaving was a coincidence."

"No, it was no coincidence. After I left you, I walked back toward my hotel. I was met outside by one of my colleagues carrying my bag. A car was waiting and I was rushed to the airport."

She turned away from the embankment and stared at the dark wall rising toward the sounds of the highway above. Fresh graffiti stood out white on the dark stone. No individual message registered. She stared, wondering about the man beside her. He was different of course from the Alex she had met in Paris. She could feel the tension in him. Perhaps, even, he was fighting for his life.

"You said at the party," she turned back toward him, "that it was important that I believed you had nothing to do with the killing."

"Yes, it is important."

"Why?"

"Only for the obvious reasons," he said. "Who wants to be thought of as a murderer?"

"It's also true that if you killed that man, I can identify you to the Western press. Even if you killed under orders your career would be ruined and the Soviet Union would finally receive the blame for an official murder."

"All that is true."

"For those reasons it's important to you that I believe you."

"Americans have been so successful in some things because they are able to ignore the complexity of others," he said, his face hard.

She faced him. "Will you find me a taxi?"

"You want to go now?"

"Yes. Unless you're prepared to tell me the truth."

"I don't know yet whether I'm ready to trust you with the truth."

"Jesus," she breathed a frosty mist into the air. "I'm going."

His arm swept up from the blackness and the open palm of his hand slapped her hard across the face. "I'm not a murderer," he said harshly.

She had fallen back against the frozen granite of the balustrade. Anger boiled within her and subsided fast as she watched his stricken face.

"I'm not a murderer," he repeated.

She struggled toward some sort of understanding.

"Not a murderer," she said. "But you *did* kill that man?"

"Yes."

"You left my room, walked across Paris in the dawn, up to his apartment room—and shot him dead?"

"All these things." He stood before her, his arms at his side.

"But you are not a murderer."

"No."

Even then she sensed the immensity of her decision. She reached out and took his gloved hand. "It is safe for us to get a drink somewhere?"

"Yes, there's a small restaurant off the Prospekt. I'm known there." They began to walk. "Is it true," he said, "that Westerners always believe there's a choice?"

"They like to believe it," she said. "Whether or not it's true, as a myth it's the basis of their society."

"Do you think it's true?"

"Not always."

He hesitated for a long time. "I think perhaps that's good," he said. "Let's forget about the restaurant."

"Why is that?"

"I think instead I'd like to take you somewhere else."

In Tom Yates' office at the Embassy Harriet Bennerman laid out the papers on the conference table. "Shouldn't you have Howard Roberts in on this?" she said over her shoulder.

Tom Yates looked up from his desk. "He'll have nothing to contribute, but I guess you're right. It'll save a lot of bitching tomorrow about being left out. Call him up, Harriet. Ask him. If he says no, so much the better."

She dialed the number from his desk phone.

"Carole's visiting with Nancy tonight," Yates said. "When you've talked to Howard ask him to put Carole on, will you?"

When Howard Roberts answered, Harriet's carefully couched invitation to the meeting had the required effect. He declined but appreciated the call. She asked to speak to Carole.

Tom Yates looked up from his desk to see Harriet's frown. "She's not there? Did she just leave, or what?"

She listened for a moment. "No, just that Tom wanted a word with her, that's all. He thought she was over with you and Nancy for the evening."

Harriet put down the phone.

"She change her mind?" Yates said.

"No. Nancy didn't know anything about Carole going there for dinner."

"Strange." Tom Yates picked up a new stack of papers.

"Would you like me to call David Butler?" Harriet asked. "He'll know where she is if anybody does."

"Sure," Tom Yates said, walking over to the conference table, "give Butler a call."

The officers attending the meeting began to drift in. Yates took his seat at the head of the table. As Harriet placed his notepad at his left elbow she bent low over him. "No sign of her at David Butler's, either," she said. "I'll call around, don't you worry."

*   *   *

They turned off the street into a courtyard lit by a single rusting wall light. Empty washing lines crisscrossed the area above their heads. The stone walls were green with damp, the wooden frame windows unpainted and split with frost; where the glass panes were broken the gaps were stuffed with rags and newspapers. At the base of a broken downpipe a patch of ice spread across the cobbles.

He held her arm tightly and guided her into a doorway. She found she could see little but a flight of stone steps and a bent iron banister leading upward. A strong smell of urine and cooking cabbage pervaded the stairwell.

"Who lives here?" she asked him.

"You'll see," he said as they climbed to the first stone landing and stopped at a door.

He knocked and they stood waiting. Inside she heard a man's voice.

"It's me, Alexei," Letsukov said.

As the bolts scraped back, Carole was half aware of a movement at the bottom of the stairs. Letsukov too had seen it. He leaned over the rail. A man in a belted woolen peasant shirt stood in the half-light at the bottom of the stairwell. One foot poised on the bottom stair, he was looking upward at Letsukov. For a moment his lips moved as if chewing on toothless gums, then he turned and disappeared back into the courtyard.

"Who was that?" she asked alarmed.

"The concierge," Letsukov said briefly, and turned away from the stairwell.

The door opened and a warm yellow light fell upon them. An old man in a tweed jacket and open-necked shirt propelled himself forward and hugged Letsukov.

She saw the old man's gray stubble rub against Letsukov's cheek, his hand patting his back. She knew, before the introductions, that it was his father.

"Come in, come in," the old man took her by the arm and drew her inside. As Letsukov shut the door behind them she saw that they were in a one-room apartment, the floorboards a dusty gray, a bed with a worn bearskin rug thrown over it in one corner, a plastic-topped kitchen table, a few chairs, a stove, a roughly hammered bookcase and some clothes hanging from a string line across an alcove. A standard lamp with an orange shade stood against the curtained window.

"I've been waiting for you to come," Letsukov's father said to his son. "I want to hear all about the funeral. You saw the parade, Mrs. Yates?"

"I did," Carole said. "I was lucky enough to have a seat in Red Square."

"Red Square!" The old man was impressed.

He turned and rummaged quickly in a wooden chest. Straightening, he tucked a half-liter under his arm. Pinched in the fingers of one hand were three glasses.

"Now sit down, Mrs. Yates," he made an attempt at an English pronunciation of her name. "This vodka is good. From the country. But not of course chilled as it should be. You, too, Alexei, sit down." They sat round the plastic-topped table.

"You didn't see the parade yourself?" Carole asked the old man.

"No . . . no. The cold . . . at my age."

"My father has no Moscow residence permit," Letsukov said. "On public occasions it would be too dangerous for him to go out."

"I see."

She found it impossible to guess how old he was as she sat listening to his son describe the parade. His gray hair was cropped short, his lined face was still hard and lean but the blue eyes were flecked with yellow, and set deep in shadow. He might have been sixty-five, even more.

"This could be a great time for us all, Alexei," the old man said ruminatively.

"Let us hope," Letsukov said.

Carole looked from one to another.

The old man laughed. "I see Mrs. Yates doesn't know our story."

"Tell her then," Letsukov said.

"Just this much," the old man emptied his glass of vodka and refilled it. "No self-pity, none. What place is there for self-pity in a man born as I was with opportunities so bright . . . so bright . . ."

Carole looked quickly at Letsukov, but his eyes were on his father.

The old man reached across the table and grasped her hand. "I was a young man in the great days of struggle, who could ask for more?"

"You were in the Army?" she asked hesitantly.

"The Army, yes. And before that even. We were building something for the rest of the world. For that great mass of victims we call mankind. No greater privilege."

He released her hand and drank and refilled his glass of vodka.

"Of course, some things we never saw. Beria the snake. Stalin the man of incorruptible evil. But we can throw off that legacy, Mrs. Yates. My mother would have said we can still make a new New Jerusalem."

"It would be wrong to pretend I understand," Carole said.

"Of course, but how can we speak, other than elliptically, of these things so close to us? Where was I . . . let me see. Berlin, nineteen forty-five. My twenty-first birthday. An agitprop officer with a front-line unit. Such fighting we'd seen in the last three years, great armies shattered and re-formed, whole villages ablaze at night, our towns reduced to rubble and bodies everywhere—by the roadside, frozen into the ice of rivers, rolled in mud under the tracks of tanks, German bodies, Russian bodies, the price of victory and defeat. My wife had been with me. Seen and shared it all. Political officer in the same division."

Letsukov turned toward Carole for the first time. "They both stayed on in the Army. In nineteen fifty-six they were in Hungary. Stationed just outside Budapest. I was eight years old at the time."

The old man nodded confirmation. "Eight years old. And my Nadya, a young woman then, your age, Mrs. Yates."

He paused, trying to recover the thread of his story. "Yes, we worked together in the political section. And then the rebellion in Budapest. I went in directly behind the leading Soviet tanks." He shook his head. "Bad things were happening. This was not Fascist Berlin in nineteen forty-five. This was a fraternal socialist society. I felt bound to speak."

He got up and walked the length of the tiny room. Standing near the bed, he smiled at Carole. "Headstrong young man. Didn't think. My wife working with me, in the same unit. Too late I saw the possibility, the certainty that I would bring her down, too."

"My father was denounced for anti-Soviet propaganda," Letsukov said. "That's to say he was told by a comrade that he was about to be denounced as soon as the emergency had passed."

"Where was our new society?" the old man said, "our new Soviet morality?"

"Was your mother incriminated too?"

Letsukov shook his head. He was looking at the old man. "No. My father persuaded her to make the denunciation herself, before the emergency was over, as the only way of saving herself and me, too."

"A child without a mother . . . in those days . . ." the old man muttered.

"She was commended for her action," Letsukov said. "My father was sentenced to twenty years in a labor camp."

"No self-pity," the old man repeated to himself. He seemed almost to have withdrawn from the story now.

"He was released in nineteen seventy-six," Letsukov said.

"And your mother?"

"She lives not far from Moscow. In the country."

Carole looked at the old man, but he had turned his face away.

"No self-pity," he said. "Not at this time."

Letsukov rose. "We must leave you to rest," he said to his father.

The old man was looking down at the table. When he looked up he was smiling. He got up, leaning unsteadily on the edge of the table, and grasped Letsukov in a trembling embrace.

Letsukov and Carole descended the stone staircase and emerged into the courtyard. Crossing to a door beside the arched entrance, Letsukov took a thin wad of ruble notes from his pocket. He knelt and slipped them under the concierge's door. Then he turned back to Carole. With his arm round her shoulders they walked through the softly falling snow.

"In nineteen eighty," he said, "my father was living, as he lives now, as an illegal. That is to say, without permission to live in Moscow. But I had to have him close to me, so it was the only way."

She wanted to ask about his mother but dare not.

"Last year the authorities began to step up the pressure on undesirables. They found my father. And soon discovered who was supporting him. But this time he wasn't sent to prison. Instead a polite colonel of KGB called me to his office. He explained my father's arrest was imminent. Yet, he said, this time it could be averted. He was an old man, this time he would never survive his sentence.

"I asked how it might be that he could remain free. They were looking for someone to send to Paris, the colonel said, an unknown face. I had just one hour to decide whether I would kill a man."

She stopped and turned toward him. "My good God!"

"I've no choice but to lay these facts before you," he said formally. "You will have to decide what you will do with them."

A green taxi sign approached through the snow. He hailed it and the cab stopped beside them. He opened the door and she climbed in beside the driver. He gave the address of the foreign compound and slammed the door closed.

Letsukov watched the taxi pull away leaving thin lines in the now heavily falling snow. Let us go directly to Letsukov's typescript autobiography in that old blue-leather traveling trunk:

I felt deeply disturbed [Letsukov wrote of that night]. This woman represented a serious danger to myself and my family. If she decided to identify me to the American authorities, the Western press would be presented with the perfect anti-Soviet story, with all the trappings it so much reveled in. For me and my father there would be little to hope from the KGB. We would have become a severe embarrassment.

Even for Moscow in December the snow was falling heavily now. Great thick flakes, swirling softly, seemed to cut me off completely from the few other passersby. I was more than a fool to have succumbed to the temptations of that chance meeting in Paris, much more than a fool. But I remember so well, even to this day, the fear and loneliness of knowing what I was about to do. Of course, in the event, it had not been so difficult. He was a proud man. He had not cringed or begged. And a religious man, too, obviously. He had made the sign of the cross just before I shot him.

And now all depended on this well-dressed, pretty American blond woman! What feeling would she take back, I wondered, to her well-heated apartment in the foreign compound? Perhaps in the back of the taxi now she was deciding my fate. My parents' fate.

To shoot a man in cold blood takes no more than seconds, hardly time for him to make the sign of the cross. But to ask afterward *why* you shot him is a question that might take a lifetime to answer. I killed Stepan X to keep my father out of prison. I killed Stepan X to save myself from that long slide down to the human rubbish tips of Soviet society . . .

Why had I left my father to tell the story? What twisted pride had held me back from telling all? "No self-pity," he had said. "Not now."

Letsukov had been just thirty years old in the summer of 1976, a Party member, an employee of the central Trades Union staff already earning nearly 1,000 rubles a month and having access to a range of foreign goods through the organization shop. His apartment was small but self-contained. Through the Trade Union House he had a choice of vacation possibilities which ranged from winter boar hunting to summers in the Crimea.

He knew well to whom he owed this life. On his twenty-first birthday his mother had poured him a large glass of vodka and sat on the side of his bed. It was six-thirty in the morning. "You've finished your university with credit, Alexei," she had said. "You have been admitted to the Komsomol and will be able to go on to be a party member. This is good. But I have things to tell you about the past. And I'm telling you so that you will never forget to whom you owe your future."

And she had told him the story of his father, who was no more than the dimmest memory by then, a memory supported only by one single faded photograph.

Three years after his father was arrested, she told him, a message came back from the camp somewhere in the far northeast that he had died in a typhus epidemic. She had traveled again and again from the village to Moscow to ask for details. But the authorities were not prepared to recognize that conditions in any camp were such as to admit typhus. No information was available, they said.

She had sat before the official in the Central Committee waiting room. "I have to know whether my husband is alive or dead," she had insisted.

The officer repeated politely that he regretted that no information was available from special camps such as that her husband was imprisoned in.

"Then I am not to know whether he is alive or dead?"

She had left the great waiting room where the distressed of the Soviet Union called for help and information about imprisoned husbands, brothers, sons.

As she started across the street, she was aware of a man at her side, the official she had just seen in the waiting room.

"The special camp you referred to," he said, out of the corner of his mouth, "suffered a severe outbreak of typhus two months ago." And he plunged across the road ahead of her.

In the village in the Moscow district lived a man named Pavel Rodontov, chairman of the local collective farm, Party member for twenty-five years, a good man without a wife. Nadya Letsukov knew that without *blat*, influence, access to authority, her son would descend into peasantry. Five months after the message came from Siberia she married Pavel Rodontov. In the absence of confirmation of her husband's death, she had first instituted divorce in absentia proceedings.

As she had calculated, Rodontov quickly took the young Letsukov under his wing. He was transferred to a school in the local town. As he got older he was elected to the local Komsomol. A university course was available to him.

Pavel Rodontov was a fat, bumbling man who had never lost the pleasure and pride of taking Nadya Letsukov for his wife. For her part she considered him a good friend. Uninspiring but ever patient he could see problems and their solution only in terms of the Party. On the village and small township level on which he operated he was however a master in the use of *blat*.

So at the age of twenty-one, Alexei Letsukov had been told the facts of *his* life. By his father's self-sacrifice and his stepfather's influence he had gained the right to a future.

And for nearly ten years it seemed he had.

Then one late summer morning in 1976 he had entered the House of Unions on Marx Prospekt at 8:45 A.M. as usual, had climbed the great eighteenth-century stairway to the office he shared with three others, and had settled down at his desk to survey the day's work. At this time he was second administrative secretary in charge of vacation arrangements for a group of ten major enterprises in the Moscow *oblast*. By this point in mid-September all vacation places were normally allocated and he was no longer bombarded with telephone calls or visits from enterprise managers trying to use their *blat* to get a pretty girl typist on holiday with them, or to extend their family number from five to ten in order to get a whole holiday apartment in Sochi to themselves. He frankly enjoyed the authority he wielded and the bottles of vodka and the Ukrainian hams that would naturally accompany any request for help.

Then that morning in 1976 the office door opened and an old man shuffled in. He was hatless and almost bald. His cheeks were sunken and of a strange gray color. He paused at the door only long enough to slip a pair of false teeth into his mouth.

Letsukov remembered afterward one of the typists calling, "Who are you, Uncle? What is it you want here?"

And the old man's reply. "There was nobody at the door downstairs. So, forgive me, I came straight up."

"And what is it you want then, Uncle?"

"I'm an old soldier," the man said, pulling at his tattered Army greatcoat as if offering evidence. "Somebody told me I have an entitlement."

"What sort of entitlement?" Letsukov's immediate superior, the First Administrative Secretary, intervened sharply. Any unestablished claim to an entitlement was like a red rag to a bull for him.

"To a sanatorium perhaps. In Sochi?"

The First Secretary laughed contemptuously. "We deal with working enterprises. You're in the wrong place."

"I was in the right place, young man, when the Fascists invaded. And you be grateful for it," the old man said sharply.

The First Secretary rose in his seat. "Don't come the old soldier with me. Get out of here. You're trespassing on State property." His voice had risen to a shout.

The old man stood his ground, slowly examining each of the people in the office in turn.

"Letsukov," the First Secretary snapped. "Check his papers. We can't have just any riffraff wandering in here. It's a breach of security."

Letsukov gestured for the old man to cross to his desk. "Sit down please," Letsukov said. "Let me see your papers."

The old soldier sat on the chair in front of Letsukov's desk. He began to fumble unhurriedly in his pockets.

The First Secretary, feeling he had adequately dealt with the intruder, collected up a file from his desk and left the room.

"Do you really think you have an entitlement?" Letsukov asked the old man.

"Oh, I have an entitlement all right. Whether it will ever be recognized is another question." He was still fumbling in his greatcoat pockets.

"You understand this is in any case the wrong office for you," Letsukov said. "But how many weeks do you think you're entitled to?"

"How many weeks is twenty years' worth?"

Letsukov frowned. "Twenty years in an enterprise?"

"The same enterprise, young man, for twenty years."

"I don't understand. Your Trade Union should have dealt with that. What sort of enterprise was it?"

The old man smiled, his new teeth white against his gray face. "I suppose you could say I was in the metal industry. Lead, to be exact."

"Safety and Health regulations, and vacations come under that heading, are very strict in any enterprise dealing with toxic metals like lead," Letsukov said gravely.

"Is that really so, young man? Well, I'm sad to say our enterprise sometimes showed a lamentable lack of care." The old man had found his papers. He handed the internal passport to Letsukov.

It was brand new, the photograph taken in the last few months. Letsukov opened it at the center page. Details recorded a period of Army service during and after the Great Patriotic War. The next page carried the red stamp of the Procurator's Office and the legend: Sentenced on December 10, 1956, to twenty years in a corrective labor camp under special regime.

He glanced up at the old man. Then with his thumb Letsukov turned to the first page—and found himself staring at his own name: *Alexei Alexeivich Letsukov.*

"It was not my intention that you should find out," his father said quietly, "but I wanted to see you just once more."

The door opened and the First Secretary strode in, his file under his arm. The thudding of Letsukov's heart was transferred down his arm, making the hand that held the internal passport tremble spasmodically. He handed back the document to his father who shoved it quickly into the recesses of his brown greatcoat.

The First Secretary had stopped halfway toward his desk and was looking at Letsukov. "Any problems?" he asked, nodding toward the old man.

"No," Letsukov said. "He's what he claims to be. An old soldier." He got up and rounded the desk. "Come along, Comrade," he said to his father. "I'll see you out of here. You want the Military Pensions Bureau, not us."

In his shirtsleeves he stood over his father, resisting the urge to reach down and help him to his feet.

The old man got up. "Thank you, Comrades," he said to the room at large, and shuffled toward the door. Letsukov followed him, close to tears. This bent old man, his father, was only fifty-six years old.

Outside on the landing, Letsukov closed the office door behind them. Glancing down quickly he saw that the doorman had still not returned.

"I must speak quickly," he said. "Your passport's stamped 'Exiled.'"

"I've travel permission to pass through Moscow on my way south. For the moment at least I'm legal."

"Do you remember the suburb of Khimki?" Letsukov said urgently.

"I can find it."

"Beside the textile factory there . . . a *kvas* bar. Can you be there at six this evening?"

"I'll be there," the old man said.

For a moment they stood looking at each other. "You know we thought you were dead," Letsukov said.

His father touched his arm. "You've hardly changed at all," he said. Then he turned and shuffled quickly down the staircase.

When he had passed through the glass doors Letsukov went quickly to the washroom along the landing. Locking the door behind him he rolled up his sleeves and ran water into the basin. Then bending forward he splashed his stinging eyes.

At six that evening Letsukov walked quickly into the little *kvas* bar. His father was sitting at a corner table drinking tea. Letsukov ordered *kvas* and sat down beside him.

His father rolled rough *mahorka* into a cigarette paper. "I've given you a shock today, Alexei. Forgive me."

"There's nothing to forgive," Letsukov said, "you know that."

"I know nothing any longer, my son. For twenty years I've fought for my life. What else do I know but how to stay alive?" He laughed. "Then again perhaps it's the only thing that's really worth knowing."

"A lot has changed, father. Here in Moscow things are better than they were."

"I can see it in the streets."

"Other things have changed," Letsukov said cautiously.

"Don't be gentle with me, Alexei. I've been to the village already. I know your mother married."

"Did you speak to her?"

"No. I saw her. Asked a few questions at the farm. She didn't see me."

"You came away?"

"What else was there to do?"

The girl brought Letsukov's drink. He lifted the *kvas* to his lips, grimacing at the burnt bread taste.

"I think she would have wanted to see you," he said. "I know she would."

"What sort of man is Pavel Ivanovich?" his father asked.

"He's a good man. He's been good to both of us. But he never replaced you. Ever."

"You'll break my heart, Alexei."

"It's true." He reached across the table and took his father's hand. It was wrinkled brown, the palms calloused. "You must see her again," he said, "before you go to exile."

His father nodded over his tea. It was not an affirmative. It was a signal of fatigue that was to become more and more familiar.

"Are you a member of the Party?"

"Pavel Ivanovich arranged it for me," Letsukov said.

His father looked up. "That was good of him. And your Moscow residence permit?"

"He got that, too."

"Your mother's happy with Pavel Ivanovich?"

"She respects him. As I do. Like me, she is fond of him, too."

The old man pushed the tea aside. "My exile is for ten years, Alexei. A small town in Central Asia. There are worse places."

"You've served your sentence," Letsukov said. "Why are you now to be exiled?"

His father smiled. "I've too many stories, my son, stories too fresh in the memory. It wouldn't do to have me hanging around Moscow on park benches. There are foreigners here, tourists, Western correspondents eager to talk to old men like me. But in my new village in Central Asia I can sit in the sun for months with never a foreigner in sight."

"But you'll see her before you go?"

It was a long pause. "You arrange it, Alexei. As soon as you can. But make it clear to her that I do not expect her to leave Pavel Ivanovich."

"And if she wants to? If she wants to follow you to Central Asia?"

"How old is Pavel Ivanovich?"

"Much older than you. Over seventy."

"Too old to have his life disrupted. I have reason to be grateful to him, not to destroy him. He has shouldered burdens in my absence. Perhaps, all that time ago in Hungary, I should have thought more of my wife and son and kept silent. Is it not a proverb in our country that silence is truly golden?" He rubbed his thumb and index finger together. "In the Soviet Union," he spoke of the country as if he were an alien, "it is a decision every man faces at least once in his life. Perhaps it hasn't happened to you yet, Alexei. When it does you will have to decide alone."

He thumped the table with his clasped hands making the teacup rattle in the saucer. "All right," he said. "Tell your mother I'm here, in Moscow. But do it gently. Do it gently."

Two days later Nadya Rodontov traveled to Moscow. Letsukov never knew exactly what happened when they met. But when he saw him afterward his father had decided he would not go to Central Asia. He would join instead the thousands of illegals living in Moscow. This way it was possible to see Letsukov's mother from time to time and to have the feeling always that she was there no more than 20 miles away.

So in that summer of 1976 Letsukov's father came back into his life. With the money he had received on discharge from the *Gulag* (one ruble a day for 7,300 days came to an impressive sum in 1976), Letsukov's father was able to bribe his way into a single room which the janitor of the building recorded as a broom store. In those days this was the way an illegal lived.

In the years that followed Letsukov could see the changes in his father. That fierce determination which had led him to the *Gulag* and then enabled him to survive it, began to lose its sharp edge. Living alone, he began to drink. His life was spent looking forward to the visits of his son and the monthly meeting with Nadya. He was not unhappy but it was as if the immense efforts of his will of the past twenty years were now beginning to take their toll.

Yet those times, too, before Afghanistan and Poland and the Soviet oil shortages, had been the halcyon days of the Soviet Union. While the West struggled with its problems of rising oil costs and ever spiraling inflation, the Soviet Union seemed blissfully exempt. The Chairman of Gosplan, the State Planning Board, had sat at his desk in the great red and gray building on Marx Prospekt and announced with confidence that the Soviet Union suffered neither inflation, energy shortage, nor unemployment—thanks to the State Planning Board.

In those years Alexei Letsukov had received steady promotions. In 1979 he had been head-hunted for a new section of the Nationalities Ministry which would be dealing exclusively with his own specialty, Trade Unions. It was a significant promotion. It required him to travel throughout the Soviet Union and from time to time to deal on the highest level with the local Party and government. Among the people he came in touch with, many local politicians and bureaucrats noted his name. Everybody liked to keep in with a man with a bright future.

The future, of course, depended on it not being discovered that his father was an escaped exile, illegally in Moscow and visited and supported by Letsukov himself. Even in those years of the good life, that fact cost Letsukov many sleepless nights. Yet the years passed and nothing went amiss. The janitor at his father's building proved completely reliable. Within a small area the old man could shop without danger. It was a sort of life.

It lasted for almost ten years. Then, like other Muscovites with connections with an illegal, Alexei Letsukov heard that the militia and KGB were conducting a sweep throughout the city. KGB men openly referred to a rat-hunt, unconscious of the irony of using an old Gestapo term.

Inevitably the day arrived when two militiamen stood in the tiny room, one watching Letsukov's father while the other thumbed through his internal passport to the page stamped "Exiled."

Letsukov had received a telephone call at the Nationalities Ministry that same day. A woman had asked him to come to KGB office 163 at the

Lubyanka after work. Her tone was briskly informative rather than unfriendly. "We are holding a man here," she said. "We have reason to believe he is your father."

Alexei Letsukov had never been through the gates of the prison at 2 Dzerzhinsky Square before. He had given the room number to which he had been called to one of the gate-guards and after a telephone call to confirm his appointment had been escorted across the cobbled courtyard.

They entered the modern part of the building built by convict labor after World War II. Before Letsukov stretched a long corridor, pale green in color and illuminated by a series of white globes suspended from the ceiling on a chromium rod. Uncertain of Letsukov's status, the escorting guard treated him with careful politeness, opening the door at the end of the corridor and half-bowing as he closed it behind him.

Letsukov found himself in a small room with a high ceiling. Painted the same pale green as the corridor, it was lit by the same white overhead globe. A scratched wooden desk and a cheap chair faced an older upright chair like doll's house furniture alone on the polished parquet.

After five minutes the door opened and a young man in civilian clothes entered. He was brisk in his introduction of himself as Colonel Pleskov, brisk in his offer of a cigarette and his request for Letsukov to be seated.

"The janitor has confessed that your father has been living at the house for four years. Since his release, in fact. He also informs us that you visit him regularly."

"Colonel, my father is dead . . . ."

The Colonel waved his hand impatiently. "I don't have to prove what I know. Kindly be silent until I have finished."

And equally briskly he had put the proposition. In return for Letsukov's agreement to his proposal he would retain his post in the Ministry of Nationalities, his father would continue to live, as an illegal, certainly, but at least in Moscow rather than in a camp in the northeast. In the nature of the assignment, nobody outside these offices would know any more than they know now. The record would be filed "Maximum Security."

One hour to decide.

In that pale-green painted office in the Lubyanka it had seemed easier to say yes. The weapon training and briefing had passed in a haze of vodka. Only on the way to Sheremetyevo Airport did Letsukov begin to ask himself who he was doing this for. It was a question that would not leave him for the rest of his life.

"What did you do tonight?" Tom Yates said as he came out of the shower.

She was sitting up in bed reading a magazine. "Nothing much," she said. "Just talked."

"With Nancy?"

"Who else?" she said. "Howard never has a lot to say."

He sat on the edge of the bed. "Where were you tonight, Carole?"

She continued to flick over the pages of the magazine. "You know where I was. Why do you ask?"

He lifted the magazine from her hands and placed it on the bed beside her. "Was it anyone I know?" he asked.

She looked at his face, flushed red from the hot shower. What point was there in lying?

"No," she said. "No one you know."

"A Russian, then?"

She hesitated. "Don't make something of it, Tom. It was just a drink. We took a drink in a restaurant he knew. A couple of cups of lousy coffee and talked."

"Russians and Americans don't just talk in Moscow."

"We talked about the funeral parade for Christ's sake. About my having a Russian mother. About his family. In a couple of hours, what else is going to happen?"

He shrugged.

"Come on, Tom."

"Okay, Carole. He was just a nice-looking guy with an interesting family story." He reached over and turned off his light. Into the half-darkness he said, "Will you tell me if you plan to meet him again?"

"I don't." She stretched a hand to his unresponsive shoulder.

Chapter Seventeen

IN THE WILDERNESS winter reigns. As the year ends, blizzards sweep across the land in a thousand-mile-long wall of swirling snow, an impenetrable white night.

And as the year progresses and the blizzards fade, this land becomes the frost's dominion. On still, brilliant nights a cold of forty, fifty, sixty degrees below zero numbs the endless snowscapes, freezing great rivers and the tears that start from men's eyes. The birch bark cracks; the hare runs its loops toward the waiting wolf; and the lights of man twinkle feebly, always in the distance.

It was yet seven days before Christmas when the old high-stacked steam engine pulling its line of rickety freight cars struggled toward the dawn rising behind the railhead town of Krasibirsk. Huddled in the last car, with forty other women, Zoya Densky awoke fighting fear. It had been the same ever since her arrest:

Even when the interrogation was over and the beatings which, to be honest, in my case were not that severe, I would awake each morning with a paralyzing dread of what the day would bring. An old man I had met in the Lubyanka, who had been arrested under Stalin and again under Brezhnev and had spent over *fifty* years of his life as a *zek,* warned me that these fears had to be combated. He suggested a few lines of Pushkin's poetry recited immediately on waking, or best of all, he said, the Lord's Prayer if I knew it, but anything to break the paralysis of fear. He knew a thing or two, that old man. He said for instance that only a *zek* bent on suicide would even think about the injustice of his sentence. In the camps he said that (a strange phrase when I think of it) man could learn that he did not live by bread alone. And learning that, he could live forever.

I suppose, of course, he was a Christian, though it meant little to me then, except that as I interpreted our talk, he meant that you could, as a *zek,* sink or swim. I intended to swim.

They unbolted the freight-car doors at a little desolate rail-stop called Krasibirsk that morning and we all stumbled out of the fetid warmth of what had been home for the last week. The soldiers, dressed in green uniform trousers, fur boots and quilted green jackets, ear-muffed fur caps and thick gloves, were a mixture of Russians and Asiatics. One or two carried submachine guns, but most carried long, roughly cut batons which they seemed to get a lot of pleasure from wielding across our bottoms. Of course most of us, at that stage, were still looking more or less like women.

We formed up in a long sullen column. "Hands behind your backs," the soldiers ordered, the first time I received that dreaded command, and we marched through the town. Few people gave us even the recognition of a hostile stare. The men, loading lorries or repairing roofs, continued work. The women in the long queues outside the shops, women like ourselves, turned away to talk to a neighbor. The first tremors of the *zeks'* hatred of all those who are free passed through me that morning.

We left the miserable township and marched through brown-stained snow to the lorry depot. It was cold but not really painfully so. In the gray dawn as we left Krasibirsk and stumbled toward the line of trucks behind the concrete slab walls of the depot, most of the women were crying.

We were ordered onto the trucks, the batons flashing across our bottoms. "Don't you dare," I said to the young soldier, as I clambered aboard. He didn't.

Until nightfall we bumped and slithered along the narrow road north, turning off only once to slide down an iced forest track and onto a frozen river. One of the women said this was the River Ob which flows north through this part of Siberia into the Arctic. At least in summer it flows. Now it seemed a solid block of ice over which the line of trucks in our convoy made good progress, their lights blazing between the riverbanks, for fifteen miles or more.

At some point in the twilit afternoon we drove off the river again and up the bank to a forest encampment where fires were burning under huge pots of soup. Every woman was issued a tin mug and spoon and pushed into line to get her issue from prisoners serving from the soup pots. It was the first time I had seen a real *zek* and it was a shock. They were mostly women, desperately thin and from the strands of hair that hung from their fur caps, almost all gray. Yet they were certainly not all that old. The number of teeth missing, too, was noticeable as they snarled at us to hurry along when we paused for a moment in the warmth of the fire. But of course the biggest shock was the contempt, even hatred, that seemed to radiate from their thin bodies. The fear welled up in me. I stepped forward, reciting to myself my lines from Pushkin. My old friend in the Lubyanka had warned me of this, too.

Oh God the first sight of Panaka! Enclosed by snow forests, it was a world alone, the long bleak huts, the mesh-covered lights along the fencing, the wisps of steam rising from urine-soaked sacking as women squatted sobbing in the latrine.

At roll call on the square between the huts I was aware for the first time of other prisoners. Shadowed bearded faces crowded at the windows of the huts. I was mortally afraid.

I became a *zek* at dawn the next day. After a night when I thought I should barely survive the cold on a wooden bunk wrapped in two cotton blankets, we were paraded outside the administration hut of Panaka One. I should explain that the well-known term "Gulag," General Prisons' Administration, is supplanted in district administrations by a term based on the name of the *oblast*. We were therefore prisoners of the Kraslag, the Krasibirsk Prisons' Administration, and our numbers were issued accordingly. Thus it was that on that morning I became Kra 97927. I also, by a supreme piece of good fortune, became assistant medical orderly on the slender basis of my year of medical studies.

The "doctor" was a woman of about fifty who had, many years before, completed three years of medical studies, but she was brisk and confident. Every medical emergency up to and including appendectomy was handled within the camp. Other problems, and they were rare, she claimed, were sent to Krasibirsk where she believed a clinic existed. Unwilling to talk about the reasons for her imprisonment, never discussing her family or hometown, she buried her thoughts in the long day's tasks, cutting, sewing, setting, prescribing, coolly and mostly efficiently. I learned, months later, that she had been given twenty-five years, and that underneath her coldness was a heart too kind to expose to this grim place. Would I, I wondered, tread the same path before my fifteen years were up?

Even with the exceptional privileges of assistant medical orderly I was pitched into camp life without ceremony. In our hut we divided immediately between newcomers and older *zeks*. It is true that among these latter some of the politicals retained shreds of old-time decency. But the hut was run by a gaggle of ex-thieves and prostitutes who were just as violent as some of the men. I remember that first day we were allocated to hut 17. Two dozen of us were lined up by a gang of knife-carrying women under the direction of a small scrawny woman whose pale skull showed through her balding dark hair. Each one of our group was stripped of her new issue of camp clothes and handed in exchange a filthy bundle from one of the thieves—torn trousers and oily quilted jackets. Then a grotesque fashion parade took place as the thieves and harlots preened themselves and complimented each other on their new outfits.

I was the only newcomer allowed to retain my clothes. Karka, the thieves' leader, had stood in front of me for a good minute before turning to her friends. "This one we leave alone. That's my orders. It's bad policy to fall foul of a medical assistant—you never know when you might need her." And she hopped around holding her belly with both hands in an obscene parody of being pregnant.

It was a relief at the time, of course, to be able to keep my clothes, but Karka's words were even more useful to me later when I faced the test that any reasonably young woman inevitably had to face in a mixed camp.

Somehow our first week passed. The work for the women wasn't really hard. While the men cut and dragged and sawed the wood the women collected all the off-cuts and sorted and graded them for despatch to toy-making factories at Perm some hundreds of miles to the southwest. But it meant, of course, that the women often worked in the same shops as the men.

Throughout that first week girls would come running into the hut after final work whistle and hurl themselves sobbing on their bunks. We got to know that it was best to leave them alone for a while. Only afterward would one of us ask who they had been chosen by—and it was of course always one of the thieves who ran the male huts. There weren't enough young women to go round and in any case the thieves demanded not just first but second and third choices as well. As you can imagine it meant the doctor became very skilled at abortion.

It was seven or eight days after Christmas, sometime into the second week, that I was called to the workshop. One of the girls had trapped her hand in a grading machine and was screaming in terror by the time I got there. A big young *zek* with a blond beard had his arm round her shoulders trying to comfort her. Even in the panic of my inexperience I was struck by the first kindly act I had seen at this dreadful place. We released the girl's hand, the blond *zek* and myself, and it was clear immediately that it was not badly damaged. The doctor arrived then and took the girl off to the medical hut while I picked up my accident bag and collected a few items that had spilt from it.

The blond *zek* was looking down at me, smiling. To this day I cannot explain how I had not recognized him before. The beard of course, and the strange dark-eyed face of every *zek*. My own nervousness, too, as we released the girl's hand. All these things I suppose.

"So you've made the long journey, too, Zoya," Anton Ovsenko said.

I stood up slowly. I knew I was trembling. I stretched out my hand, but with a minute movement he waved it aside. *"Zeks* don't shake hands, Zoya. We're all much more and much less to each other than that."

I could see he had changed, and not just physically. He had learned things about human beings which are given to few people to learn.

I ached to tell him that he could trust *me,* that I already believed in my youth and innocence that I could surmount this place.

"We must be friends," I said swallowing hard.

"Of course." But his tone was distant. Perhaps he already knew what was about to happen next.

I turned sadly away and made for the door. Emerging from behind a machine a man stood in my path. He was of medium height, balding, with the easy smile of authority. Only his clothes showed he was a *zek.*

"One moment, Zoya," he stopped me with a hand raised.

I made no effort to ask him how he knew my name. Perhaps already I had developed that sixth sense without which no *zek* survives.

"Do you know who I am?" he asked.

I shook my head.

"I run hut 12. And 14. And any other hut you care to mention."

I looked round wildly. Five or six men had gathered, among them Anton. "It's true," he said flatly. "Not much happens here that Uncle Vanya doesn't give permission for."

"You're going to be mine," Vanya said in his easy, matter-of-fact tone. "I'll send someone over to collect you from your hut after lights out. Be ready."

I looked again at Anton, somehow imagining he would spring to my defense. But that was an imagining from another world. His face was blank.

I turned back to Vanya. The words of our scrawny hut leader, Katka, were thundering in my head.

"No," I said. "No, Vanya."

"Don't be a fool, girl."

"When I take a man, I'll choose him."

"Don't be a fool," he repeated. But his lips now were twisted angrily.

I was shaking. But I held on tight to my bag. "You can send one of your men for me," I said. "And I'll come."

"Good. That's better."

"But remember this," I blurted. "The very first day you need treatment, medication, anything, I'll feed you enough poison to kill a thousand Uncle Vanyas."

His black eyes never left my face.

"Or imagine, Citizen," I said, "imagine one day you catch your thumb in a machine, like this girl this afternoon, and you need a little operation under anesthetic. It won't be just your thumb you're missing when you come round!"

The surrounding men burst out laughing. It seemed minutes almost, then Vanya smiled. "Now that's something I couldn't risk," I could see he was covering his fury. He grabbed me by the shoulder and pushed me toward the door. "Get on your way, you big tart," he said. "I can choose *any* woman in this camp. *You,* I can do without."

I stumbled and tripped forward. Slowly I got up. Vanya was laughing, or trying to laugh. His thieves gathered round him, were taking their cue from their leader. Anton stood to one side, nodding toward me with surprise and, I think, approval.

Early in the second week of December Natalya Roginova disappeared. At functions and receptions for those foreign leaders who had stayed on in Moscow after the funeral, Kuba strutted prominently. But of Roginova there was no sign. The Western press was in speculative ferment, but only old former U.S. President Richard Nixon was right when he announced in a CBS interview that he saw no mystery at all. At a time like this, he said, a politician gets back to the grass roots to scatter promises of a bright future for anybody prepared to hitch to his wagon. Richard M. Nixon should know. Now, of course, it has been established that in a grueling hundred hours of visits that crisscrossed the country, Roginova saw the Party Secretaries of every one of the remaining fourteen republics in the Union (she herself was Secretary of the largest, the Russian Republic). What deals she made will never be precisely known.

In Soviet, as in international, politics she remained an enigma. Like

Khrushchev during Stalin's reign she had never been more than a loyal lieutenant to the leader and the Party. Only gradually did some begin to suspect that, again like Khrushchev, she might well have surprises in store for the Russian Empire and the world.

It was early evening but already dark. The old man sitting in Moscow's Vossitaniya Square had no watch. From time to time he looked up at the vast skyscraper block opposite, watching the fall of snow across the lighted windows, worried that it would be too heavy for her to come. Heavily bundled in an old Army greatcoat and with a peaked leather cap with earmuffs protecting his head, he hardly felt the cold.

There were still plenty of people in the square, he was glad to see. Women returning from Moscow center with heavy shopping bags. Others joining the queue for the cinema in the skyscraper opposite. He strained his eyes to read the hoarding carrying details of the evening's performance, but he knew it would mean nothing to him anyway. In the last years life had passed him by. He only looked across at the cinema queue to stop himself constantly peering through the falling snow in the direction she would come from.

He knew it must be getting late. He had arrived earlier than he should, but he couldn't bear the thought of the wasted minutes if she got there first. It was a long journey of course. And even once she reached the Belorussian station it was two or three stops to Barricadnaya Metro. Even while he thought of the journey he cast an almost furtive glance along the pavement. His eyes were certainly not what they were! And yet that small figure that seemed to appear and disappear in the crowd . . .? He stood up. Then sat down again. A militiaman passing showed no curiosity in the bundled figure sitting on the bench. Or in the old woman who joined him and clasped him in her arms. In his gray greatcoat and tall *shapka* the militiaman strode on through the crowd.

"Nadya," the old man took her face in his hand. "I thought perhaps the snow would be too heavy. In the village it's always worse than here."

"Would I let the snow stop me?" she said. "Now let go of my face and let me give you these things before I forget. Some pork cutlets . . . already cooked but if you want them hot, make sure you cook them through again, thoroughly. And some soup . . . did you bring a bag?"

Obediently he took a creased plastic bag from his pocket. She put the cutlets and the jar of borsch in it and followed them with a round of butter and some cheese. Finally, and with evident reluctance, she took a liter of vodka from her bag and transferred it to his. "Now just a glass in the evening. Promise me?"

He smiled. "I promise."

"At heart you're a crafty old peasant," she hugged him. "I don't know why I've believed you all these years."

At Barricadnaya station Alexei Letsukov circled the statue of the worker-soldier for perhaps the tenth time. The cold was biting through his topcoat. He decided to take another walk through the connecting tunnel between the two Metro stations. There at least it was warmer than out in the open.

He thought of his parents on the bench outside the Widows' House. It was not warm there either, but he doubted if they would notice. Once a month was not often. And whatever the weather it was never long enough for them.

As he turned toward the columned Metro entrance a convoy of four official cars raced down the reserved lane in Barricadnaya Street. He stopped to watch them jump the red lights and speed west to some warm well-lit dacha outside the city.

Letsukov shuddered with cold and anger. He found it impossible at times to contain the bitterness he felt against the Red *vlasti* when an old couple like his parents had been reduced to a monthly meeting in a public square.

Perhaps things, somehow, would change. And if they did, perhaps there would still be the chance of a few years together.

He walked the length of the tunnel to the old Red Presnya station. Then turned and walked back. As he emerged from Barricadnaya his mother was walking toward him, dabbing at her tears with an embroidered yellow handkerchief.

By the middle of December Natalya Roginova appeared back in Moscow. On December 16th she attended the Politburo meeting with, under the rotating chairmanship arrangements which had been established by Leonid Brezhnev, General Kuba in the chair. Here she fired her first heavy salvo.

"Collective Reporting" was her term for it. Her proposal, which was carried by a majority of that meeting (Kuba and two others dissenting), was for a review of the state of the Union by all ministries at this crucial point in its history. A perfectly reasonable proposal on the surface. But people like Politburo administrative assistant Rinsky, one of those charged with planning the big meeting for December 20th, saw clearly the trap Roginova was planning for his colleagues:

Perhaps I should explain first of all something about our peculiar system of government [wrote Rinsky]. There were in fact two systems of Soviet government—one real, one imaginary. It seems strange now but nobody thought it was in the least odd in the early 1980s. Perhaps because all Soviet life in those days had its image and its dark reality.

Let us first take the *image* of government. The Supreme Soviet had 1,500 elected members, half from constituencies throughout the country, and half, like the U.S. Senate, based on the States or Nationalities of the Soviet Union. In a rough sense therefore the Supreme Soviet was the Congress of the Soviet Union. This in turn elected a 39-member Presidium, which in terms of the image was the government of the country.

Now to understand real power in the Soviet Union it is necessary to appreciate that this vast elective apparatus had, in itself, *no authority whatsoever*. Because, parallel to this system was a different, but not always totally separate reality: the Communist Party of the Soviet Union. Its 16 million members joined the Party by invitation only; blackballing and rejection were common. It was in fact a massive and exclusive club. At the top of this club stood the Central Committee, 287 members, and at the top of the Central Committee was the Politburo of the Party, fourteen of those, most equal among equals. This was Soviet reality: the Politburo of the Party ruled Russia and its dominions while the Presidium and the Supreme Soviet nodded eager agreement. The 1977 Brezhnev Constitution of the Soviet Union did no more than formally recognize what had been the case since Lenin's day: the dictatorship of the proletariat was a mockery of resounding hollowness. The dictatorship of the Party was hard, blunt fact.

So the man (or woman) who ruled the Party as its General Secretary ruled the Soviet Union. And the death that had just taken place left that vital post unoccupied.

Now to get back to Roginova's Collective Reporting. The actual ministries who executed policy would be on the spot. The Party who initiated policy, by the image and reality dualism of Soviet life, could be in no way responsible for any ministerial incompetence that the Collective Reporting might reveal. Thus Party General Secretary of the Russian Federated Republic Natalya Roginova had no accounting to make. But Minister of the Bureau of State Security Semyon Kuba had been neatly toppled from his seat among the judges. What exactly Roginova had in mind for the December 20th Collective Reporting none of us could precisely guess . . .

Leadership issues apart, the other Soviet sensation of that month was the critical reception in the West of the serialized form of Kuletsyn's novel, *To Be Preserved Forever*.

American publisher Hal Bashford had been as good as his word. In the

United States and Britain a serialized version of Kuletsyn's novel was rapidly catching the popular imagination. In Germany and France the demand for it was already building heavily.

Western correspondents in Moscow were urged by their home offices to get an interview with Valentin Kuletsyn. The correspondents themselves had not heard of him and often showed great ingenuity in tracking him to the village of Barskoye, outside Moscow.

Even Bukansky's genial spirit could not suppress a slight note of bitterness at Kuletsyn's reception of his Western success:

How much vodka can a man drink a day? I know it's killing me, a half-liter by noon, another by midnight. I ward off troubles with the clear fluid; with it I celebrate victories. These days, of course, the victories are few and small. A trivial success when I gain Ministry acceptance for some second-rate but honest poet of the Dnieper Marshes, his lines full of birdsong and penscratch. I can publish, the Ministry says, with a suitable introduction on our Dnieper Marshlander's Party background. I am triumphant, so I drink vodka. I am sick at the triviality of it all, so I drink more vodka.

Then I meet Kuletsyn. An authentic Russian voice. A rolling, ungainly ingrate who speaks pure poetry. Well, the risks I have taken are small compared with the reward. The world will know Kuletsyn. Today I can *know* the world will revere him. Understand him? No! But equally no matter. I, Igor Bukansky, a vodka-soaked trimmer, publisher of much trash, womanizer, fool . . . I have made sure the world will read Kuletsyn. I reach for the bottle on my desk. I will call in Lydia. She will understand. At least I think she will understand. She sleeps with me for English chocolates, Czech fur boots, a German tape deck—what else is there to sleep with me for now? But still I tell myself she understands.

Earlier today I saw Kuletsyn. I tell him how the West had reacted. I see him now, as if he's in the room.

"Igor Alexandrovich," he says. "What can it matter what the West thinks?"

"Your safety depends on it," I say to him. "They will not arrest a man well known in the West. You can go on writing."

"Already," he says, "I have had Western motorcars in my village. Is invasion by the press the only Western measure of success?"

"No," I said, "dollars too."

He stiffens, turning his head from the thought.

"You'll be a rich man, Valentin Sergeivich," I tell him. "You'll find the Soviet government will be very pleased to let you bring your dollars home. Ill-gotten gains though they are in the eyes of the censor."

"I have no use for dollars."

I stand up, angry. "Yes, Valentin Sergeivich, we Socialist artists are all deeply offended by the reek of dollars. When you inform me that you've given all yours to the Egyptian poor, I'll believe that you're as different from the rest of us as you believe you are."

He stands before me in bedraggled clothes. His claim, of course, is to be the conscience of old Russia. And I in my thick carpeted office with the Italian furniture, I believe in this scarecrow genius. I believe in his passionate denunciation of the Soviet system, even of people like me. And yet he isn't, in the sense I am, a true peasant born. His father was a mathematician, a schoolteacher. What does he know about peasant Russia, about the spring stirrings in our land? More than me, I'm sorry to say. Oh, his details can be wrong. But the heart's right. Am I to play the envious Lippo Lippi to his Raphael? No. I have taken my decision. The man before me is the greater patriot, the greater writer. I have no wish to offend him. Or rather I try to suppress it.

"Most of all, you will remain free, free to write," I urge him.

Ah, that sardonic smile.

"I can go on writing in a labor camp," Kuletsyn informs me.

"But not under six feet of earth." I am angry and humble. Why is genius so often vouchsafed to the self-obsessed? Am I too kind for genius? Is that the fatal flaw?

Alone again, I ring the desk bell and, when she comes in, I tell Lydia to bring me a bottle—and herself.

She is looking at me strangely. "Igor Alexandrovich, there must be no bottle for you. You must go immediately to the *banya,* take the hottest steam you can bear."

"Lydochka," I tell her, "I am celebrating a triumph. A secret triumph."

"I can guess," she said. "But this is more important. General Strelin's aide just phoned. The general invites you to dinner tonight. A private room in the Officers' Club. I am to inform you that Natalya Roginova will be present."

Some 20 miles west of Moscow city center the silver aspen onion domes of a small white-painted country church seem, by some trick of the light, to float unsupported, like inverted balloons above the snowscape. Here at Archangelskoye, on an estate once owned by the princely Golitsyn and Yusupov families, stands a magnificent yellow-ocher palace set in a great park and approached by a series of Italianate terraces. Until the early 1980s visitors from Moscow would wander through sumptuously furnished public rooms past paintings by Tiepolo and Van Dyck, part of the great art collection of the Prince Yusupov who rebuilt Archangelskoye.

But the conveniently short distance from Moscow, the comparative ease of security arrangements and the facilities for government meetings had attracted some functionary of the Kremlin majordomo's office. In the summer of 1983 the last tourists were ushered from the grounds, chain-link fencing was erected to enclose the great park and only the floating dome and gables of the church remained visible to the ordinary mortals who rode the 541 bus from Tushinskaya.

On the morning of December 20th, the park and terraces lay under a thick blanket of snow, but the drive from the main gate had been cleared early, long before the first of the sleek black official cars would begin to arrive.

We administrative secretaries [recounted Peter Rinsky] had been at Archangelskoye since early the day before and a whole army of butlers, valets, cleaners, cooks, waiters and maidservants had arrived almost a week earlier. We had been told to prepare for a meeting which might take one day or equally six. Rest rooms and offices had been allocated to the principal ministers, suites to the members of the Politburo, and the conference sessions themselves were to take place in the elegant, galleried Oval Hall.

My friend would smile wickedly at the name. Must we *always* insist on outdoing the Americans? he'd ask.

By six o'clock that morning when I came down into the forehall the chaos was indescribable. It was the security men's fault as usual. *They* were insisting on checking every document box that the various ministry secretaries were bringing in; the secretaries were equally insisting that KGB junior officers lacked sufficient security clearance to examine the boxes. KGB colonels and above were dragged from their beds in Moscow to arrive unshaven, their uniforms unbuttoned, swearing and cursing at everybody in sight.

In the midst of all this the cleaners, a group of the toughest women you're likely to see even in Moscow, were pushing their vacuums like bulldozers before them, their long electric leads tripping anxious political secretaries and caterers dragging in crates of champagne. The din was unbearable. Threats of immediate arrest by the KGB colonels were openly laughed off by the women cleaners. (I would not have liked to arrest one of *them.*) The majordomo, mad with panic, checked his watch against the great sunburst clock every thirty seconds and begged, pleaded and screamed at everyone to clear the forehall immediately.

The Oval Hall was no better. Here Security was supposedly making a final check for electronic devices but seemed more intent on a shouting competition between themselves to confirm the identity of each other.

There was apparently some ludicrous rumor (Oh, how I wished *I'd* started it! sighed my friend) that the Americans had installed an electronic listening device in the Oval Hall. Some lunatics actually wanted to tear down plasterwork when their detecting devices located a deeply implanted eighteenth-century iron nail. The majordomo, back to the wall, arms thrown wide defensively against the plasterwork, forbade KGB technicians to approach. The women cleaners laughed and cheered.

By nine o'clock all the junior ministers had arrived with their droves of secretaries and personal assistants. By nine-thirty the senior ministers had arrived and been installed in the suites of rooms on the ground floor. At ten exactly the last cavalcade purred along the drive and silence fell in the forehall where the ministers were lined up, like the domestic serfs of some aristocratic household, to receive the members of the Politburo.

Roginova and Kuba entered first, the others straggling in an octogenarian gaggle behind them. Coats were taken and the *vlasti*, the powers that be, moved along the line shaking hands, embracing, and exchanging a few words with each of the senior ministers. Naturally we guessed that Roginova planned a bombshell, but we were ignorant of the details.

They filed into the Oval Hall. Coffee and cherry cake was served. The waiters were ushered out by majordomo Pletnakov. Relief showed on his bulging red cheeks as he closed the huge double doors.

Inside the Collective Reporting began.

Now we administrative secretaries who were the senior civil servants present were each, as I mentioned earlier, attached to one of the Party or ministry figures in the Oval Hall. Most of us, of course, were highly experienced in such meetings and had frequently drafted the speech of the minister concerned. Thus we knew, within a matter of minutes, how long any presentation might take.

On this occasion Minister Bukin was to speak first. His particular responsibility was oil energy exploration and production and his administrative secretary assured us that a minimum three and a half hours would be necessary for his presentation. This of course would be the usual three hours of self-adulation and a half-hour of distorted statistics threaded in. Nobody expected the truth, so nobody told the truth. Image and reality.

Consider then our surprise when after less than fifteen minutes the double doors burst open and a red-faced Minister Bukin stumbled into the forehall. His voice was hoarse with humiliation as he summoned his administrative secretary. He required, he stormed, a digest of his speech, maximum length of fifteen minutes. All hard fact and . . . the word "truth" bubbled on his lips but refused to erupt into our Soviet world of make-believe.

Bukin was the first of many that morning. Natalya Roginova had struck, and in a way which Russian bureaucrats could not handle. She had demanded a true accounting. A short blunt statement from every minister. They reeled one by one from the conference chamber, lost as village illiterates required to recite Pushkin. My friend could hardly contain himself. The following is the text of Roginova's attack on Bukin:

Comrades, Members of the Politburo, comrade ministers, comrade marshals . . . I base my text on the pamphlet of the ever-illustrious I.V. Lenin: *What Are We to Do?* because analysis of the economic, social, military and foreign position of the Soviet Union indicates that we have reached yet another of those great divides which history in its inevitable progress presented to our forebears in 1921 or 1941 and now to us as we move into the second part of this decade.

Comrades! No future can be more golden than our own. But we must know how to apply our principles to that future. This is what I. V. Lenin tried to teach us. This is what we ignore at our peril. In my village the peasants say the future is a lump of unformed clay. Perhaps they're right. But we know in the theoretical echelons of the Party and government that history decrees that clay cannot go unshaped. It will be molded by the arbitrary forces of market capitalism. Or again, here in the Soviet Union, by the effort of Socialist will that we alone can produce.

Yet the Russian peasant will be the first to admit that to mold and knead that unshaped clay we must know much about it. Will it crack in summer's heat or the first frosts of winter? Does it contain stone? Is it mixed with moss or straw? Will it redden in the kiln of history? Or feebly lose its color?

These questions we must apply equally to the substance of our own future. Comrade Minister Bukin spoke first this morning of the oil-energy resources of the Union. He gave us figures of exploration drilling by the projected foot. Figures for current reserves and production targets into the 1990s. Afterward we applauded the efforts of himself and his ministry.

According to Comrade Bukin our oil-energy future is safe in the hands of Comrade Bukin.

Why is it then that our military so often discusses the problem of an ever-reducing fuel supply? Why is it that our Foreign Ministry contingency planning is entirely based on access to foreign oil supply? Why is it that our Nuclear Power Program is predicated on oil-energy shortages? Do these Comrade Ministers perhaps not *believe* the statements of Comrade Bukin?

Comrade Bukin tells us that the Soviet Union is the world's largest oil producer. And we applaud. But Comrade Bukin forgets to tell us that our oil production has not increased since 1980. He forgets to tell us that for five years production has stagnated or declined in all major oil-producing regions except Siberia, and that even there the massive Samotlov field last year passed peak production.

Comrade Bukin invites us to applaud a production level for this year of

10.5 million barrels a day. But he fails to remind us that in 1980 Soviet production was running at 11 million barrels a day.

Let us look to the future. Even with all the exploration successes in the Barents and Kara seas is it not true, Comrade Bukin, that Soviet oil production will continue to decline? And as we struggle for oil in the deep waters of the Caspian Sea, is it not *certain* that production will never again reach the high point of 1980?

Comrade Bukin points to our massive drilling program. This year the Petroleum Ministry has established a target of 70 million feet. Again we all applauded. But Comrade Bukin has not told us that his ministry has never achieved a drilling target since 1976!

No matter, our reserves are surely vast. Is not the Tyumen *oblast* in western Siberia a true source of hope for the future? Perhaps, but only once we have mastered the techniques of oil recovery through the permafrost of the north. American Intelligence sources put this at 1990 or after. Are they right, or is the ever-optimistic Minister Bukin?

Comrades! This year for the first time since the days of Joseph Stalin we have been unable to export oil. Next year the Soviet Union must become a net oil importer. In order to meet our own requirements and nearly 2 million barrels a day promised to the Democratic Peoples' Republics we will require to import over 25 billion dollars' worth of oil. Even adopting the levels of optimism of Comrade Bukin, it is certain that we will be unable to pay without using reserves for more than half the oil imports we need.

And what then if we choose not to import oil supplies on this level? Then comrades, the shape of the Soviet future, that peasant clay I spoke about, becomes clearer. Without oil, both industrial and agricultural production must decline. Shortages, more serious than we now know, will be faced by every Soviet citizen. Has Comrade Bukin considered that? Has Comrade Kuba considered how security will be maintained? Have the Marshals of the Armed Forces considered that a declining gross national product must mean a declining military budget? Has the Foreign Ministry considered the effect of draconic reductions in our support efforts to Ethiopia, Cuba and Vietnam? Or how the Peoples' Democracies in Europe will survive on a fifty percent reduction in Soviet oil imports?

Comrades, this crisis is upon us. It will require from us no less than a complete reshaping of our Soviet goals. My belief is that we face a future no less uncertain than in the interventionist period of our glorious past or than in the days when the Fascist armies were launched across our frontiers.

I have chosen to speak only of the problems facing our oil industry. Yet there are others in agriculture, transportation, mining and metals. In all these vital areas we are faced with the necessity of a massive program of structural reform. Again I will take as an example our energy problems. At this moment they are managed by no less than sixty government departments and ministries. Chief among these are Comrade Bukin's Petroleum Ministry, the Ministry of Coal Industry, the Ministry of Chemical and Petroleum Machine Building, and the Ministry of Construction of Petroleum Enterprises. When I am asked by foreign visitors who is our Energy Minister, Comrades, I cannot even remember the *names* of all those who bear responsibility for this crucial area of our economy.

Let it not be thought that I have singled out Comrade Bukin for unfavorable comment. There are many others whose Ministries invite similar examination.

Comrades, the Party has much dead wood to clear away. Only then can we face a Socialist future with the confidence that our history and our Soviet people deserve . . .

Natalya Roginova's analysis, based on a research paper published by the Central Intelligence Agency as early as August 1981, was largely accurate. What we did not know until the Archangelskoye Conference was that she had chosen the Soviet oil problem as the arena in which she would launch her bid for power.

Essentially she had divided the Soviet senior leadership between the bureaucracy, including Kuba's KGB, on one side, and the Party and its own analysis of the future on the other. Perhaps she had reason to believe that the military would remain neutral in the struggle. She already knew from her flying visits to Party Secretaries throughout the Union that she had *their* support. As the resignations and retirements and sudden illnesses of senior ministers began to be announced at the conclusion of Archangelskoye, it seemed as if Natalya Roginova was carrying a majority of the septuagenarian Politburo along with her into her version of the Soviet future.

Yet still, in the West, and throughout the vast reaches of the Soviet dominions, nobody knew what exactly that version was.

Chapter Eighteen

At Sheremetyevo, Lydia handed Bukansky his briefcase.

"I'll bring you back a pair of fine London boots. Dark-red leather," he said. "English size seven."

"Bring yourself back," she said. "And don't drink too much while you're there."

He looked at her in surprise.

She looked down. "I'm sorry, Igor Alexandrovich. I shouldn't have said that."

With his index finger he lifted her chin. "You keep your mind on the boots, Lydochka," he said.

She smiled. "I will."

"And someday, who knows, I'll get a chance to take you with me somewhere."

She smiled again. "Someday," she said.

She watched him walk through customs with an airy wave to the chief officer. So huge, he seemed almost to block the door to the departure room. Then he was lost to sight.

The arrival of Igor Bukansky in London on Aeroflot A71 was noted by Scotland Yard's Special Branch with neither great interest nor concern. All Western intelligence dossiers indicated that the editor of *Novaya Literatura* was over the hill. The extent of his alcoholism was variously estimated but all reports agreed that he had long lost the confidence of the Soviet leadership. His visit to London was known to be the result of a long-standing invitation by the Writers' Guild of Great Britain to speak at their Awards Dinner.

The invitation had no political significance. Rather it was aimed at developing further cooperation between Britain and the U.S.S.R. following the recently successful coproduction, *Dickens' London.*

In retrospect some of the officers of the Writers' Guild who sat with Bukansky at the top table in the ballroom of the Dorchester Hotel that night are prepared to say that he seemed quiet and preoccupied. Certainly he was observed to be drinking nothing more than mineral water until the awards were made and the President of the Guild welcomed the guests.

At that point Bukansky took a large whisky, drained the glass and stood up to reply. In his halting English he delivered a totally unexceptionable speech on coproduction and cooperation. He complimented the award winner and the producers of *Dickens' London* and offered fraternal greetings from the Soviet Writers' Union.

Then he looked toward the future. The world, he said, could not afford a war, the balance of nuclear forces being what it is. He noted with regret that since the high point under Leonid Brezhnev in the late 1970s détente had suffered badly. He professed to be unable to understand why this was so. Cold War attitudes, he said, were all too easy to adopt. Rigidity of viewpoint was safer (he seemed to be pointing the finger at no particular side) than flexibility. But flexibility, he suggested, was necessary for survival . . .

By this point most of his audience were wondering when he was going to finish and let the dancing begin.

Flexibility, Bukansky was now reading from a prepared script, could offer a totally new view of the world as it approached the year 2000. We had seen levels of military expenditure that even the richest countries were unable to endure. We had seen the West and the Soviet world poised on the brink of the nuclear abyss for over three decades.

And what had flexibility to offer? That of course was for the political leaderships to decide. But as a writer, looking to the future, Bukansky saw the possibility of a new détente, of that peaceful coexistence of which Nikita Khrushchev had first spoken. He saw the possibility of peaceful competition replacing armed rivalry in Africa. He saw the possibility of a reconsideration of the problems of central Europe. Even a separation of NATO and Warsaw Pact forces on the frontier of the two Germanies. Yes! Even a reunited Germany if adequate guarantees of nuclear and conventional disarmament were to be offered!

Bukansky reached for his refilled whisky and offered a Russian toast: To the president and officers of the Guild. And to that political cooperation on which the survival of all of us depended . . .

Fifteen minutes later the news hit Fleet Street. And fifteen minutes after that it was being pored over in newspaper offices in New York, Washington, Bonn, Paris and Rome. The London *Daily Telegraph* pulled down its front page and led with a four-column headline: Russia offers deal—German unity in exchange for NATO withdrawal?

The opening paragraphs read:

Last night as principal guest of the Writers' Guild Awards Dinner at the Dorchester Hotel, influential Russian editor Igor Bukansky suggested the

Soviet Union would be prepared to withdraw from East Germany if a new united Germany were to become a demilitarized zone.

This would undoubtedly be the most far-reaching Soviet proposal on the German question since the Potsdam Conference of 1945. If West Germany accepted, and it is difficult to see how Bonn could refuse, it would involve the withdrawal of American and British forces from German soil and a dramatic reduction of German forces.

Whether NATO could possibly survive such a blow is doubtful. Whether the United States would be prepared to continue to maintain forces on the European mainland is equally doubtful.

Indeed it seems now the most obvious move for the Soviets to make, divesting themselves of an increasingly troublesome ally in East Germany, and aiming a dagger at the heart of NATO at the same time . . .

The piece went on to discuss Igor Bukansky's possible standing with the new collective leadership and, acutely, in a summing-up paragraph, detected the hand of Natalya Roginova behind the proposal.

Throughout the world, radio and television news editors were demanding that their stringers in London get some comment from Bukansky. But Bukansky was already on his way back to Moscow.

In NATO headquarters in Brussels senior officers hurried to the first of a series of late-night meetings. In Bonn politicians looked at each other aghast. They knew NATO could not survive German withdrawal.

Natalya Roginova had played her second trump card.

Tom Foster Yates thought the whole embassy had gone mad when he entered the new building that morning. A messenger, clutching his arm, almost dragged him toward the elevator. Every telephone within earshot seemed to be ringing. A group of agitated correspondents were demanding clarification on some issue from a retreating press officer.

His secretary, Harriet Bennerman, had already assembled a slim file of overnight international comment.

Tom Yates dropped into his chair and opened the file. As usual Harriet had underlined in blue pencil the more significant passages. He turned the pages quickly, reading only the underscored lines:

No more pathetically obvious ploy could have issued from the Kremlin in the days of Brezhnev himself. Let there be no mistake: This is a ploy aimed at China.

Peking Radio, reported by *Agence France Presse*

The most constructive alternative to have been presented by any country in the history of East-West relations since World War II.

>Tony Wedgwood Benn, MP, London

A one hundred division armoured thrust at the heart of NATO could not create more havoc.

>Mrs. Margaret Thatcher, London

If the West falls for this one, it deserves all it gets.

>Richard M. Nixon, San Clemente, California

With this one proposal the new Russian leadership could change the face of German politics. How could the ruling Social Democrats refuse an offer which would liberate 20 million of their Eastern countrymen? Would they *want* to refuse an offer which would certainly bring them a vast new increase in votes from the East. If the Russians are serious this may well be the end of the NATO alliance as we have known it.

>*London Times*

On the question of disarmament in Central Europe it must be said at the outset that if Germany is unprepared to defend itself it cannot expect the United States to shoulder its responsibilities.

>U.S. State Department spokesman

Reunification in exchange for a disarmed Germany? This must remain for the moment a hypothetical question. The State Department does not comment on hypothetical questions.

>The same U.S. State Department spokesman
>ten minutes later, after "consultation"

It is unlikely that France would consider the relocation of United States military forces on French soil.

>Élysée Palace spokesman

Who can any longer deny the Russians are serious when they claim they want peace?

>European Campaign for Nuclear Disarmament

In the U.S. Embassy it fell to Tom Yates to write the crucial position paper.

In it he attempted to assess the forces at work within the new collective leadership. His conclusion that in London Bukansky was kiteflying for

Natalya Roginova and some supporting group within the Party was widely accepted when it reached Washington.

Meanwhile, a special emissary had been sent by the Administration to Bonn to gain at first hand the German Chancellor's reaction. But Helmut Schmidt was too acute a politician to provide any answers at this stage. On German television the night after Bukansky's speech to the British Writers' Guild he laid down his approach. There is, as yet, no Soviet proposal. A Soviet citizen, not even a member of government, has made certain remarks about German unification. It is true that well-placed Soviet citizens abroad do not normally speak publicly without prior government approval. Nevertheless the object of this apparent new departure could easily be no more than an attempt to disrupt NATO during a period of its increasing military strength. If that is so it would be unwise for the German Federal Government to speculate. Until the Soviet Union chooses to approach the Federal Government officially, what was now widely called simply *The Proposal* did not exist.

Nor could the U.S. President's embassy or the British ambassador get anything more out of Helmut Schmidt.

For Carole Yates these days before Christmas were a period of intense excitement. On December 22nd her husband, Tom, recognized by the administration as one of the U.S. Moscow embassy's most reliable new Kremlinologists, was called to Washington to give the President a personal briefing.

Carole had seen him off at Sheremetyevo Airport. As she waved to him through the barrier and turned back toward the car park, Alexei Letsukov was crossing the concourse toward her.

In the weeks since she had last seen him she had found he occupied a large part of her waking thoughts. In some way beyond her present understanding he had become a mirror to her face. He had killed a man. And knowing that she still had talked with him, had held his arm, drank coffee in a restaurant and left him with some regret. Through him she found herself immersed in a moral problem beyond her experience as an American woman. There at home morality was sexual or at most an item not included in an annual Internal Revenue return. It was whether to buy a cheap set of tires for the car, knowing *almost* for certain that they were stolen. In this past month the triviality of her moral anxieties had sickened her. She had wanted to talk to Tom about it, but of course it was impossible. How could she now say to her husband that to sleep or not with a stranger seemed on the same level of moral choice as a slice of chocolate cake when dieting?

The last meeting with Letsukov had thrown her into much deeper turmoil than the first. That certainly she knew. Any residual guilt for the night they had spent together in Paris had been totally obliterated. Even the possibility of damage to her husband's career (which had not in fact materialized) had been wiped from the slate. What now remained were two interlocking questions, almost the same yet each with their separate limits: Should Letsukov have agreed to kill the man Stepan X? And secondly, could she condone his having done it?

And here she found herself in even deeper, more troubled waters. Sitting alone in the apartment or walking sometimes along the canal bank, she had decided she could condone the act once done. But could not have, beforehand, condoned his decision to do it.

The whole incident of the last meeting with Letsukov had sent a continuing shudder through her world. She found she wanted desperately to meet him again, not for romantic or sexual reasons, but because he was now the one person to whom she could talk about what had become *her* problem.

The effect on her marriage had grown cumulatively throughout the weeks since the funeral. At first Tom Yates had seemed to have forgotten her meeting with Letsukov. Their lives, privy to some of the details of the great power struggle going on around them, had become tinged with that wartime urgency which can make marriages and mend minds. But Tom Yates was no fool. He could sense somehow that his wife was now living on two levels of separate absorption. And because he was a Westerner he had come, reluctantly, to the conclusion that she was in love.

In her diary Carole Yates makes clear that she would have denied it vehemently. Even when she stood before Letsukov on the concourse at Sheremetyevo Airport.

"I've been seeing off a delegation from the Azerbaijan Republic," he said. "And you?"

"My husband has been called back to Washington for consultations."

They both remembered Paris.

"Yes," she said. "It was the same then."

He took her to the *kvas* bar beside the textile factory at Khimki.

"Kvas," he said, "is a sort of peasant brew, made by dripping water through burnt bread. It can be very potent."

"Do they serve vodka?"

"Of course."

"Then I'll have vodka."

"And coffee?"

"Made by dripping water through burnt bread?"

He did not smile.

The half-liter was served in a bottle set in a dish of ice. He took the protruding neck of the bottle and poured vodka into their glasses. Around them Russian workmen furtively eyed her Western clothes.

"I've never been to a place like this before," she said.

This time he smiled. "No, I don't expect you have. Officially it's the canteen of number 3617 garment factory, Khimki. The factory was moved last year to the south. Somehow the canteen remained."

"Can anybody come here?"

"More or less."

"You're very distant."

"I don't mean to be. On the contrary, I want to thank you for not telling the American embassy what you know about me."

"You're sure I didn't?"

"Yes. By now I would have known."

She drank her vodka and placed the glass back on the scarred wooden table.

"Do you have friends?" she asked him.

"Not many."

"Perhaps Soviet life doesn't encourage friendships."

"I don't see why not."

"What are we, Alex? Not really friends. Certainly not lovers."

"No."

"So why did you even bother to approach me at the airport? I hadn't seen you. You could have walked away."

"Yes," he smiled. "But I didn't."

"Why?"

"Why lie to you of all people?" he said, suddenly cheerful. "I didn't walk away because the moment I saw you I wanted to sleep with you again."

She shook her head. "No."

"I'm sorry," he said after a moment, "that was insulting. I assumed too much."

"Yes."

"What I said was nevertheless true."

She shrugged.

"You want something from me," he said suddenly, "I can feel it, but I can't guess what it is."

"I want to know how you felt after Paris."

"About you?"

"About what you did there."

He shook his head.

"Why not?"

He paused. "Because it goes beyond shame, Carole."

They left the *kvas* bar and took a taxi to Gorky Park. The pathways, hosed down with water by the city authorities, are converted by the winter cold to long skating alleys.

"Would you like to try?" he asked her, looking at the couples skating hand in hand through the avenues of frosted branches.

They hired skates and set off toward the Krimsky Val. After a few moments he took her hand. He skated with slow, easy movements matching his pace to hers, supporting her whenever she seemed about to lose her balance.

The cold wind brushed her face, but the effort of skating warmed her. A pale sun was setting somewhere behind the Kremlin, lights flickered in the branches of the trees and cast long shadows across the snow on either side of the frozen pathways. Couples with hands or arms entwined floated by them, their skates hissing gently over the ice. Despite the change of season she found it easier to imagine that they were again in Paris together, skating through a snow-covered Bois de Boulogne.

It was past dark when they handed in their skates. Standing beside the wooden hiring hut, they watched for a few moments the figures floating silently through the avenues of treetop lights.

"I would like to see you again, Carole," he said slowly. "But I don't need to be reminded this isn't just Paris all over again."

"No, it's not just Paris all over again."

They began to walk arm in arm toward the exit from the park.

"When we first met in Paris," she said, "I thought I still loved my husband. I don't any longer. It means I'm vulnerable, Alex. What I'm saying is that even now I know how dangerous it would be for me to meet you again." She stopped walking and turned to face him. "I know how ridiculous I must seem, anticipating this sort of danger."

"This sort of danger being that we fall in love?" he said.

"That *I* fall in love," she smiled.

"Risk it," he said. "I will."

"Yes," she said. "Me too."

Chapter Nineteen

IN THE LAST DAYS of December, General Semyon Kuba was invited to the Soviet Marshals' dacha at Klim in circumstances of some secrecy. Attending the Bolshoi program of Russian Dance that evening, he had left in the middle of the last act.

Officers of his own KGB had cordoned off a small area behind the theater and here Kuba had changed from his limousine into an altogether less impressive vehicle, a gray Rumanian Fiat.

At the Marshals' Club Kuba was welcomed by old Marshal Kolotkin. There were no young admirals of the Soviet Navy nor were there any of the younger Air Force Marshals present in the assembly room. There were, however, among the uniformed officers, a number of civilians whom Kuba immediately recognized. Most prominent among them was the burly shape of V.S. Bukin, the Petroleum Minister. Beside him, the rumpled face of Nikolai Baibakov, Chairman of the State Planning Committee. There were others, too, men from the Party apparatus and some of the older members of the Soviet Academy.

Kuba knew, without being told, that one strand held together all these men of power in the Soviet system. They believed that since the death of Stalin the Soviet Union had lost its way. Above all they blamed Nikita Khrushchev. They blamed him first and foremost for his speech to the 20th Party Congress denouncing the crimes of the man who had led them since the death of Lenin. They blamed Khrushchev for his wild boasts and for his peasant fooling before the world at the United Nations in New York.

There were men among the group assembled to meet Kuba who could barely remember the Stalin days. There were older men who had been deeply involved in all the leader had done. But there was no division of feeling between them. They believed the Soviet Union must be led back on the right track. They believed in a strong leader. They wanted to believe in Semyon Trofimovich Kuba.

Champagne was served by the Marshals themselves. When every glass was filled, old Marshal Kolotkin, senior surviving soldier of the Patriotic War, Hero of the Soviet Union, raised his glass to Semyon Kuba.

His old eyes, yellow and tear-filled, squinted across the room. He seemed to be having difficulty with his speech. His jowls flapped noiselessly.

"Comrades," he said in a voice heavy with emotion. "Salute with me this man. And . . ." he raised a hand to stop them. "And, in that salutation, honor the person of another man, dishonored in our times."

They drank and responded enthusiastically. Again Kolotkin gestured for silence.

"I am eighty-nine years old," he said. "But I care as deeply today about our glorious Soviet power as I did when I was a young man at the barricades. In those days we Bolsheviks placed our Soviet power in the hands of an almost equally young man. This was a responsibility known to none before him. A sixth of the earth's surface, a hundred and a half million people. He did not flinch. The leader I speak of took the Czar's Russia by the scruff of its neck and made of it in twenty years the mightiest power on earth. There are two sides of a gold piece, fear and respect. *Our leader did not flinch.*

"I will not talk in the same breath of the leader who followed him. But I am forced to talk of the events of three days ago. Comrades, a number of senior officers of the Soviet Army were addressed in the strangest conditions. Some might say in conditions chosen deliberately to exclude certain of the most senior officers present this evening.

"Comrades, it was put to them that Soviet power was in a decline. Comrades, it was put to them that adjustments would have to be made. Comrades, it was put to them that the vision of our youth was no more."

The old Marshal swayed in anger. His face reddened. "Comrades, it was put to them that the achievements of J. V. Stalin had no place in our Soviet future," he thundered.

Overcome with emotion now, Kolotkin took the arm of one of the younger technocrats and waved for his glass to be refilled. He was breathing heavily and, all in the room could see, unlikely to be able to finish his speech. He raised his glass again. "There is another future . . ." He was staring at Kuba, not three paces in front of him. "Lead us into that other future, Semyon Trofimovich. Lead us along that path which the father of the Soviet Union trod."

The old man staggered forward and clasped Kuba, spilling champagne down the back of his jacket.

The guests of the Marshals of the Soviet Union made a half-circle round the two men. The sound of clapping was like the beating of the wings of doves rising in the air.

They sat in front of the stove in his apartment off the Arbat. In the two evenings he had brought her here since their meeting at the airport she had come to feel more for the tiny kitchen and the cramped space of the one living room than for her own spacious apartment in the foreigners' compound. The feeling was just another sign to Carole that the danger she had spoken of in Gorky Park was already upon her. Although Letsukov had not so much as kissed her, every small physical contact between them had become charged with anticipation.

It was clear to her that Letsukov had decided that she must make the first move. He seemed content for them to sprawl on the bed together (there was no room for a sofa or armchairs in the living room) and talk and listen to music. They were, of course, both waiting until the memory faded of their anonymous coupling in Paris. And both knew that it was for Carole to give the sign.

Two nights before the new year as they sat after dinner with glasses of the whisky Carole had brought, Letsukov had got up and gone to the small bureau in the corner of the room. Opening the drawer he took out a small package wrapped in brown paper and handed it to her.

She was sitting on the side of the bed. "What is it, Alex?"

"A New Year's present."

She lay the brown package in her lap. She knew he was ready to talk about Paris.

He leaned his back against the wall. "When I returned to Moscow," he said, "I could barely remember the name of the American woman I had slept with that night. Even now I remember nothing of being in bed with you. Nothing important. But I had sacrificed the life of an unknown man. I was required to do it by a KGB officer. But this officer served the same State I served."

He crossed the room and sat down next to her. "You can have no idea of how easy it is for us to *avoid* thinking. For us, Russians, it's the same thing as avoiding madness. We've somehow learned to live both with our pride in Soviet achievements and the daily evidence of Soviet failure. For many years I was no different from any other Russian. The two-headed eagle was the symbol of the Czars. But that ability to look both ways at once was even more necessary for Soviet man. I'm not condemning it. I'm not defending it. It's the way I was, too."

She took his hand. "Until Paris."

"No. I want you to know the truth, Carole. Perhaps even after I arrived back in Moscow I could still have played the Soviet game. I knew no other. The shame I feel is not just for what I did in Paris. The real shame I feel is because I know that I could have still, even *then,* have pushed that from my mind."

Tears had filled her eyes. He put his arm around her and pulled her close to him. For a moment they sat with their heads touching.

"Last summer," he said, "I had to go to Leningrad to interrogate a prisoner. A man with one head, not two, looking left and right at the same time. I've not got far yet. But I know now that there is a road for me." He paused. "I wanted to tell you that before you opened your present."

She turned in the crook of his arm and reached up a hand to his face. Her long fingers stroked the line of his mouth. "Shall I open the present now?"

"Open it now."

She sat round to face the stove and unwrapped the brown paper. Inside was a star-shaped brooch, enameled white and royal blue within its gold mounting.

"I saw my mother yesterday," he said, "I told her about you."

Carole's eyes were still on the brooch. "What did she say?"

"She said, as all mothers do, be careful. And she gave me my grandmother's brooch to give to you."

She laid the brooch aside and reached out for him. With their arms round each other they fell back on the bed.

When he kissed her she had no memory of his kisses in Paris. When her hands reached inside his jeans she had no memory of the warm contours hardening in the palm of her hand. When he entered her, it was for both of them, as if for the first time.

Along the banks of the frozen Vega River the branches of the alders were heavy with rime. Sedge and rushes rising spikily from the ice crunched underfoot. A pair of ducks flew low, their necks outstretched, wings beating furiously.

Member of the Politburo, Deputy Prime Minister, General Secretary of the Communist Party of the Russian Federated Republic, Natalya Roginova, stood alone by the riverside. Her eyes followed the line of the stone packbridge and the road, barely discernible under the snowdrifts, to the cluster of wooden houses on the hill. The twin onion domes of the church gleamed blue and gold in the last rays of the afternoon sun. She knew every wooden izba in the village, every inch of unpaved road, every man, woman and child who worked the farm there. She knew even of the visiting priest and of the secret reconsecration of the church last year.

It was her village. Fifty-four years ago she had been born there in the stable block of the great ruined mansion which had once been the center of her father's estate. As the daughter of an aristocrat she could hardly have been expected to have thrived in those hard years, but her father had been no ordinary aristocrat. Long before the October Revolution he had proclaimed his belief that the land of the Russians should be for Russians. He had distributed his lands to the peasants in the villages he owned. He had moved with his young wife into the stable block of the mansion and with his own hand burned down the great house one bright night in the summer of 1910. His brothers and uncles had denounced him as a lunatic when he had hired himself as a laborer to one of his own peasants. Yet his young wife, Natalya's mother, had refused to leave the lunatic. She, too, the family said, was touched with madness. The Czar's police took an interest in the case. For seven years the young couple were exiled to Siberia. In 1917 they returned in triumph, unique almost in those days, as aristocrats welcomed back by the local Party Committee.

In the starving, war-torn twenties the lunatic rose to be General Secretary of the *oblast*. Natalya was born in 1932, five days after her father was executed for anti-Party activities. Reaching her early twenties, a deprived, second-rate citizen of the Union, a worker on the local collective, Natalya Roginova, one day in 1953, was informed that her father was to be rehabilitated. Joseph Stalin had died earlier in the year. The new men were to make amends. From a name unmentionable in the village, except in whispers, Roginova's father was accorded a small stone monument and his wife and daughter the honors and privileges of a hero of the Revolution.

She seized her chance with both hands. The local Party, in ideological disarray after Stalin's fall from grace, welcomed her as first a member, then an activist, then as First Secretary. In her thirties she was a tall, passingly attractive girl who used her talents, her sex and her utter ruthlessness on occasion, in relentless pursuit of advancement.

As a woman in that land of equal rights, nobody took her seriously. They believed that an insurmountable natural barrier existed. Time and time again, with one Party appointment after another, Natalya Roginova proved them wrong.

She turned now from the riverbank. She had left her carload of personal guards up on the road outside the village. They were strictly forbidden to show themselves in the vodka-house. She liked to preserve her reputation as one who could be among the people as her father had been, safe in their affections. And in truth she was.

Through the whitened pines smoke rose from the chimney of a log cabin and in the twilit afternoon a paraffin lamp gleamed at the single window.

Already the snow carried a thin crust of ice which crunched underfoot as she followed the path up toward the cabin. So many times in the recent years of her rise to power she had wondered whether her mother refused to come to Moscow deliberately. Or whether she stayed on in her timber izba in the pine woods because she knew that even after almost three-quarters of a century her St. Petersburg society bearing and her rich aristo accent could only do harm to her daughter's progress. Approaching ninety now, she still stood unbent at the izba door as Natalya approached.

Inside it was stiflingly hot. On the glowing stove the samovar bubbled. The two women sat smiling at each other across the rough three-legged table.

"Why do you do it, Natasha?" her mother said. "I ask you not to send a ham and you sent two. I tell you I have forgotten the taste of caviar and you send a kilo. My little daughter, this is not wise. I should not be the best-fed woman in Trevchina."

"You're not," Natalya said. "Whatever I have sent you, I arrange tenfold for the village chairman. For distribution, I tell him. What he does with it is up to him."

"Those are not the politics of your father."

"No."

"Perhaps that's why he was known as the lunatic baron."

"Perhaps," Natalya said.

The two women drank tea and talked about the village; who had died, who had given birth, last year's crop failure, the prediction of a savage winter, the alders having lost their leaves before the hawthorn this summer.

At last the old woman said, "Now that the funeral is over, who will rule us in his place?"

"Who knows?" Roginova murmured.

"Will it be my little Natashenka?"

"Who knows."

"Will it?" the old lady said sharply.

"Either myself or Semyon Trofimovich."

"Then it must be you."

"All ambition for myself apart, I believe it must be. I am the only one of us in Moscow who has a vision of the future."

"*Our* vision still?" the old lady asked.

"Yes."

"A lunatic vision," the old lady said happily.

Dinner that New Year's Eve at the Bennermans was for eight. Apart from the hosts, Jack and Harriet Bennerman themselves, the guests included the Larsnes from the Swedish embassy and Skip and Betty Rider from the Australian Broadcasting Corporation. Carole Yates and David Butler made up the eight.

The Bennermans were known for some of the most luxurious dinner parties in a town where all foreigners lived at near aristocratic level. Harriet was rich. Her stepfather, an ancient Midwest construction millionaire who doted on her, had died last year leaving her his fortune. The Bennerman marriage was still reeling under the blow. Jack Bennerman, on $29,000 a year from the government, urged restraint. Harriet, with a monthly income greater than her husband made per year, saw no reason to restrict her orders from the specialist shops in Helsinki that shipped goods to Moscow-based foreigners. Her weekly order list would include fine brandies and rare years of port and claret. She was proud of keeping what David Butler called an excellent table.

The Riders were the center of interest. They had recently returned to Moscow from a cultural visit to Azerbaijan, which happened to coincide with the funeral.

"Frankly, with the funeral coming up in a few days we'd expected the visit to be canceled," Rider said, "but you know how these things slip through the Soviet bureaucracy."

Jack Bennerman scribbled a note and passed it to Rider. It read: "What about Boris?"

Skip Rider shrugged his indifference. "Boris" was the common term for the listening devices installed in all apartments in the foreigners' compounds.

Bennerman got up from the table and switched on a small radio which was perched precariously on a high pile of books. His belief was that the device in this room was located in an ornate wall-light fixture, but everybody present was aware that he may well be wrong.

"Okay," he nodded to Rider. "Boris can relax with some music for a while."

"We arrived in Baku three days before the funeral . . . great weather, well above freezing and the sun out for hours at a stretch . . ." Rider began.

"I'd hoped to buy some of the local shawls and bedcovers they make down there," his wife said, "but we were plunged immediately into the usual round of visits."

Skip Rider grimaced. "You know the sort of thing. This is the Akhundov Library. It houses three million books. Before the arrival of Soviet power illiteracy was ninety-five percent and books were the preserve of the foreign oil barons and their local lackeys. Now illiteracy is unknown and so on and so on . . . And where afterward? To the old city? No, to the skyscraper apartment blocks on Nizami Street, as if anyone wanted to marvel at tower blocks."

"But, dear boy," David Butler said. "Those tower blocks are all of twenty years old, and haven't yet fallen down. Clearly you can't see Soviet achievement when it stares you in the face."

Rider smiled. "I should have realized. But the restrictions of our bourgeois world view made those first two days just about the most tedious in our lives."

Betty Rider nodded emphatic agreement.

"By this time," Rider went on, "the boyars had woken up to the fact that there would be foreigners about for the local funeral parade and it became pretty clear that they had no wish for us to be around. So with that delicate touch the Soviets are noted for, they inform us they have arranged a visit to Bilgya for the next day. Now I have to tell you that Bilgya is one thing only, a none too pretty bathing beach. And though this isn't Moscow weather, we're still only a few degrees above freezing for Christ's sake. So we protest."

"And how." Betty Rider confirms.

"So that night our guide, Anatoly, comes in, beaming relief. Protest accepted, he says, a mistake had been made. So we get to see the funeral? Betty asks him. No, he says, we are going to Kobystan to see the unique cliff-face carvings there."

"There was nothing we could do about it," Betty said. "The *vlasti* had made up their minds. No foreigners were to get to watch that funeral parade. And Anatoly just couldn't be shaken on the point. So at six the next morning we get into the car and set off for our fifty-mile drive to Kobystan."

"But we didn't get very far," her husband came in. "We're driving along the Moskovski Prospekt when the steering goes crazy and the driver announces we've got a flat. Anatoly is troubled, but not too troubled until a second or two later the driver announces someone has stolen the spare. Then Anatoly loses his head and starts yelling at the Azerbaijani driver. Some very nasty little racist tidbits he comes up with, and before we know it the crowds on the sidewalk are all gathered round us and a young student type, obviously Azerbaijani himself, has got Anatoly by the scruff of the neck and is beating six bells out of him."

"Did the crowd think you were Russian, too?" Carole asked.

"Oh no," Rider said. "The driver took care of that. But I tell you, I've never seen things get out of hand that fast. Within minutes the car was on its side, the wheels were being stripped off. Two mili-men in uniform who tried to control things were getting punched out against the wall. By the time we got clear the car was on fire and the militia sirens were screaming in toward the Prospekt."

"So you were free to enjoy the funeral?" Bennerman said.

"Exactly. And what a funeral it turned out to be . . ."

"The funeral of Soviet hopes in Azerbaijan," Betty Rider said. "We hung around keeping away from the hotel and the Intourist Office while the crowds got thicker and thicker on the Lenin Prospekt, which is the main drag there. And I guess about noon the whole thing started. It was a mini May Day Parade on Red Square here in Moscow. A quarter of the flags and banners. A podium for the local boyars erected outside Subunchinsky station; an empty coffin, you know, all slightly provincial and a bit of a joke. Until the bands start playing and the first regiment gets its marching orders."

"In Russian, of course," Betty said.

"Russian orders. And an obviously completely Russian regiment from an Air Force Cadet school and some Russian funeral lament played by the band. The crowd went wild. They may be Moslems but they had certainly been hitting the vodka. They broke through the Azerbaijani mili-men guarding the route and stormed across Lenin Prospekt. I didn't know whether to laugh or cheer. One minute you've got these smart young Russian cadets goose-stepping like they owned creation, and the next they're drowned in a sea of Azerbaijanis, knocking off their caps, tearing at their collars, punching and booting them down the Prospekt. You talk about the problem of the nationalities, this was it before our eyes."

"So there never was a parade," Carole said.

"Not in Baku there wasn't. And I just wonder whether there was in a lot of the other national capitals."

"In Tallinn Estonia it was called off at the last moment," David Butler said. "In Frunze, the Kirghiz Republic capital, rioters called for a return to the old Kirghiz town name of Pishpek. In Kiev they just got away with it by using virtually all-Ukrainian military units and playing Ukrainian national songs."

"How the hell did you get hold of all that?" Bennerman said.

Butler rolled his eyes. "I have friends everywhere," he lisped deliberately.

"You never passed it on to me," Bennerman said aggrieved.

"We sent it straight to Washington, via London as an A report," Butler said.

"Bastard. Are you trying to ruin my career?" Bennerman said, mollified.

Butler rocked back in his chair, his watch-chain stretching across his stomach. "Superb dinner, Harriet. I shall guard the memory of that sixty-one Margaux for the rest of my days. I shall have to," he added, "there is no chance of it being repeated."

"Unless you come here again," Bennerman said. "My newly rich wife has three dozen bottles stacked in the kids' playroom."

"And why not?" Harriet flared.

"You won't find me protesting, honey," Bennerman said.

"Do not call me 'honey,' please. And that's exactly what you were doing, protesting."

Around the table everybody knew she was drunk. It wasn't uncommon these days.

"No," Bennerman said slowly. "I wasn't exactly protesting. Tell you the truth, I get a belt out of it, too, when someone like David here drinks the stuff. He actually knows the difference between Château Margaux sixty-one and the contents of a piss-pot."

"It's all the aftertaste," Butler said. "And one would hope the color."

Nobody even smiled.

"Listen," Harriet leaned toward her husband. "I drank much more great wine with my horny-handed Midwestern stepfather than . . ."

"Horny was he?" Bennerman said. "Well, it's the first time you've mentioned that."

"You bastard."

Carole looked desperately at David Butler, but he shrugged.

"Listen," Harriet said, pouring herself another brandy, "count yourself lucky."

"I do," Bennerman said. "My wife just inherited several million dollars."

"So does that make me any different? Okay, maybe I even buy myself a really decent dress . . ." She plucked at her low-cut gown, half spilling her breasts, ". . . for the first time in my life."

"Tell them it cost six thousand dollars from Paris, dear," Bennerman murmured.

"Okay, it cost six thousand dollars from Paris," Harriet shouted. "But that's *all* I do. I spend money. *My* money! I'm not screwing around Moscow with Russian bureaucrats. I'm not being felt up in the back of some Zhuguli-Fiat by some smooth Moscow gigolo. I'm not risking your career. I'm buying a few bottles of wine and a party dress, goddammit!"

Carole sat white-faced.

David Butler leaned toward her. "Do you know, Carole darling, I think it's probably time I took you home." He put his lips close to her ear. "Boris would never approve," he whispered.

Driving her home, David Butler was unusually silent. Then as the car crunched to a stop at the traffic lights just before the foreigners' compound, he turned at the wheel.

"Do you feel like a nightcap?" he asked.

"Your place or mine?"

"Neither," he said. "You must come to my club."

She laughed as he pulled away from the lights. "I don't believe it," she said. "Now you're going to tell me you've an authentic British gentlemen's club hidden away here in the heart of Moscow."

"Not exactly, dearest," he said.

They left the car in a small back-street courtyard, walked back onto the main Prospekt and hailed a taxi. Even then they had a maze of side streets to negotiate after letting the cab go.

The rebuilding of Moscow is a planner's dream turned nightmare. Skyscrapers lurch from street level into the frosty air. New buildings exhibit all that tattered sadness of London's failed architectural confidence of the fifties. But these buildings were only built three or four years ago. Between stalks of concrete, older structures remain. Courtyards are reached through coach doors, broken cobbles beneath the snow threaten ankles, rusting iron stairs lead down to basements where cobblers or home matchbox makers plied their trades in the days of the Czar.

Those days seem but a muffled cry away if you stand in such a courtyard, the snow softly falling, the icicles hanging from the low eaves like rows of sparkling Damoclean swords in the lamplight. Music penetrates the clapboard walls, an old song, a slurred male voice. If a drunk slumbers in a doorway, you kick him hard, an act of kindness in such numbing cold.

"I never knew such places still existed," Carole said as Butler led her by the hand toward a basement staircase.

"Indeed, dearest," he said. "They not only exist, they flourish."

The iron staircase had been sprinkled with salt. It spiraled down to a chipped deep-red painted door. The bell was hidden behind the thick Russian architrave. Butler found it and pressed it four times.

"Does it work?"

"It works."

They waited two or three minutes. The basement led on the left into two dark coal-holes, the doors long rotted away. Broken splints of wood hung from twisted hinges. Standing there, Carole had an overwhelming feeling that she was being observed.

A lock clicked. Bolts were drawn back. The battered red door opened and a man with an open-neck silk shirt and gold chains to the navel stood in the doorway. He was short, dark-skinned and his wavy Mediterranean hair was flecked with gray.

"This," said David Butler, "is Mother Hubbard."

It was a gentleman's club sure enough [Carole wrote later], but not the sort I'd in mind. In London or Amsterdam or San Francisco Mother Hubbard's would perhaps have been a gas. In Moscow I could not believe my eyes. There were few foreigners there, and those that were all spoke excellent Russian. There were no women except myself.

Mother Hubbard couldn't have been more attentive if I'd been Tony Curtis in his "Viking" days. He brought excellent vodka and smoked sturgeon on blinis and sat with us. "Why should only the *vlasti* live well?" he said gulping a whole vodka with that special ring-finger elegance which was pure self-parody.

It didn't take me long to see where at least some part of David's extraordinary knowledge of the Moscow scene came from. Among the chatter and gossip I heard names that astounded me.

I had always half-believed that David was a member of the Intelligence section in the British Embassy, although his official title was cultural attaché. When I asked him pointedly if his security people knew he came to Mother Hubbard's, he raised his hands in horror. "Darling," he said, "I'd be shot at dawn if they knew I frequented places like this!"

But I still didn't entirely believe him.

Mother Hubbard had left us to greet other guests. I was still busy looking around at my first glimpse of gays with 50-inch chests and broad Slavic features.

"Tell me about Alex Letsukov," David Butler said.

I had drunk Scotch and wine and cognac at Harriet Bennerman's. I'd drunk vodka with Mother Hubbard. Perhaps if I'd been sober I would have said nothing, or little. As it was, when David Butler asked, I told him.

He sat for a long time without speaking. I found I more and more admired this man. "What have you told your husband?" he asked after another sip of vodka.

"He knows I met someone from Nationalities after the party they gave. He doesn't know it was the man I met in Paris in the Spring."

"Have you faced the fact that he's probably KGB?"

"I don't have to face the fact," I said dishonestly. "I use him for sex."

"Don't be a silly bitch," Butler said. He wasn't smiling now. "If he's KGB, only one side of this relationship is being used, *you.*"

"I have an instinct about this man," I said.

"Infallible." He signaled for more vodka.

"You think I'm wrong?"

"How could I pretend to know. The KGB use sex as they use psychiatry and beatings and blackmail. You have to be an eighteen-year-old bourgeois Marxist to believe anything else."

"And his father? He was real enough."

"I agree the mise-en-scène sounds a little too subtle for the Bureau. But it's not inconceivable that they've at last recruited one creative spirit."

"You're angry."

"I think your husband's a nice man. I think you're frigging around with things you don't understand. I am also . . . inordinately fond of you."

"What are you saying?"

"I'm saying be careful, for God's sake. There's too much Russian in you, Carole."

"What does that mean?"

"It's not by chance that they play card games for lives. It's not by chance that they invented Russian roulette. Anything can be a game to them—life, sex, death. Perhaps because in their history almost everything has had to be a game."

"For Christ's sake David, you're drunk. I don't understand you."

He sat back. "I'm drunk. But I still mean what I say. Give up your Letsukov. Stop playing your Russian games."

"I'm an American, damn you," I said. "I don't understand all this talk of games."

"There is a manual," he said, "published by dissidents now in the West. It suggests how, as a psychiatric prisoner, you should answer the questions the doctors put to you. Never use a common expression like 'It's enough to give you nightmares' they say."

"Why not?"

"Because the doctor's next question will be about these obviously serious nightmares you suffer."

"Is this true?"

"It's true. But what's important is that the dissident authors cannot escape from the purely Russian idea that the patient is playing a game, however deadly. After all, that doctor doesn't *need* your answers. He can go away and write up a whole batch of answers for you. But you see, Russians savor the game."

"I'm leaving," I said. "I'm drunk and unhappy and I'm leaving."

He stood up. He was swaying slightly. Outside, in the basement area, with the snow falling on our shoulders, he said, "Could you accept the remote possibility that a man could love all men, and one woman?"

I slid my arm through his. "No, David, I'm sorry, I can't."

Chapter Twenty

IT WAS LATE when Natalya Roginova left her mother's izba. She walked alone carrying a lantern on a stick like any peasant from the village. Briefly in the 1970s, electric flashlights had deposed the lanterns, but batteries had become unobtainable and the old lantern pole, the base fitted snugly into a leather cup on the belt, had made its return.

She reached the bridge across the frozen Vega and stopped to lean against its low stone wall. On the hill the streetlamp at each end of the village glittered in the cold, dry air. At the meeting of the Politburo tomorrow the issue of the First Secretaryship of the Party would be resolved. She knew that she had built up sufficient following to make the post hers. And then, provided the military remained neutral, she would deal with Kuba's leadership of the State Security Ministry. By the New

Year her position would be indisputable. And then? A lunatic vision her mother had said. But to Natalya Roginova her vision was a solid, practical necessity which happily married well with her own deep love of Russia.

The world would reel as the shape of the Soviet future became clearer. But she must carry the Army with her, that she knew.

She continued on up the narrow path through the birchwoods. In summer the brightness of the greenery was breathtaking. As a young girl she would stand here near the top of the hill and look out across the rolling landscape unchanged by Czar or boyar or commissar. This was the Russia she loved, the *Rodina* of her dreams. She understood clearly how even defectors to the West might take with them in their hastily packed bags a casket of its soil.

Ice cracked on the branches above her head. The lantern ring squeaked on the pole. The light fell yellow on the banked snow. She found the path she was looking for. She had decided not to pass through the village again on her way to the car. Old Petya would insist on taking her to the vodka-house and it was a point of honor to her to drink like a man. But tonight she needed a clear head.

She stumbled through the thick snow, the lantern swinging wildly above her head. Somewhere to her right a boar crashed through the frozen thicket and ran along the edge of the wood.

She was aware suddenly of a nagging sense of unease. The boar? Why should that alarm her. She had seen and heard a thousand boars. Except during the rutting season they fled at the first sign of human beings. As this had done.

As this boar had done? She stopped dead. The lantern jerking forward. The boar had turned along the edge of the wood. There, on her orders, should be waiting her three carloads of personal guards. On a fine night like that some at least of the guards would be lounging against the vehicles smoking and talking. And yet the boar had run that way! Her countrywo-man's instincts told her that that was impossible, that the only explanation was that the guards were no longer there.

She lowered the lantern and turned down the wick until the yellow flame guttered and disappeared. She had no doubts what was happening. Nobody could live through the days of Stalin and still have doubts. She must get to the village. Old Petya would find a way to get a message to the *oblast* Party headquarters. She had been an overconfident fool to expose herself in this way.

She turned back down the path. The frozen thickets shook again, this time with the weight of a man. A torch beam crossed the snow and settled on her face. Two other men stepped forward with bright lights in her eyes.

"Natalya Roginova," one of them said, "By order of Comrade General Kuba, you are requested to come with us."

She turned bitterly without speaking and continued on up the path, the three men ranged uneasily around her. At the edge of the wood she glanced quickly in the direction of the boar's run. Her cars had gone. Around the tire marks the trampled snow was stained red.

The next morning's *Pravda* led the pack. The inside front page carried a lengthy article entitled "The Cult of Personality in the Arts." It was a vicious attack on Igor Bukansky, on his early poetry and his later editorship of the magazine *Novaya Literatura*. It condemned Bukansky for his life-style and his use of his position to elevate himself to a literary pasha in Moscow. The last paragraph called for his replacement as editor of *Novaya Literatura*.

To Muscovites who as yet knew nothing of his visit to London, the article was a mystery that many took a delight in solving. The reintroduction last year of jamming of Western broadcasts closed that avenue of information. But Marina Lorotkin's Moscow Television News Review at midday provided a further clue. Bukansky's pursuit of the cult of personality, it was alleged, had taken his insidious influence into some of the highest regions of Soviet government. It was undeniable that he had assiduously cultivated the friendship of anyone in government circles unwise enough to encourage him.

To many Muscovites the picture was now taking shape. It remained only for the central figure to be placed against the threatening background.

That evening's edition of *Izvestia* provided the required information in a five-line announcement at the bottom of page 4: Minister of Petroleum Bukin, while retaining his responsibility for all inter-Party questions, has assumed the posts which ill-health has forced Natalya Roginova to relinquish.

So that was it. In Washington and the West European capitals heads of state secretly sighed with relief. The proposal for German reunification had emanated from a Party group led by Roginova. But she clearly had been unable to carry the rest of the Politburo with her. The proposal was dead. The NATO alliance would live to fight, or not, another day.

At his comfortable dacha in the Lenin hills outside Moscow, Igor Bukansky awaited arrest. He was well prepared. By the door he kept a small shabby canvas bag. In it was a change of underwear, a toothbrush, a thick sweater with torn elbows which he had once used for gardening, and a pair of Canadian fur-lined boots which he had carefully scratched and stained to make them less desirable to an examining KGB officer. He knew that any books he took with him would be confiscated, pencil and paper likewise. But he had spent one whole evening splitting with a razor blade the cardboard lining of his case, sliding into the gap ten 100-ruble notes and gluing the cardboard back together. He had also taken advantage of a tip given to him by a senior minister in Stalin's day. With a metal cutter he had snipped through two gold rings, opening them wide enough to fit around the base of each big toe, then wrapping them round with a covering of adhesive plaster. For so many years shoes had been of such appalling quality in the Soviet Union that KGB examining officers seldom spared a glance at corn plaster during the initial strip-search.

His preparation for departure made, Bukansky settled down to enjoy what time was left to him. He knew it would be short. At the beginning of the week Saratkin, the stoat-like pseudo-poet who was the recognized KGB representative on the committee of the Soviet Writers' Union, had delivered a slashing condemnation of his handling of the editorship of *Novaya Literatura*. The criticism included allegations that he, Bukansky, had become so seduced by the false attractions of Western diversity in literature that items of truly Soviet literary standard were rarely to be found in the magazine. In long speeches the subservient jackals on the committee had supported the stoat. Unanimously they had voted for Bukansky's replacement as chairman of the Foreign Committee.

There had been other signs, too. His three maids had tearfully left that morning as had his chauffeur and gardener. Each one, under KGB orders, had parroted an excuse he was not expected to believe.

But the freezer was full of steaks, the kitchen cupboards still stacked with foie gras. Five crates of excellent vodka sat in the cellar and, slightly surprisingly, in response to his phone call (it was the last he was able to make to Moscow, the phone was cut off that afternoon) his secretary Lydia had arrived from the office.

He had expected that she would have already seen which way the wind was blowing and fabricated a sudden illness. But she didn't. Bukansky had smiled to himself. Perhaps this attractive little gold digger, too, was in the pay of the local KGB. Well, no matter. She had given him a lot of pleasure in the last two years.

She sat opposite him now in the Western clothes she loved. Nothing gave her more pleasure than to be taken for a German or American woman in the street. Every time it happened she would recount to Bukansky the full details as if each incident confirmed her successful study of the copies of *Vogue* and *Harper's* that Bukansky brought back for her from abroad.

He leaned across her sleek blond head to pour her champagne. Busy with the arrangements for his departure he had drunk much less than usual. Perhaps a little more than a half-liter all day. Undoubtedly she had not seen him so sober for over a year.

He stood behind her, his hand on her shoulder, then leaned forward to slide his flat palm down the front of her smooth dress. She turned her head automatically and smiled at him.

He took his hand away and crossed the room to the wall safe. Spinning the combination he pulled it open. From inside he took a new packet of 100-ruble notes, 5,000 in all.

He walked back to the sofa where she was sitting and picked up her handbag. While she watched him with cool gray eyes, he opened it, dropped the money inside and snapped the bag closed. It was English leather bought in the hotel shop on that last fatal trip to London.

"You've been a good girl, Lydochka," he said. "But now the presents from the West have come to an end. You know that."

"I know you were criticized by Saratkin at the meeting of the Writers' Union."

"Word travels fast. I'm certain to be arrested."

"What will happen to you, Igor Alexandrovich?" the girl asked.

"Who can tell?" He poured himself a large glass of vodka. "I'm nearly sixty years of age. I was born among peasants in a peasant village. Without the Revolution I would have remained a peasant, a serf almost as my grandfather was. Instead . . ." he swept his great arm out in a gesture which included the warm spacious room and herself. "I'm not complaining, Lydochka. Nevertheless, some things I lost on the way. My innocence, certainly. What talent I had, perhaps."

"Were you ever married, Igor Alexandrovich?"

"No . . . No. I'm not sure why."

The girl studied him carefully. "Perhaps it's because you have always considered women are there to be used. Just another of the good things of life there for the taking."

He smiled. Three days ago she would never have dared to say such a thing.

"How old are you, Lydochka?"

"You know very well, Igor Alexandrovich."

"Twenty, of course," He paused. "But just consider that you might have chosen something of the same course as myself."

"I haven't," she said firmly.

"Think how you love Western clothes. Think what you'll do for Western clothes . . ."

"Please, Igor Alexandrovich . . ."

"You were barely eighteen when you came to work for me."

"Yes," she said, her mouth hard.

"Do you keep a diary, Lydia?"

"Yes," she said.

"Every detail of how I corrupted you?"

"That is not my view."

"No, you had a choice. Of sorts." He walked to the bookcase and pulled out a bound manuscript. He opened it at the first chapter. "Just read the beginning," he said. "I'm going to bed. When you've read that first chapter come up and join me. Or not. As you choose. But *choose,* Lydochka."

He laid the book on her lap and left the room.

She read:

On the night of my seventeenth birthday we crashed through the remnant of the SS Charlemagne Division opposite our sector and rode on the back of the self-propelled guns of a Guards Artillery Brigade into East Prussia.

That night we marched and fought until dawn and all around us in the darkness we could feel and hear the reality of Soviet power. The greatest Army that the world had ever seen was blasting its way into the heart of Fascist Germany. I, who could have been still at school, saw the dawn of my eighteenth year on the edge of a great plain with small neat townships among well-tended fields.

As I scooped my ration of *balanda,* the gruel issued at first light every day, Mischa Kropoyan, our sergeant commander, came back from company headquarters.

"Throw it away, lad," he said, his thumb jerking contemptuously at my mess can. "Don't waste your appetite on that muck."

He was barely two years older than me but he had fought at Stalingrad and Kharkov and a whole string of grinding battles from 1943 on. He was a front-line soldier to his black-nailed fingertips, a wily Georgian if ever there was one who would scrounge and browbeat and steal for his own men. Me, he treated in an almost fatherly way, coaching me through the winter's battles until I, too, gained that curious sixth sense for survival that makes a front-line soldier.

"Listen, Uncle," I said, "I'll throw this *balanda* if you can be sure we'll get a bread ration today."

He took me by the arm and drew me to the edge of the low escarpment. "See all those farms," he pointed across the ordered plain before us, "in every one of them hams hang from the fire rafter. Bottles of schnapps cluster in polished cupboards. And hiding in the barns and cellars, women. All for us, Igor. Today, your Uncle promises you, will be the last day of your virginity."

I suppose I blushed, because he clapped me on the shoulder and bellowed with laughter. "It's official," he said. "Whatever's down there is all for us."

"Official." I thought of my straitlaced Soviet father, a collective farm foreman. The only Soviet official I had really known.

"In this life," Mischa said, dropping his voice, "you have to learn to read between the lines. Listen, I have just been to company headquarters. Usual orders for the day's advance, estimates of opposition, ammunition resupply schedules, all normal workaday stuff. Except one little item. Soviet military personnel entering former Reich territory are to have the right to send home one parcel of six kilos every month. Officers much more."

"I don't understand," I said. "Six kilos of what?"

"Exactly, little brother," Mischa grinned. "How long is it since you have owned six kilos of anything? Not since you put on a brown side cap and pinned a red star to the front. So the six kilos, Igor, can only come from down there, from those neat little villages. Of course in their wisdom our military authorities know it. And you can be sure they also know that there's no way on earth to encourage a front soldier to take the ass of a pig and leave the ass of a woman."

I was shocked because I believed Mischa was right. Those six-kilo parcels were an official license. What would my father have to say about that?

Yet if I was shocked I was also greedily excited. Looking down on those farms that morning I thought not of six kilos of dresses for my sisters or shoes or curtain cloth for my mother, or even smoked hams. I thought of the women huddled in the cellars, and Mischa's promise. And I tossed the mess can of *balanda* into a bush as the company bugle blew the order to move forward.

We advanced all morning, our loudspeaker trucks up front with the infantry blaring sentimental German songs interspersed with demands for surrender from the pockets of German troops still fighting on. I never admitted it, of course, but I couldn't help admiring the last-ditch bravery of the men of this beaten Army.

At a village called Regensmarck a new unit of shock infantry passed through our battalion and we received orders to consolidate on this line. Mischa nodded toward the single street of houses in front of us and winked. "As sergeant commander," he said, I've decided we'll leaguer up in this village for tonight."

A pair of T-34s rumbled through the village, shock troops fanning out protectively around them. From the shuttered houses there was no movement.

Mischa let the tanks reach the ridge beyond the village and motioned us forward. My legs were trembling. "Work through from house to house," Mischa had said. "Any Fascist opposition gets the bullet. The rest . . ." he rolled his dark eyes, "is for us."

I found myself with Loshkin and Krassansky, a pair of small leathery Siberians a dozen years older than me. We had circled round to the back of the village main street and broken into the garden of a larger house than most of the others.

"Cover me," Krassansky said. And he ran forward to hurl two grenades in quick succession. Shattering the glass of a ground-floor window they exploded inside with a dull double crump. The kitchen door flew open. Perhaps it was already unlocked.

Loshkin and Krassansky disappeared through the smoking doorway. I followed.

I was in a large wall-papered kitchen, the walls scarred by the flash of the explosions, the lace curtains still smoldering. A wooden dresser contained row after row of undamaged blue plates. A blue-enameled stove occupied one wall.

Upstairs I could hear Krassansky whooping with delight. I entered the hall as he came bounding down the stairs wrapped in an embroidered bedcover through the folds of which the barrel of his tommy gun poked. "Nobody up there," he said. "But just take a look at the way Fascists *live!*"

Then from the cellar we heard Loshkin shout. "Women!" he yelled, "down here, you two."

Krassansky leapt past me trailing the bedcover and disappeared down the cellar steps. For myself I hesitated.

I could hear the women pleading below. Behind me one of the lace curtains smoldered into flames. I tore it down and stamped it under my boot.

"Bukansky," Loshkin called up the cellar steps. "Come and get a piece of this."

I started down the stone steps. I was sweating; trembling, too. As if some fever was upon me, as indeed it was. From the darkness came the squeals of women. I strained my eyes. White legs thrashed beneath the heavy brown shapes of the two men.

A woman was standing beside me. Blond hair pulled back from her forehead. Heavy breasted under a white apron.

"Frau, komm," my voice issued from between suddenly parched lips. I gestured to the darkness of a corner with the barrel of my Thompson.

She shook her head. "I'm an old woman," she said in Russian. "I could be your mother."

I am not a violent man. To this day I find it hard to believe the surge of anger that passed through me. I poked hard at her belly with the barrel of my machine gun. She rocked back against the wall.

"Over there," I shouted.

"At least," she said quietly, "let us go upstairs. Not here, in front of my daughters."

To this day I don't know what my answer might have been. Mischa's voice bawling down the stairs has swept everything else from my memory. "Counterattack," he yelled. "Panzer SS."

The clatter of machine-gun fire and the thud or mortars sounded in the village street. I dragged Loshkin from one of the girls. Krassansky was already on his feet tying his rope belt. My woman was smiling, willing death upon us.

I ran upstairs and the whole house seemed to fall around me as the shell struck. I was the only one in the house to survive . . .

Upstairs, amid the opulence of his fragile present, Bukansky undressed slowly. Would she come up? He stood at the window in his heavy robe, looking down at the sticking plaster on his toes. He had no more to offer her now. Tomorrow she would be looking for a new job, a new protector, a new source of Western clothes for her young body. But would she come up now?

He looked up. Through the double-glazed window imported on special permit from Sweden he could see the sidelights of two cars moving slowly down the drive. He knew he should dress quickly.

But first he had to know. On this last night it had become of sudden desperate importance. He went quickly to the bedroom and opened it. Across the gallery he could see down into the room. She was sitting where he had left her, the manuscript closed on her lap.

At the thundering on the door she jumped to her feet, the book flying from her lap.

He came forward onto the gallery. "It's all right, Lydochka," he said. "It's me they've come for."

She stood trembling.

More than anything he wanted to ask her whether she would have come upstairs. Instead he gestured toward the door. "Let them in, Lydochka. I'll get my clothes on." he said.

They came in bustling with importance. The girl was sent home immediately by the plainclothes major in charge. Bukansky was dismissed to a corner of the room while a systematic examination began of his papers and his books.

Sitting at a small Alexandrine writing desk Bukansky watched the men clumsily dissecting the corpus of his life. What would the fools make of it? What would they make of his two years with Lydia?

While he waited he took a pen and began to write:

What sail can cross the passage of these years?
Not mine.
What masted clipper slaving south
Could bring you back,

> Show you the journey's end
> Before good time
> Show you the dockside laborer
> And his plight,
> The seeping brick of gaslit streets,
> The cries of children
> Hungry in the night.
> You from that sunlit world of youth
> Must see *my* world and find its wealth uncouth—

"Citizen Bukansky," the major gestured to the door. "It's time to go."

Chapter Twenty-one

IN KULETSYN'S NOVEL, *To Be Preserved Forever,* there is a young man who revels in being a poor student. He wears, most times we meet him in the book, a traditional Russian student cap, a belted linen shirt outside his breeches and leather knee-length boots. He neither drinks vodka nor chases girls. His contempt for Western standards is overwhelming. Toward the end of the novel, he enters a seminary and begins to study for the priesthood.

From this brief description it might be thought that Kuletsyn's book describes a time a hundred years ago or more. But it is set in the 1980s. His student is a figure who became more and more common on the University campuses of Russia in those years. Like Kuletsyn's student, these young men and women were deeply stirred by feelings for the Russia of the past, for its onion-domed churches, its villages, its sheer rustic simplicity. It is, of course, a medieval vision which keeps at bay the encroachments of the twentieth century.

Probably nobody in the government at this time saw the growth of Rodinist feeling for what it really was. Far from being imperialistic and expansionist as the Soviet leaders thought and hoped, this 1980s brand of Russian nationalism looked inward. Its beliefs gave no encouragement for young men to go and build an empire in Central Soviet Asia or the

Caucasian republics. Instead they encouraged a surly sense of superiority toward anyone who was non-Slav.

It was a mood which in the 1980s was spreading deep into the Russian consciousness. Black Africans at Moscow's Lumumba University were jeered at on the streets. Chinese faces were considered particularly offensive and almost equally Soviet citizens from the Chinese border areas. Street-cleaning babushkas spoke resentfully of Georgian farmers or the ever-increasing numbers of Uzbek workers.

The 1979 census showed clearly what was happening. In nine years the urban population had grown from 136 to 164 million. Concealed in this apparently innocuous figure is the fact that a massive part of this emigration to the towns was from the south and central Asian countryside to the *Russian* towns. The falling Slav birthrate had made it essential to attract workers north. The alternative, the partial resituation of Soviet industry in the south-central dominions, was unthinkable. But as the Soviet Union entered the eighties the social tensions created by the presence of the new workers became increasingly apparent. In Russian cities like Gorki and Sverdlovsk groups of Asiatics spent their lonely free time hanging aimlessly around the railway stations or, in the summer at least, on the benches of the public parks. Always in groups of a dozen or more, ill-dressed even by Russian standards, many barely able to speak more than a few words of Russian, they seemed to many inhabitants of the northern towns to be inalienably foreign and more than a little menacing.

Assaults on Russian women increased. Or at least news of them spread like wildfire around the city. In the ancient Russian city of Vladimir, 150 miles from Moscow and now a center of the electrical and chemical industry, a 16-year-old Russian girl was gang raped and battered to death on Third International Street, the city's main thoroughfare. A group of 16 Uzbek laborers from Chemical Enterprise 7 were arrested by the militia that night. By noon the next day without a word having appeared in the press or on radio, a group of 400 women surrounded the Police Station on Podbelsky Street screaming for the Uzbeks to be brought out.

The women were dispersed only with serious difficulty and after militia reinforcements had been brought from other stations. But by nightfall they were back in even greater numbers. Again they were dispersed, this time with light water hoses (effective since the incident took place in winter).

But the violent feelings of the women of Vladimir were not doused by the water spray. That night five Uzbeks were attacked at the rail station by a group of women. Seven more Asiatics were chased by a mixed Russian crowd and caught and badly beaten on Sacco and Vanzetti Street.

The next day stories flew around Vladimir of a wave of attacks on Asiatics in the local factories. If even a quarter of the stories were true it was clear that the situation was getting out of hand. The *vlasti,* God forbid, were losing their grip.

Then, the following day, something unprecedented in the history of Soviet journalism took place. The newspapers were almost completely devoted to the case of the raped girl. The militia inspector in charge broadcast locally giving details of the finding of the body, the postmortem, even the few leads the investigating team had to go on. But the Uzbeks, he insisted, who had been arrested outside the Planetarium on Third International Street were arrested for drunkenness, and at no time was there any suggestion of a mass rape which was the allegation which had swept through the town.

There was, he claimed, no point in demonstrating outside Podbelsky Street station. The Uzbeks had been given 12 hours in the town's drunk-tank and released. Meanwhile a real suspect had been arrested, a Russian of subnormal intelligence whose semen count coincided with that of semen in the victim.

Never before had such detail been broadcast. We have no record of how effective the inspector's broadcast (three times repeated in one day) proved in pacifying the anti-Asiatic feelings in the town. But the Vladimir rape story within a month or two had spread widely through Russian industrial cities, acquiring even more horrendous detail and always ending with the assertion: Of course it was Uzbeks who did it.

The backlash among the nationalities was slow in developing. But it came from a core of hatred of the Russians that went back to the last century. Now stories of their treatment, of their second-class citizenship in this Union of supposed equals, flowed back to the national republics. Anti-Russian outbreaks like that in Baku on the day of the funeral parade became more common.

In response, Kuba was able to push through a reluctant Politburo further budget increases for an expanded Bureau of State Security. At this time, too, he assumed the responsibilities of Minister of the Interior, making official his control of the militia.

Of the remaining power blocks in the Soviet State, the Party and the Army, the first was already in disarray following the arrest of Natalya Roginova. The Army, paralyzed by uncertainty and rent with deep divisions between its more junior and senior general officers, for the moment sat tight and watched.

On one issue only it refused to budge. Its Politburo representatives still refused to endorse Kuba's claim to be appointed General Secretary of the Communist Party. Thus the Party remained headless while Kuba's paramilitary formations increased in number and authority. And the

Army looked on uneasily at developments it felt it could neither encourage nor dissuade.

Chapter Twenty-two

IT WAS RAINING. On the rooftop opposite he could see the melting snow sliding down toward the guttering. Another year. A year far different from those times a decade ago. Now he despised his youthful self. "Silence," his father had said, rubbing his fingers together in the Russian way that first day he had returned, "is truly golden." So perhaps is youth.

Letsukov turned up his coat collar and crossed Dzerzhinsky Square toward the guardhouse on the gate. "I have an appointment with Colonel Pleskov," he said.

The guard picked up something in his tone and rose, saluting smartly. Within minutes he was being escorted down the long pale-green corridor with the white globes on chromium rods.

Colonel Pleskov was already in the room. He was as brisk as ever.

"You've been meeting an American woman," he said. "Mrs. Carole Yates, wife of . . ." he glanced at a paper on the desk, "Thomas Foster Yates, First Secretary at the American Embassy."

"Yes." Letsukov remembered vividly the Colonel's earlier phrase: "I don't have to prove anything."

"The relationship dates perhaps from a reception on the day of the state funeral." The Colonel smiled, obviously pleased with himself.

"It does."

"What sort of a relationship is it, Letsukov?"

"The usual sort."

"Sexual."

"Yes."

"Do you discuss political questions?"

"No, Colonel."

"I believe you."

"Thank you."

"Only because I've examined photographs of the lady."

"I see."

"But political questions could be introduced."

"I don't see the point."

"The point is that her husband is an American diplomat. We have some reason to think he is highly thought of in Washington."

"I can't help you, Colonel. I have never discussed Mrs. Yates' husband."

"Then you must."

Letsukov sat in the upright chair, the wet topcoat dripping onto the parquet floor. "I must?"

"Yes. It's a unique opportunity. Use tact. Ask questions. We can provide you with a more luxurious apartment to go to if that's what the lady is used to."

"It's a casual relationship," Letsukov said. "A few times only. There's no reason to believe it will last."

The colonel stood up. "You must make it last," he said smiling. "And why not? I have seen the photographs, as I said."

Letsukov stood.

"You're leaving for a trip to the Ukraine next week," the Colonel said.

"I shall be away a month or more. By then Mrs. Yates may well have found other friends."

"I think not," the Colonel said jovially. "Absence, the Americans say, makes the heart grow fonder. We could, of course, cancel your visit—but I don't think it would be wise. In any event we are not pressing you. Let me have your first report when you get back to Moscow."

"I repeat the relationship may not last," Letsukov said. "For the moment she finds it exciting to . . ."

"To sleep with an uncouth Russian?"

"Perhaps there is something of that in it, yes."

"Not that you Alexei Alexeivich are an uncouth Russian."

Letsukov eyed the young Colonel.

"I know these foreign women," Pleskov said. "They're looking for something different. They've got everything—they need more." He extended his hand. "A report once a month. And if you need that apartment, rich curtains, a silk bedspread, a touch of the old Russia, just let me know."

Letsukov left Dzerzhinsky Square and walked quickly in the direction of the Plevna Gardens. Gray-edged, the watery snow on the rooftops dripped into the gutters of the Polytechnical Museum. Ahead, in the Plevna Gardens, Carole was waiting for him.

He felt he had reacted convincingly to the Colonel. Not too much guilt. Not too much anxiety to cooperate. Walking through the drizzle his thoughts were full of the young American woman whose life had become entwined with his. The images bombarded him: of Carole pacing the room, brushing her blond hair with short vigorous strokes; of Carole asleep beside him; of Carole naked in the shower; of Carole laughing, talking, joking; of Carole with all that sheer capacity for happiness which he had never met in a woman before.

He had changed in the months they had been together. Infected by her optimism he had begun to see that hope for Russia was inextricably connected with hope for himself. He had begun to see that the Soviet system could only continue to exist while Russians like himself worked for their own private success within the system. Only now did he see how deeply pessimistic that willingness to conform had been. Lenin himself, he thought wryly, would have rejected it for the serf-like attitude it was. But then Letsukov was aware that he had achieved this epiphany only through his love for Carole.

To Alexei Letsukov to be in love was an experience which defeated all comparison. He had not in the past lacked for the company of women. So often he had used the act of sex as a temporary salve, to assuage guilt, to suppress anxiety or to erase disappointment. In Paris he had used Carole herself that way. But with a wonderful tenacity she had drawn them both above that first encounter, enabling them to remeet on different terms, allowing his caution both as a Russian and a Soviet man to evaporate slowly in the warmth with which she encircled them.

And now that warmth was to be pierced by the grubby probing fingers of the KGB.

Letsukov stopped at the Plevna Monument. He stood with the light rain falling on his fair hair and trickling down his forehead.

As I stood at the Plevna Monument that evening [Letsukov wrote], I saw myself at a crossroads of my life. However wary I was of the Russian addiction to the bitter taste of sacrifice, I was forced to recognize that as long as I continued to see Carole I would be of more than usual interest to the men at the Lubyanka. Yet if I were to take the opportunities which my work offered, to become involved in the Free Trade Union Movement, I could not afford to be an object of interest to the KGB for a totally separate reason. I could not, in short, put brave men at additional risk so that I might continue to enjoy a closeness which every day seemed to grow between this American girl and myself and which every day we saw more confidently as love.

She had that habit, perhaps that free North American habit of any woman in love, of running toward me and throwing her arms round me when we met in the open.

I remember to this day the sound of heels approaching, the perfumed warmth of her embrace and the breathless questions as she clung to me.

"It was nothing," I said holding her away, "a formality."

"But you're not called to the Lubyanka every day," she said anxiously. "What was it?"

She already knew that I was to leave next week for a month's visit to the Ukraine.

"It was about my trip," I said. "I have to visit some KGB prisoners in Kiev. Apparently I have to have special permission."

"That's all it was?"

"KGB bureaucracy."

She looked at me doubtfully. "You're not holding anything from me?"

I shook my head. "The KGB are very careful about who they let see their prisoners," I said. "But don't forget they've good reasons to trust me."

She took my hand and thrust it deep into the warmth of her silk-lined pocket. And together we walked through Moscow with the brief treacherous scent of spring in the air.

In the cities of the Ukraine that spring, the queues for potatoes were 30 and 40 yards long. When meat appeared in the State butcher shops the Militia was called to control the crowds. Factory workers protested and issued declarations and even organized lightning strikes. But the lack of worker organization made the task of the KGB easy. Yet the interrogating officers were themselves misled by the efficacy of their own methods. Under torture men confessed to membership in the Free Trade Union Movement or the Ukrainian National Army. Under more torture they indicted others. In this situation the KGB reports passed on to Moscow were bound to be a self-fulfilling prophecy.

Yet the ferocity of the secret police methods was effective in another direction, as Letsukov was to discover in the Ukraine that spring:

It had seemed to me that, ideally placed in the Trade Union section of the Ministry of Nationalities, I would have a role in the exchange of information among the brother movements in the different republics. But of course I had not even begun to understand what it was like to live outside the law of the Soviet Union. Without underground credentials to offer, clearly no one was prepared to take a Ministry investigator into his confidence.

I took risks. In the Ukraine I visited relatives and friends of prisoners and offered help. But I had lived my life *within* the law, even when acting as an executioner for the State. To act as an illegal, to gain the confidence of other illegals, I slowly realized, I would first have to pay my dues.

On my last day in the Ukraine I was interviewing workers who had been arrested for calling for a strike in a small leather-making enterprise in

Poltava. The affidavit of the informer, the stoat, had interested me particularly with its claim that the workers had mentioned the name of Joseph Densky. I interviewed a certain Stepan Bolek first. An older craft worker in his early sixties, with a gray stubble on his cheeks and hands as brown and tough as the leather he worked, Stepan Bolek regarded me warily in the square concrete interview room. It was a small suburban militia station, it may or may not have been wired to record conversations. But I had dues to pay. I could no longer avoid taking risks.

"Comrade Bolek," I said to the old worker before me, "I have one question to ask you. Are you in touch with Joseph Densky's movement in Leningrad?"

"I have never heard of this Joseph Densky," the old man said.

"The informer claims you used his name."

"He is lying."

"They usually do," I conceded to his evident surprise.

The old man watched me in silence.

"Comrade Bolek," I said to the old man in front of me, "I wish to do you a service."

Bolek curled his lips contemptuously. "Why should you want to do me a service, Comrade?"

"There's no time to go into my reasons. You would like to know the name of the stoat who informed on you and your friends. I have that information. The depositions against you were all signed by Galgradsky the tanner."

The old man shook his head. "Perhaps," he said. "Perhaps not. But how is this information likely to help me now?"

"It can help others. You can get the information to your friends outside."

Bolek gestured to the bars on the high windows.

"You have means of getting a message out. Galgradsky the tanner. Remember."

"I'll remember, Comrade."

"And now I want you to do something for me."

Bolek's lips twisted. "I thought you might, Comrade."

"I believe you are in touch with Joseph Densky's movement. I want you to get a message to the movement. I know that first whoever is deputizing for Densky must trust me. Tell them I am willing to perform any task which establishes that trust. You understand?"

"I understand very little, Comrade Letsukov."

"Then understand this. I am not offering myself as a sacrificial lamb. My position in the Ministry makes me more important to the Free Trade Union Movement than that. But I am prepared for sacrifice in a cause in which I deeply believe."

"You're talking to the wrong man, Comrade. I have never heard of Joseph Densky's movement."

I stood up. "If you are a member of the Free Trade Union Movement, and I believe you are, you will find a way to deliver that message to the leaders in Leningrad." I reached forward and shook his hand. "I will be waiting for their reply, Comrade Bolek."

Chapter Twenty-three

THERE WERE TWO girls with whom Zoya had made friends. The three of them together had managed to maneuver their bunks into a corner of the hut which was recognized as separate territory by the rest of the women. Hung with gray cotton blankets, the corner became a room apart within which the three girls were able, sometimes for hours at a time, to keep reality at bay.

Anna Bratlova was the closer to Zoya in upbringing. A student of literature at Tashkent University (although of impeccable Slav origins), she had in her second year met a young Zambian student named George Maccari at the English Language Club. Maccari was very far from the browbeaten product of colonialism that she had quite naturally assumed. He accepted no condescension from Russians and frankly proclaimed that the English language had produced the richest literature in existence. Anna Bratlova was at first aghast. How could he praise the culture and thus indirectly the society of his oppressors? But George Maccari had a fiercely independent spirit. Through him Anna began to learn of the diversity of the West. And by the time she realized she was in love with him she had already departed on that journey of the spirit from which no traveler returns. Worse, she was too young to dissimulate. In the compulsory Diamat (Dialectical Materialism) paper in her third year she had attempted to discuss rather than recount. The Dean had called her before him after marking the papers. He was a gentle, hesitant man but he forced himself to talk about her relationship with George Maccari. It was, he said, clearly affecting her studies. Her low marks in Diamat had confirmed his fears. Political reasons made it difficult to ask Maccari to

leave. (He was the son of Zambia's leading Marxist.) But good sense
decreed that she should stop seeing him.

And if she refused?

The Dean sadly shrugged.

Maccari told her they must stop seeing each other. She found the idea
impossible. He asked her to marry him and apply for an exit visa, but in a
second interview the Dean made it clear that this would not be an
acceptable solution.

She was invited to discuss the question at the local KGB office. A suave
and educated major spent the afternoon combatting Maccari theses.

Still she and Maccari continued meeting. That autumn she had discovered she was pregnant. For a short while it seemed as if she might,
after all, receive the exit visa.

The suave major spent another afternoon with her and explained,
hinted rather, at the important work a Soviet citizen might do in
neocolonialist Zambia as the wife of a young and ambitious politician.

She discussed with George Maccari the idea that she should pretend to
accept. They agreed it was the only way to obtain a visa.

They married in Tashkent. The child was born in their final year of
school. The new Maccari family presented themselves at the emigration
post at the airport with every possible document stamped and signed.
George was instructed to take the baby through to the departure lounge.
As a Soviet citizen there were one or two further formalities for Anna.

Three hours later she was still sitting in a room alone in the airport
lounge. At one point she thought she heard George's voice raised,
shouting his refusal to board the plane.

Later two men collected her and took her down to Tashkent's Militia
Station 21 in the former Drunken Bazaar. She was charged with no
offense. No explanation was offered. She was given food and waited. For
a whole week it continued. She began to shout and scream to anybody
who passed her cell grill, but it did no good. At the end of ten days she
was loaded with other women into a boxcar heading north. It was the first
days of spring, and the woods on the way to Panaka were greening.

She claimed Zoya saved her from madness. It was a month or more
before she had got to know the tall beautiful medical orderly. She was shy
about talking to her at first because she knew from the crude jokes in the
hut when Zoya was absent that many of the women wanted her for
themselves. But for Anna Maccari it was quite different. She saw strength
there. The strength to stand against the thieves and prostitutes who ran
the hut.

Slowly they became friends. It was for Anna a dependent friendship.
She would clean Zoya's bedspace and stand guard over her cotton
blankets as she aired them each morning. It soon became almost more

important to protect Zoya's meager possessions than her own.

Strangely, it was Zoya who was able to provide the answer to Anna's sudden separation from her husband. In the camp last names were seldom used, patronymics never. Only through roll call would the full name of a fellow *zek* be known, except by chance conversation. And Zoya, as medical assistant, never attended roll call. In this way it happened that although a friendship was steadily growing between the two, Zoya was still unaware of Anna's last name.

She knew Anna had married a foreigner and gradually, as they began to gain confidence in each other, she gleaned hesitant tidbits about her life with him in Tashkent. But no *zek* at that time gave information freely. Complaints against Soviet justice could double a sentence and although, ironically, Anna still had no knowledge of the length of her sentence, she was as fearful as some of the one-year call girls of offending authority.

Then one night, slightly drunk on a little watered lab alcohol which Zoya had smuggled into the hut, Anna told her story.

It was the name that jolted Zoya's memory: George Maccari. And she was able to tell Anna of a visit that her husband's father, also named George Maccari, had made to Leningrad while she was still a student. As First Secretary of the Communist Party of the Russian Federated Socialist Republic, Natalya Roginova had entertained the visiting Marxist dignitary. Even in newsreels it was evident that they had got on well together. He was a tall good-looking African in his early fifties. She, perhaps a little older, had sacrificed her life to politics. The Leningrad student population had much enjoyed Maccari's week's stay in the city. Outrageous stories began to circulate about the two of them. There was little doubt that they contained no scrap of truth. But it was the first and only occasion when a scrap of sexual scandal, true or false, about a senior member and Party apparatchik had ever reached the ears of the people. And they had reveled in it.

Soon it all passed, was forgotten. But not by some, not by the elephantine memories of the men in the Lubyanka, in the *Children's World* as some Moscovites call KGB headquarters after the famous toy shop across the square. There, in this children's world, memories are preserved forever, raw, undigested.

So that when Natalya Roginova fell from power, George Maccari in far off East Africa fell from grace. And there was no longer need to allow a Soviet citizen to accompany her son and husband out of the country.

It was not a very important incident, nor was Anna Maccari's link with the deposed Roginova anything that might be considered a serious threat to Kuba's leadership. But the link, however tenuous, was there. And among the many KGB mottoes quoted in the streets and marketplaces, none has produced more *zeks* for their camps than *Better Be Safe Than Sorry*.

After Zoya's explanations Anna felt an immense relief. She was still, after all, a product of the system and she had nurtured the debilitating belief that it was somehow her fault. That she had failed her husband and son. But now her gratitude to Zoya was boundless.

The third girl in the trio of friends was the Leningrad call girl Laryssa Navratovna whom we have met before during the Blue Bridge riots of the previous year, and who was arrested during the great demonstration of November 7th.

Hardy and independent as Leningraders can be, she refused all blandishments from the thieves and harlots' corner (to which by profession she might be thought to have belonged) and gravitated instead toward Zoya and Anna. Within a few weeks her stories of the *vlasti* with their trousers down and her raucous friendliness had made her totally accepted by the other two.

Of course Laryssa Navratovna's arrival did not go unnoticed by the men [Zoya recalled]. I myself was happily exempt by my position as medical assistant; Anna received under duress the occasional "favors" of one of the guard sergeants which effectively prevented a *zek* claiming her; but Laryssa with her plump prettiness was not going to be long unspoken for in this place. I think she'd been there less than a week when it happened. It was after lights out, and we three were behind our blanket screen with an end of candle and a liter of lab alcohol to comfort us when we heard a light tapping on the window. One of the women from the other end of the hut went to the door, the lock of which presented no problems to our experienced thieves. Indeed, every hut in the camp owned homemade keys to their own door.

We could hear the whispering for a minute or two but took little notice. After dark in Panaka One the guards watched the perimeters and turned at least something of a blind eye to nocturnal visits to the women's huts. Perhaps they had been told that you can't press too hard on the lid of a boiling pot.

We heard the door creak open and further whispering. Then to my alarm, soft footsteps approaching our corner. The blanket was pulled aside and I was astonished to see Anton and his friend Bubo duck beneath the string.

Bubo was carrying a parcel which he placed on my bunk. "Good evening, ladies," he said. "May my friend and I sit down?"

I gestured to the pile of crates in the corner and they each upturned one and sat round our table. The candlelight flickered on Anton's blond beard. Once or twice I tried to catch his eye but he seemed to be only interested in what Bubo had to say.

Bubo in turn was now addressing himself exclusively to Laryssa Navratovna. "My dear lady," he said in a courtly manner I'd only seen in books, "even in this place we have the established customs of the house."

"I'm glad to hear it," Laryssa Navratovna said. "Even more glad if you gentlemen are prepared to respect them."

"We are indeed. I especially."

Laryssa raised her eyebrows coquettishly. Even deprived of makeup she managed to look like a cheerful Leningrad tart. I found myself feeling very proud of her.

"And what are these customs that you so deeply respect?" she asked.

"First come, first served," Bubo said.

Laryssa burst out laughing. Anton at last glanced at me, but shyly as ever.

"So?" Laryssa was still chuckling to herself.

"So I've come to make you the usual offer."

"Offer?"

"There's no force involved," Bubo said seriously, "I'm making my offer, request, call it what you will, now, before anybody else gets a chance. It's up to you whether you act upon it. Or when."

"What is this offer your friend's making?" I leaned across to Anton.

He turned to Bubo. "It's his offer," he said gruffly. "Let him explain."

"The offer is to be my woman," Bubo said simply.

"Then I accept," Laryssa said. "But if I'm not well treated I shall sue for divorce, that's a warning. Will you fight for me?"

"If necessary. Why do you ask?"

"The one they call Uncle Vanya has already been sniffing around."

Bubo nodded. "I'll fight."

"Good," she laughed now. "And what else can you promise me?"

"I've brought a half loaf," Bubo took the parcel from the bunk, "to celebrate."

"And we have vodka here," I said.

"Then let's begin the wedding feast," Anna spoke for the first time, her eyes sparkling uncharacteristically.

"Your friend here, I suppose he's to be best man?" Laryssa was shooting quick glances from Anton to me. "Or did he come over on an errand of his own?"

It was a long silence. "I came as witness, of course," Anton said at length. For the first time he turned full face toward me. "You should not be offended."

I poured the lab vodka, spilling it over the wooden table in my sudden discomfiture. "Offended? How could I possibly be offended, gospodin," I said, deliberately using the old-fashioned means of address.

Laryssa burst out laughing. To the shouts for silence from the other women in the hut we sat there in the candlelight and toasted Bubo and Laryssa's happiness.

In these spring days Semyon Trofimovich Kuba emerged from under his stone. References to him in *Pravda* increased from perhaps one a day to at least a dozen. It was by now commonly accepted that Natalya Roginova was under arrest or dead. Her position as First Secretary of the Russian Federated Republic was now taken by the florid-faced Bukin who had been elevated to Prime Minister and elected to full membership in the Politburo. Natalya Roginova's name was now quite simply never mentioned. If a head of state visited Moscow it was Kuba who received him, flanked by other members of the Politburo, but clearly the first among equals in the familiar fashion of Soviet collective leadership.

Western Kremlinologists speculated, but answers eluded them. Clearly Kuba had defeated his arch rival Natalya Roginova. But did that mean he had carried the rest of the Politburo with him? Or were the armed forces, for instance, standing between him and the full fruits of unchallenged leadership?

No one in the West knew for certain. In the meantime they continued, government Kremlinologists and journalists alike, to dig into the background of this squat, shambling figure with the high cheekbones of a Slav and the slanting eyes of a central Asian. Few, at that time, came very close to the truth.

Semyon Trofimovich Kuba had been born in 1917 or 1918, almost certainly in western Russia, the son of a Slavic mother and a Siberian soldier of the Czar's retreating Army. His mother was the daughter of an adequately well-off corn merchant and the difference in status between her and the Siberian muzhik suggests the possibility of rape. Certainly she took the child's grandfather's name for his patronymic. Semyon could have come from anywhere. At that time his last name was Garodsky.

As the winds of war and civil war reached gale force the mother was blown toward the south. Perhaps she was, as Kuba would sometimes claim, an infantry officer in the new Red Army. Certainly she died in the battle against Denekin's Officer Corps at Tsaritsyn, later Stalingrad, later still Volgograd.

There is no record of the next years. Only a child's fitful memory. Possibly, as he claimed, Kuba was adopted by a Red Army unit; he claims memories, at the age of six, of the bitter war fought by the Uzbeks against the invading Red Army in 1924. But he was also known to claim a similar experience of the equally bitter civil war that finally forced the Georgian peoples into the Soviet Union.

In the 1930s the picture becomes clearer. Barely 14, but we can guess hardened and experienced far beyond his years, Kuba (by now he had discarded his own name and adopted Kuba, a former code name of his hero figure Joseph Stalin) took part in the "struggles against the kulaks."

There is no need to say much more about the barbarity of the forced collectivization of the country's villages. In practice it was a piece of calculated savagery only comparable with Hitler's final solution. In Russia and the Ukraine peasants starved to death, literally in their millions. It is now virtually certain that the 20 million Soviet dead claimed by Stalin to have been suffered by Russia in World War II include some millions at least from the forced collectivization period. The ten-year census of 1938 was never published in full. By the time of the 1948 census the Hitlerite Legions had intervened to be awarded some of the blame for the huge death toll.

Kuba's rise from 1938 when he entered his twenties was rapid. As an NKVD (an earlier designation for KGB) officer he served at the front for four grueling years. There is no reason to doubt that his medals were less than justly awarded. There was no need to build him into a military figure as had been done earlier with Khrushchev and Leonid Brezhnev. He fought with and exhorted the retreating armies of Stalin and fought and exhorted again as the Russian masses, responding now to the call of a socialist *Rodina,* marched through their own blood back toward the Nazi border.

At the age of 27, as the war ended, he had paid his dues. Under Beria he now began to rise rapidly in the secret police nexus. He was assigned as commandant to a labor camp and acquitted himself well. A period on the Finland border followed when he reduced the number of Soviet escapes to almost nil. He also increased the number shot trying to cross the frontier by at least three times. Called to Moscow, he was appointed a colonel in counterespionage. He acquitted himself again well enough to survive Beria's execution by Khrushchev and in the early 1960s was given responsibility for the Fifth Chief Directorate at the Bureau of State Security's Lubyanka Headquarters.

Under the Soviets the Fifth Directorate was a key post. He controlled first the Jewish Department, an area always open to lucrative bargaining with the West. He controlled the clergy, sects, State criminals, and most important of all, the intelligentsia and the nationalities. It is a matter of some interest which groups were considered worthy of inclusion in Fifth KGB Directorate responsibilities. It provides an interesting and surprisingly accurate commentary on the state of things to come.

As Chairman of the Fifth, Kuba proved an immense success. He informed the whole organization with the slogan: "When in doubt take no chances whatsoever." During the years before the Helsinki Accords it worked well. And afterward, trembling on the edge of promotion to general, and though he had never traveled outside the borders of the Soviet Union, he was appointed head of foreign Espionage, Chairman of the First Chief Directorate, KGB Lubyanka. It was not a period of the Soviet Union's greatest espionage successes but by now Kuba was sufficiently well placed to protect his rear against any but the most formidable Party attack.

He was of course a senior Party member himself and on succeeding Andropov as Chairman of the Ministry of State Security he had been appointed first candidate member, then full member of the Politburo.

A child of the Revolution, he saw the Soviet Union as beset by enemies, foreign and domestic. There was no greater term of approbrium in his limited vocabulary than "envious cosmopolitan." Cosmopolitans envied the West its goods—but somehow in Kuba's mind envied the Revolution its success at the same time. Natalya Roginova he saw as one among many.

He never paused to ask what the Revolution was or what it had done for the Soviet people, that question in itself would have been close to treason. He saw the Revolution as an icon to be defended. An icon of such rarity that no one could question its beauty. Cosmopolitans who looked too closely at the icon, he regarded as obscene violators of its intrinsic spirit.

Under Stalin, when the handsome Yezhov controlled the secret police and Russians in their millions trudged in rags through the Gulag gate, the age came to be known as the Yezhovschina, the days of Yezhov. Now, as the Kuba purges gained pace, men began to talk of the Kubaschina. The term was not inappropriate. A massive building program was ordered at all Gulag camps throughout the Soviet Union. The door knock at midnight became almost as familiar under Kuba as it was under Yezhov or his successor, Beria. The Party structure in the national republics shuddered under waves of arbitrary arrests. Loyalty and disloyalty again lost their meaning.

The execution squads too were at work, secretly in prison courtyards or among smoking rubbish dumps on the edge of town. With an awesome rapidity men learned again to refuse to talk to their neighbors and to keep packed bags by their beds against the expectation of arrest. Denunciations increased daily—and were acted upon. As winter became spring, and spring summer the security forces of Kuba's Bureau extended their grip on the land.

It is said that where three Russians are gathered together the man in uniform naturally deals the cards. Authority is the traditional adhesive of the Russian State. But it is not *respect* for authority. It is the joy in its exercise.

And so, sadly there was once again in Russia's unhappy history, no lack of men prepared, on behalf of their masters, to wield the knout.

Perhaps in these days of the Kubaschina some dissident estimates of five to seven million unfortunates behind the wire is correct. The lower figure would certainly not have included the penal brigades, the only part of the concentration camp population for which a figure is known. Within six months of Roginova's fall these soldier-prisoners, mostly from Russia's southern dominions, numbered close to half a million men. At the height of the Kubaschina no one could guess it, but these lowly, half-starved penals were destined to have, within months, a decisive impact on the course of history.

Chapter Twenty-four

SHE AWOKE THAT morning and lay in bed trembling with excitement. It was the day Letsukov was due back from the Ukraine.

Brilliant sunshine flooded through the bedroom windows. No childhood memory equaled the happiness she felt. She got up quickly, took a shower and dressed. Sitting over a first cup of coffee she realized it was still barely seven o'clock. She smiled wryly to herself. It was going to be a long, long day.

At seven-thirty Tom Yates emerged from the bedroom, yawning. He sat is his robe at the kitchen table while she poured him coffee.

"I've been doing some calculations," he said. "I'm building up a healthy stock of leave. I thought we might fly down to Italy for a couple of weeks with Jack and Harriet."

Carole carefully poured herself more coffee. "Seems a waste," she shrugged, "when there's so much to see here."

"For Christ's sake, Carole," he said, "you spend half your time complaining that you've seen all there is in Moscow, and now you don't want to leave."

"Perhaps I just don't take to the idea of a solid fortnight with the

Bennermans." She sat at the table and picked up her cup. "They're more your friends than mine, Tom."

"You'd sooner take off somewhere with David Butler you mean?"

"Frankly, yes." She felt a mounting excitement.

"While I go to Italy with the Bennermans."

"If that's what you want to do."

"Goddammit, I don't feel I know you any longer, Carole."

She would have liked to have been able to tell him that their marriage was over but she was still dependent on the status that being his wife conferred. There was no other way of remaining indefinitely in Moscow.

She sipped her coffee, eyeing him across the table. "I don't want to go to Italy, Tom."

"Okay, I'll go by myself," he said angrily.

She found she felt no guilt, only, as the day wore on, a gnawing impatience for the late afternoon to come. At the airport she was almost two hours early. She sat on a hard plastic bench watching the painfully long drawn-out movements of the clock hand.

The Kiev plane was on time. She had already chosen her position beside a vast concrete pillar, not too conspicuous but with a clear view of the arrival gate. As the passengers began to file through she felt a sudden, sickening charge of apprehension. There was no sign of him among the first group of men. No sign of him among the stragglers. No sign of him beyond the barrier among the final knot of airline officials.

She returned for the next Kiev flight, and the next. The following day she returned again to the airport for each flight, and between times drove back into Moscow to his apartment in case, for some reason, he had arrived by train.

On the third day her husband left with the Bennermans on a hurriedly organized trip to Italy. Her time was now her own and to her fears and disappointment and apprehensions was added a yawning sense of waste.

Five days later she was driving past his apartment at evening when she saw a light. She was trembling as she parked the car. Climbing the stairs her legs shook violently. As she pressed the bell she found she was supporting herself with the other hand on the doorjamb.

The door opened and he stood before her. She drew back, stunned at the coldness of his face.

"I had some leave due to me," he said when she was sitting in the small familiar room trying to bring the flame of her lighter to the tip of her cigarette. "I took the opportunity to go down to my mother's village."

"My husband had some leave due too," she said bitterly. "He took the opportunity to go to Italy. He'll be back tomorrow."

*   *   *

I suppose [Carole wrote long afterward], that if there is a difference between loving and being in love it is this: that to be in love is to accept the total vulnerability of endowing another person with the responsibility for your happiness. I was in love with Alex. I had freely handed to him powers which I had never parted with before. And when he withdrew from me I suffered in a way I had not imagined possible. It's true that there were times in the next few weeks when I felt he was suffering almost as much as I was. We met less and less frequently. We behaved more and more as intimate strangers. Sometimes I exploded and his misery seemed to match my own. I hung on and on, humiliated, but I knew beyond all doubt that it was the end of the affair.

Chapter Twenty-five

IN MOSCOW IT was the beginning of a hard summer and, everybody could see, likely to prove an even harder winter. It was now known in government and Party circles that a combination of last year's harsh winter and the drought of this spring had resulted in the dreaded double crop failure.

Soviet grain supply, since Brezhnev turned Khrushchev's Virgin Lands policy into a qualified success, depended both on the traditional bread-basket in the Ukraine and on an entirely new source of supply which had been developed in the western Siberian lands of Kazakstan. If both crops were successful, the 200-million ton average for grain crops could be handsomely met. Partial failure, as in 1979, might lead to a crop as low as 179 million ton. For the current year 245 million tons had been optimistically forecast.

In fact the spring weather had already made it certain that even the 1979 figure would not be reached. Before the Politburo was the utterly menacing possibility of a total grain crop of less than 160 million tons.

American, Canadian and Australian grain imports might once have filled the gap. But that was in the days of 1979–80, when Soviet oil exports to the West, at the rate of over a million barrels per day, were earning substantial amounts of foreign currency. The other major source of foreign earnings, tourism, had suffered a massive reduction by the progressive restrictions on foreign visitors which Kuba had insisted upon from the time of the Leningrad riots. Today, with closely watched guided tours to Moscow as the foreign visitor's only option, earnings from tourism had been reduced to a trickle.

The final source of income on which the embattled Soviet leadership might call was the country's still not inconsiderable gold reserves. Already the Soviet Union had dipped deeply into its gold holdings to pay for vital Western technology, but the trap was already apparent: The more Soviet gold was sold on world markets the more the price of gold fell. In the past four years the Soviet economy had already found itself caught between spiraling costs of imported technology and falling gold prices on the international market.

What then was the solution to the immediate shortage? The slaughter of millions of cattle, pigs and sheep? The immediate increase in the availability of meat would be welcome—if it could be transported to Soviet tables. But the aftermath would be the virtual disappearance of meat from the Soviet diet during an extended re-stocking period.

Gathered under Kuba's chairmanship for the July meeting, the aged and baffled members of the Politburo told each other that they never realized that the Soviet economy was on such a knife-edge.

Kuba argued for further gold sales and the purchase of foreign wheat, but the Central Bank adviser made clear that at current gold prices this was not even an option if the minimum grain shortfall to be made up was between 40 and 50 million tons.

On the night of July 19th, after the meeting had already continued for over five frustrating hours, the Politburo of the Soviet Union took the portentous decision to impose immediate bread rationing throughout the Russian dominions.

In the camps the changes began, as ever, with the issue of rations. Even under the harsh work conditions of Kolyma and East Cape the rations were lowered for each *zek*. The results were perceptible within a month. The thieves who ruled the huts throughout the whole archipelago of shame began to exert pressure on the politicals. Within each hut they attempted to establish two scales of rations: one for thieves, one for politicals. As the rations were cut again, the political majority in camps throughout the Gulag system rebelled against their oppressors. Men fought with knives and axes, killing silently in the darkness of their huts. Sometimes the politicals triumphed and operated a fair distribution system. Or they would triumph and steal the rations of the defeated thieves, as they had had their rations stolen. In some camps the two sides arranged an uneasy truce; in others they united. But in every camp the tension between guard and *zek* increased. The relative ease of the late seventies and early eighties was gone. Guards patrolled in pairs, machine pistols cocked. Incidents in which *zeks* were shot "trying to escape" became more and more numerous until the mandatory enquiry became more and more perfunctory. To the old *zeks* to whom the days of Stalin were a familiar horror, the times were changing back again in one of those fearsome, cyclical movements which so far have seemed to be the very history of Russia.

In the Kraslag area of responsibility, which included the Panaka complex of camps, the major general in charge favored only one solution. If the camp's timber cutting and sorting norms were not met, rations should be reduced. If that caused disturbances, then mutiny should be treated in the approved manner. The enquiry, if any, would be conducted by the officers of the camp concerned.

In these months [Anton recorded] life became harder than ever. Our rations were cut. Our work norms remained the same. Perhaps for us in Panaka One it was easier than for some others. But I remember vividly the day we went to do repairs at Panaka Five, the camp for penal brigades we had built that winter. There the poor devils had the faces of ravening wolves. They were mostly, if not all, Asiatics and they begged us on their knees, begged *us,* for a crust of bread.

Our masters had created a pyramid of privilege. In it everybody had their boot on somebody else's face. Slip once in our honored society and the weight of boots on your face would be doubled. So the slogan was: Conform! Enjoy your ration of privilege, however meager! Despise the man below you! Use your boot to secure your place!

Yet those faces of the penal brigade troops were unforgettable. Even the armed guards feared the naked hatred of these emaciated bundles of rags.

As we marched back behind the lanterns in that light summer night, our guards were less attentive than usual. Hands behind our backs, I walked next to the tailor from Bratsk. He was older than me, not an educated man, but somehow I felt in need of his experience.

"How can it be, Bubo?" I asked him. The guard, paces behind us, said nothing. "How can man do this to his fellow creatures?"

Bubo reclasped his hands behind his back, limping heavily.

"Anton," he said. "One thing is sure. There's more ignorance and indifference in the world than there is naked, lunatic cruelty."

"Is that all it is then? Ignorance and indifference?"

"No," he said. "It's systems of government that allow ignorance and indifference free play."

"You're not a Communist then, Bubo?"

He blew misty breath through his closed lips. "How can I tell? When

Communism devises a system to prevent the rise of a Stalin, or one of our present monsters, I'll look around and think about it. But until then it's not the proletariat of Karl Marx, it's the KGB in their camps that control the means of production. Isn't that so?"

We trudged on. The lanterns swinging at the head of the column reminded me of a colorful old picture my mother used to take out and look at, of a group of robed men in Jerusalem with lanterns on poles gathered round the figure of Jesus Christ. With his long beard and emaciated body he looked just like any of us *zeks*.

It was late when we arrived at our Panaka. We had eaten at the penal brigades' camp, a millet stew and a few grams of rotten bread, and we weren't entitled to another meal. The hollow ache in the stomach was commonplace by now and some of the older men were suffering other symptoms. Their speech was slurring and their eyesight definitely failing. I was 26, had a few pounds of fat to burn off when I was arrested (thanks to being the son of a peasant mother), and now and again in the last few months the assistant medical orderly, Zoya, slipped me a handful of pills and a few pieces of mutton fat. Perhaps she did it for a few of the others as well.

We were checked through the gate and stood wearily on the square while they went through the totally unnecessary ritual of roll call. No lights showed in our hut, but I could imagine the scene of the thief Vanya and his friends gathered round a lamp, shielded with blankets, playing an inevitable game of cards. Russians, they say, will drink anything and play for anything. That night I was to find out how true it was.

We entered the hut, Bubo, myself and perhaps ten others. Ravenous and exhausted, we made our way past the blanket fence shielding the kerosene lamp and the hunched figures holding their fistful of cards. I knew Vanya had food in his bunk. He controlled the distribution in our hut and made sure that there was always a little extra for him. Of course his thieves got more than their share, too, but we politicals, the majority, didn't protest because Vanya never overdid it. He trod a careful line between the greed of his thieves and the desperation of the rest of us. And of course we valued our lives.

I rolled on my bunk, my stomach spasms outlawing any chance of sleep. I knew from a change of tone among the cardplayers' whispered voices that the game had ended. I had no curiosity about who had won what. Vanya kept a tight hold on the gambling. The most a man could stake would be his day's ration. In other huts, other camps, we knew the appalling levels the stakes reached.

The cardplayers were getting to their feet. They, the thieves, lived down at the far end of the hut, barricaded together in case of sudden attack. But one of them was moving toward our end of the hut. I lay tense, sliding my hand downward to where I kept the blade of a kitchen knife rammed between the bunk boards. Strictly illegal of course, because Vanya decreed that only thieves could carry knives.

The faintest of shadows fell across my face, then passed on. The man stopped at the three-tier bunk next to mine. Bubo the tailor occupied the top tier. I had no idea who the man was. But despite Vanya's rules I knew, I thought I knew, what was happening. The thieves had gambled for a life. Except to stake their own lives which they sometimes did in the camps, there was no more desperate gamble. The loser was bound by the game's rules to kill, that same night, the man whose life he had staked. The rules, and they were inflexible, required that the man to be killed should be a serious opponent. Bubo, tall and powerfully built, was a candidate.

The shadowed figure moved forward. As the lamplight gleamed on the knife-blade I kicked. The man went forward onto his face and I jumped from the bunk down onto his spine. The uproar was immediate. Men scrambled in terror across other bunks, shouting for mercy from the killer of their dreams. The forbidden electric light was switched on. In other huts the shouts were taken up; lights, equally forbidden, sprang on. The guards raced from the administration hut, fearful despite their weapons, and uncertain from where the uproar had emanated.

In the light I could see that the man on the floor was Kaufmann, a Volga German and Vanya's number two. I kicked and kicked at his head, crashing it against the timber base of the tier of bunks. It seemed to flop from side to side as if on a rope.

Bubo was next to me, facing the thieves' end, a spar of wood torn from the bunk in his hand. "It's now or never," he was shouting. "The politicals must run the huts!"

I got my knife-blade and followed him. Ten or more others were with us holding stools or broom handles or even swinging buckets above their heads.

We fell upon the thieves, smashing at their skulls with our rough weapons, tearing the knives from their hands. Outside the guards were firing in the air. From every hut came chanting and shouting. We fought until the last thief lay cowering or unconscious before us.

"From today, Anton and me rule this hut," Bubo announced as the guards broke in. "And only politicals carry knives."

Naturally there was an enquiry, and strange to say, I think for once we got more than our fair share of justice. Or perhaps we just got justice and I had lost the ability to see it when it was staring me in the face.

There were two men dead, the Volga German and another thief. Several were injured, all none too seriously. But before the enquiry opened Bubo made it clear that anyone who told the truth would be dead by midnight the same day. The story, therefore, was reduced by Bubo to its essentials. A fight had broken out in the hut. Most of the men were involved. The dead thief had killed the German and then collapsed himself from a knife wound the German had inflicted moments before.

Nobody of course believed a word of it. But in their wisdom the camp authorities decided not to pursue the matter. For the fight itself each man in our hut received a hundred hours extra labor. All but Vanya and the remaining thieves thought the price was cheap.

For Zoya, protected by her position of medical assistant, her first summer at Panaka passed learning the rudiments of medicine. The doctor remained as unapproachable as ever, absorbed in her daily tasks, fiercely proud of the work she did and prepared to defend any diagnosis and treatment she gave. She was not always right but without her the situation in the camp would have been more desperate than it was. The authorities recognized this, as did Zoya herself.

Yet there was one independent triumph which Zoya could claim. Each morning among the line of men waiting for medical treatment there would be one at least who complained of a burning rash on his arm or leg. Ointment and return to duties, the doctor's treatment, proved useless. The rash would develop seeming to constrict the blood vessels, crippling the man, and too often causing the whole limb to decay from the body.

In these extreme cases the doctor would reluctantly send the *zek* to the hospital at Krasibirsk, but no report on the patient was ever received back at Panaka and the rash continued, believed by the *zeks* to be contagious and resulting in a man or woman being cruelly isolated in their hut, cut off from the few human contacts that sustained life.

It was Zoya's triumph to diagnose the cause of the dreaded rash. And it was done on the basis of a play she remembered by the University Drama Club about working conditions in feudal Russia. One scene had referred to a medieval affliction called Saint Anthony's fire, a burning rash which would blacken and rot the limb from the body. As an enthusiastic medical student she had taken an early opportunity to ask her lecturer about it and been told that it was now believed to be in some cases erysipelas and in others ergot poisoning caused by a fungus growth on winter-stored rye.

She had presented this possibility to the doctor and surprisingly it had been agreed that the storage conditions in the camp bakery would be examined with the authorities' consent.

Apart from the rats and thousands of mice in the storage compound outside the camp they had found huge mounds of rye from that last summer and perhaps the summer before coated with a heavy gray-white fungus.

There was no facility to analyze the fungus and indeed no one skilled enough to do it. But the authorities agreed that the worst of the infected rye should be dispensed with and the rest used by the bakery detail in strict order of its arrival in the camp. Whatever the accuracy of Zoya's diagnosis it is true that before long the incidence of the rash diminished and finally virtually disappeared.

Anna Maccari had come to the medical hut on some official errand during the afternoon after the visit to the rye store. The evidence of her happiness was in her face.

"The whole camp's talking about you, Zoyushka," she bubbled. "They're calling you the little doctor, the one who's going to annihilate the rash."

"Let's hope they're right," Zoya said. She stood up from the worktable where she had been mixing the thick tarry ointment which the doctor had devised to treat the rash.

"I'm certain you're right about the rye store, certain of it," Anna said.

Zoya stretched her aching back, her arms above her head, her breasts strained against her linen camp shirt. Suddenly she was aware of Anna watching her:

As I stood there stretching I was acutely aware of Anna there beside me, of the look on her face. She moved half a step toward me and slipped her arm round my waist.

"You know I love you, Zoyushka," she said.

As gently as I could I removed her arm. "You must choose a man, Anna. A good man," I told her.

She gestured toward the huts outside. "I hate men," she said. "All men."

"Even your husband?"

"That's another world, Zoya," she stammered passionately. "It doesn't exist for us. You're always saying we must live in the world we have here, at Panaka."

"At Panaka, at least, we have a mixed camp."

"Is that good? Is it good to have thieves and rapists on your doorstep?"

"There are some good men here, Anna. Some men at least who are trying to remain good."

"Anton," she said without bitterness.

I hesitated. "Yes, Anton."

She moved toward the door of the hut. "Tell me one thing, Zoya. If things were different, if Panaka had not been a mixed camp . . ."

I crossed and hugged her tight. "Anochka," I said, "Don't ask silly questions. How can I possibly say?"

Never once after that, in all the time we were together, did she ever mention the incident again.

Chapter Twenty-six

THE ANNOUNCEMENT OF bread rationing on August 1st was a more severe blow to Soviet citizens' confidence in the Party and government than anything since the revaluation of the Stalinist past undertaken by Khrushchev. To a people who had never been told that grain purchases from abroad had been a common support of the Soviet bread supply for 15 years, it seemed inconceivable that their country could not provide sufficient bread for its people.

Against the background of this sudden shock, Soviet citizens now looked again at the increasing shortages and rising prices of vegetables and meat. Previously they had thought in terms of distribution problems which would gradually improve. Now they gradually ceased to believe in a plentiful supply and began to speculate openly on the introduction of rationing for other foodstuffs as well.

Hoarding of canned goods began. Within a month even the previously well-stocked shelves of herring and cheap, mostly unwanted fish products began to empty. In the new supermarkets which had been built to accommodate the expected plenty of the 1980s bright lights lit long empty shelves.

At the free markets prices rose in response to the new fears. Occasionally there were riots and the peasants' produce was torn from them and carried away before the militia could reimpose order.

And with the end of summer came the announcement of draconian fuel economy measures. Factory heating levels were to be reduced by 20 percent. In the Central Asian and Caucasian Republics this would be no serious hardship, but the workers of Leningrad and Moscow, of Gorky and Pskov, knew exactly what sort of winter they had to look forward to.

Where, they asked, was that progress on the promise of which all Party propaganda had been based? Where were the consumer goods, supplies of which were supposed to be rising by eight percent per year? Long before, it had been the subject of amused comment by foreign visitors when Soviet drivers stopped their cars as it began to rain and leapt to fit the windshield wipers which they kept in the glove compartments for fear of theft. Now a truck would lose its tires in an overnight parking lot, apartments would be rifled for hoarded food and vodka, a man's suit or his wife's one party dress.

To Carole Yates it seemed that Muscovites had never looked more gray or had been more rudely determined in the food queues that lined many of even the most important thoroughfares.

And steadily the number of bombings increased. Westerners driving through the new districts of Moscow would often report a traffic detour or roped-off area, or would even hear an explosion and its hollow returning echo. Workers in the area adopted an attitude of callous indifference. A distant explosion would as often as not elicit a muttered "There goes another shock-worker." The truth was there was a deep well of sympathy among Russian workers for the Rodinist attacks on the Asiatics, and even on the government offices responsible for bringing them north.

Perhaps it is not surprising, therefore, that the militia, too, in that last summer of the Soviet Union, seemed different. Before, they had strutted in Red Square and along the Kirova Ulitza, proud of their uniforms and their function as guardians of Soviet society. Now they seemed hard-eyed and sullen. If one militiaman rebuked a Muscovite for a minor offense, two other policemen would be at his shoulder in seconds, anticipating trouble.

Leaving Letsukov's apartment one evening Carole had driven straight over to see David Butler. She had been crying in the car and it was evident to Butler as he let her in.

"I think," he said, "we should go out for a short walk, Carole."

In the Plevna Gardens she took his arm. "I can't imagine," she said, "how I ever thought I was in love with Tom. I'm beginning to understand that love is something much more bitter and necessitous than anything I felt for him."

"Is Letsukov in love with you?" Butler asked.

"Sometimes I'm sure of it. Other times he can spend a whole evening pushing me away, emphasizing our differences. And then an hour later . . ."

"In bed?"

"Usually. But we've had much more than that between us." She paused. "I'd leave Tom, I'd leave America, for Alex."

"And he?"

"I wouldn't ask anything from him. He hates the Soviet system, I know that. But he's trapped by it."

"It's a world of moral choices far more complex than the world we live in, Carole."

For a few moments they walked in silence.

"I've no advice to offer you, you know that," he said.

She smiled sadly. "I suppose I was hoping. But that's the school kid in me still."

"I do, however, have a suggestion. That is that we go to Mother Hubbard's and we both get blind drunk."

"I accept," she said.

Miserably they disentangled their limbs. Letsukov reached to the bedside table and took a packet of Belomors. Lighting one he lay back while she watched him smoke.

"We must do something to save what we had," she said desperately.

Letsukov drew deeply on the cigarette. "We come from different parts of the world, Carole. Don't ask too much of either of us."

She got up and began to dress. He watched her as he always did. When he finished his cigarette he got up too and put on a bathrobe. She knew it meant that he would not come down with her to find a taxi.

In the room it was half-dark. She finished dressing and walked to the window. She felt stifled by the narrow compass of the room, and by all that had gone before.

"Shall I put on the light?" He was sitting on the bed in his robe. He had lit another cigarette.

"No." she said. She reached down and picked up her purse. Feeling inside she found a lighter and a half-packet of American cigarettes. She lit one and stood smoking by the window.

"There's a man down there," she said, without turning. "He's standing in the doorway opposite."

Letsukov came to the window and stood for a moment, looking down. "I think I see him."

She glanced sideways at him. "I'll go now," she said.

On the back of the chair she could just make out her coat. She picked it up and threw it over her arm. "Are you worried about that man down there?" she asked Letsukov.

"No. Why should I be?"

"Most Russians would be."

In the dark she saw him shrug. She was close to bursting into tears.

"I can't believe we've been so profligate," she said. "I can't believe we've spent all that feeling we had between us."

She watched his shadowed figure, willing him to speak. "Say something, Alex. Say something to me."

"I can't." His voice was little more than a whisper. "I've nothing to say."

She reached out and touched his arm. "I'd like to come and see you again. Just one more time maybe . . ."

Beneath her fingers his arm was motionless.

"No." she said. "Clearly not."

She walked past him to the door. "Good-bye Alex."

There was an ancient elevator in the old prewar apartment block, but she ignored it. Running down the stairs her heels clacked on the carpetless stone. In the lobby she pulled on her coat and hurried outside searching the street for a cab.

She had completely forgotten the man in the doorway opposite. But now as she stood on the sidewalk he came away from the shadow and crossed the street to enter Letsukov's apartment building behind her.

Slowly she walked 20 or 30 yards along the street then crossed over to the other side. From there she could see into Letsukov's second-floor window. His light was now on. A man in a leather jacket was standing with Letsukov in the doorway of his room.

So it was over. Whatever the significance of this mysterious visitor, her affair with Letsukov was over.

She continued to walk down the street with slow paces, her hands deep in her pockets. It was a pleasant late summer evening, not too cold. It was a pleasant late summer evening and her affair was over. Over as abruptly as it began all that time ago in Paris.

She could see the green light of a taxicab approaching. She hailed it not caring if it stopped. The cab brakes squealed. The door opened. She got in.

At first Letsukov had thought that Carole had come back. He had crossed quickly to the door and opened it, still wearing his bathrobe.

"Comrade Letsukov?" A tall young man in a black leather jacket said.

"Yes. Who are you?"

"May I come in? I have a message for you."

Letsukov drew back the door and let the man in.

"I've been waiting hours out there. I'd begun to think the woman lived here."

Closing the door Letsukov looked round to see the stranger had thrown himself comfortably into an armchair and was stretching his legs.

"Very nice though, Comrade. Foreign? American I'd say."

"Who *are* you?" Letsukov asked again.

"A fair enough question," the man nodded. "I might be one of those thieves you read about all the time now. But I'm not."

"Are you from the police?" Letsukov said.

The man laughed. "Not me, Comrade. Why? Were you expecting someone from the police?"

"No."

"Ah . . . it's the way I am, is it?"

"Perhaps."

"Offensive to you? You learn very quickly in the KGB, I was a sergeant once. My name's Mart."

"What sort of name is that?"

"It's an Estonian name, Comrade, what we used to call a Christian name."

"All right," Letsukov said, "why are you here?"

"Give me a cigarette," the man reached across and took Letsukov's packet of Belomors.

"Before I was KGB, I was a merchant seaman. Traveled the world."

Letsukov recovered his cigarettes from the stranger and took one from the packet.

"You travel a bit yourself, I hear, Comrade. Paris even."

Letsukov lit his cigarette. He was sure that, despite denials, the man was from Colonel Pleskov's office in the Lubyanka. No doubt demanding a further report on his affair with Carole.

"I traveled to Paris a long time ago," he said.

"So I heard. And topped someone while you were there, you bastard."

"Save yourself the hypocrisy. You know better than anyone why I did it."

"I don't know why and I don't want to know," the man said airily.

"I'm entitled to be given your rank and full name," Letsukov said. "If not, I phone the militia station right away."

"I've no rank," the man said. "And I've no full name, it's safer. And if you try to get out to that phone I'll tear you to pieces. I learned to fight in Hamburg, New York and the old London docks. A member of the Soviet Merchant Marine has to."

"Tell me what you want, and get out."

"If I had my way, I wouldn't have come here in the first place."

He got up, took Letsukov's cigarettes and again lit himself a cigarette. He was probably in his early thirties, blond and hard-faced.

"I've come from Leningrad," he blew a plume of smoke into the room then drew again on the cigarette, holding it between index finger and thumb like a worker.

"We've been working on your case, Comrade, my friends and me. You once made certain offers of help to the wife of Joseph Densky."

Letsukov remained silent.

"More recently you were in the Ukraine. Making more offers of help. But . . . how far are we to trust you?"

Letsukov inhaled sharply through his teeth. "If you're who you say you are, you have to decide that for yourself," he said.

The man went back to the chair and sat on the arm. "Do you know Estonia?" he asked.

"I've been to Tallinn."

"I was born there," the man said. "Do you know the KGB general in command?"

"He was present at a reception for a few moments when I was there."

"General Avgust Pork, there's a name to frighten children. Have you got any vodka, Comrade?"

Letsukov brought a glass, and a liter from the kitchen.

"General Pork has been very active lately," the man unscrewed the bottle and poured a large measure into the glass. "He's been up to his favorite trick, beating workers in the little room below his office."

"Trade Unionists? Joseph Densky's followers?"

"Keep your mouth shut and listen," the man said. He gulped a mouthful of the vodka, swilled it round his teeth and swallowed it.

"Yes, you've got influence all right or you wouldn't get such good vodka. Where was I? General Pork and his favorite tricks. Workers, Comrade, nationalist workers. But then everyone's a nationalist in Estonia and Lithuania, all except the KGB, of course, and some of *them*, too. I was."

"You carried out the beatings for Pork?"

"I never killed anyone, Comrade. I never murdered a nationalist in Paris."

Letsukov brought himself a glass and poured some vodka from the bottle. "Get on with it," he said.

"These workers Pork has been beating up this week, perhaps some of them have been talking, giving names. We want to know, Comrade. We want to find out if anyone talked."

"So that you can warn the men in danger?"

"That's right. So what help can you give us?"

"You want *me* to find the names?"

"We want you to tell us how successful Pork has been. If there are any names, we want them."

"That's not possible," Letsukov said.

"Your office deals with these things, yes or no?"

"Listen," Letsukov put down his vodka, "we would have an account of every examination. The Tallinn report is no doubt in the office at this moment."

"So?"

"But I no longer deal with Northwestern regions. My area has just changed to the Caucasus."

"You can still get that report."

"You don't understand. It would mean breaking into a file cabinet."

"So what?"

"Suspicion would immediately fall on someone in the office."

The Estonian looked at Letsukov with contempt. "I told them," he said, "I told them in Leningrad, that you'd be one of two things, a Bureau spy or a weak-kneed coward. What do I care if suspicion falls on you?" His voice was menacing. "What's your career against fifty, sixty, a hundred arrests in Estonia?"

Letsukov sat on the side of the bed looking into the sharp-cut lines of the man's face.

"When I was with the Bureau," the Estonian said, "we used to break in wherever we wanted to. Other government departments as often as not. Sometimes we'd set a fire going and with any luck burn the place down. You do that Letsukov and your department head is going to think it's a KGB job. He'll ask them, they'll deny it. He won't believe them, they won't believe him. Everything gets so mixed up, believe me, that it'd take a spider to unravel the web. And a hundred Estonians go underground, with any luck, just in time. You'll do it, Letsukov, because if you're what you say you are, you don't really have a choice."

Letsukov finished his vodka. "Yes, I'll do it. Give me a week."

"A week, you bastard? Did you take a week in Paris? By that time Pork's men could be knocking on the doors in the middle of the night."

When Carole arrived back at her apartment Harriet Bennerman was sitting on the sofa in the living room. Tom Yates was sitting opposite her in an armchair but his cigarette stubs were mixed with hers in the ashtray next to her.

"You're back early," her husband said as Carole took off her coat. "I thought Architectural Club meetings went on into the small hours."

"Only if David Butler invites us back. He had work to do later this evening."

"How is David?" Harriet asked. "I haven't seen him for ages."

"He's fine," Carole said. "Matter of fact, he was talking about inviting you and Jack over to one of his Armenian meals. Us too," she added to her husband.

"I can't take fat guys flouncing around in caftans," Tom Yates said.

Harriet stood up. "I'd better be on my way, Tom. I'll get that typed up by the time your conference is through tomorrow. 'Night, Carole."

"See you, Harriet," Carole said and walked into the bedroom. She stood for a moment looking at the neatly made bed. The blankets and coverlet were folded under in a style known as hospital corners. But she could have sworn that their rather slapdash Ukrainian maid had never done a hospital corner in her life. She had no way of telling how she would have felt if she had not been so miserable about Letsukov. She let her imagination dwell for a few moments on the picture of Harriet's fat arms encircling her husband's neck, drawing him down onto her vast pneumatic breasts, but the idea was more ridiculous than painful to her. And in any case, she couldn't be sure. Perhaps the maid had been doing hospital corners ever since they had arrived in Moscow.

She took a shower, swallowed a sleeping pill and got into bed. Ten minutes later when her husband came into the bedroom she was asleep.

Chapter Twenty-seven

AT FIVE MINUTES past five the next evening, Letsukov stood at his office window overlooking the Ulitza Razina. The Examination Department of the Nationalities Ministry, Trade Union Section, had been moved from its former eighteenth-century splendor and now occupied the sixth and seventh floors of a nine-floor block whose cracking walls and window frames parting from the surrounding plaster proclaimed it as being of recent construction.

In the next room he could hear the busy tapping of his secretary's heels as she crossed and recrossed the office, locking files and feeding papers into the shredding chute. He had taken his coat from the hook in the outer office while she was in the cloakroom and he was banking on her assumption that he had already gone home.

He could hear her clearly, humming to herself. Then she crossed the room for the last time and locked the connecting door between their offices. So far so good.

He waited until he heard her heels pass along the corridor outside, waited even until he heard the lift door slam. Then he took his own keys and let himself into the outer office.

Given the Department's security grading the technical constraints were not great. There was no electronic alarm system. The file cabinets were sturdy but by no means impossible to pry open. The most effective security element was the key system. By this the most important files could only be opened by the Department head and the official dealing with that subject. Thus although Letsukov dealt with KGB reports on Free Trade Union activities, his area (Southern Republics) excluded him from the Estonian file. The metal cabinet would have to be broken open.

The only real immediate risk was the security patrol. He knew that the three men comprising it were, as often as not during the day, to be found drinking *kvas* in their office on the floor below. But he had no idea how conscientious they were in the execution of their duties after the staff had left.

He went to the door leading into the corridor, unlocked it and opened it an inch or two. He could see the whole length of the dusty alley between the lines of locked doors. No one. He closed and relocked the door and took a strong pair of pliers from his pocket.

He knew the Estonian file well. The year before he could have unlocked it and copied out the names he wanted. There would have been no possibility then of detection.

He inserted one end of the pliers into the lock and levered. The soft metal around the lock opening buckled. He increased the pressure. Something snapped and fell down inside the cabinet. Concentrating on the noise within he had forgotten the danger from noise outside. He went back to the office door. It was of thin hardboard construction. He could hear nothing.

Returning to the cabinet he took the handle and pulled. The lock now rattled inside and the file drawer opened a fraction. He pushed the head of the pliers into the gap and levered hard. The lock snapped and the file drawer slid open. Estonia—security—reports, the pink cardboard tab read. He lifted out the folder and opened it to the latest filing. There was the report signed by General Avgust Pork, KGB, Tallinn. One prisoner only had given information, three names and details of a Friday-night factory meeting. General Pork intended to move against the factory meeting if it was still to be held, in the hope of a bigger bag of dissidents. After the meeting had been raided he would arrest the three men. Any action against them any earlier would obviously have the effect of canceling the meeting.

Friday, two days' time. Three men saved. Only three.

A key turned in the lock. Letsukov heard the guard sergeant's cough as the door opened.

Red-faced, the security man stood coughing into a handkerchief. "Sorry, Comrade Letsukov," he said, wheezing and wiping his watery eyes. "It's bronchitis the doctor says. Gave me a very severe warning last time I saw him."

The coughing began again and, unable to speak, the guard made an awkward apologetic bow and stepped back into the corridor, closing the door behind him.

Letsukov sat at his secretary's desk listening to the coughing of the sergeant echo in the corridors. He copied out the three names and pushed the piece of paper into his pocket.

He had saved three. And sacrificed himself. What point in starting a fire? He found it difficult to think clearly. He was trembling.

A fire. At least that might disguise the fact that he had been after the Estonia file, might give those three men just a few more hours?

He broke open two more filing cabinets and piled the reports around the wooden desk leg. Lighting the papers he watched the flames rise and begin to die away. He threw on more papers but again the blaze quickly reduced them to a smoldering pile. In self-disgust he took his coat and left the office.

At the elevator he saw the guard. "I was telling you, Comrade," he pressed the elevator button, "I was telling you what the doctor told me. Give up smoking he said or you'll be dead in a year."

The lift came and Letsukov took it to the ground floor. A meeting on one of the lower floors had just broken up. Officials and secretaries flowed out of the building onto Razina Street.

The Estonian, Mart, stood in the middle of Red Square and ran his eyes along the Kremlin wall. He had decided to see it once in his life. He had no wish ever to see it again.

He looked at his watch. Just after seven o'clock. Dusk was falling. Over the Kremlin, searchlights leapt into the sky isolating the bright red banners of the Soviet Empire undulating in the evening breeze.

He didn't trust the bureaucrat Letsukov. Any man who killed for the KGB would certainly betray for the same masters. Yet he had no choice but to go back to Letsukov's apartment. It was still possible that Densky's wife was right.

He was aware of a figure shuffling up beside him. He looked down and saw a fat, balding man standing next to him. He was paring down slivers from an apple with an Army jackknife and eating off the blade.

"Your first time in Moscow, Comrade?" the fat man said.

"The first time," the Estonian agreed cautiously.

"Greatest city in the world."

"True enough."

"Beautiful girls," the fat man pointed to one of the milling tourist groups standing in the square. It was a mixed factory party with eight or ten young girls with tight skirts and carefully curled hair.

"Beautiful," the Estonian said.

"Where are you from, Comrade?"

"A long way from here. Up near Estonia, Pskov."

"I thought I recognized the accent. Now don't go, Comrade," the fat man laid a hand on the Estonian's arm. "You here with a factory party, or on your own?"

"Why are you asking?"

"Because in my business it's best to know who you're talking to. A factory party is it?"

"The others have gone off to the circus. That's not for me."

"For the little ones, I agree. What sort of thing is it interests you, Comrade? Those beautiful girls, for instance?" He cut a slice from his apple and slipped it adroitly into his mouth.

"Every man's interested in beautiful girls," the Estonian said. "Good night, Comrade."

He began to walk away but the man hurried after him. "Not so fast, Comrade. You may be losing an opportunity here."

"What sort of opportunity?" He kept walking.

"You like films? I can take you to a place where they show films, American films, that'd make your mouth water. Girls doing it with girls—everything."

"Fat man, I was in the Soviet Merchant Marine. I've seen porn films in the city where they were made."

"Ah . . ." the man was clearly disappointed. "Then listen, you want to make a few hundred rubles?"

"I'm not a film star." They had almost crossed the square. The twisted, sugar-candy domes of St. Basil's rose above them.

"My name's Sasha," the man said. "They call me Fat Sasha."

"Do they?"

"Now this is a really good deal," Fat Sasha threw the apple core away. "How long are you in Moscow for?"

"A few days."

"Good enough. Don't walk so fast. I can't talk."

The Estonian walked on, if anything increasing his pace.

"Do you know what a surprise party is?"

"No."

"I'll tell you. Some of the wives of Red Army, Soviet Army I should call it these days, senior officers give parties. They have places you wouldn't dream of out in the country. Colonels' wives and above. These ladies, not always old, they have everything. You think of it, they've got it."

"Except one thing."

"But they're real upper-class women. Furs, champagne . . . diamonds. They give these parties for each other. Surprise parties."

"And they invite you, Fat Sasha? Is that the surprise?"

"Never . . . more's the pity. But they like a half-dozen young waiters. You take the point. You have to do your bit after dinner is served with any one of them who chooses. But it's not often that one of our boys leaves without three hundred rubles in his pocket."

The Estonian's hand came down on Fat Sasha's neck gripping it like a pair of iron fire-tongs.

He squealed in pain wriggling to get free. In the shadows beside the cathedral the Estonian gripped harder. "Listen, Fat Sasha, I ought to take you along to the nearest militia station. Porn films you're offering, sex parties . . . and you're slandering the wives of Soviet officers."

He pushed the fat man against the wall. "Yes, I could take you in or beat you to a pulp here and now."

Fat Sasha flinched.

"Or there is another way."

"I've got money," Sasha dipped his hand into his pocket and pulled out a roll of ruble notes. "A hundred rubles," he said.

Groups of people drifted past them, too far away to see what was happening or too indoctrinated with the necessity to avert their eyes.

"No, you can do something for me," the Estonian said. "Keep your pimp's money, I've got an errand for you instead."

Carole turned the car into the lane beside Letsukov's apartment building and cut the engine. It was a four-year-old British Jaguar which they had bought from David Butler when they first arrived in Moscow, but its red paintwork still stood out among the drab gray and black Volgas like a gleaming beacon of the West.

For a few minutes she sat in the car pretending to debate to herself whether she would go up. He had made it clear enough last night that he wanted the affair to end. But something, apart from the misery that she found she felt at not seeing him again, something else troubled her. Every time she had felt she was getting closer to him, he had deliberately pulled away.

She thought perhaps it was the American in her that needed an explanation. Certainly it was not the Slav element in her makeup, if indeed that existed in anything but a biological sense. Or again perhaps she was simply trying to invent an excuse for one more meeting.

She didn't welcome the idea that she would probably humiliate herself. But she was prepared to risk it. She got out of the car and walked round to the front entrance.

The janitor was standing on the step, sniffing the evening air. Climbing the stairs she reached the landing and stood opposite Letsukov's door.

She could turn now and go. But the sounds of movement inside were a powerful magnet. She stepped back across the landing as if to reduce the compulsion to knock on the door.

The ancient lift rattled, rose one floor and stopped. A fat man pulled the gates half open and eased himself out onto the landing. He was heading for Letsukov's door when he saw her. He must have recognized by the clothes she wore that she was a foreigner. He hesitated, took a step back, another forward, and stood by the door.

She smiled at him. Somehow reassured, he knocked.

When Letsukov answered he saw them both at once. He had no idea who the fat man might be. Even in his confusion she thought he seemed pleased she was there.

Fat Sasha was more confused than either Letsukov or herself. He leaned forward in a squeaky stage whisper and said something in Letsukov's ear. She heard "an errand, the Estonian . . ." perhaps other things she afterward forgot.

He had been pleased; he was now furiously angry. He stood in this doorway, white-faced, hesitant . . .

"Go inside, Carole," his voice was sharp. "I have some business with this man."

She walked past them both into the apartment. Letsukov stepped out onto the landing and pulled the door shut behind him. It was a few moments before he returned.

"Obviously I should not have come," she said.

"It would have been better if you hadn't. Why did you?"

"I think," she said carefully, "I wasn't satisfied that you really didn't want to see me anymore."

He was silent.

"A mistake," she said. "Yet another."

He walked toward the kitchen. "I still have some of the coffee you brought. Would you like some?"

"Yes," she called through to him. What frightened her was just how desolate she would have felt if he'd asked her to go.

Fat Sasha left the apartment building and hurried across the street. A few yards to his right a lane, corresponding to the lane on the other side where Carole had parked the Jaguar, led between wooden warehouses. Sasha turned quickly into the darkness and stopped. He had made a bad mistake with the merchant seaman, he knew that. Even now he could be badly beaten up in this ill-lit lane and lose his hundred rubles.

That iron hand gripped his neck. Involuntarily Sasha squealed.

"Quiet, you fat pig. Did you get it?"

Sasha pulled from his pocket the piece of paper. The Estonian dragged him across the lane to a hanging lamp. Taking the paper, he read it, screwing up his eyes.

"Just three," he said to himself. "It's possible. Yes, it's possible."

He released his grip on Sasha's neck. "On your way, Fat Sasha. And be careful in the future who you talk to in Red Square."

Sasha waddled in a fast trot down the lane. In the street a militia car braked when the driver saw his running figure.

The driver hung his head out of the window. "Sasha," he called. "Over here."

The militiaman's eye caught the dark figure of the Estonian hesitating in the entrance to the lane. "And you," he roared.

The back door of the car flew open. A young militiaman came out ready to give chase. The Estonian strolled casually forward. He could see the second man relax, his hand moving away from his pistol holster.

"So what's on tonight, Sasha?" the driver said, one elbow across the sill. "And let's have a look at your friend's papers for a start."

"No friend of mine," Sasha said.

The Estonian fumbled in his inside pocket. The militiaman stood impatiently, legs slightly apart.

"What were you two up to then down the lane?"

"Even duchesses have to piss sometimes," Sasha said.

"And you?"

"Even duchesses," the Estonian said.

His hand left his pocket to pass an internal passport to the young militiaman. His knee came up at the same time into the gap between the parted legs.

In the apartment they both heard the militiaman's cry of pain. Letsukov, emerging from the kitchen, saw Carole looking down into the street below.

"What is it?"

"The police are holding the man who came to see you," she said as evenly as she could. "There was another man who ran across the street somewhere. I think he must have broken away from them."

Letsukov took her by the arm. "Carole, you've got to go."

"You're in trouble, Alex."

"If that fat man tells the militia he was here, I'm in a lot of trouble. So go Carole, now."

"Wait a minute," she was looking down at the scene below. "They're letting your fat man go. It's the other one they're interested in, the one that got away."

The young militiaman had hauled himself back into the car. As it pulled away on squealing tires, Fat Sasha hurried off in the opposite direction.

She turned back to Letsukov. "I'll go now," she said, "if you'll answer one more question."

He was handing her her coat.

She took it and picked up her purse. "In some ordinary place," she said, "like Boston, Massachusetts, would you still be asking me to go?"

He took her and kissed her lips. "Good-bye, Carole," he said. "It's got to be good-bye."

With a roar like an avalanche the whole side section of the office block on Razina Street tore away and hurtled down into the car park below. Within minutes the flames, which had been contained in one floor of offices, had swept up to the three floors above. While the gathering crowds watched in amazement further sections of the concrete walls sagged like melting snow and fell, revealing burning rooms and smoke-filled corridors like the dollhouse of some pyromaniac child.

Zelmetsky, Letsukov's department head, was informed at 8:20 P.M. He immediately telephoned Letsukov to come down to Razina Street. "The militia says it's chaos there, papers flying all over the street," he said.

With mounting hope, Letsukov raced in a taxi toward the office building. Militia cleared the way through the huge crowd when they discovered who he was.

Zelmetsky was talking to the fire brigade officer when Letsukov joined them. The fire was under control now, in fact had burned itself out. But above the fifth floor, the firemen dared not go.

"Expose it to heat and the concrete they use these days just turns to dust," the fire officer said. "You can't hold up a nine-story building with dust."

"We have to get closer," Zelmetsky told him. The whole of that sixth floor carried the confidential papers of my department."

"Comrade, there's going to be a risk when you approach any shell as cracked as this one. But I think we've seen the worst now. Find yourself some helmets and I'll see what we can do."

When the first section of wall had collapsed it had carried with it the whole platform floor of the offices on that side of the building. Letsukov's office no longer existed. Clambering over the wreckage he began to feel a new optimism. Among great jagged pieces of concrete, a chair would be smashed like matchwood, a filing cabinet caved in with locks burst open and charred papers fluttering across the ruins.

For two hours he and Zelmetsky climbed across the debris collecting documents. Letsukov could see no sign of the Estonian cabinet but from those others he saw, he felt confident that no one would waste a second look at a broken lock. Even better, the fire officer told them it would be virtually impossible to locate the precise office where the fire started. His own theory was an electrical fault. It was the cause of over half the major fires in Moscow these days.

In all, the fire officer said they were lucky, especially with casualties.

When the wall section collapsed there was only the 14-man guard unit in the building.

Letsukov stood among the rubble, like the others dust-covered, his face smudged with the soot. "Were any of the guards killed?" he asked slowly.

Most escaped without injury the fire officer told him. But two guards on the sixth and seventh floors fell with that corner. Killed outright. A third, he said, had been trapped among smoke and fumes. He was bronchitic and the doctors had apparently said he was unlikely to last the night.

Three men killed, then. For three men saved. In his torn, dirty clothes Letsukov walked back home as dawn began to break. He was now sure he was safe. A bulldozer had exposed the missing filing cabinets before dawn. Among them, buckled almost in two, was the Estonian cabinet, its top drawer burst open like so many of the others. Letsukov and Zelmetsky had emptied it of files and abandoned it among the debris. To Zelmetsky it was a good night's ork.

A good night's work. Two dead and one dying. By now probably dead. He had refused offers of lifts from Zelmetsky and the militia. He preferred to trudge back across an empty Moscow as dawn broke behind him. Three men dead, three men saved. Was that still the inexorable equation of his life?

Investigating officer Gregory Sergeivich Platonov had been a policeman for the best part of 40 years. As a young militiaman he had patrolled some of the toughest districts in the high-dam town of Bratsk when the ardor for socialist construction wore thin and the fights and knifings were an every Saturday night occurrence. After that he had served as a desk sergeant in the north Urals town of Perm before being promoted to Moscow in the early seventies as a junior investigating officer. Here he had seen and heard things that made the cropped gray hair rise on the back of his neck. He could hardly believe the way some people lived. But he had kept his head down as they say and stuck to his job. For five years he had been in robbery, and it was there that he had seen some of the apartments of the senior Party men.

Then in 1977 he had been transferred to the Arson Squad. Being the sort of man he was he had applied himself diligently to his work, studying fire reports, working closely with the Fire Service and specializing in what was called "negligent arson," which perhaps in some other societies might be known as "accident."

He had inspected the site of the Razina Street fire the morning after it occurred. In overalls and metal helmet, the architect's drawings in his hand, he had clambered over the wreckage and climbed up to the dangerous sixth and seventh floors. He liked to work alone.

The problem, in terms of establishing culpability, was to identify the precise starting point of the fire, and that was difficult when the collapsed section included at least six separate offices.

He sat, six floors up, his legs dangling over a broken lip of concrete, a mound of rubble below him, and puzzled over the electrical wiring plan. Nothing seemed to fit. At least not if the Fire Service report was to be accepted.

Platonov's function was to examine the site of a fire and accept or reject the fire report. Normally he found himself in agreement with the fire officers, but on this occasion he simply could not see by reference to the wiring plan and by the visible evidence that an electrical fault could have been responsible.

There in front of him, across a great gap where the floor had collapsed, was the evidence in the torn metal conduit that at least the electricians had worked according to building regulations. He had questioned the officials and secretaries who worked on the sixth floor and nothing suggested illicit electrical machinery or any form of overloading. Yet a fire *had* broken out, in one of three offices almost an hour after everyone had left.

Two of the guards were dead. The other was in hospital.

Platonov walked down the concrete stairway and emerged at the service door onto the great pile of rubble. For an hour or more he worked over it, levering up slabs of concrete, sifting dust, examining charred pieces of office furniture. He did not need his laboratory to analyze the concrete mix to tell him that, whoever else was responsible, the construction brigade was certainly an accessory. But there were far too many examples of bad building in Moscow to make any action worthwhile.

He gave instructions for all items of furniture, scraps of carpet and electrical fittings to be collected from the rubble, and to be removed to the examination sheds. Then he left for the site of the second fire that night, an Asiatic's hotel in one of the new districts that might or might not have been an arson attack by the Rodinists.

Chapter Twenty-eight

LATE INTO THE long summer nights the sound of axes chopping echoed through the birchwoods. Chainsaws buzzed, men shouted warnings and trees toppled slowly to crash among the undergrowth. Even in this wood-scented, free-seeming air, men worked with that slow, grinding determination which is all that's left when malnutrition and the threat of death by shooting hang over them.

Even Anton's once heavy frame now showed an outline of ribs and collarbones. Smaller men, less well-fed on arrival at Panaka, took on a hunted skeletal look, moved dangerously listless from the path of falling trees and crouched gasping in the thickets when the guards' backs were turned. Death was now commonplace and a severed hand or split kneecap might come to any man no longer capable of concentration.

But hard as conditions were in Panaka One, they were ease itself compared to life in the Penal Brigade's camp at Panaka Five. Like some insatiable and ever-swelling tumor, Panaka Five had grown throughout the summer until it now contained over 30,000 men. No attempt now was made to put them to work. Their ration scale was far too low to make even light regular work a practical possibility. But more than that, tools became weapons in the hands of the penal *zeks*. Caged like animals they became a terror to their guards. And the guards replied in the only way they knew. A camp whipping was a daily occurrence. To run chained behind the cart soon broke the marrowless legbones of undernourished men. On the camps' notice boards it was officially stated that cannibalism was punishable by shooting.

The camp commandant was a distraught former Soviet naval officer who had been transferred to camp duties for incompetence at sea. He was no more competent on land. And his responsibilities in terms of human lives were many thousand times greater. When new penal detachments arrived unannounced from the Perm Military District, he would telephone Kraslag headquarters at Krasibirsk and beg for a ration allocation, or for a hundred yards of sewage piping or a supply of roofing felt to build new huts. But a system which could not organize fruit in Moscow in September lacked the will to supply Panaka with the basic necessities. The ex-naval officer, incapable, to his credit, of becoming inured to cruelty on this scale, took his own life that summer after a tour of the new open graves he had ordered to be dug.

By autumn it was beginning to penetrate the thinking of some of the more aware of Kuba's followers that what Natalya Roginova and the revisionists had been saying before her arrest was that the Soviet Union as it now stood was no longer a viable politico-economic unit.

They had thought that at the Archangelskoye meeting she was *predicting* an oil crisis, they now became dimly aware that she had been *describing* an oil crisis, one that the Soviet Union was already suffering.

Bread rationing, the Oil Energy (reduction of use) Measures announced in September and the Restricted Travel Measures of October began to point toward a siege economy.

As the autumn rains slashed across Western Russia and in the north and east the temperatures began to drop, the Soviet economy creaked and groaned like a huge beam, finally overladen. Bread rationing affected the individual and the family, and fuel rationing to factories and enterprises throughout the Soviet Union began to bite sharply into the already pathetic levels of production.

Among Semyon Kuba's problems at this time must be numbered the appearance and phenomenal growth of the underground trade union newspaper *Iskra,* "the Spark." It of course escaped no Soviet citizen that *Iskra* was the title of Lenin's own revolutionary paper. But what made the new version's suppression impossible to achieve was the fact that *Iskra* appeared to be printed in dozens, perhaps even hundreds of different cities. The main part of the newspaper was clearly based on the Moscow original, but regional news was included by local editor-printers. The techniques of Lenin's *Iskra* and of *Pravda* were thus brilliantly combined.

For the first time now in the Soviet Union, through *Iskra,* Free Trade Unionists could speak to each other. For the first time reports of strikes and injustices were reported. The BBC Overseas Service began to quote *Iskra* and Western news agencies recognized the veracity of its reporting. Throughout the autumn, as the reputation of *Iskra* grew the KGB constantly redoubled its efforts to trace its presses and distributors. But the cellular system and the *Pravda*-like editorial organization continued to elude all KGB efforts. Still, as autumn faded, the editor of *Iskra* occupied a high position on the Lubyanka's list of wanted men.

In the marketplace the shortages from decreased production raised both black market and free market prices and the Soviet worker was no longer earning the wages necessary to pay.

What was true of consumer goods production was equally true of agriculture. After a temporary meat glut in early October when wholesale slaughtering took place, meat disappeared completely from shops in hundreds of cities across the Soviet Union.

Then the problems of transportation intervened. Back in the days of Leonid Brezhnev the leadership had warned of an impending transportation crisis. The age of railroad locomotives and freight cars, and above all the poor quality of their maintenance, were already affecting the efficiency of food distribution when the Soviet Union entered the eighties. Five years later when the corruptly administered Transport Restrictions were added to the burden of the railways, the system quite literally ceased to function over whole areas and districts for periods of up to two or three weeks at a time.

Thus one of the most bizarre developments at this time, and one which

Western commentators totally failed to predict, was the advent of the local temporary famine.

When first reports from *Iskra* began to reach Western Europe most governments were frankly skeptical. Shortages, even localized severe shortages, they knew existed, but famine in a developed state like the Soviet Union? Hardly possible, was the verdict of most specialists. They took even the low current figures for grain production in the Ukraine and the Virgin Lands, added emergency purchases from the United States and Canada, calculated dairy food production and added cheese and butter sales by the European Common Market and announced in their reports that no citizen of the Soviet Union could be even remotely close to malnutrition.

But to be of value to a family food must reach the kitchen table. Vast stores of grain in the black earth regions of the Ukraine are of no value to the workers of, say, Novosibirsk. A glut of butter and cheese in Belorussia is no guarantee that Bratsk, east of the Ural Mountains, is similarly favored. In these months the harsh truth emerged that the food distribution system of the Soviet Union, in particular by rail, had in many areas temporarily collapsed. Vikenty Lossov was a stationmaster at the small but important junction of Stara in the Kazan *oblast:*

I was over retirement age at the time, of course, but that's not to say I was too old for the job. The local chairman had come to see me himself and asked me to return to work. The stationmaster who succeeded me had just been kicked out. It seems he'd left unprotected trainloads of grain in the sidings for two months. Just forgotten about them. And you can imagine what the rats and the rain did to that consignment.

I don't mind admitting I was flattered. Nearly seventy years of age and being asked, personally mind you, by the local chairman! I'd had forty years of experience. During the war against fascism I ran four junctions just behind the front. And in those days we had to deal with old equipment, worn rolling stock, and air attack as well as the usual Russian problems of flooded lines or solid frozen points. Just a staff of five and myself. Eighteen, 20 hours a day were normal. But then we knew what we were working for. We knew that every rail-car of mortar ammunition or anti-tank shells was going to be used to drive the fascists back where they came from. And the returning trainloads of our wounded, well, you didn't sit on your backside and watch the samovar bubble when a hospital train had to be expedited.

Things had changed a lot since the time I retired ten years ago. The younger ones just didn't care. No pride in the work any longer. But even so I was completely unprepared for what I found when I went back to Junction 616 in January of that year. Chaos, my friend, would be a pretty

way of describing it. I don't even know how to start. The staff had grown
from 50 to 300. Yet the siding tracks looked as though the Messerschmits
had been over the night before. Five full trains were *derailed* in the sidings
themselves! Pilfering, I'd seen plenty of before. But this was full-scale
looting. Farmers would come in with trucks and shovel the grain off the
wagons and nobody thought to stop them. Loco repairs? On the day I
took over, the manifest showed 15 shunting engines on the junction.
Fourteen were unusable through neglect and lack of basic repairs.

That same day I was shown what they called "the dump." When a train
carrying perishables broke down in the junction area, its load—fruit,
cabbages, potatoes, whatever—would be shoveled onto a vast rotting
dump of vegetables—after all the still edible stuff had been looted, of
course.

And nobody cared! We'd come a long, long way since the days of
Stalin. That peasant Khrushchev started it all, that's when we lost our
pride in ourselves, making a fool of the country in the United Nations,
boasting that every Soviet citizen would have an automobile and a
refrigerator and a television set. Why did we want to be like the capitalist
West? Under Stalin we were different—times were hard, but we had the
world's respect. That first night when I got home to my wife, I don't mind
telling you, friend, I wept . . .

Of course transport conditions throughout the Soviet Union weren't all
as bad as Junction 616. But especially in the autumn thaw, large areas of
north and northeastern Russia were vulnerable to complete, if only
temporary, transportation collapses when road transport became impossible on immense stretches of mud highways. Although we even now have
few details, it seems certain that while no large-scale famine was suffered,
virtually all foodstuffs could, and often did, disappear from a whole
district for a period of up to a month at a time. By then airlifts, military
supply echelons and farmers with an eye on a quick capitalist profit would
frequently flood the area with foodstuffs. But the memory of that local
brief famine would remain, even if public order had been effectively
maintained. But it wasn't always so.

Bita K. was a young Uzbek worker who had come north on the promise
of highly paid factory work in the labor-starved plants outside Perm:

Naturally I had never seen a winter like that, with snow up to fifteen
feet thick and great drifts along the highway between my hostel lodgings
and the plant. And when the spring thaw came the mud seemed to be
everywhere. You couldn't drive a truck along the main street without it
sinking up to its axles. A man on a horse would get sucked down just as
quickly.

I can't remember when it was we began to realize things were really short. I suppose in the hostels the meals had been getting worse and worse, potatoes would disappear from the evening meal, or cabbage even, but I seem to remember there was enough bread. But then one day it was announced supplies had not arrived and we were given 1 ruble and 50 kopecks to go out and find a café.

Well, we Uzbeks didn't normally go out much at night. The Russians in the town weren't all that friendly and when our work brigade first arrived there were a lot of very violent incidents. They say there's no racism up here in Russia, but I can tell you different.

Anyway, that night we went out in force, fifty or sixty of us from my brigade section alone. I suppose some of them struggled through the mud and found a beer hall that served *kasha*. My group didn't. We ran into trouble straightaway with a line of Russian women outside a food store screaming at us that we were using up food meant for them. Then the men appeared, some of them even local Russian workers of our own plants, and a nasty fight started in the mud of the main street.

That was the first night. The next day supplies still hadn't reached the hostel and the factory canteen was serving only a short ration of soup and tea. By the evening we were starving but most of us Uzbeks didn't particularly want trouble so we stayed in the hostel playing cards and talking about lamb sizzling on a spit the way we cook it back at home.

The next day was Saturday. Usually there's not a Russian to be seen at the plant that day because we Uzbeks works the Saturday shift for the extra money to send home. The Russians say they can't buy anything with it anyway.

But that Saturday when we reached the plant, two or three hundred Russian workers were there already. They'd elected some sort of soviet and sent a delegation to the plant manager. Unless food supplies were provided for the town, no one would turn up for work on Monday. And they soon made clear what would happen to the Uzbeks if they tried to work that day's shift.

Well I speak Russian as a section leader in my work brigade, and I translated for those who couldn't understand what was happening. The factory manager, it seems, had guaranteed a good canteen meal for any man at work. Somehow he'd got some supplies. But that was no good for the Russians. They wanted food for their families because it seems that although in the hostel we'd been getting more or less enough for the last few weeks, things in the town had been getting worse and worse. And a lot of families had been going really hungry.

So the Russians wouldn't work for one canteen meal a day—and the Uzbeks, with no families to worry about, saw this as the only way of getting something to eat.

When the Uzbeks announced their decision to the Russian workers' soviet, the Russians went mad. They came at us with iron bars and spades and anything they could lay their hands on and we scattered through the town. It was the last day I saw the plant for a month.

But in the hostel there was no food. From time to time a trainload of fruit or cabbage would arrive in the town and be stripped bare before the authorities could distribute it properly. And for us Uzbeks there was only one thing to do. Like hundreds of groups of Russians we went into the country around.

I can't pretend I'm very proud of what happened in those weeks. I think of myself as an educated man, I believe in the teachings of the Prophet and know that theft is forbidden by the Koran. But hunger, real hunger, is an evil driver. In bands of thirty or forty we began to roam the sodden farmlands. At first we bought from the peasants. But soon the prices became so high we began to threaten. Then when our money ran out (we weren't earning anything at the plant, remember) we just took what we wanted. And those peasants had everything. While we were starving hungry they had sheds full of potatoes and pigs running in the downstairs styes. More food and fuel than we'd seen even before the shortages.

Well, the peasants didn't give up without a fight. Sometimes we arrived at a village to find the men of the collective farm organized, ready to resist with axes, hammers, even guns. And then it was murder or maiming before we triumphed or were driven off.

Sometimes we'd have the women, too. There didn't really seem any reason not to, and most of the Uzbeks in any case had not been near a woman since the beginning of their contract period.

But let me just make it clear, it wasn't just us Uzbeks. Or the Tadzhik contract workers from the plant next to ours. The Russians were doing the same. And when they hacked their way into a village they didn't spare the women either, I was told.

I suppose it went on for about a month altogether. The militia arrived after the first week and I heard the Russian workers attacked their headquarters and fought a pitched battle in the middle of the town. However true it is, we weren't worried by militia until almost the very end of the famine when thousands were drafted into the area with helicopters and light-armored track vehicles. Apparently the Army itself was already sealing off the whole *oblast*.

I heard that deaths, not through starvation, just through the violence, amounted to over 2,000 in our factory town alone—and the peasants must have suffered at least as heavily. But rumors run like hares and I can't tell you anything more because we Uzbeks were all rounded up and returned home as the supplies started coming in again. Nobody ever asked *my* labor brigade to volunteer for work up north again . . .

*   *   *

The Kirov Clinic was once a compact classical mansion built in what is now the Lyublino suburb by the architect Gilardi in the years before Napoleon's advance on Moscow. Its elegant facade had now been extended by two low concrete wings, the brutal ugliness of which was enhanced by the double row of square barred windows which each contained.

From his room in the west wing, Bukansky could look out over the park. By climbing on his chair he was able to see the creeper-covered corner of a stone pavilion, a statue of Diana the Huntress and the edge of a small ornamental lake.

He had occupied this room since his arrest and, squeezed against the side of the window, he had watched the snow melt from the lead roof of the pavilion, and the first sprouting leaves of lilac by the side of the lake.

He had suffered no more than a few cursory interrogations and was fed adequately, although no vodka had passed his lips since his arrest. He was consequently fitter than he had been for some years. But there are no compensations for captivity.

In the early spring he had been visited by a doctor, or at least a man in a white coat who introduced himself as a doctor. He had come into the room and sat casually on the bed while Bukansky observed him, his head cocked to one side.

"May I at least know what this place is, doctor?"

"It's the Kirov Clinic in Lyublino. That must have been made clear to you when you signed your arrest papers."

"I signed no papers. I was given none to sign."

"Unusual," the doctor said, "if true."

"It's true."

"I'm here to examine you," the doctor said after a moment or two. "I have to write a report on your condition."

"I've no complaints," Bukansky told him. "I'm very fit. A mouthful of vodka wouldn't go amiss, however, if you have such a thing in that black bag of yours."

The doctor placed the bag beside him on the bed and opened it. From inside he took a bottle containing some white tablets. Unscrewing the top he shook some into the palm of his hand. "Take these," he said.

"What for?"

"You'll find they'll calm you."

Bukansky smiled. "I'm calm enough already, doctor."

"They'll help you suppress your desire for alcohol. Your craving."

"I have no craving, doctor. And my desire for alcohol is now no more than that of any citizen you might run into on Red Square."

"That could be considered an offensive exaggeration of alcohol problems in our country."

Bukansky laughed. "I'm saying I'm all right, doctor. A couple of months in here have cured me of any craving. Let's get on with the examination, shall we?"

The doctor lifted his hand. "First I would like to discuss with you your attitude to the West."

"What has that to do with a medical man?"

The doctor took out a notebook and silver pencil and scribbled a few lines. "I wanted to ask you," he said, bringing his eyes up from the notebook, "if in any way you have materially altered your attitudes to the West?"

"No," Bukansky said cautiously. "I have no reason to alter my view that the West is an essentially anti-Soviet power grouping. That has always been my view."

"You have not then found, after serious reflection in the Clinic, that your view of the West has changed?"

"Doctor," Bukansky said urgently, "my view has not changed because it has no need to change."

"Ah," the doctor scribbled in his notebook. "But you obviously, Citizen Bukansky, appreciated what the West calls 'the good things in life.'"

"Yes, without considering them the *best* things in life."

"And what would you consider the *best* things in life?"

"Our own Soviet achievements."

"Then why did your magazine, *Novaya Literatura,* spend so much time praising the 'good,' and ignoring the best?"

"Are you going to examine me, doctor?"

"When you have answered my question."

"The magazine, under my editorship, did not take that view."

"You deny it?" the doctor said in apparent astonishment. "I could show you issues of your own magazine that look like a collection of fashion plates for capitalist clothing enterprises in Paris and New York."

"I'm happy to see you, and possibly your wife, read my magazine."

"I studied it," the doctor said coldly. "I found it interesting to note how many references you chose to make to the so-called arts of the German Federal Republic."

"I considered some of their recent architecture and design to be of high quality, especially by their young socialist designers."

Again the doctor bent his head and scribbled.

"This obsession with Western life," he said at length, "clearly remains with you. A form of nostalgia perhaps for the things you've lost."

"The only thing of value that I've lost, doctor, is my freedom."

"In the sense *you* mean it, another Western concept."

"What sort of a doctor are you?" Bukansky said.

He stood up. "My position is senior medical adviser here at the Kirov Clinic. My specialty is psychiatry."

He picked up his bag.

"So the examination is concluded." Bukansky looked at him with contempt.

"The examination is concluded."

"Will I see your conclusions?"

"Of course. As soon as I have determined what treatment is appropriate."

He rapped on the door and a guard outside opened it.

"One moment, doctor," Bukansky stood next to him by the door. "Do I understand that at this point at least I am a patient, not a prisoner?"

"That is true. Any restraint is for your own protection."

"Of course. I am naturally interested in my friends . . ." Bukansky said cautiously.

"Yes?"

"As a patient do I have the right to contact any of them by letter?"

"I will make enquiries."

"Do I have the right to know if any of them have made efforts to contact me?"

"Do you have one, or several persons in mind?"

Bukansky hesitated. "Several."

The doctor's blue eyes stared into his. "No," he said. "Nobody has made any effort whatsoever to contact you."

Bukansky turned away. "Thank you, doctor," he said.

The doctor paused by the door. As if as an afterthought he said: "One more matter I must raise with you, Citizen, before we conclude the examination. I'm sure you are aware of the process of Soviet law in these matters."

"Tell me."

"We have just been conducting, as required by law, a forensic-psychiatric examination of your condition. This is at the legal request of the investigative organs of the State and the procuracy."

"I am comforted, doctor."

"The next stage is for your case to go to court."

"On what charge?"

"But of course there is no charge," the doctor smiled reassuringly. "What the court has to establish is whether or not you are accountable for your actions."

"Which actions?"

"The actions which caused investigative organs originally to ask for your psychiatric examination."

"Do you know a book called *Catch-22*, doctor?"

"A Western book?"

"Yes."

"I am unfamiliar with it."

"Please go on, doctor . . ."

"Your defense counsel . . ."

"I was unaware I had one, or needed one."

"He was appointed by the procuracy at the time of your hospitalization."

"Should he not have discussed matters with me?" Bukansky said. "I might have been able to help."

"It is not desirable, Citizen. I must repeat this is not a criminal case. The court is simply charged with the responsibility of deciding whether or not you are accountable."

"If I'm non-accountable, what happens?"

"You remain in hospital for treatment, of course. But let me continue, Citizen. Your defense counsel had decided to call an important witness in your favor."

"Who is this witness?"

"He has decided to call Lydia Petrovna, your former secretary."

Bukansky said nothing.

"Presumably she will testify to your complete accountability."

"I think she found me sane, doctor, yes."

"You have the right to refuse this witness."

"Why should I do that? I believe she will be prepared to testify in my favor. That's to say in favor of the view that I am not mentally deranged."

"It's true," the doctor conceded, "it would not look good in court if you had rejected such a witness."

"Then I accept."

"Very well, Citizen. Then I, too, will exercise my legal right to a prior examination of the witness."

"What for?" Bukansky tried to cover his alarm.

"We must be satisfied that the witness is not suffering herself from a psychopathic condition."

"You have the right to bring her to one of your hospitals?"

"Undoubtedly. Under RSFR Notarial Law, articles six-six, six-seven, she can first be examined by her own doctor."

"But will anybody tell her that? Will my so-called defense counsel?"

"A Soviet citizen is presumed to be familiar with Soviet Law."

"I see," Bukansky said. "But in any event you will bring her here and examine her?"

"Yes."

"What will you find, doctor?"

"How can I tell," the doctor said, testily. "When I have not yet conducted the examination."

"You must have already made up your mind."

"That is an aggressive slur on my professional standards, Citizen Bukansky."

"I am not prepared to be responsible for any Soviet citizen being brought to this place," Bukansky said.

"You have no choice, Citizen. Under the law I am empowered to conduct an examination."

Bukansky looked at him steadily. "Thank you for explaining the position so clearly to me, doctor. Kindly inform my defense counsel that I reject the witness."

Chapter Twenty-nine

IT WAS A brilliant northern summer evening, the end of a day of intense heat. The men had just returned, in long marching columns, from the woods. Zoya, sweeping out the medical hut, had glanced through the window to see Bubo, Laryssa and Anna talking together on the edge of the parade square. Something in their manner alerted her immediately. Then Bubo began to walk toward the medical hut, his face grim.

Zoya dropped the broom and ran toward the door as Bubo entered. He took her arm firmly. Closing the door behind him, he said, "It's Anton. He struck one of the guards."

Zoya fell back against the wall.

"It was Sergeant Balutin. He was whipping one of the men half to death."

"What will happen?"

"Balutin had him stripped and tied to a tree. He's to stay there until morning."

"The mosquitoes."

Bubo nodded. A man might just, might only just, withstand the swarms of huge Siberian mosquitoes. But by the morning he would be unrecognizable.

Zoya sat on a wooden bench, her head in her hands. When she looked up she had controlled her tears. "The gold ruble," she said. "The old Czar's ruble that Anton's mother smuggled to him. Do you know where it is?"

"It's wedged between the boards in the wall of our hut."

"Can you get it for me?"

He asked no questions. Five minutes later Zoya was standing in the guard hut in front of Sergeant Balutin.

"I can pay you," she said. "Pay you well."

"I have a different woman every night," he sneered. "How can *you* pay me better than that?"

Zoya took a deep breath. "Money," she said. "Gold. A ruble from the old Czar's days."

The sergeant paced the hut. "Let's see it," he said finally.

She knew the risk she was taking. From her waistband she produced the ruble.

"It's against regulations for prisoners to have money," he said.

"Its against regulations for guards to accept gifts."

The sergeant stood before her, considering.

"Too many men saw the prisoner strike me," he said. "I can't release him now."

"Then let *me* go," Zoya said. "Tomorrow morning, when the detail arrives on the site, he'll still be bound to the tree. Nobody will know he wasn't there all night."

Balutin reached out his hand and took the ruble. "I'll escort you through the gate," he said. "Be back before roll call."

It was five miles through the summer woods. Half walking, half running, a blanket tied to her back, food, mosquito netting and ointments in her shoulderbag, Zoya covered the distance in less than an hour.

She found him as Bubo had described, strapped to a tree, naked.

His head jerked from side to side vainly trying to disperse the swarms of huge mosquitoes. His face was distended until the eyes had closed; his body was already raw, the genitals swollen.

She stood before him too shocked to speak.

"Who's that?" he was trying to force open his eyes.

"It's me, Zoya." She drove clouds of mosquitoes from him.

"Zoya . . ." his lips distorted in an attempt at a smile. "Zoya . . ." he repeated as she undid the straps and drew him down onto the soft moss.

Working quickly she pegged out mosquitoe netting around him, then crawled inside, dragging the blanket and her shoulderbag with her.

She was not sure if he was entirely conscious in those first two hours as she gently spread the oils over his face and body. As the sun dropped to its low point on the horizon he drifted into a fitful sleep to awaken rubbing at the swellings on his arms and legs. But his eyes could open now and the outline of his lips seemed slowly to be reforming.

Twice more during that summer night [Zoya recounts], I reapplied the oil to his body as he lay there silently watching me. Perhaps I lingered more than was necessary, but who can blame me? In those moments I was no longer a *zek*. I was a girl in love.

In the early northern dawn we looked at each other, our lips inches apart. The swelling on his face had reduced during the night. He leaned forward and kissed me gently.

"There aren't words to thank you for what you've done," he said.

"You know why I came here, Anton," I said. "I won't pretend I had a choice."

He looked at me without speaking.

"What keeps us apart, Anton," I whispered, "is it memories of your fiancée, your past life?"

"It's our present that keeps us apart, Zoya," he said. "What part can human feelings have in this place?"

"Laryssa loves Bubo," I said. "He loves her."

"Bubo is made of harder stuff than I am, Zoya. For me every day is a struggle not to surrender to this dreadful place."

"But to love someone is not to surrender to Panaka."

He shook his head. "You must be wrong," he said. "It doubles the fear and the compromises that have to be made to be always thinking of another. Beneath his love for Laryssa and his friendship for us, Bubo rests on a rock of hatred for this system. He can never be compromised. Bubo once told me, that if he had one foot in Paradise, he'd withdraw it to take vengeance on Moscow."

"There's more than one way of surrendering to Panaka," I said.

"And more than one way of fighting back." He leaned over and kissed me again. A different, longer kiss. Then we rose and I strapped him again, naked, to the tree.

During that last late summer and autumn of the Soviet Union Carole watched, from a distance, the affair between her husband and Harriet Bennerman develop. She had little interest and even less concern to find any. Occasionally she would discover the bed made with Harriet's ludicrous hospital corners. Once David Butler had tried to tell her, but she had cut him off. She had no wish to know.

Sometime in late September, Jack Bennerman had invited her to lunch at the top of the Rossiya. For half an hour, over a bottle of wine, they had skirted the subject. She could see his exasperation building as she avoided opportunities to begin to talk about Tom and Harriet.

Finally he had said, "Look, Carole, I think you know why I asked you to lunch today. Let's get it out in the open for Christ's sake. Your husband and my wife have got something going between them."

She nodded. "They're having an affair, yes."

"Jesus, that's pretty detached."

"How else can I put it?"

"It doesn't worry you?"

"No."

The waiter brought a plate of dubious stew. It was listed on the menu as *boeuf bourguignonne.*

"I think it's a lot more than just an affair," Bennerman said.

"You think they plan to take it somewhere? Divorces? Marriage?"

"That's the way it's heading, Carole."

"And how do you feel about that, Jack?"

"You want an honest answer, between friends?"

"Yes, preferably."

"When Harriet inherited the money last year," he said carefully, "I was knocked sideways. It's just so goddam much! And every week there'd be new letters from her New York lawyers saying the audit on this or that plant or holding had been completed and she was now worth another hundred thousand dollars more than the last estimate. It was crazy money."

"But?"

"Money's nice to have around. Even crazy money. I don't seem to have so many objections these days."

"You want to stay married to Harriet?"

"I want it all ways, Carole. Who doesn't?"

They both pushed their stew aside and Bennerman ordered a half-pint of vodka.

"If Tom asks for a divorce," Carole said, "that's okay with me. Perhaps I'll even ask him first, I don't know. But I don't want to leave Russia just yet and so I'm happy enough to hang on in."

"So we've both got our reasons for turning a blind eye to what's happening."

"I suppose so."

"We ought to see more of each other, Carole, you and me."

"To go over the latest evidence? No, I don't think so, Jack."

"Just to see each other," Bennerman said.

She looked at him uncertainly. "We see each other on the party circuit almost every week."

He shrugged. "You and me . . ."

"No, Jack."

"You've still got this Russian going?"

"No, that's long finished."

"So why do you want to stay on in Moscow?"

"I don't know, Jack. In many ways I hate the city. I hate the life I have here. I hate the drabness all around me, the queues, the rationing . . . I'm exasperated by Russians in the street or the Metro . . . but I still feel I want to stay. Perhaps it's because I'm part Russian, or part Slav, anyway. I feel there's something happening here. I feel I want to stay to see it."

After she left Jack Bennerman, she walked through Red Square. The Kremlin was no longer open to visitors but she could see from where she stood at the far end of the crenellated wall the rising colorful domes of the churches around her. She was American, she told herself, she didn't believe in anything but a commonsense destiny, demystified, more Anglo-Saxon likelihood than anything else. And yet she could not, standing in Red Square, believe her future lay anywhere else but in this city, or at least in this country. She knew how much her feelings were shaped by the wish to see Letsukov again, but even so she found the idea of a return to her old life intolerable.

Compared with the great dissident trials of the last two or three years, it is sadly true that Bukansky's coming ordeal was exciting little comment in the West. And for Kuba's men that is what counted. For the objectives of the trial were purely domestic. First, while Natalya Roginova remained under household arrest and had not yet been brought to trial, Igor Bukansky would serve as a proxy for her, a warning to any of her supporters who might think the Kuba regime was weakening. Second, the trial was intended to administer to all those in literary authority—publishers, editors and journalists—a timely warning that it was dangerous to stray from the narrow Party route to literature and to indulge in excesses of the imagination which had nothing to do with socialist realism.

The big question mark was Kuletsyn. In less than a year his fame in the West had grown prodigiously. *To Be Preserved Forever* had been translated into almost every known language. In the English-speaking world the paperback sales were now being counted in millions; in Germany, Italy, France and Scandinavia the novel was a massive best-seller, so that even under the Kuba regime, Kuletsyn's position had become almost impregnable.

But for almost six months now he had refused to speak to anyone. Western journalists received a flat refusal when seeking interviews. It was believed that he was writing a second book. But nobody could be sure. Those relatively few western newspapers which reported the coming trial of Bukansky, however, had no doubt that only Kuletsyn's intervention would ensure the worldwide publicity that Bukansky would need if he were not to end his days in a labor camp.

It was for this reason that on a late autumn morning Lydia took the train from Moscow's Belorussia Station out to the village of Barskoye beyond the Lenin Hills. She had pondered her strategy for several days. He was, after all, her uncle. If she arrived at the little station at Barskoye and telephoned him, he would be bound to see her.

The train as usual was late. But it was a matter of indifference to the stationmaster. In the hot summer days he sat outside the station hut, his leather cap tipped over his eyes, a glass of *kvas* raised to his lips. For the rest of the year he remained inside, except on Mondays when a mail package would be hurled from the guard's van.

Today he stood in the clapboard hut watching the train pull away. He sucked on his long-stemmed pipe. For a few moments he allowed himself to think of the train's destination. Minsk, the Belorussian capital . . . he had fought there in the war, retreating and advancing. Forty years ago, as a 19-year-old village boy. To this day he wore his long gray Army greatcoat, the one they'd issued for the great parade in Moscow. It was tattered now around the sleeves and belted with an old necktie, stained and with a few buttons missing, most of them even. But it enabled him to identify himself as an old soldier, who had drawn the lot of honor and taken part in that great Red Square parade before Joseph Stalin.

Out of the corner of his eyes the stationmaster saw a movement. He knew immediately who this Western-dressed young woman had come to see. Who else but the famous author who lived in the woods beyond the village? The fact that his book was unavailable in the Soviet Union never occurred to the stationmaster. He assumed it was queued for in all the big Moscow bookshops. Any author who had Western journalists telephoning him all the time could hardly have less of a success in his own capital city.

The telephone link, he explained to the young woman, was an ex-Army fitting. Before the war there had been no telephone in Barskoye. Now there were two, one to the chairman of the collective farm and the other to the Comrade Writer Kuletsyn. He opened the connection and vigorously turned the handle on the side of the instrument.

He handed the old brass-ended telephone to Lydia. She listened for a few minutes to the strange emptiness of the line, then the receiver was lifted from the hook.

"Yes?" She recognized her uncle's voice.

"Uncle Valentin, it's Lydia, your niece . . ."

"Yes." She could see the frown.

"I'm at the station at Barskoye village. I want to come out to see you."

"Out of the question."

"It's vitally important."

"I'm working, Lydia."

"You know why I want to see you?"

"No."

"I have to come, somebody depends on it." She put down the phone and turned to the stationmaster who had been openly listening on the extension.

"Can I get a taxi?"

"He doesn't want you to come," the stationmaster said gravely. "The wishes of an important writer should be respected."

Lydia gave him a frosty, Moscow glare. "A taxi, is there one?"

"That facility we don't possess as yet," the stationmaster said.

"How far is the house?"

The stationmaster hesitated. He was impressed by the tone. He decided it would not be wise to fall foul of so imperious a young woman.

"How far is the house?" she repeated.

"A half-mile or so on the other side of the village. And the road is still good, there's been no rain yet this autumn."

The peasants of Barskoye talked about it for weeks afterward. Estimates of the value of her clothes varied from exaggerated to astronomical. Wise old women said she was an American despite the stationmaster's assurance that she spoke Russian and was the gospodin writer's niece. Some of the men claimed they had definitely seen her on television. This was considered a more reasonable explanation and the event was known henceforth as "the day the television lady came from Moscow."

The road was as the stationmaster had predicted, still hard from the summer, the dust damped down by autumn dews. Lydia followed the track along the edge of the birchwood, astonished at the number of birds flitting across her path, hovering in the air above the meadows or singing among the trees.

She could already smell wood-smoke when she heard the axe. A small track led off through the wood and she decided to take it. Immediately she was plunged into scented shadow. The sound of chopping was louder now. She walked on over the thick springy ground, her high heels digging deep into the mulch.

The drift of smoke was steel-blue in the shafts of sunlight. Misted by sun and smoke she saw a figure swinging an axe at the base of a dead tree.

He stopped as she called to him and stood waiting for her to pick her way into the clearing.

"I asked you not to come," he said.

"You can spare me a few minutes, Uncle Valentin," she said placatingly.

"You interrupt the rhythm of my work."

"You were chopping trees," she said accusingly.

"It constructs the rhythm of my day's work. It's as much part of working as running a pen across paper."

She thought how bizarre he looked. In the West, she supposed he was already a millionaire, yet he wore old Army breeches and boots and a gray collarless shirt under an open waistcoat. Perhaps he was not allowed to bring his foreign fortunes into the Soviet Union?

"I'm here now," she said. "Offer me a glass of tea at least. It's warm weather for this time of year."

"After the tea you must go."

"Willingly. I can't wait to get back to Moscow."

He gave her a withering look. He disapproved of almost everything about this girl, her morals, her lack of seriousness, her aping of Western fashions, her un-Russianness . . .

"Why have you come to see me?" They were walking side by side through the wood.

"You must know," she said.

"I know nothing of the life beyond Barskoye. What is there to know?"

They passed the fire he had made from the smaller branches of cut trees and the air became suddenly clearer. A wooden hut could be seen at the end of the path, the window and door lintels carved and painted.

"Igor Bukansky is to be put on trial next month."

"Yes?"

She felt a surge of anger. Carefully modulating her voice, she said, "He needs your help."

They reached the hut and he pushed open the door, leading the way inside. It was dark and smelled of flour and kerosene. He opened one of the shutters. "How can *I* be of help? He needs a lawyer, a well-prepared defense."

"You know that that could only reduce a sentence by a few years. No, he needs you to speak out for him."

He stood facing her, his head to one side, his blue eyes sharp above the slightly hooked nose. "Like the Western journalists, you are trying to make of me something that I am not. You are trying to make me into a political influence. I mean political in the narrowest sense. Party political."

"A man's liberty may depend on you speaking for him."

"The maintenance of my own sense of values may depend on my not becoming involved."

She sat down suddenly. She had never liked this man, this remote, posturing uncle, her mother's younger brother. But she knew she had to try.

"Let's not talk about politics or values," she said quietly. "I don't understand your point of view. I only understand simple things. Igor Bukansky is a good man. He has helped many people. Ordinary people like the doorman at our office when his small child needed special treatment for a postoperative infection . . ."

"This has no relevance to our discussion," Kuletsyn said.

"Then tell me what has, Uncle Valentin? I think I must be too young to understand."

He poured tea into two glasses. "Igor Bukansky was once a poet," he said. "Sometime in his youth, he chose a different route. He chose to join the Party, to have Western-style offices, secretaries . . ." he waved his arm toward her, "a country dacha . . . This was his choice. I chose to travel a different, harder route. While he drank champagne, I drank the water from the well, while he flew the world a free man, I was the despised *zek,* the prisoner. But even in the camps I kept my freedom. Even as he traveled the world he lost his."

He had begun to pace the bare wooden floor. "What you are asking is that I give up the freedom, the independence, that I have carefully carved from the hard material of my life. You are asking me to join Bukansky's world. To make a political plea for mercy."

She shook her head.

"A writer must keep his eyes on higher things," he insisted. "His responsibility is not with politics, which is the ephemeral art of the present. His responsibility goes both backward and forward in time. It is to preserve the emotion of the past and construct the spirit of the future."

She was crying.

"You will not understand, my niece, because you have already delivered yourself into Babylonian captivity. For your Western finery you have offered your body to our masters . . ."

"No."

"How can you deny it? The very chains hang round your neck."

A butterfly landed on the windowsill, its large pale-blue wings heaving as if with the efforts of flight.

"Will you speak for Bukansky?" she said.

"I will not."

She stood up. "I beg you," she said.

Kuletsyn stood opposite her, across the table. "Igor Alexandrovich made his choice. I cannot allow it to alter mine."

The sunlight fell on her hair and on the movement of her shoulders. "I've nothing to offer you, have I?"

The butterfly flitted across the room, circling their heads before it disappeared through the door. She took a half-pace toward him.

"How dare you! Get out of here, you whore," he said. "Get out of here and leave me in peace!"

Chapter Thirty

ON SEPTEMBER 18TH, in the preliminary hearing of the closed court in the case of Igor Alexandrovich Bukansky (in absentia) it was judged that the defendant was non-accountable. In the underground newspaper *Iskra* the judgment was condemned as a travesty of justice. In *Pravda* Bukansky was accorded five lines.

After the hearing it was recommended by the doctors who gave evidence that Bukansky should be transferred to Moscow Psychiatric Hospital 36 where facilities existed for the specialist treatment of psychopathic negativism from which the defendant was suffering.

Each week Lydia had applied to the local militia station for the date of his trial. But not until seven days after the hearing had she discovered the trial had already taken place. She had returned to her apartment and sat for over an hour in the deepest depression. Since her visit to her uncle she had not been able to fight off these depressions. Sometimes she would go to bed at six or seven in the evening and stay there until the next morning when it was time to work. She found no interest in television or in friends. She missed Bukansky in ways she never conceived possible. She would wake up in the night crying at the enormity of her helplessness.

The police had not left her alone, either. On most occasions now when she returned home she would find some strange object in the apartment, a man's cap in the bathroom, five or six cigarette ends stubbed out and crushed into the carpet, or worst, most sinister, a glove between the sheets of the made-up bed. It was, she knew, the KGB's doing, but it worked. She found more and more that she preferred not to come home to the apartment. Instead she would stay with her elder sister on the other side of Moscow.

Within a few weeks she found herself unable to go to work. She ate little now but drank at least a half-liter of vodka every evening to help her go to sleep. Every Wednesday she returned to the militia station to ask for permission to visit the hospital and every Thursday she went to the hospital with the same request. Each told her it was necessary to seek permission from the other. Her head span after three visits and she returned home to open another bottle. Only now it was a liter bottle and she began drinking earlier in the day.

Her looks and appearance deteriorated, too. Her Western clothes began to lose their sheen, get shabbier. Her makeup, if she used it, would be excessive, a wide gash of red across her mouth. In the suburban area where her sister lived she was now known for her unsteady walk and frequent outbursts of weeping on the streets.

She talked a great deal about him too, until her sister was bored with constantly repeated stories of Igor Bukansky. She had never in any case approved of Lydia's affair with this older man and she made a few half-hearted attempts to introduce her to some young workers in the area. But Lydia was always too indifferent or too drunk to make any impression on them, and her pregnancy was already beginning to show.

Before autumn she was seeing a doctor twice a week. He had forbidden alcohol and prescribed tranquilizers. She had simply taken both.

She was to be seen now in the local vodka store, two fingers held high in the hope someone would share the price of a bottle with her. A few weeks later her sister's husband asked her to leave.

She could not live alone, not in that apartment. Each night she cried her way through a bottle of vodka and passed out on the bed. She dreamed or drunkenly plotted, she no longer knew which, to travel to Barskoye village and burn all her uncle's treasured manuscripts, but alcohol sapped her initiative and her hate.

Not long after it sapped her love, too. At first it became difficult to remember the outline of his face. Then, in a frenzy of frustration, she would pace the apartment forcing herself to remember his full name. Then as she drank more, the details of their life together faded. She would examine her broken, scratched Western shoes admiringly. Or as she stumbled out in the morning, peremptorily require the janitor's wife to inspect the quality of her now torn and stained Paris dress.

No more than a few miles away across Moscow, Igor Bukansky spent his days in the free association room of Psychiatric 36. His fellow patients dribbled and laughed and poked their fingers at him, as he walked among them telling simple jokes or showing childish tricks. Often he thought about Lydia and wondered who now was buying her Western dresses and it was the only time he was unhappy.

He had never been treated with sodium amytal or any of the other possible drugs. Twice he had seen young men being taken down corridors, babbling drunkenly in an attempt to fix and retain their reason. Both young men (he never knew their names) had seemed normal enough when they had stood in line with him to be registered. One he believed to be simply a witness in a coming hearing for a Sverdlovsk dissident, and he thought again of Lydia.

Of course he feared the drugs, but he had long ago spent an evening with his friend Dr. Felperin discussing the nature of the chemicals most favored and rehearsing their effects. Perhaps even then he had been preparing himself for his ordeal.

In the first week at the 36 he had been escorted to a room, more an office than a doctor's surgery, for his reception examination. The doctor had invited him to sit down, then had taken up a pen and begun to write. Without looking up he had asked, "What is the date today, Citizen?"

"I'm not sure," Bukansky said casually. "Sixteenth . . . seventeenth?"

"Ah . . . and what day of the week is it?" The doctor's face was round and smiling, but his lips were thin so that he managed to convey an accurate impression of his total insincerity. For a moment Bukansky studied the pink moon face, unable to restrain his amusement.

"It is Wednesday, doctor."

"Tuesday, Citizen."

"Doctor, today is Wednesday. If, however, you say it is Tuesday, then I agree."

"What is a hundred minus ten?"

"Why do you try to insult me?" Bukansky said casually.

"I ask you a simple question," the doctor was looking at him now, smiling patiently.

"The answer to your question is ninety," Bukansky said.

"Good. What is the meaning of the expression 'you're riding in the wrong sleigh?'"

"You're in the wrong place . . . pursuing the wrong course . . ."

"Do you ever apply it to yourself?"

"Do *you*, doctor?"

The smile disappeared. The doctor looked down at his papers. "I have here a complaint you wrote to Nikita Khrushchev personally. This was in the days when he occupied a position of power in our country."

"I wrote to him, yes."

"Can you remember the content of your letter?"

"I see no need to repeat it since you have it before you."

"But do you remember it, Citizen?"

"I complained in my letter of August nineteen sixty-two that I was being subjected, that's to say the magazine was being subjected, to excessive critical comment from unqualified sources."

"You referred to the Bureau of State Security."

"I did."

"Why did you write the letter?"

"I don't understand your question, doctor."

"Ah . . . it's a simple enough question. What was your purpose in writing the letter?"

"I said I did not understand your question. My meaning is that I did not understand why you asked the question since the answer is in the letter itself." Bukansky spoke as if to a child.

"But what prompted you to write the letter?"

"I was receiving daily batches of mindless criticism . . ."

"Mindless, ah . . ."

"Yes. And if you'd seen that rubbish you, even you, would have agreed it was mindless. I couldn't produce a magazine in those circumstances. I couldn't breathe in those circumstances."

The doctor nodded. "Did you experience this difficulty in breathing before nineteen sixty-two?"

Bukansky stood up and strolled to the door. "I've had enough for today, doctor. You have a limited talent to amuse."

"Patients who prove non-cooperative can be treated in other ways, Citizen."

"The *fiksatsiya,* the chemical straitjacket?"

"A course of drugs, yes."

Bukansky looked down at him for a few moments. "Don't ever find that you've been riding in the wrong sleigh, doctor. To change over when the horses are at full gallop could be very, very dangerous."

At the time [Zoya wrote later] we in the northern and northeastern camps had no idea what was happening in Moscow. The big change in our lives dated from the day Colonel Rospinev became commandant of Panaka. He was small, white-haired and obsessive about his appearance. I remember two things above all about the first day I saw him, the glistening polish on his boots and the angle of his red-topped military cap, tipped slightly backward to give him that extra inch of height. No, I remember three things. The last was that he was carrying a dog-whip. God knows what his orders were, but I'm certain that he never even considered the possibility of an uprising. He would attend morning appel every day, slapping the whip against his polished boots, and he would personally detail the work allocations.

I used to watch from the sick bay window to see what Anton was assigned to that day. I could often see the looks that passed between the guards behind the colonel's back. The point was they never felt safe out in the woods unless there were enough of them with any one detail to back each other up. And there just weren't that number of guards anymore.

Even worse, from their point of view, was that the colonel was splitting the details so that often thirty men would march out with only two guards. And they would be allocated to a cutting zone too far away to shout for help from the next detail. For the prisoners it meant an easier life. Two or three of them would slip away into the birchwood for an hour or two's rest, to be replaced later by the next group when their time was up.

It didn't take me long to realize that our little colonel had his eye on me. Three inspections of the medical hut in one week was enough to show something was brewing.

Laryssa, as you'd expect, encouraged me. "Go on," she said, "he's so small you'd hardly know he was there."

And the truth is, for what I could have got out of it, I might have done it if it weren't for the thought of Anton.

But that, I suppose, is what being in love's all about. Not that I seemed to be getting very much response from the brute.

Of course Bubo knew what the brute was thinking all the time, but I'm sure he'd been forbidden by Anton ever to talk to Laryssa about it. Laryssa had never kept a secret in her life.

Well, that's the way things were. I was chasing one man, and being chased by another. Because by now there was no doubt at all that our little colonel was hot in pursuit. Not only would he make over-frequent visits to the sick bay, but one day he stopped me in the narrow space between the ends of two huts.

I curtsied as you're required to for a camp officer.

He was looking me over. "You're a fine-looking girl, Zoya. I can see camp life suits you," the fool said.

I curtsied again. "Thank you, Comrade Colonel." I made to turn away, but he stopped me, holding the upper part of my arm and slapping his dog-whip against his boot as ever.

"How would you like to go into town, Zoya?" he asked, smiling like a fox.

It was nearly a year since I'd seen the outside of Panaka. My face must have given the answer.

"Good," he said. "I want you to begin collecting the medical supplies yourself from now on. And while you're there, I'll give instructions to the guard to take you to my apartment. My wife has asked me to find a good, clean camp girl to do the heavy washing for her."

He strode off well pleased with himself. For my part I was uncertain. The thought of seeing even dreary Krasibirsk for an afternoon was magical. And the heavy washing was a cheap price to pay for the privilege. But would his wife be there every time? Or would I find one afternoon our little colonel slipping back early from the office?

I longed to talk to Anton about it but I was afraid he would ask me what it had to do with him. So I put up with Laryssa's rolling eyes and on a morning when the birch leaves were glinting gold in the sunlight I climbed up beside the driver of a camp truck and drove out of Panaka on the road to Krasibirsk.

Freedom is a far headier draught than vodka. I sang all the way to

Krasibirsk. In Lenin Square the driver left me to go alone to the Medical Center and for ten delicious minutes I strolled through the streets looking at the girls of my own age, free even in this miserable town.

Of course I was soon seized with bitter resentment. I was sitting on a bench outside the Medical Center. Perhaps it was mostly the excitement of it all, but I watched those other girls and I sobbed my heart out.

A nice old man came along and gave me a Belomors, and sat by my side patting my back while I smoked it. He could tell by my camp clothes that I was a *zek,* but he said nothing except, just as he stood up to go, he looked down and smiled. "Remember one thing at least, girl," he said. "You're young." I think I'm very lucky with my old men.

I collected the pathetic allocation of medical supplies and rejoined the driver in the square. His breath was smelling of *kvas* and I just hoped he hadn't taken vodka with it. It was a long drive back to Panaka.

The colonel's apartment was large but barely furnished; the colonel's wife was small and overdressed. She had a thin slit of a mouth, a sharp nose and receding chin which contrived to make her look more foxlike than her husband. And she hated me on sight.

I tackled the washing in the copper tub with a will and was required afterward to scrub the bare board floors of the long hallway. It was made clear to me that I was not allowed into the kitchen unless she herself was present. She offered me no food, no tea.

I did not sing on the long drive back. I was the victim of the most acute depression I had felt since coming to Panaka. And I was sure that, in some curious way, that heartless woman in the apartment was as responsible as the afternoon's reminder of my loss of freedom.

But Anton was at Panaka. And my friends.

It was at this point that Semyon Kuba decided that he was strong enough to dispose once and for all of the threat still posed by Natalya Roginova. Or perhaps he decided that he would never be strong enough until he had. One of the most interesting documents of that period was an account by Roginova of her single interview with Semyon Kuba during the period of her imprisonment:

I was taken from my own place of imprisonment to one of Kuba's dachas on a pleasant soft autumn morning. Even through the darkened glass of my own car I remember the sunlight on the vast clumps of alders along the country lanes and the astonishment of the peasants in the villages as our convoy swept through. It was clear that Kuba had decided I was too dangerous to be exposed to the main highways.

Semyon Trofimovich greeted me at the door of his timber dacha looking like nothing so much as a benign country landowner of the last century. I

was led into a small office with plain planked floors and two armchairs
arranged facing each other.

I had not been too seriously deprived of information during my
imprisonment. I was well aware of the principal developments of the
Kubaschina, the vast increase in the labor camp population, bread
rationing, fuel restrictions, the notorious Labor Direction Law which was
now forcing young Transcaucasians and Central Asians to work in the
factories of Russia and the Ukraine.

We sat in the two facing armchairs.

"The time has come," Kuba said, filling his pipe, "to regularize your
position." He gave me a friendly, browned-toothed smile.

"You mean, to have me shot?"

The smile faded. "There are more than enough charges I could bring
against you."

"You don't have enough support from the Party in the national
republics or enough support from the younger Army generals to shoot
me, Semyon Trofimovich," I said, "or I would be dead already. You're
looking for a means of disposing of me other than by shooting. What are
you proposing?"

He fiddled with his pipe, lit it, watched the cinder glow in the bowl and
drew on it with an air of great satisfaction. To anybody who had known
Stalin it was an old trick. But Kuba's preoccupation was not with the
functioning of his pipe.

"I'm proposing," he said at length, "a statement of error. A statement
made by you before the Central Committee in special session."

"What form should the statement take?"

"It could be quite general," Kuba said. "It should mention your failure
to appreciate the demands of the national republics for greater protection
against Western-inspired bourgeois nationalist movements."

"What else?"

"It should state that you now see that the establishment of the national
parade divisions in each republic was an insult to the conception of a
Soviet Army."

It was easy enough for me to see now in which direction Kuba's worries
lay.

"Is that all?" I asked him.

He began the long process with his pipe again. I waited for what was
coming next.

"Your recantation," he said, "should end with a call for a stronger
leadership. It should end with a call to appoint me First Secretary of the
Party." He paused. "And President of the Soviet Union."

I must have smiled because he smiled back.

"So you still need my support," I said. "Even now."

"After you make the statement you will be assigned an important ministry. Agriculture or Fuel Supply."

"There will be no statement." I said.

"You refuse?" Cinders showered onto his uniform jacket.

"I refuse."

"Then you will be sent for trial."

"As a Western agent?"

"Yes."

"You'll get no confession from me, Semyon Trofimovich. And without a confession you will be back where you started."

Kuba stood up. "I don't need a confession from you," he said. "I'll have a confession from someone else, equally damaging. His confession will leave the judges no alternative but to indict you immediately afterward."

He could only mean one man—Bukansky.

Chapter Thirty-one

IN EARLY SEPTEMBER a site was carefully chosen for a meeting which Semyon Trofimovich Kuba considered (rightly as it transpired) as the most important of his life.

Built overlooking the Black Sea just west of Odessa, by an eccentric American architect named George Washington Baxter, the Royal American Hotel, as Baxter had chosen to call it, had all the florid elegance of a fin-de-siècle Chicago cathouse.

The very isolation which had originally deprived it of a thriving clientele guaranteed it against requisition for worker housing in the early days of the Revolution. It had been, briefly, a brigade headquarters for the British interventionist force and wineglasses and beer mugs can to this day sometimes be found in London antique shops bearing the legend "Royal American Hotel, Odessa."

But apart from these early losses to military souvenir hunters, the Royal American stood untouched, although decaying, into the 1930s until, some few years before the war, the First Secretary of what was then the Tatar Soviet Socialist Republic took over the building as his dacha. But before the resumption of peace and plenty, Stalin's deportation of the Tatarpeople had left no role for the First Secretary.

Lavrenty Beria was the next occupant, persuaded by one of his local satraps that the now nameless building should be converted to a school for training senior security staff.

A renovation program was put underway. Stonework was repointed, roofs and gutters renewed, broken windows replaced. Inside the building cherry red carpeting was cleaned and found to be in surprisingly good condition. When the new curtains were hung and rotting mattresses replaced, George Washington Baxter would have had no difficulty in recognizing his original interior decorations.

But in 1953 Lavrenty Beria was executed in one of Khrushchev's swift steps to power, and the Royal American Hotel was once again deprived of a function.

Thus it was that the Royal American, its former name still etched in stonework across the bar, the stars and stripes still carved in mahogany on the ornate newel posts, passed through the possession of the head of KGB, mostly unused, until a subordinate of General Semyon Kuba selected it, as suitably neutral ground, for the private conference of Central Soviet Asian party leaders he called in October of that year.

The government caterers moved in from Odessa. A full staff was supplied by the local KGB directorate, guards were posted and a specialist staff from Moscow wired each room.

Bizarre as was the setting of the conference, for General Kuba, the outcome was vital. The six men invited were the leading Party figures in the most important Transcaucasian and Central Asian republics of the Soviet Union: the Caucasians—Georgia, Armenia and Azerbaijan; and the Central Asians—Kazakstan, Uzbekistan and Turkmenistan. Among the leaders, only one, from Kazakstan, was a Slav, reflecting the regrettable political necessities of the last few years.

The first session had been arranged for the afternoon at the conclusion of a banquet luncheon at which Kuba's most faithful associate, Minister Bukin, would be host. General Kuba himself would join them for the afternoon session.

In the still florid dining room they sat at a long table, the heavy cloth concealing mahogany legs carved with intertwined erotic figures. After caviar and rack of lamb, Bukin began the toasts: to the Union, to the nationalities, to each of the six guests in turn. Bukin knew exactly what Kuba expected of him as cheerleader for the afternoon's conference. But then so did the six men seated around the table. They responded to each toast. But offered none themselves.

At 3:30 P.M. Kuba's convoy of automobiles drew up outside the dining-room windows and a few minutes later an aide opened the dining-room door.

Mikoyan, the Armenian, a nephew of former Deputy Premier Anastas Mikoyan, has left this account:

For myself I remember Joseph Stalin well. Family connections, one great-uncle, a deputy premier, another the designer of the MIG airplanes, gave me access to many Kremlin occasions even when I was only sixteen or seventeen. Naturally Stalin dominated every event at which he was present. Some things about him I remember; the yellow teeth when he smiled, the strange side-to-side walk as if each leg in turn was shorter than the other, his habit of surreptitiously (as he thought) wiping his nose with the back of his hand, his appalling Georgian accent, the way he would make jokes about having people shot. But some other things I remember: how he charmed foreigners just by pretending to listen to their opinions about the Soviet Union and how the whole of Moscow fell silent with dread when his death was announced.

He was a great man, make no mistake about it. My Uncle Anastas once said to me, "Only great men are immune to the suffering of others." But then he was a man, *the* man, of his times. And in his times suffering was part of the nature of the beast.

Why am I talking of Joseph Stalin? Because as we sat there after lunch that day and the door was flung open to admit General Kuba, it was Joseph Vissarionovich I saw in the doorway, short, in plain uniform, a hooked pipe beneath a heavy mustache. It was deliberate, of course, right down to the rolling walk as he approached the table and the warmth of his smile. He was here to listen to our opinions, and like Stalin with the foreigners he would no doubt listen, pulling on his pipe. But I at least knew that would be the end of it. For the moment he needed our support. So be it, he must be made to pay.

We retired to the conference room with coffee and Armenian brandy. "Better than the French," Kuba toasted me.

We began with a speech from Mikhail Bukin. He dealt with the immediate past. He had moved from cheerleader to trumpet blower. From the day of the funeral, he said, the Soviet Union's path was clearly marked. Before us, a matter of four or five years ahead, we could all see the time when the Soviet Union would be by far the mightiest power on earth.

This, we all saw, was a restatement of Stalin's dream of the 1950s, of Khrushchev's boast of the 1960s, and of Brezhnev's claim of the 1970s.

Targets for the new five-year plan were to exceed the United States in almost every area of production. Gross national product would climb by a prodigious ten percent. The military budget alone would expand from seventeen to twenty-one percent.

Throughout this self-deluding litany, Kuba puffed his pipe, nodded agreement or confirmation and occasionally looked across at one of us and raised his eyebrows as a target percentage was mentioned as if to say, "There, you doubters, what d'you think of that?"

From this image of a halcyon future, Bukin passed on to the purpose of the conference. Party organization would have to be strengthened to achieve those massive economic goals. There could be no place for anyone who toyed with the idea of statism.

In the months since Natalya Roginova's arrest, statism (from status quo) had become the accepted term within the Party for what was taken to be her view: namely that the Soviet Union should shed some of its most burdensome foreign policy commitments and concentrate on social and technological improvements in vital areas of the economy and Soviet life.

"Only a powerful, dominant Party can lead a powerful, dominant nation," was Bukin's slogan. I watched Kuba nod judiciously and flick a few grains of hot ash from his jacket in the way I'd seen Stalin do a dozen times.

Then Bukin came to the heart of the matter. Collective leadership was a principle we all endorsed, he said. But to be effective a troika has to have all horses pulling the same way. In the Politburo the collective leadership was hesitant because, since the justified disgrace of Roginova, the Party had been headless. Nearly a year after the funeral we were still without a Chairman of the Party and a President of the Soviet Union.

Statist elements, Bukin said, in the highest bodies in the Soviet Union, had consistently blocked the election of Semyon Trofimovich Kuba to the positions which analysis of the problem proved were rightly his. The future demands that the guiding hand of Semyon Trofimovich should be unfettered.

The future insists, he went on, that First Secretaries of the Republics play a fuller part in the guidance of affairs. I refer, he said pointedly, to an enlargement of the Politburo to include the most senior Party members in the republics.

Ourselves, of course, he meant. At the end of the speech, Bukin was red-faced and sweating. Every word had been carefully chosen and Soviet men that we all were, we knew precisely what was on offer. For us, a place as members of the highest council in the land. For Kuba, our support in his election to General Secretary of the Party and for the purge of Roginova's supporters which would inevitably follow.

There was no time for consideration. While we all sat around the table applauding the speech, each one of us was desperately calculating his own position. Each man had only one objective, not to leave himself at the end of the conference as one of a minority against Kuba. That way lay the knock in the night once Kuba's purge began.

And yet I think it would be true to say that of the six representatives of the Nationalities present, not one favored the elevation of Kuba. We had all received a visit from Natalya Roginova in the days before her arrest, and I believe every one of us had pledged ourselves to the course she had outlined.

Perhaps here in the outlying regions of the U.S.S.R. we saw things more clearly than in Moscow. Certainly Roginova encouraged us to think so. We knew that plan *targets* were not steel ingots, or bushels of wheat or barrels of oil. We knew that the wonders of production achieved in the hard years of Stalin's reign could never be achieved again after the demythologizing of the Soviet ideal which Khrushchev's attack on Stalin had made inevitable.

At least, and this every man around the table kept to himself, we knew that these targets could not be reached without a fundamental reshaping of Soviet society. And that is what Natalya Roginova had offered us. After Stalin, Lenin was to be dethroned, and perhaps after him, Marx himself. What she had offered was a true federation of the peoples of Stalin's Empire, an opportunity to jump clear of the past, ahead even of the present. At least, this much she had said to me. But what had she said to the others?

And now, as Semyon Trofimovich leaned forward to speak, we all knew that we were being pressed back in time, to a past we no longer believed in.

It fell to me to answer first. I saw the stem of the pipe, gray-wet with saliva, point crookedly across the table.

"Comrade Mikoyan," Kuba said formally. "Let us have first an Armenian view of these great issues."

I spoke desperately, trying to gauge the likely response of the others. The only one I felt at all sure of was Bashmani the Uzbek with whom I'd had a cautious, skirting conversation a month earlier. All the rest kept their eyes down. By not so much as a pursed lip did they register that they heard my words.

"None of us can be unaware of the difficulties with which the members of the Politburo have had to contend since death removed a firm hand from the tiller," I began. "In the Armenian Republic the inevitable introduction of bread rationing has strengthened disaffected nationalist-bourgeois elements. Party recruitment programs have fallen well short of target in each of the last two quarters and civic discipline has reached an unprecedented low."

I saw Kuba shake his head angrily. His own KGB were responsible for the maintenance of civic order. He must have known well what had been happening in Armenia in the last two months.

"All this," I continued, "reflects just those leadership conditions which Comrade Bukin has outlined."

A nod of agreement now from Kuba.

"Weaknesses in the Party structure must be removed forthwith."

The Uzbek Bashmani looked across at me, his round Asiatic face expressionless.

"Every Communist must see the truth of Comrade Bukin's analysis. A united Party must lead a united nation."

Bukin frowned, wondering whether that was precisely what he had said.

"To the great end that Comrade Bukin revealed to us in his speech, the inclusion of the senior Party leaders of the republics in the Politburo must greatly strengthen the collective leadership under Semyon Trofimovich's guiding hand."

Everybody present was aware that I had said nothing about an endorsement of Kuba as General Secretary of the all-Union Party. But on one issue I had to be clear first.

"It would be an error to disguise from ourselves the disagreements of the immediate past," I said. "I think all Party leaders would agree that Natalya Roginova still commands a certain following in the . . . lower ranks of our national Party organizations."

"Natalya Roginova is a broken reed," Bukin said angrily.

"Nevertheless it would be helpful to know the Politburo's intentions toward her."

Bashmani nodded agreement. The other delegates allowed themselves a judicious pursing of the lips.

Kuba leaned forward. In a voice meant to convey certainty, he said, "Natalya Roginova will be brought to trial for anti-State activities. In particular, for her formation of the national divisions which have damaged the concept of unity in the Soviet Army."

"Is she prepared to confess her errors?" Bashmani asked quickly.

"There's no necessity," Kuba said. "The confession of the renegade Igor Bukansky will produce all the evidence needed that her activities were guided by Western governments."

"Treason is a capital charge," Bashmani said.

"A capital charge," Kuba nodded grimly. "She will receive a capital sentence."

We knew now which way we must go, we Party leaders. Around the table no man doubted Kuba's will to power. But it was Bashmani again who opened that small chink in Kuba's armor.

"Bukansky," he said, "has of course already confessed."

Bukin shot a quick, worried look at Kuba.

The KGB general smiled his brown-toothed smile. "Accept my assurances that he will, Comrades."

I stepped into the breach. If Bukansky had not yet confessed, we still had time, time not to change the endorsement Kuba required from us, but at least to extort a concession.

"I must now speak for everyone present from the republics," I said.

For the first time the heads rose, the lines of their mouths were tense with fear.

"I have spoken of our increasing difficulties in the autonomous republics. In particular I have spoken of the inevitable introduction of bread rationing. But you should know, Semyon Trofimovich, that there is one issue in all the southern republics more threatening to good order and Komsomol recruitment programs even than bread. That is the issue of the Penal Brigades."

Bukin glanced again at Kuba, but the general kept his eyes upon me, puffing clouds of smoke which almost obscured his face.

"Semyon Trofimovich, it is a matter of fact that in the last three years the Soviet Army has experienced its own disciplinary problems. We know and understand the causes. Conscripted soldiers from the southern republics are often less technically educated and always less familiar with the Russian language than Baltic or Ukrainian or Belorussian recruits. The strain therefore falls on them. It is a widespread subject of anti-Soviet rumor mongering that raw recruits have been disciplined for failing to understand orders given in the Russian language."

Bukin leaned forward. "I am unable to see in what way this affects the issue we were discussing," he said. "As chairman of the conference . . ."

"Let Comrade Mikoyan speak," Kuba growled.

"Thank you, Semyon Trofimovich," I said. "The issue here, Comrade Chairman," I turned to Bukin, "is precisely the issue you analyzed: the need for strength and unity in the Party structure. I have heard of Komsomol leaders taking dissident and anti-Party attitudes after release from military service."

I strove to address the hanging heads around me. "Comrades, we know that for every Armenian or Georgian or Uzbek who serves in a Penal Brigade, a whole Armenian or Georgian or Uzbek family becomes disaffected.

"And how many are now serving in Penal Brigades? Is it a hundred thousand? Or two hundred thousand? I know in some of the other republics the situation is worse than in my own. But unless we grant nothing less than a General Amnesty the all-Union Party unity which we seek is a chimera."

The hanging heads jerked upward. Bukin scowled. Kuba twisted his heavy lips round the stem of his pipe. I had made my point. The price of our support should be a General Amnesty to the Penal Brigades.

Why did I do it? I'm an Armenian first and foremost and I don't see the sense or justice of imprisoning Armenians because they don't speak Russian. But we Armenians are a practical race. I had read the KGB reports, I had spoken to the peasants in the hills. Whatever ignited the nationalist feelings of these few years remains a mystery. But there was no mystery about the fact that the Penal Brigades were fanning the flames. And where would I be if the house caught fire? I, the chief Soviet representative in Armenia?

Bashmani spoke next in, as it happens, heavily accented Russian:

"Comrade Chairman, I endorse the words of yourself and Comrade Mikoyan. Party unity in the autonomous republics is threatened by the existence of the Penal Brigades. I will not mince words. In Tashkent people speak openly of slave labor. Returnees claim that in their Penal Brigade there was hardly a Slav to be seen. Conditions are such that men will do anything for food. In these conditions longer and longer sentences are being handed out. Even worse than men returning with their stories of the penal camps are those who do not return.

"You know that in Uzbekistan we are conducting a campaign against religion. We have agitprop units regularly visiting the villages. But the enemy has chosen his ground cleverly. He tells the peasants that the penal camps are against the word of Allah. Are you surprised if the ignorant peasants believe him?"

In the end only the Georgian First Secretary hesitated to commit himself. Bukin, carefully watching Kuba's reaction, said it was, in the interests of Party unity, an issue which should receive serious consideration. But Bashmani showed more courage than any of us.

"It cannot receive further consideration, Comrade Chairman. It is the subject of Party Decision. It is agreed that the unity we all seek, under the guiding hand of Semyon Trofimovich, cannot be achieved while this issue stands in our way."

There, it was out in the open: a General Amnesty now and Kuba would get the endorsement he needed to defeat the waverers in the Politburo—as soon as the Roginova trial was successfully concluded.

Semyon Trofimovich prodded at the tobacco in his pipe bowl. "The present figure for all Penal Brigades," he said, "is four hundred thirty-four thousand men."

Even the Georgian gasped.

Kuba nodded to himself. "Obviously we cannot declare a General Amnesty and send them home overnight. The first step would be to improve conditions in the penal camps. The second, to issue a general order that military personnel must no longer be sent to outside punishment camps.

"As for the timing and implementation of the Amnesty, the November 7th celebration of the Revolutionary Anniversary would be the ideal moment. It would serve to link Party history with an act of mercy. But this timetable imposes harsh burdens on our camp administrations. Preparations for release and transport would have to be seen by the prisoners to be far advanced. I myself would prefer May Day next as the date for the announcement.

He glanced round the room. The others stared ahead, stonily. "Perhaps not," he said ruminatively. "Perhaps this is something we must put behind us. There will be no amnesty for politicals, of course." He paused. "November 7th, then. I will issue instructions."

So we eight men around a table in the former Royal American Hotel, Odessa, all unwittingly set in train the stupendous events of that winter.

But whether Semyon Kuba was to receive from us the Party and Presidential authority which would enable him to ride the tiger, depended on the will of one man—Igor Alexandrovich Bukansky, Patient of State Psychiatric Hospital 36, Moscow.

The Swans Fly West

Chapter Thirty-two

I WAS RIGHT about the little colonel [Zoya continues her story]. After the second or third visit, he came up to the truck just as we were about to leave for Krasibirsk. Very casually he handed me a key. "That's to the apartment," he said. "My wife's away this afternoon. Let yourself in and tackle the washing. I want no slacking," he added with what he hoped was a twinkle in his eye.

Krasibirsk no longer depressed me. I hated the stares at my camp uniform, but I would sometimes meet the old man as I took my ten minute walk around the little town and he would buy me a few slices of sausage if there was any in the shops or a half loaf to chew on. From him I learned for the first time that bread was now rationed.

I also learned that he, too, had been a *zek,* sentenced to ten years under Stalin and then to ten years exile in Krasibirsk. By the time he was free, he said, he had no longer any wish, even to leave Krasibirsk, where he had worked as a carrier, carting goods by horse wagon often over vast distances to townships even further east.

He said that Siberia, this land of death and chains as the writer Gorky had called it, had a strange hold over him.

I was grateful to him because he succeeded, in those few minutes on two or three occasions, to make of Siberia something more than just a place of dread. He talked about the great virgin swamp and woodland, the taiga, a thousand miles deep, four and a half thousand miles long. He talked about the birch and larch and willow and cherry trees with the love of a man who had walked freely among them, his feet flattening the spring crystal flowers that grew among the moss.

He told me, too, about the native-born Sibiriaks, not the Gulag spawn as he contemptuously referred to the people of Krasibirsk, but the people who came from Russia by force or choice over the last 200 years and are now so completely Siberian that their folklore is from the Tatars and their songs are convict songs.

To him this was the true meaning of Siberia, the land of the *raskolniks,* the dissenters, the free spirits.

But it would not seem so, he conceded, to me, a camp girl, looking from behind the wire at Panaka.

I went to the apartment and let myself in. To tell you the truth I was terrified that the old woman would come back and find me there. I know she wasn't expecting me because I had to collect the washing from the linen bin and strip the sheets off the bed myself. Usually she had it all ready for me.

I had finished the linen bin ten minutes after I arrived. I was working fast, determined if possible to get out before the colonel arrived back. I hurried into the bedroom and crossed to the unmade bed. There were some papers lying on the crumpled counterpane and I picked them up to put them aside. I had actually placed them on a small table next to the bed before I realized what I had read. The heading, in red letters, had spelled out the words *General Amnesty!*

I think my legs actually buckled with excitement as I snatched up the papers. Then the most awful disappointment flooded me as I read the subheading: *A General Amnesty for Penal Brigades.*

Conditions were to be immediately improved in all Gulag areas. Kraslag orders were to transfer military prisoners to Panaka One in order to reduce overcrowding in Panaka Two, Three, Four and Five.

I heard the outer door click and my eyes flew down the page. Politicals and criminals (they were *not* included in the amnesty) from Panaka One were to be evacuated to East Cape! The furthest, most dreaded camp complex in all Siberia.

I knew the colonel was standing in the doorway. I placed the papers on the side table and stood up.

He was white with rage. If he'd had his dog-whip with him he would have beaten me on the spot. As it was he paced the room screaming threats and abuse.

I was trembling with fear. Quite obviously these orders were intended to be a closely guarded secret until the amnesty day.

He could have had me shot on some pretext, and I'm not really sure why he didn't. Not because he was still thinking of getting me into bed, all thoughts of that nature had clearly flown from the mind.

Perhaps he knew I was popular in the camp and that a formal execution might spark off trouble. Then again a formal execution would mean a report to Kraslag or even Gulag headquarters. God knows why, but suddenly the little man's attitude changed and he invited me into the kitchen and gave me milk and sausage.

The General Amnesty, he explained, was a high-priority secret. That was only the two levels below the most important secrets in the Soviet Union, he added with visible pride. He had realized by now that I did not know the date of the coming amnesty and I think this fact influenced his attitude.

I stuttered out that I had read that we politicals were to be sent to the East Cape.

He nodded in a fake sympathetic way. Up there he said the purga blows and anybody caught out in it is finished in minutes. "But . . ." he lifted a finger, ". . . I think I can see a way out for you, Zoya," he mused almost to himself.

I had never in my life seen such a vain, frightened little man. He made me feel less frightened myself.

"Conditions are to be improved for the military prisoners. You saw that in the report?"

I nodded.

"I am detailing a shock-brigade of carpenters to build latrines at Panaka Five immediately . . ."

"A shock-brigade of carpenters!" How I had come to despise these terms! His shock-brigade would be a resentful gaggle of *zeks* with hardly a carpenter among them. The lies in our system went deep.

"They will also be building a medical hut. That hut will have to be staffed, Zoya. You understand me?"

He was actually offering me a deal!

"If I went to Panaka Five, how long would it be for?" I felt brazen now, not in the least afraid of him.

"I can't tell you that, can I?" He smiled apologies. "High-priority secret, remember."

"I would need help there."

"You would. An assistant."

"Two," I said.

He blinked.

"The medical responsibility would be heavy," I said pompously.

He nodded. "Very well. Two assistants."

I could put it to Anna and Laryssa tonight. But not unnaturally, I had another thought in mind. "The shock-brigade of carpenters, where will they come from?"

He seemed to find the question perfectly reasonable. "They will be chosen from the best workers in Panaka One."

"The only *zeks* I would trust to build a medical hut that didn't fall down in the first wind is hut forty-seven," I said.

I was leaning against the stove now, drinking my milk. For the first time I saw what fear of an even higher authority does to men in authority themselves. I might have been a carpenter-engineer discussing the problem with him.

He took out his notebook and made a note of hut 47. Then he stood up straight and cleared his throat a few times. "You understand that if anybody at all learns of the General Amnesty before I announce it, I will have you shot," he said.

I knew now he didn't mean it. But I also knew enough to make an abject apology for reading his orders, and to give him a promise of secrecy which I had no intention of keeping.

He looked at his watch. Frowning, his lips moved, calculating . . . My heart sank as he nodded to himself.

"A glass of vodka, Zoya," he said. "To put the seal on our little accord."

He poured vodka into two large glasses. We stood opposite each other in the kitchen and drank.

"You were very lucky it was me who found you reading the document, you realize that, Zoya?"

"Yes, Colonel."

"Lucky because I don't mind admitting that I've taken quite a liking to you since I became Commandant."

He moved across to where I was standing. Any reasonable man would have seen that the mere difference in our heights made seduction laughable.

He reached out and hooked a finger into the waistband of my trousers. "I would go so far, Zoya, as to say that I've been very much looking forward to an opportunity to be alone with you."

I could feel the tug of his finger, pulling me toward him. I resisted cautiously.

"You know what I mean, Zoya?"

"Yes, Colonel," I said unhappily.

He increased the pressure and drew me forward. His other hand snaked round my waist. On tiptoe he kissed me on the side of my neck.

"Such a tall girl," he murmured. Then releasing me, he took my hand

and led me into the salon. He pointed to the huge sofa from some other world, its stained red velvet outlined by scrolled mahogany.

He came down beside me and began fumbling at my shirt. Disgust made me tremble.

"Relax, relax," he muttered, "no need to be afraid of Lavrenty Andreivich . . . there . . ." Painfully, he grasped my breast.

With more skill than he showed in his lovemaking he hooked the heel of one boot within the instep of the other and drew it off. Then with his stockinged toes, eased the second boot down to a position where he could shake it free.

I, poor wretch, was supposed to be unaware of this maneuver until he leapt suddenly to his feet, tore off his uniform jacket and began to unbutton his military breeches.

"Take your clothes off, girl," he snarled at me, pointing jerkily with his free hand at about the level of my waistband.

I was not a virgin. Few Russian girls of my age are. But I was not very experienced, either. What he saw on my face, or thought he saw, I shall never know. Perhaps all his middle-aged desire flooded from him, or perhaps he was even further enflamed by what he interpreted as virginal diffidence.

I shall never know because at that moment two long bursts of a truck's klaxon sounded in the street outside.

Can you ever feel sorry for a brutal little bigot like that colonel? Perhaps I'm pretending to myself.

There was nothing I could do. I stood there, fully dressed, while the colonel dragged up his breeches, pulled his jacket on with one hand while trying to button himself with the other. When the colonel's lady entered the apartment he had one boot half on flapping like an expiring fish on the carpet.

She struck out at me as I ran past her, bloodying my nose, to the great amusement of the driver waiting in the street below.

Russians love a scene. All the way back to the camp he would break into bellows of laughter, causing the truck to swerve dangerously from side to side on the road until he succeeded in controlling himself.

It was late when Zoya arrived back at Panaka. The guard escorted her to the door of her hut and with another bellow of laughter locked her inside. She stood for a moment or two in the darkness listening to the even breathing of the hundred and twenty women around her. The Far Cape was a fearful prospect. Some of the women had been *zeks* in Stalin's days and knew the East. From the stories they told, perhaps exaggerated with the perverse pride of old *zeks,* few returned whole in body, practically none in spirit.

She felt her way along the retaining timbers of the line of plank bunks until she reached the corner. Ducking under the blanket she felt free of the fetid air of the main hut, although the air in their small corner could smell no different.

Laryssa was awake immediately. With a gentle shake Zoya woke Anna. She desperately wanted to tell them the full story of the afternoon, but she concentrated only on the all-important details. First the news of the General Amnesty, then that to improve the conditions for the Penal Brigade Panaka One was to be taken over by them. The criminals and politicals, they themselves, were to be transferred to the East Cape. Unable to see anything but the gray outline of their faces, she still felt their horror in the grip of their hands on her arm. Quickly she explained that the day of departure at least could be delayed. And maybe for Anton and Bubo, too.

Laryssa rolled a few shreds of *mahorka* in a piece of paper and lit it. "Surely it's madness to volunteer for the Penal Brigade's camp?" she said. There was no lightness in her voice now.

She handed the cigarette to Anna. Zoya watched the glowing end warm her lips and chin. "I think Zoya's right," Anna whispered. "Anything that delays our transfer east, we should take."

The three women sat in silence passing round the soggy roll of paper.

"If Bubo goes, I go," Laryssa said finally.

"If Bubo goes it will be because Anton has decided to go," Zoya said. "In that case, I go."

Anna took the last draw on the cigarette and crushed it out on the plank of her bunk. "I don't have a man to follow anymore," she said. "So I'll follow you."

That night the three women slept together in one double bunk. During the night they all woke frequently and pressed each other's hand and asked, "Are you all right?" Even in that short night, dawn was a long time coming.

At first light Zoya left for the medical hut where each morning she would wash and drink tea before the sick parade which took place immediately after roll call.

She had already arranged for Laryssa to tell Anton to report sick with a fever. It was the only excuse a *zek* could make which would not have the guards driving him with dog-whips to the work place. In their ignorance, all fevers could be typhus and typhus killed guards and *zeks* alike.

The line of prisoners outside the medical hut was no more than eight men when Anton joined them. Some were cases of festering wounds which were passed straight through to the "doctor." Others were simulated fevers which Zoya treated with, at the most, an aspirin and a pass for two days' excused work. At the end of the line Anton came in and stood awkwardly. "I've got a fever, Comrade Medical Assistant," he grinned. "Or so you tell me," he added in a whisper.

Zoya glanced toward the doctor's room. Her door was shut. She was attending a man who had had his knee shattered by a falling log.

"I have to speak to you," she said. "I've some information I got in Krasibirsk yesterday. They're planning to move us from Panaka. We don't have time to speak here."

"My detail is in the woods at the river bend all day," he said. "Can you come there?"

"Do you know the old wooden jetty?"

"Yes."

"I'll be there as soon after midday as I can. Can you get Bubo to cover for you?"

"Of course."

She stood looking at him, wanting to touch him. "At midday then," she said.

During the long morning she faced the thought for the first time that Anton and Bubo would decide not to come. There was, after all, no guarantee of how long it would be before the General Amnesty was declared and they might all find themselves having delayed their departure for a month and then transported to East Cape among a totally new, and inevitably hostile, group of *zeks*.

As the hands of the medical room clock rose toward midday she prepared her excuses for the doctor who had been writing up reports in her office most of the morning.

Then at 11:40 she was called into the inner office.

The doctor sat behind her desk, her gray hair pulled back in a severe bun.

"Sit down, Zoya," she said without looking up.

Zoya sat.

The doctor continued writing for a few minutes, then threw the pen aside. Her lips were trembling with anger. "In a place like this," she said, "do you consider one human being owes anything to another?"

Zoya looked at her fearfully. It was the sort of question she just could not imagine the doctor asking.

"I don't understand, Comrade Doctor," Zoya said respectfully.

"No," the older woman shook her head bitterly. "No, you don't understand."

Zoya sat silently, watching her.

"This morning I received a telephone call from the camp commandant," the doctor said. "He told me that the Kraslag had ordered an improvement in the Penal Brigades' conditions."

"Yes?" Zoya said with a cautiously interrogative lift to her voice.

"You know already," the doctor said violently. "Panaka One is to be dispersed. Or at least transferred."

"Yes," Zoya said more firmly this time.

"I was ordered to remove from the transfer list the chronically sick. You're to stay with them. I know what that means, Zoya. It means Panaka One is to be transported east, probably to the far east." She was trembling. "To East Cape, you bitch, isn't it?"

Zoya rose from her seat in fear. The doctor's face was suffused with anger. She was standing behind her desk, plucking at a thick strand of gray hair which she had torn from the tape that held her bun.

"You offered yourself to him, didn't you? You used the fact of a twenty-year-old body to cheat me of my own chance to live. I'm fifty-five," she screamed. "I've another sixteen years to serve. Can I last sixteen years at East Cape? I've got a family, don't you understand, children I haven't seen for nearly ten years." Suddenly she was pleading. "Please Zoyenka, please, I have every right to stay."

Overcome with an uncontrollable trembling, Zoya watched the doctor standing before her, her face crumpled in supplication.

"You're young, Zoya," the doctor said more quickly now, "You'll survive. You'll hardly be into your thirties when your release is due. You can survive East Cape. Tell him that, Zoya," she pleaded. "Tell him you'll go. Let me stay, for God's sake."

It was a moment Zoya Densky never forgot in every detail of the bare-boarded office, the misted windows and the woman with the flying strands of gray hair.

I turned [she wrote afterward] and ran from the office. Perhaps the doctor thought I was going straight to the colonel to beg him to keep her at Panaka, I don't know. I was too ashamed for myself and mortified for another human being to think. I ran to the gate and blurted out to the guard that there had been an accident at the river bend location. He looked at me quickly, not even thinking to ask how I knew. Opening the side gate, he let me through.

Perhaps I kept running to burn the shame out of me. I knew, good as that woman had been to me, that I would never let her take my place.

At the river I stopped. Leaning against a tree trunk I coughed and spluttered, my head hanging. After a few moments I sat down. Birds flitted from one high branch to another. A faint sweet smell of decaying leaves rose all around me. The great river Ob, flowing north from the middle of Siberia, was here a broad untroubled stream so clear that I could see the long fingers of dead branches reaching up from far below the surface.

Slowly I recovered my breath. A squadron of swans sailed majestically toward me. I watched them as, on some unheard command, the long necks stretched, the beaks pointed and the huge wings beat the surface of the river. From the confusion of great white wings and churning waters they rose into the air, suddenly graced again with that serenity, as in languid flight they banked across the birch treetops on their long journey west.

From within the wood Anton's voice called me. Had he seen the swans' flight too?

I got to my feet and reached the path he was following.

"Did you see the swans?" I asked.

He smiled. "Yes," he said. "It means winter is coming."

"Where do they go, do you know?"

"All the way to Western Europe. Denmark . . . some of them even to the coast of Britain."

"Denmark . . . Britain . . . Would they cross Leningrad?"

"Perhaps. Close enough to look down on the Nevsky Prospekt or Vasilyevsky Island."

"Do you know why I asked you to come here?"

He rested his long back against a tree and slid down into a sitting position. "Laryssa managed a few words with Bubo. She says there's to be a General Amnesty for the Penal Brigades."

"And the politicals and criminals in Panaka One are being sent east."

"And if we wanted to, we four could stay?"

"We four and Anna," I said.

"If we stayed we don't know how long it would be for."

"No. Perhaps a month. Perhaps all through the winter." I hesitated. "If we were sent east there's no guarantee we would go to a mixed camp. There are very few."

He nodded. "I know."

I sat down next to him. "This way," I said, "we can stay together."

He turned onto one elbow and reached out to put his arm across my waist. "And that's important to you?" he said.

"More important than anything."

He was looking up at me. "For me, too," he nodded gravely.

I think the floodgates opened then. I threw my arms round his neck and we were kissing and rolling in the hollow between the trees.

It was a release from everything, from dirt and corruption and slavery and Panaka and from the pathetic woman begging for her life in the medical hut.

Deep in the growth of green river grasses we rolled together and stopped.

"First," he said, "we must be married."

I sat up, brushing grass and twigs from my hair. "Married, how?"

He reached out and stroked my face. "When they sent us here to Panaka," he said, "they put us beyond all laws of states or churches. They took one sort of freedom from us, but in doing that, they gave us another."

I looked at him, questioningly.

"If we choose to get married," he said, "we will."

I took his hand. "I choose."

He covered my hand with his. "I also choose."

"Zoya Ovsenkovna." In these wide woods I whispered my new name.

"Can you hear the sound of bells ringing, Zoya?"

"Yes."

"And the clatter of the dishes as the wedding feast is laid?"

"Yes." I reached out and plucked a piece of grass. "In my grandmother's village, the bride's mother would twist a piece of grass like this, and say, "May my Zoya handle her Anton as I twist this grass around my finger."

"Then so be it," he smiled and pulled me toward him.

That afternoon we consummated our marriage among the high birchwoods until the blasts of the guards' whistles were carried on the wind, summoning us back to our other life.

Chapter Thirty-three

IN LATE SEPTEMBER General Semyon Kuba received a report he had anxiously awaited. In consultation with the Moscow procuracy one of his most trusted assistants at the Lubyanka, Colonel Y, had reached the following conclusion: that it would be entirely possible to bring former Minister Natalya Roginova to trial for anti-Soviet activities given several broad conditions:

I. That the trial, but not the summing-up and verdict, should be held in camera on the grounds that matters of Soviet security were being considered.

II. That charges of exploiting her position to maintain an un-Soviet and luxurious life-style be dropped as politically inflammatory at this time.

III. That the chief witness be hospital patient Bukansky.

IV. That the witness Bukansky should make a statement to the Western press confessing to his contact role between Natalya Roginova and certain Western governments and agencies.

Kuba initialed the document. Before sending it back to Colonel Y he scrawled across the bottom: "Ensure that Bukansky is prepared to make the necessary statement."

At the Lubyanka Colonel Y received Kuba's reply by afternoon messenger and ordered his car immediately. Arriving at Hospital 36, he was quickly shown into the office of the senior psychiatrist.

The psychiatrist was not reassuring. "Patient Bukansky cannot be said to be responding to treatment. He remains pathologically unrepentant. I must tell you, Colonel, that the Soviet doctor Timofeyev describes dissidence as 'a disease of the brain which develops slowly.' In other words, the Patient Bukansky not only shows no sign of repentance, he's getting worse."

Nevertheless the colonel insisted on seeing Bukansky, and to the doctor's intense irritation, alone.

"May I say that for a patient you're looking remarkably fit, Igor Alexandrovich," the colonel said after he had introduced himself.

"I'm in excellent hands, Colonel."

"That's as may be," the colonel said briskly. In a few sentences he told Bukansky of Roginova's forthcoming trial and the role he was expected to play. "Within a month of the trial," he added, "I can assure you you will be out of here. You will then be free to live wherever you choose in the Soviet Union as long as it is outside the tourist areas."

"I am then to be the principal witness."

"There will be a large number of supporting affidavits. But the greater part of the trial will be held in camera. Your evidence will be given a prominent place in the summing-up and a select number of Western journalists will be allowed to visit you immediately afterward."

"For confirmation of my evidence."

"Yes."

"All very well, Colonel," Bukansky said. "But what conceivably can my evidence be worth?"

"Leave that to us."

"You don't understand me, Colonel. On September eighteenth of this year I was officially declared by a properly constituted Soviet court, non-accountable. Insane. I hardly think the Western press will find me an impressive witness!"

Colonel Y's second report to Kuba concluded:

I explained to Bukansky that the verdict of the September 18th court could be set aside by a further hearing. He then openly threatened to behave at the press conference after the Roginova trial in such a way as would convince the Western press that the September verdict was totally justifiable.

In view of the negative attitudes expressed by patient Bukansky, it will be necessary to discover further arguments which might cause him to modify his presently recalcitrant position.

She knew from her husband's face that there was trouble. He came into the apartment and stood at the kitchen door, his topcoat still on, his hands deep in his pockets. The Ukrainian maid smiled with her steel teeth and offered tea. He shook his head and looked toward Carole. "Get your coat," he said. "I feel like a walk."

She moved past him into the hall and nodded. "Okay." It was normal procedure among the foreign community to leave the apartment if something important had to be discussed. Slipping into her coat as he watched her, Carole was suddenly, painfully reminded of the way Letsukov used to watch her while she dressed.

They left the apartment and descended in the elevator. Whether or not the lifts were bugged was a matter of some debate among the Moscow foreign community. Nobody took the risk.

They remained silent as they walked through the compound gates, past the militiaman on guard duty and turned along the street.

It was a cool summer evening. The Moscow crowds flowed past them on their interminable foraging expeditions. This month a sudden shortage of electric light bulbs had struck the city. Last month it had been key blanks, tap washers, washbasin plugs and combs. Sometimes the shortage would end with a massive delivery from some state enterprise beyond the Urals and the shelves would be full of the sought-after items for a few weeks. Then, equally mysteriously, every comb or light bulb or washbasin plug or key blank in Moscow would seem to disappear overnight.

Carole watched the faces hurrying past: young and old, middle-aged factory workers and clerks, all with that stolid, determined look. They had only quarreled once, Letsukov and herself, when she had said how sorry she felt for Moscow women. Alex had seemed unable to distinguish sympathy from condescension. And yet sympathy was what she felt. Like most of the foreign community she had come to love those Russians she had met casually in restaurants or, with more difficulty, in their homes. Perhaps it was her own part-Slav origins, but she found she responded totally to the rambling talk, the excess of vodka, the songs, the desperate determination, almost always successful, to have a good time. And yet these were the same people who pushed and struggled in the queues, who bumped hard against you in the street without apparently noticing and certainly without apology.

She glanced again at Tom. His face was set and angry. She had no idea what he wanted to talk about. Some piece of office back-stabbing perhaps? She didn't imagine it concerned her. Since she no longer saw Alex she had lost that edge of guilt.

The crowd thinned as they reached the edge of the park.

Still walking he turned his head toward her. "Sometime last week the French pulled out a low-grade Soviet defector from their embassy in Paris," he said. "French Intelligence had been dancing with him for a month or so trying to up the ante."

"What does that mean?"

"It means that they were trying to get him to bring over some better material when he came."

"Were they successful?"

"No."

They walked in silence for a few moments. The huge Rossiya Hotel rose above them.

"Most of his stuff was not much more than useful gossip," Tom Yates said.

"Except . . . ?"

"Except a couple of items for us to look into. One of them reached my desk this afternoon."

"I'm listening."

"KGB here in Moscow," he said slowly, "are working on a contact in the U.S. Embassy here."

"Jesus," she said. "Is that possible?"

"I don't know. I'll tell you how French Intelligence gave it to us. A Russian bureaucrat, not more than fairly senior, is reported to be having a torrid affair with one of our embassy wives."

She looked at him wordlessly.

"KGB got onto it some time ago and ordered the bureaucrat to develop her as a contact."

They walked on in silence.

"Are you that embassy wife, Carole?"

He had spoken flatly, looking not at her but into the faces of the Muscovites that flowed past them.

She breathed in the cool air. "We're a big establishment, Tom. There are a lot of wives."

He nodded. "But the Russian bureaucrat in question works for the Ministry of Nationalities."

She knew already the report referred to her before that final confirmation. It was two months ago that Letsukov had made it clear they should part. And now of course she knew why. They stopped by the Rossiya Gardens.

"I'm going to be absolutely straight with you, Tom," she said. "Up until a couple of months ago I had been meeting Alex Letsukov. That last time he told me he did not wish to continue. It was, although I didn't know it then, his way of keeping the KGB off our backs.

"You goddam bitch," he said softly. "Do you want to kill me? In the job I mean?"

"I didn't think enough of that aspect of it. For that I'm deeply sorry."

"There are other aspects as well for God's sake."

"Of course there are."

"Those are the ones you're not sorry for. Is that it?"

"I'm sorry we have to talk here out in the open."

"We live in Moscow. Or didn't you notice?"

She shrugged. "What do you want to do, Tom?"

"I want to bat you all the way from here to the apartment."

"Would that help?"

"It'd help me."

She put her hand on his arm. "Look, Tom, I know what I've done. It's out in the open now. Tell me what you want."

"I want a divorce," he said. "And I want you to get on the next plane out to New York."

She saw the world close in around her. "I won't do that, Tom. Give me a few days."

"So you can get yourself and me deeper in it?"

"I want to see him just once more, yes."

"I want you out of here, do you understand me? Harriet's getting onto UPDK for an exit visa first thing tomorrow morning."

He realized what he had said. "I had to tell her," he grunted. "So that the travel arrangements could be made."

"You told her the whole story?"

He shrugged.

"You told her about the divorce?"

"Why not?"

"Before you told me?"

"Let's walk," he said.

They turned and walked along Razina Ulitza. She felt a bubble of laughter rising inside her. She knew it was inappropriate, even cruel, given the fact that she had put his career in jeopardy. But the thought of

Harriet with her steel-rim glasses and tweedy earnestness made it difficult
to keep the bubble from bursting.

"You've been cheating too, Tom, haven't you? With Harriet?"

"Absolutely not."

"Our Ukrainian maid doesn't turn hospital corners, Tom."

"What the hell are you talking about?"

"I know you've been sleeping with Harriet, Tom."

"Once," he said shortly. "While you were out getting laid."

"More than once. But now we know where we stand."

He walked on, hands in his coat pockets, head down.

"Do you really want this divorce? Or does Harriet?"

He turned toward her. "We both want it, Carole."

"I see."

"But it still alters nothing. In normal circumstances what you now
decide to do with Bureaucrat Letsukov would be your business. Try and
understand that here and now, in Moscow, it's mine."

"I still want to see him again, Tom."

"Then I'll inform the Embassy of what's been happening to date."

"You've already done it Tom, haven't you? This afternoon."

"Okay, I've done it. It was the only way."

"Harriet must be some tough girl."

"You'd admit that she's a hell of a lot more suitable as a Foreign
Service wife than you."

"I'd admit that," she said, almost gaily. "And I'm still taking those few
days."

It was a night of shouting and screams and men and women sobbing
hopelessly. While a bitter wind swept down from the north the *zeks* of
Panaka One were assembled on the square between the huts and issued a
loaf and a bottle of water each for the journey east. Like infinitely pathetic
refugees they clutched the few possessions they had acquired during their
stay. An old political held a tattered copy of the Bible beneath his quilted
jacket; a woman stared at a crude hand-colored picture of a child,
someone else's child; one carried a single spare boot, another a bundle of
rags wrapped in brown paper.

The whip-guards, ferocious in their nervousness, called the *zeks'*
numbers in batches of twenty or thirty and pushed and whipped them
toward requisitioned lorries or horse-drawn carts.

The colonel-commandant paced the square anxiously, flinching from
the growling guard dogs, as tensely keyed as their masters. There had
been nineteen suicides during the night, the last and most inexplicable
reported to him was Madame Ustinova, the camp doctor.

When the last horse-drawn cart trundled through the gates its canvas covering was already dusted with the first thin snow of winter.

The colonel climbed into his car and drove himself along the rutted track in the direction of Panaka Five. These were hard times for him. He knew that high in the Gulag command circles they were watching him and others like him for any slipup in the whole Amnesty operation. Those who succeeded would definitely be marked for promotion.

Almost a month earlier Anton and Zoya had driven this same road.

I had not been to Panaka Five for almost a year now [Anton recounted], and I suppose I imagined that not much had changed. But as our leading cart trundled round the bend in the forest road and approached the barbed wire I was reminded of nothing so much as the films of the fascist concentration camps that had been shown and reshown throughout my youth. Belsen was one name I remember, and a place in Poland called Auschwitz. A gray-brown sea of men heaved listlessly behind treble-wire fences. The huts that we had built showed great gaping holes where timbers had been ripped from them to feed winter fires. And the smell . . . it obliterated totally the last autumn scents of the forest from which we were emerging.

These men were savages. When we arrived they were still half-starved, the eyes full of hatred, staring from gaunt faces. Among the shaven heads, the universal gray skin and the protruding ears, it was almost impossible to tell at this stage of their malnutrition a Central Asiatic from a Slav. Only by the eyes might one know, and there were precious few blue eyes in Panaka Five.

We so-called carpenters, and especially Bubo and myself who had been fed medical rations by Zoya during the harsh summer months, felt almost ashamed of the flesh on our bodies, although to be truthful it could not be called excessive.

To be working all day with my wife, Zoya, was an unexpected bonus. But as "doctor" she stomped around the hut we were building, asking for extra benches here and more plank beds there. And at night in the separate tented camps we occupied in the woods, the guards stood out in the exposed late autumn winds and we, the zeks, sat inside round our improvised wood stoves. Every night in Panaka Five Zoya and I spent together in our own tent.

Only Bubo really made contact with the penals. As their rations improved and work schedules were gradually reintroduced, Bubo would take a group of the fittest out to the woods to fell timber for the huts we were building.

Still, none of us had any idea of the date of the General Amnesty. It was clear enough that the men were becoming fitter now as each week passed, but their snarling hatred for the guards and the ferocious guard dogs was unabated.

When the medical hut was finished Zoya and the other two girls, Laryssa and Anna, worked fourteen hours a day cleaning the most dreadfully neglected wounds, isolating dangerous fever cases and even, under the new rules, sending the worst penals to the clinic in Krasibirsk. Much more leeway was now allowed in reporting sick (indeed, in Panaka Five it had hardly existed before). Each morning from the roof of the hut I was repairing, I would watch the lines outside the medical hut of men still thin and bent as if old, in tattered gray uniforms and sinister black summer skullcaps with long earflaps designed to protect the shaven head against mosquitoes. How Zoya ever controlled them in there I shall never know.

Through Bubo we soon got to know a little of what was happening in the camp. Naturally among the penals some form of organization had developed, as it always does. A Siberian (where exactly he came from we never knew) named Barkut was the most feared among the penals' leaders. If anything I suppose he looked like an unusually tall Mongolian. He had developed, Bubo told me, some sort of violent religion which selected penals were forced to adhere to on pain of death. Among his terrifying fraternity he was known as Barkut Khan.

The Khans, as we called them, had little or nothing to do with us. How many Khans there were in this camp of 30,000 men we did not know, but from stories Bubo heard in the woods, Barkut claimed hundreds. Since a man had no choice, once selected, it seemed possible.

Meanwhile the weather changed. The winter came in with all its solitary fury. We *zeks* built a small hut for ourselves on the site of our tent-camp and divided it into small rooms. So still Zoya and I spent every night together. And every night we prayed that the Amnesty would not be declared on the morrow . . .

Chapter Thirty-four

AT DAWN AFTER a heavy night's snowfall a young Rumanian lieutenant emerged from his billet at the comfortable Belescu farm just outside the town of Satu Mare and saw a black tank facing him across the half-frozen Somescu River. He waved to it. The machine gunner, upright in the open hatchway, cut him down with a five-second burst.

Troops of the lieutenant's platoon tumbled out of the Belescu's barn and were shot down by white-cloaked soldiers rising from the roadside. An hour later Rumanian troops on the Negresti-Satu Mare road were violently attacked by a motorized infantry company and the vital crossroad was taken.

It was certainly some hours later before the headquarter unit of the Rumanian division in the undermanned Northwest Defense Area received anything approaching a coherent report. By midday, when the Rumanian reserve army was alerted, the Hungarian invasion was already well under way.

Nobody in the East or West, no speculating journalist, military planner or position paper writer had even considered the possibility. While the attention of the world in the late seventies and early eighties had been concentrated on the more flamboyant nationalism of Poland, the Baltic States and the Ukraine, developments in Hungary and Rumania had gone largely unobserved.

Take Hungary first. After the burst of national feeling which had led to the 1956 rebellion and Khrushchev's brutal suppression of it, it was generally agreed in the West that Janos Kadar, the Moscow puppet prime minister, had slowly but effectively divested himself of his strings. Of all the Eastern satellites Hungary seemed the most content, Hungary and Rumania, among the most quiescent.

The world had paid no great attention to the United States' offer in January 1978 to return the Crown of St. Stephen to Budapest. The symbol of Hungarian independence and legitimacy for Hungary's rulers for over a thousand years, the crown had been saved from the hands of the SS and smuggled to Austria at the end of the war. From Vienna it had been sent to the United States for safe custody.

There is no doubt that Hungarian feelings were deeply stirred by the return of St. Stephen's Crown, and it is likely that outlets, other than the obvious and dangerous anti-Soviet one, for nationalist expression began to be sought at about this time.

There was one just such outlet to hand. At the collapse of the Austro-Hungarian Empire in 1918, Transylvania, for centuries a province of Hungary, had been transferred to Rumania. The peace treaties at the conclusion of World War II failed to rectify this casual allocation of half a million Hungarians to the rule of a foreign power.

Now turn to Rumania. Since the war there had been a potent strain of nationalism emanating from Bucharest. Claiming descent from a Roman colony established in Dacia by the Emperor Trajan, Rumanians consider themselves linked to Western Europe by an essentially Latin language and culture.

In the nineteen seventies, coal miners in the Jiu Valley, which produces most of Rumania's coal, had struck, demanding better conditions and improved food supplies. Ministers were jeered at and Ceausescu himself failed to gain a hearing from the miners. By promises that were immediately broken and a sweeping program of arrests, the strike was put down. But word of the strike spread throughout Rumania and in order to counteract the rumor, the government propaganda campaign chose the only issue which would unite all Rumanians. A new drive was conducted to "assimilate" the recalcitrant Hungarian minority.

The Hungarians were quick to respond. Hungary's leading poet, Gyula Illyes, accused the Rumanians of "apartheid and ethnocide." He in turn was accused by a Rumanian Central Committee member of having an "anti-Rumanian" obsession.

The war of words continued, but nobody considered the possibility that the Hungarians would resort to any more violent strategy. In the early eighties a partial trade embargo was imposed by the Kadar government, but lifted within months, almost certainly under pressure from Brezhnev. Then a series of events occurred, and almost like cogs finding their place, started the movement of the wheel.

In Rumania, Ceausescu was faced with a new and more serious demand for better conditions by the Jiu coal miners. These men, who had been little more than retrained peasants at the time of the last strike, had now the advantage of a further eight years together and were now much closer to an industrial proletariat. Organized and formidable, they faced the government with their demands. Bucharest knew only one real strategy— to bring in the troops. And as the winter began, a significant part of the Rumanian army was concentrated on Jiu in an attempt to force the miners back to work.

In Hungary, too, the cogs had deftly fitted. Janos Kadar had retired after nearly thirty years as the head of the government. The new leadership was younger, more belligerently nationalist. They took the opportunity of Rumania's discomfiture to demand a solution of the Transylvanian problem.

Still, in the West there was little belief that the Hungarians were in earnest. In Moscow, economic difficulties and the continuing power struggle focused all attention inward.

The Hungarians, emboldened by Moscow's silence, took a further step. They demanded an independent principality of Transylvania, jointly administered by Hungary and Rumania.

From Bucharest came a howl of pain. But the government was in no position to do more. The Jiu strike was now spreading to the national transportation system and to the industrial suburbs of the capital itself.

Hungary, after thirty healing years of Janos Kadar's rule, was now the most confident of the Soviet satellite leaderships in the affection of its people. But in the last months it had launched an unprecedented campaign in the press and on television against Rumanian "atrocities" in Transylvania. The new nationalist leadership had unwittingly overstepped itself. For a people whose intense feelings of nationalism had been effectively frustrated for the best part of thirty years, the situation was intolerable. They demanded action.

It was a tiger the new leaders lacked the experience to ride. They appealed to Ceausescu to come to a conference in Budapest. He refused in a violently anti-Hungarian speech. The Hungarians, in reply, moved army units toward the hitherto undefended frontier. Ceausescu spared three divisions from internal security duties to face them.

Incidents occurred daily. When fifteen Hungarian Transylvanians were sentenced to death for military espionage on behalf of Budapest, the Hungarians pushed four armored divisions across the border in a "defensive operation on behalf of Hungarian Transylvania." Twelve hours later the two countries were at war.

That same night over Radio Free Europe and by every other means they could exploit, the Ukrainian National Army of Liberation announced its support for the Hungarians and promised that their partisan units would immediately attack across the Ukraine-Rumanian border in the direction of the Rumanian towns of Suceava and Iasi.

Even before instructions arrived from Moscow the announcement caused consternation at the Soviet Army's Ukrainian Command Head-quarters at Zitomir and KGB headquarters in Kiev. Were military and KGB units to cross into Rumania in pursuit of the Ukrainian National Liberation Army? And if they then met advancing Hungarian troops, whose side were they on?

Before dawn the Rumanian government had protested in the strongest terms since 1945 about the presence of bandit forces on their soil.

In a purely reflex action the generals of the Soviet Army ordered ten first-line divisions to the Hungarian and Rumanian border during the morning of Day One. By evening both Hungary and Rumania had protested to Moscow at what had seemed to each of them like a Soviet threat on behalf of the other.

Meanwhile the two small armies clashed in skirmishes and brigade-scale battles. Strong points were occupied and attacked. As the hours passed the fighting units became more and more inextricably intermeshed.

And still there had been no admonitory word from Moscow.

*   *   *

But it now became clear that Moscow's new military problem was not to be confined to the Soviet Union's southwest borders. News was now to arrive in Moscow which indicated that the Chinese government might be taking advantage of the situation to flex its muscles.

At Aerial Reconnaissance School A, Sverdlovsk, the three interpreting officers left the viewing theater and made their way back to the conference room.

"We all agree that it's a positive movement?" the senior officer asked.

The others nodded.

"A force of between thirty and fifty divisions?"

"Our estimate must be based on the vehicle complement per division. To know that, we have to know whether they're first-line of readiness or not," one of the officers objected.

"Which is why I propose a figure of between thirty and fifty," The senior officer said. "I don't think we can do better on satellite information alone."

His fellow officers assented.

The senior officer picked up his telephone and was connected to the cypher room. "Moscow T-1," he said. "Reads: Satellite observation twenty-one hundred hours this date. Between thirty and fifty Chinese divisions on approach march Amur River border areas IV, V, VI. To arrive border twelve to eighteen hours. Message ends."

In Marshal Dimitry Ustinov's Kremlin command headquarters the news from the Amur River border area came as a bombshell. He had just ordered the dispatch of ten first-line divisions to the Hungarian-Rumanian border to await the Politburo's decision on intervention. Now, what appeared to be a direct threat was developing in the East.

Amur IV, V, VI described that section of the border where a Chinese salient some 400 miles deep and 200 miles wide pushed into the belly of the Soviet Union. At its deepest point it was barely 50 miles from the Trans-Siberian Railway. There was no area which could cause greater alarm to the Moscow military planners, or would be more difficult to defend against a sudden armored thrust.

Contingency plans were consulted. Even if the Chinese intended no more than a relocation of forces in this area the planners considered a minimum reinforcement of twenty-two divisions necessary.

At midnight that night the new enlarged Politburo met for the first time. They had been due to meet the following day when Kuba thought to push through his appointment as First Secretary of the all-Union Communist Party. But at the midnight emergency meeting military affairs naturally took precedence.

Even Kuba must have seen the contrast between the aging members of the Politburo, already tired before the midnight session began, and the younger members from the republics, including now the western republics.

Kremlin secretary Peter Rinsky certainly did:

It was after all only midnight, although the chances are, I suppose, that all the old men had been in bed for an hour or two when the call came. Had they not been such a unique gang of murderers one would have felt sorry for them.

At that first meeting of the expanded Politburo, secrecy, I'm happy to say, went out the window. At two-thirty they took a break. The doors opened and, instead of the decorous shuffling of old men, the young ones came charging out like bulls still arguing amongst themselves.

My friend and I kept our ears at full prick and afterward I think managed to piece together what had happened. The Defense Minister had proposed immediate reinforcement to the China border to counter some troop movement along the Amur River. Naturally with our existing problems in Hungary and Rumania this was going to put a severe strain on manpower.

The solution Defense proposed and Kuba endorsed was to call up class A and B reservists despite the fact that Mikoyan the Armenian and others had warned frankly that severe resistance would be met in their republics.

Others felt that their political position at home would be threatened if the first Politburo meeting they attended resulted in a mobilization decree which would fall most heavily on the non-Russian republics.

The Ukrainian First Secretary seems to have tried to bring the two sides together. He feared an American response, and with the Ukraine in a vulnerable position if the West should decide to support Hungary *or* Rumania, he suggested a mobilization confined to the *Russian* Republic where nationalist feeling against the Chinese was strong.

This of course was a ground-breaking suggestion. To my knowledge it was the first time that it had been suggested that the Union should tackle its problems on an individual republic basis. Naturally the Central Asian and Caucasian republics were delighted at the idea. Let Mother Russia deal with Mother Russia's own problems!

They had coffee and sandwiches and went back for the second session. Even through the thick soundproof doors we could hear Kuba shouting. There must have been some fine blood-thirsty threats handed out that night.

The meeting broke up at four in the morning. Everybody now seemed drained of energy. Kuba, leading them out, was grim-faced.

It was only next morning that we knew who'd won the day. To our country's problems of bread rationing and oil and transport restrictions was now added a nationwide mobilization of Class A and B reservists to contend with.

I suppose people like ourselves make a life of sorts wherever we happen to be. Naturally in Moscow in those days there was no question of being open. As I've said, for the golden boys it was seven years in a camp. But nevertheless we had our meeting places. The best by far, not a million miles from Red Square, was "Mother Hubbards." One or two of the foreign community were "members" and Scotch and English gin were available most nights. Mother Hubbard himself was well aware of the risks. But then the prices reflected it.

Certainly the fun had gone out of the place recently. In the last few weeks we were like a clutch of old hens clucking around anyone who had any information to give. And most members had something. They were, after all, well placed in various circles of government and Party and one, Vladimir, (nobody asked his other names) was a colonel in the KGB. At least, this we believed, and he never denied it.

I think it was David Butler, the Englishman, who started the whole thing. I remember it was a particularly drunken evening and five or six young Georgian dancers had been introduced by Mother Hubbard, just to keep the adrenalin running and the drinks flowing. Of course we were all desperately competing and the champagne was popping every few seconds. Mother Hubbard was looking happier than he had in weeks.

I was sitting with my friend at one of the alcove tables watching the young Georgians overwhelmed by the hospitality on offer when the Englishman Butler walked in. Whether his embassy knew he was golden I can't say. But then the English take such an extraordinarily relaxed view of these things. I instance the case of the dreadful Anthony Blunt. Not only was he *not* sent to a camp for being golden, but he seemed to have got away scot-free when it was revealed that he'd spied for the murderer Beria as well. That's liberalism for you!

I must say truthfully that David Butler was a very different kettle of fish. No one in the club regarded him as other than a totally loyal Englishman, and many of us I know used him (with his own knowledge) to feed a little detail here and there into the Western pipelines.

Well, this evening Butler sat with us and, although each of us no doubt had one eye on the Georgian dancers, the conversation quickly took a serious turn.

David Butler said frankly that he thought the Soviet Union was facing its greatest crisis since the Hitler War. In food, energy and transport, the crisis had already arrived. By the end of this winter its effects would be literally incalculable.

To that could be added the problem of internal nationalisms, which the Soviet Union was now experiencing. Nobody believed these feelings could be suppressed by a Stalinist. Or at least, he added, nobody in their right mind.

And now the Transylvanian crisis.

I suppose it was nervousness about the future that made us tell him that the reservists were to be mobilized. He would know by tomorrow anyway.

He foresaw, accurately as it happened, serious problems in the autonomous republics when the mobilization orders were announced.

Until that evening, I suppose, we, even in the government, had not taken the idea of a collapse of authority in any way seriously. But David Butler convinced us we should. His view was that the night of the funeral was no more than a rehearsal for what was to come. He claimed that Kiev and Tallinn and Russian towns, too, like Leningrad and Sverdlovsk were already sporadically rioting against the militia. It could start in Moscow anytime. A prudent man, he said, would make some arrangements, even if they later proved unnecessary.

Frankly, my friend and I were impressed. David Butler, we knew, was no scaremonger. And our own experience confirmed what he said. We decided it was time to take our vacation entitlement, as far away from Moscow as possible.

As I said, it was a drunken evening. We saw no more of Butler. He was one of the lucky ones (trust him!) to fix himself up with one of the young Georgians. But perhaps in compensation or commiseration, Mother Hubbard himself came over to sit with us. And within seconds, gossips that we are, we were talking about leaving Moscow for a few weeks.

Well, Mother Hubbard knew exactly the place. The Georgian port of Batumi on the Black Sea. Mother Hubbard touched the graying side of his wavy black hair. "And of course," he said, "if you wanted to go further west, I could always arrange a fishing boat to Turkey."

We were shocked. It hadn't for one moment occurred to us to leave the country. But as soon as Mother Hubbard left us, we plunged into the idea like a pair of excited schoolgirls. The thought of living in France, in Paris! And although Mother Hubbard's remark had been a casual addition to the idea of going to Batumi, we both knew that he meant it. These Georgians are an amazing people. The families are so close-knit that they are able to trust one another completely. Like New York Sicilians.

We could think about nothing else. Before we left we called Mother Hubbard over.

"You *were* serious?" I asked him.

"About what, Peter?" He'd forgotten already.

"The fishing boat."

"Quite serious. If you are."

"We won't be robbed of everything we have?"

"No. But you'll have to pay heavily."

"How much?" my friend asked anxiously.

"Ten thousand rubles each."

It was a great deal of money.

"But if you've got Western currency tucked away, it can be done for one thousand dollars each."

We went home, the two thousand dollars ringing in our ears. Hidden in the apartment we had exactly that sum in hundred-dollar bills from the sale to an American diplomat of an icon that had been in the possession of my friend's family for generations.

Chapter Thirty-five

THE SIGNS OF the fast approaching General Amnesty were not difficult to read. After Anton and Zoya had been at Panaka Five just over a month, twenty truckloads of Army uniforms arrived. They included quilted jackets and boots. Eight huts of penals, at about 200 men to a hut, were issued new clothing. Two days later these first 600 men were bundled onto a long convoy of waiting trucks in the middle of the night. By dawn they had gone. The Amnesty operation was under way.

The next morning it was announced that they had been transferred to another camp. But for all the smoothness of that first night's arrangements it was no longer possible to keep the secret. Railway officials in Krasibirsk knew the trains were traveling west. They told the whip-guards, the whip-guards threatened the penals (in excess of their authority) to withdraw the Amnesty from them. The word blazed around the camp. And the fretting impatience of men who had been previously resigned to years of imprisonment now brought Panaka to that dangerous pitch which the colonel-commandant had feared all along.

Even if he were able to command the trucks and horse wagons and rolling stock to transport 2,000 men a week, it would take fifteen weeks to evacuate the whole Panaka complex.

But 2,000 men a week from Panaka alone was totally beyond the capacity of the rail lines, forty wagons was far beyond the capacity of some of the ancient steam locomotives to pull. The colonel, desperately trying to face the future, saw no possibility of the evacuation being complete until the spring, or even early summer. But equally he knew that he could never maintain camp discipline that long.

Even worse, since he was required to evacuate the whole complex within six weeks of Amnesty Day, how could he still requisition rations for prisoners who according to Gulag orders were no longer at Panaka? And if he was unable to requisition rations, how would he control 30,000 starving men with only 1,000 guards?

Each camp commandant had been given authority by the Gulag command in Moscow to decide at what point he would announce the General Amnesty. The colonel had already been in touch with his fellow camp commandants throughout the Kraslag area and discovered that in smaller camps of perhaps 5,000 penals each, commandants had already announced the Amnesty and established a lottery to determine the order of evacuation. This seemed to be working effectively, and in the last weeks up to 5,000 penals had already been committed to the railway system. Where they now were between Krasibirsk and Moscow the camp commandants neither knew nor cared. Once the men had left the Kraslag area they were no longer the commandant's responsibility.

At Panaka the colonel saw no alternative. He officially informed Kraslag headquarters that it was impossible to achieve the six-week evacuation schedule unless Panaka was given priority in the requisition of rail transport.

That same day he posted notices throughout the camps in his command announcing the Amnesty and setting up a lottery system. With an optimism he did not feel, he proclaimed that the Panaka complex would be fully evacuated in fifteen weeks.

It was the day of the first heavy snowfall of winter. The colonel stood at the window of his office in Panaka and congratulated himself on the quiet which had fallen over the camp. He watched the huge flakes swirl down and begin to settle across the appel-ground. He even, with the warmth of the stove on his back, began to think again of Zoya.

He heard the telephone jangle in the sergeant-clerk's room next door and waited for the hand-cranked whirr of his own receiver. Turning from the window he crossed to the desk, lifted the receiver and adopted his telephone voice.

"This is General Satolov at Kraslag," the voice on the other end of the phone said.

The colonel smiled respectfully into the mouthpiece. "Yes, General."

"I've been discussing the Panaka problem with Gulag main headquarters. There are of course several other complexes of your size. Some even containing more prisoners."

"I understand that, General."

"On the other hand, the peculiar problems of discipline in the large complexes has been recognized at Gulag. Your own report was not unimportant in this change of view."

"That is kind of you to say so, General."

"My decision is therefore, Colonel, to withdraw all transport facilities from the smaller camps in the Kraslag area and to allocate all available transport to you."

"Excellent."

"In addition, one thousand border guards are on their way here to Krasibirsk and will arrive this afternoon. Your camp guards will therefore hand over responsibility to KGB Border at Krasibirsk railhead."

"This relieves a great many of my concerns, General."

"Good. You will receive all this in writing tomorrow. The point of my telephoning now is that I have motor and horse-drawn transport available here for a further two thousand men. And the train bringing the border guards can return with your contingent."

It was the last thing the colonel wanted to hear. He had fixed the day of the lottery for three days ahead. Could he now organize it by tonight when the transport would arrive at Panaka?

He nevertheless thanked the general profusely before replacing the receiver.

He sat down heavily in his chair. He had already issued orders to his clerks for the work to begin on the lottery. Rolls of gray roof-insulation paper were now being cut into small cards. His system called for each one to be numbered and as it was selected from the lottery box by the prisoner, for his own Kraslag number to be written on the back. Without that precaution, murder would be committed to acquire a higher number.

But there was no possibility of arranging the lottery today. He had seen how slowly his clerks were working on the lottery cards. And even if they'd been ready, large numbers of men could not easily be moved around the camp in driving snow.

Wrestling with the problem, the colonel came up with a partial solution. He would order the cooks to issue a double ration of soup and bread tonight. He would also cordon off the group of huts closest to the gate and at two hours after midnight transfer the occupants into the convoy of vehicles which he would keep hidden a half-mile away from the camp.

Less uneasy than before, he called in Major Kalemnev, his second in command, and issued his orders.

In their hut in the woods outside the main camp, the *zeks* sat in the biggest room morosely drinking Zoya's lab vodka. Now that the evacuation program had been announced, they saw their future at Panaka extending no more than a few weeks. Indeed, there was already no real function for the men. It was possible they would be leaving any day while the three girls stayed on to continue their duties in the medical hut.

Every hour or so two of the men would take shovels and go outside to clear the snow from the door. Pushing Laryssa gently from him, Bubo stood up and took a shovel. Anton reached out for the other shovel and followed across the hut. The two men dressed in workcoats and caps and with a quick nod from Anton, Bubo hauled open the door. Plunging through the burst of windborn snow, they pulled the door closed after them. They were stumbling in a drift already over two feet high.

Gaining their balance they stood together in the snow. It was just before dusk. Panaka Five was stretched out immediately below them in regular lines of huts on either side of the appel-square, the third side of which was closed by the administration huts and the medical room.

The snow was already settling on Bubo's thick eyebrows. Leaning on his shovel, he gestured to the camp below. "Perhaps all is not lost, Anton," he said grimly. "Surely our masters won't let such a fine camp go to waste. Perhaps we'll be invited to stay."

"Perhaps," Anton said without conviction. "They've amnestied the penals for whatever reason. But we wouldn't be short of ordinary *zeks* for company."

They began to shovel the snow from the door. It was good to work outside and the cold still lacked the ferocity of the deep winter temperature. By the time they had finished, the falling snow seemed to be thinning. They could see now right across Panaka, past the main gate until the winding road was lost in the gloom.

They were just about to reenter the hut when Bubo stopped Anton with a hand on his arm. Anton turned, following the movement of Bubo's head. There, far out beyond the camp, a line of slowly moving lights was visible.

"Headlights," Bubo said.

One by one the lights disappeared as the road wound among pine and leafless birch.

"There must be fifty of them or more," Anton said.

"So another contingent leaves tonight." Bubo dug his shovel into the bank of snow and thrust his gloved hands into his pockets. "When I was at the camp this afternoon nobody was expecting to go tonight."

Anton shrugged. "It's getting colder," he said. "I'm going in."

For another twenty minutes Bubo stood outside the door watching the winking lights as they appeared and disappeared following the bends and undulations of the road. He could not have said why he stayed there as darkness fell. Perhaps because to a *zek* all information was precious. Or might be. When he finally turned to go back in, the convoy had halted about a half-mile along the road out of sight of the main camp, and had extinguished its lights.

But Bubo was not the only prisoner to have seen the moving lights.

Before dark each evening food from the cookhouse in the camp was carried up by cart to the compound where the *zeks* and their guards lived on the hill. That evening two of Barkut's "Khans" had been detailed to go with the cart. Marching beside the whip-guard who led the horse, one of them had glanced back over his shoulder and seen distantly what Bubo had first seen. He had said nothing. But by the time they had unloaded the soup boxes at the compound, he knew that a large convoy of carts and vehicles was hiding behind the bend in the road just beyond the camp.

In his office the colonel received the report of the convoy master, a young Captain, with some satisfaction. The trucks and carts were well hidden off the road and ready to be called up at any time.

The colonel even enjoyed the drama of the situation in explaining at length to the young captain that he would be unable to authorize food to be taken out to the drivers. For camp discipline, he said, it was utterly vital that no one should know until the last moment that a convoy was leaving tonight. The captain, slicing his sausage with his sharp knife, agreed.

Outside the office window the appel-square was well lit. All Panaka guards were on special duty, and as hut after hut of penals trudged across to collect their double ration it was comforting to the colonel to see the stocky figures of the guards, bundled in their overcoats, standing in pairs at every hut doorway. From where he sat at his desk he could see, too, the timber structure of the watchtower rising above the main gate. The platform itself was in darkness, but the knowledge that two light machine guns pointed onto the main square was a further comforting element in what, until now, had been an unnerving day.

It was eight o'clock. There were another six hours to go before the loading operation began. The colonel took from his desk a quart of vodka. He felt that he himself certainly, and the captain even possibly, deserved a warming glass while they waited.

There was no similar calm in the huts. Men gathered in groups wolfing their double ration, spitting soup through broken, gapped teeth, even dropping precious crusts of bread in their anxiety to join in the speculation about the convoy. Why was it hiding? How many men could it take? Who were they to be when the lottery was not to be held until Friday?

In the circumstances it is not surprising that they believed that in some way they were about to be tricked. And if that were so, could it mean that the whole idea of a General Amnesty was just a device to keep them quiet while some other barbarity was planned for them?

Months, years, of near starvation and isolation do not make for rational judgments. When the doors were locked for the night and the lights extinguished, lookouts were posted in every hut to keep watch on their neighbors. Men lay on their plank beds still speculating, seething with anger at yet another betrayal by the system.

At just before midnight Major Kalemnev, the colonel's second in command, entered the office with no more than a perfunctory knock.

The colonel, flushed with vodka, was in the middle of a story to the captain about the young woman doctor at the camp and the passion they had conceived for each other.

He was irritated at Kalemnev's appearance in the doorway. He never knew exactly what the major had heard about the day in his apartment in Krasibirsk when his wife came home.

"What is it Kalemnev?" He lifted his head peremptorily.

"They've heard," the major said. "They know the convoy's waiting."

The colonel rose to his feet in alarm and anger.

"How have they heard?" he roared. "How do you know they've heard?"

The young Captain looked respectfully away.

"I keep a number of informers, Colonel. I see it as my duty as second in command to know exactly what's going on among the penals."

"Your duty, of course it's your duty."

The colonel sat down suddenly, with a furtive glance toward the square outside. "What are they saying? It seems all quiet out there."

"I think they're waiting to see what happens to the convoy."

The colonel poured himself more vodka. He stood up, glass in hand, and began to pace the room. After a few moments while his subordinate watched him, he stopped, tipped the vodka to the back of his throat and hammered the glass down decisively on the desk top.

"No point now in delay," he said. "Kalemnev, assemble all guards, cordon off huts 60 through 70 as we originally planned. Place a two-man guard on the door of each hut. If there are disturbances inside, the guards are to tell them that the evacuation schedule has been speeded up, but that any man attempting to break out of the hut will be immediately shot." He turned to the young captain. "Bring the convoy up to the main gate right away."

The two officers departed. The colonel poured another glass of vodka and stood at the window looking across at the darkened huts.

For half an hour he stood there watching the guards take their positions and the dark line of soldiers cordoning off the huts closest to the main gate. There was no need to panic. His organization would maintain discipline.

At midnight the trucks arrived outside the gates. The doors of huts 60 through 70 were opened and men were thrust forward through the open gate and pushed and kicked onto the trucks. From some of the other huts came shouts of fury. Lights were switched on and off. But the discipline of the guns and dogs at the hut doors held.

One after another at the main gate the trucks were crammed with men before driving forward to take their place on the road leading back to Krasibirsk.

Then, in the outer office, the telephone rang. At this time of night it had to be important. The colonel ran into the other room and snatched the receiver from the sergeant-clerk. The general's voice was on the line.

"My dear fellow," the general said, "has that convoy left yet?"

"No, General. We're just loading now."

"Then don't."

"Don't?" The colonel's mouth dropped open. "Don't load your men. Keep the vehicles there tonight. I'll give you clearance to resume loading tomorrow."

"General, this is a delicate operation. Discipline must be maintained . . ."

"Certainly it must be maintained, Colonel. That's exactly why I'm telephoning you, don't you see?"

"No, General."

"My dear man, we can't receive your penals here in Krasibirsk."

"Why not?" the colonel said angrily.

"Because the KGB border guards who were to escort them west have not yet arrived."

"But they were due today."

"You've been too long out in the woods," the general snapped. "The train that arrives on time is a rarity. Keep those men at Panaka until further orders."

The line was dead in the colonel's hand. He turned on the sergeant-clerk. "Get me Major Kalemnev," he shouted. "Get him over to this office immediately."

He stumbled back into his own room. There was an inch of vodka in the bottle. He poured it into his empty glass and drank it down.

On the rise beyond the camp Anton, Bubo and the three girls stood outside their hut watching the loading of the penals.

It had stopped snowing and the night was now clear and cold. The little group stood together, each with a blanket draped round the shoulders.

Below them in the bright lights of the appel-square they saw Major Kalemnev running toward the administration building.

Anton pulled Zoya closer to him with an arm round her waist. She looked up at him. "We must never stop hoping," she said. "So far, just think how lucky we've been, you and me."

Minutes later the major reappeared, running now even faster, he burst through the cordon of guards and began to shout orders to the officer in charge of the convoy. They were too far away to hear the words, but they saw the line of loading penals falter in its movement toward the trucks, curl back on itself like a snake, then suddenly dissolve into a chaos of men running toward trucks and carts, fighting to get a place aboard.

Down on the square Major Kalemnev found himself overwhelmed by struggling, snarling prisoners. He was kicked to the ground and trampled on as they rushed to the empty trucks.

From the administration building the colonel came running across the square, bareheaded, a pistol in his hand.

He screamed orders for the cordon guard to face the main gates.

Behind him the huts erupted into uproar. He could hear shutters being smashed, men shouting and the sinister chanting of the Khans.

The cordon dissolved in a struggling mass of penals and guards. Rifle shots sounded, thin and tinny in the clear air. The locked doors of one of the huts burst open and men poured out on the square.

Guards retreating toward the administration hut fired a magazine of bullets into the running men. Dogs circled and barked and snapped in panic.

Windows shattered and, monkey-like, men clambered out. Every minute saw another 500 men running wildly onto the square.

From the watchtower the guards fired a long burst and penals tumbled and dropped and somersaulted across the snow-covered tarmac. A second and third burst drove men back into the shelter of the huts, but directly below the watchtower the confusion of struggling guards and penals made it impossible to fire into the melee.

A heavy truck charged forward bumping over the bodies of fallen men. Skidding across the blood and snow, the penal driver aimed the hood at the wooden supports of the watchtower. As the truck crashed among them, the tower jerked back and then slowly forward, like a falling birchtree, into the mass of fighting men.

Flames sprung from the administration hut. Clerks lay among the burning filing boxes with their throats cut.

On the hill, Bubo was at the guard-post of the *zek's* compound. Four terrified guards faced him with their rifles.

"We're *zeks*," he was shouting, "not penals. They'll be up here next. Let's leave now, Brothers. Let's go into the woods. For God's sake, you can see what's happening down there!"

The young soldiers' rifles wavered.

"Save your lives, Comrades. And ours."

Shots and screams and chants and triumphant shouts rose from the camp.

"It's your lives, too, Brothers," Bubo said urgently.

On the square lights shattered one by one. Flames roared from timber huts and men swirled around shouting and singing. Underfoot were trampled bodies of the guards, their throats gaping, their boots ripped off them. The colonel's cadaver, hanging by the neck from a timber of the collapsed watchtower, was punched and knifed and hacked at until the uniform was in shreds and the pool of blood beneath his stockinged feet melted the snow in a great dark circle below the swinging corpse.

For the penals of Panaka Five, it was their night of revenge.

As dawn broke the square was empty except for the bodies of the guards and their dogs in the churned and blood-stained snow. A great fire burned by the main gate and three, perhaps four or five hundred men slept around it, wrapped in blankets and the topcoats of the murdered guards. In those huts which were still intact, thousands of other penals dozed, their backs against the wall. Sleep was the only luxury they had been accustomed to in quantity. Few had the stamina to see the night out.

Among those few were Barkut Khan and his men. They visited each hut commandeering weapons, issuing orders for the morrow. As the penals stumbled, red-eyed, back onto the square, the Khans were in command. Their orders were for the whole camp to march on Krasibirsk. Those trucks and horse-carts which had not escaped the night before would be loaded with the contents of the clothing, food and ammunition store. Any man who disobeyed Barkut's order would have his throat cut.

In the *zeks'* hut above the camp they heard them coming, chanting, shouting, bellowing as they scrambled up the hill.

The four young guards, their rifles pointed at the *zeks,* trembled and dropped their weapons and ran for the door. Somewhere outside as they tried to tear their way through the barbed wire, the penals caught them and cut their throats.

In the hut Bubo stood forward. "We are prisoners like yourselves," he shouted at the group of men. "We have a right to live."

"He was a good work leader out in the woods," a voice shouted from the back.

A small man with a summer black mosquito helmet dangling over his ears waved a rifle. "We've no quarrel with the *zeks,*" he said. "We've come on Barkut's orders. We're taking your women."

Though Bubo and Anton fought until they were unconscious, the other *zeks* held back. Can you blame them? Zoya asked.

Why should they have died for us? We were dragged outside and thrown onto the back of a horse-cart, Anna, Laryssa and myself, and among the chanting men carried down to the main gate where penals crowded the road, ready to march.

I think we must have been assigned a protector, or perhaps several. A young penal, Anatoly, who drove our cart, found us a covering of blankets and some bread and cold soup for the journey, and any penals who grabbed at our arms were quickly beaten aside by the men marching behind the tailgate.

That evening we reached Krasibirsk. There was some rumor, perhaps invented, that a thousand KGB guards were expected. But as the penals swarmed through the streets into Lenin Square, there was no sign of militia or KGB.

Anna, Laryssa and myself were locked in a small hut made of railway sleepers in a siding next to the station, so we saw nothing of the events in Krasibirsk that night. But we heard shouts and screams and shooting and could smell smoke as it penetrated the gaps in our timber hut.

When we were released in the morning, half the penals seemed to be still drunk. And Anatoly, laughing, brought an armful of women's dresses, old-fashioned with long skirts, and insisted we put them on.

During that day we were moved into the waiting room of the railhead station where perhaps sixty young and not so young women had been imprisoned. They were desperate for information which we, in any case, could not give. And sorry as we felt for them in one sense, they were not *zeks*. They had continued living their lives while we, 30 miles away, served our time in Panaka. Many of them though had worked as cleaners or cooks or secretaries at Kraslag headquarters. No, it would be untrue to say we felt overmuch sympathy for them as they told of rapes and beatings during the night. How hard we had become! But after all for them it was just one night!

The KGB troop train turned out to be more than a rumor. When the penals looted the local Kraslag general's office they found evidence that a train was due that day. Hundreds of penals, even thousands, scattered across the countryside. But many thousands of others, probably under pain of death from Barkut Khan, stayed in Krasibirsk. At three in the morning the KGB train arrived. From the waiting room we saw the old steam engine drag itself into the railhead station. It was too long to enable it to line up with the 100 feet of platform, and yawning, stretching KGB troops stood in the cattle-car doorways ready to jump down.

From where we were, crouched in the darkened waiting room, we saw bullets split and rip through the woodwork of the cattle cars, we saw KGB men pitch forward from the doorways and we saw hordes of penals storm forward with knives and axes, hurling themselves on the border troops as they tried to jump down onto the lines.

We hid our eyes from the worst. But I heard afterward from Anatoly that those border guards who had survived the first onslaught were all butchered in the warehouses opposite before morning. The terrible screams and pleas for mercy which we could not block our ears to testified to the truth of Anatoly's account.

Oh God, it's so easy to forget. Was it on the third morning that we were ordered onto the train? Two women were assigned to each cattle car of fifty men. But still Laryssa, Anna and myself were held apart, assigned to a cattle car where clearly Anatoly was still to guard us.

We were going west. That's all Anatoly would tell us, probably all he knew. We were going west and they now had real guns. Not only the border guards' small arms but the twenty 60-mm guns on the light tanks which were also part of their equipment. Until then I had forgotten that all the penals had been soldiers before their imprisonment.

No modesty. Of course we suffered that night. Not like the other women. But still, many times . . .

Chapter Thirty-six

IN TRANSYLVANIA THE Ukrainian Liberation Army proved to be hard fact. It was not large, hardly more than two brigades in numbers, but groups of Ukrainians were crossing the border into Transylvania every day now to join the battle.

The Hungarian government saw the danger of embracing their unasked-for allies, but the Ukrainians, although only lightly armed, were providing a valuable diversionary element in the battle. More important, their presence had had a totally stultifying effect on the policymakers in the Kremlin. The Rumanians demanded the bandits should be dealt with by the Soviet Army, but refused to allow the Russians across their borders. They clearly had no confidence that they would ever be able to eject them. Hungary rejected all Soviet demands for the forcible return of the Ukrainians pleading that they could not spare the troops for the operation.

The response to the war of the Hungarian minority in Rumania had been such that the Ceausescu government now faced an internal rebellion as well as an invasion by foreign forces. In the largely Hungarian belt of counties stretching across Transylvania and deep into Rumania itself—

Bihor, Cluj, Mures and Harghita—Hungarian partisans were attacking Rumanian troop formations as they moved toward the front.

In Hungarian-speaking areas there was hardly a family without relatives in the Magyar homeland and Hungarian tanks were welcomed with emotional scenes in the villages along their line of advance. Equally emotional was the Rumanian reaction which saw in the possible loss of Transylvania the reduction of the national territory by almost half.

Two Soviet delegations were dispatched in the first week of the war to the two capitals. In Budapest they were received quietly and asked to await developments. Without firm instructions from Moscow they had no option. In Bucharest the Soviet cars driving the delegation from the airport had been identified on the streets and stoned by the populace. In Rumania it was already widely believed that the Soviet Union had prompted the Hungarian attack and that the Ukrainian National Army was nothing more than a disguised Soviet military formation. Such are the complexities of Balkan politics.

But in Moscow, grave as the Transylvania crisis was in fact, people in the city were much more concerned with the new evidence of the Chinese threat. Almost a quarter of a century of propaganda had enflamed the Slavs' distrust of the East to a deep loathing. Russians respect numbers. The sheer size of the Chinese population was enough to impress the average Russian citizen.

Yet detestation and fear of the Chinese, far from unifying Soviet citizens against the external threat (it had been used successfully as a deliberate technique many times in the past), now had the effect of drawing Russian citizens together against the backsliding republics of the Soviet Union and against a government which appeared to be too weak to control events. The autumn of desperate shortage of food and fuel had revealed that anarchy which lies just below the surface of Russian conformism.

Yet the Moscow Carole Yates walked through as she left the foreigners compound that evening seemed little different than the city she had come to know in the last few months. A cutback in power had just ended and the streetlights were on again. Office windows were brightly lit, the queues lined the shop fronts and the buses roared busily down the *prospekts*. At the Metropole Hotel she hailed a taxi.

It was, as so often in Moscow, a woman driver. "You're a foreigner, gospodina," she said as Carole got into the seat beside her.

"I'm American."

"Ah, then you have these troubles, too, with your blacks. For us it's Asiatics. I won't even allow them in the taxi. Never want to pay the full fare. Bargain with you, straight out of the bazaars, they are. And the money they earn! Just here for the long ruble, depend on it. Russia for the Russians is the way we should be. Look at the rubles we hand out to the rest of the world. We're supporting Africa, you know. Every bag of grain they eat, over half comes from Russia. And *we've* got bread rationing! Are you surprised? These Czechs and Rumanians and Bulgarians aren't much better. Cadging education from us because it's the best in the world, naturally. Then they go back and stir up trouble at home! And then who has to help them out?

"But you can't beat the Asiatics for plain ingratitude. Who built them up? We did, of course. Before the coming of Soviet power they were nothing. Camel dealers, bazaar thieves. You heard about the Vladimir rape? Yes, well that tells you a few things. In my district which is crawling with them, a young girl daren't go out by herself at night. And some not so young." She howled with laughter. "Although I suppose for some of the old ones it's their only chance!"

Leaving the taxi at Nogina Street, Carole walked back toward Solyanka Street. He would have to come that way.

For the next half-hour she had threaded back and forth between the side streets behind the Ulitza Solyanka, trying always to keep the crucial corner in sight. At just after five o'clock she saw him under a lamp across the street in front of her. She ran forward, her boots slipping in the hard-packed snow. Bundled figures of Muscovites turned to stare after her.

"Alex," she called, "Alex!"

He reached the curb and turned suddenly, extending his arms to catch her.

"I know what they asked you to do," she was saying into the fur collar of his coat. "I know why you wanted to stop seeing me."

He led her quickly into a deep alleyway. A faint blue light shone on piles of stacked wooden crates. In the darkness between them, he kissed her.

"My husband, Tom, found out," she said. "The KGB wanted you to report on me." The words bubbled out of her.

"I couldn't tell you," he said.

"You didn't trust me enough to tell me."

"Carole," he said hopelessly. "Understand for God's sake. I didn't have the *right* to tell you."

"You still didn't trust me with your safety."

"No, not just for my safety. Others, too."

"Your parents?"

He didn't answer. "I'm glad you know, Carole," he said. "But it can't make any difference."

"Alex, I'm leaving Moscow in a few days. Can *that* make any difference? Can it?"

She watched the struggle played out on his face.

"When do you leave?" he asked after a few moments.

"Thursday. I would have gone tomorrow but I'm having some customs problems with jewelry I brought in. On these trivial things . . ."

"Hangs a thread?" he said. "Is that the English expression?"

"No, Alex," she smiled. "But in this case it will do."

The wind through the alley made the wooden crates creak.

"I must go now," she said. "I just wanted to tell you I know."

He reached out and touched her face. "Could you be free tomorrow afternoon? And tomorrow night?"

"My husband wants a divorce. I'm free."

It was the same journey Zoya had made in the other direction almost a year before. Throughout the second day Anatoly had brought the three women drink and had allowed them off the train at the frequent stops made to clear the line ahead of snow. He had now made it clear that the three women were for the entertainment of Barkut himself.

They lay among the filthy straw in the cattle car peering through the wooden slats at the interminable snow-covered forests that hugged the track. It was impossible to keep despair at bay. And equally impossible to think of escape. Even when they were allowed out into the snowdrifts to wash, Anatoly came with them, his rifle in the crook of his arm.

During the afternoon stop Barkut came. Hardly glancing at the other two, he reached down and seized Anna by the wrist. Dragging her after him he jumped down onto the track.

He took her there before our eyes [Zoya said], Anna made no attempt to resist. It would have been futile anyway. When it was over he got to his feet and walked away tying his cloth belt.

We could see she was crying but quietly, not uncontrollably. She stood up and we stretched out hands to pull her up beside us. I suppose neither of us had even noticed the penals gathering behind her, until one of them grabbed her round the waist and hauled her back down onto the track.

Struggling wildly she was dragged back to one of the other cars. We screamed at Anatoly to help. But he stood in the doorway of the boxcar shrugging. "She's theirs now," he said, and slid the slatted door closed.

The train bumped and clanked forward through the remainder of the daylight and into the evening. Sometimes we thought we heard Anna screaming in the boxcar behind us, but over the rattling of the train, the shouts of the penals and the occasional burst of automatic fire loosed into the night, the man-muffled scream of one woman would not carry far . . . perhaps after a while we pretended not to hear. There was nothing whatsoever we could do to help.

With Anatoly there were five men in the boxcar with us. Throughout the afternoon they had been drinking vodka from the store of bottles in the corner, but apart from a few lewd jokes, they had paid little attention to us. Perhaps it was because they feared Barkut's return at any one of the many short stops. Both Laryssa and myself knew it would be different during the night.

Anatoly was sitting with his back against the side of the car, dozing across the rifle crooked in his arm. My first intention was to steal one of the bottles of vodka now rolling in the straw. In the light of the swinging kerosene lamp, as I edged toward the nearest bottle, I realized that the other four men were asleep, too.

Perhaps that's how escapes are made. I stretched out a hand and with the tips of my fingers rolled the bottle within reach. Then moving back to Laryssa I indicated the sleeping men. She understood immediately. As the train slowed yet again, we got to our feet. I picked up a stale and dirty half loaf and shoved it into the pocket of my quilted zek's coat. The door slid back easily. I followed Laryssa out into the black night.

I suppose we were lucky. We landed a few feet apart in a drift deep enough to break our fall. Even the vodka bottle was intact.

We crawled toward each other and watched the train disappearing along the single-line moonlit track. An hysterical feeling of exhilaration seized us both. We laughed and guzzled vodka until the tears streamed down and froze upon our cheeks. Then both together it seemed we stopped laughing. We were both, I'm certain, thinking of Anna.

We had absolutely no thought of where we might be. From somewhere north of Moscow, at Vologda I think, the line ran almost due north through Kotlas and Pechora, then, as if shying away from the dreaded Gulag area of Vorkuta, it crossed the Ural Mountains to head through wastes of frozen marsh and birchwoods to the railhead at Krasibirsk on the River Ob. The purpose of the single-track line was, I suppose, to transport copper (mined by zeks) from the new field on the northern reaches of the Ob and the Panaka timber into the industrial centers of the Urals. I had traveled the route out to Krasibirsk the December before but there was nothing to recognize in these unending forests.

We decided to keep to the track and trudge on west. At this stage we hadn't decided whether or not we would stop the next train.

It was too cold to snow, but our quilted jackets kept us warm enough. For the first ten minutes we kept looking behind as if expecting a train, but soon we trudged on, the act of stepping over the railroad ties punishing our calf muscles.

We found it comforting to hold each others gloved hand as we walked.

It was perhaps about midnight when we stopped and built ourselves a windbreak from the lower branches of young fir trees. Then with another capful of vodka each, we settled down to sleep.

Chapter Thirty-seven

CAROLE TURNED UP the radio in the sitting room until it blared through the apartment. Tom Yates, already dressed for the cold outside, his briefcase in his hand, frowned irritably. The turned-up radio meant she had something important to say. He took off his fur hat which was already intolerably hot in the apartment.

"What is it?" he asked her.

"I won't be back tonight, Tom. I thought I should tell you."

He stood before her. Sweat was already beading his forehead.

"Change your mind, Carole," he said, "and I could change mine."

She reached out and squeezed his arm within the thick material of the coat. "No, Tom. I won't be back tonight."

He nodded and pushed the fur hat on his head. "In that case I'll see you tomorrow," he said.

When he left she turned down the radio and went to the hall closet selecting the shabby coat and fur hat she wore for her visits to the market. Her market bag was already packed in the bedroom, the green oilcloth sides cracked with wear.

At eleven-thirty she stood with a group of Muscovites on the platform at Pavelets Station. In her worn cloth coat and carrying the battered shopping bag she merged easily with the Russian women returning to the country after an early morning shopping foray to the capital.

The train was shunted into the station barely a half-hour late and the peasants and a few skiers with their short Russian skis strapped to their backs pushed and scrambled their way aboard. In a crowded compartment Carole found herself pressed into the corner of the wooden slat seat. Her companions, women mostly in their fifties and sixties, their heads bound with cloth scarves after their rabbit fur hats were removed, settled down to crack hard-boiled eggs and gossip about their morning in Moscow.

There were two young soldiers in the compartment, too, and the women offered them eggs and bread and asked them about their villages. After a while one of the women produced a liter and it was passed around, emptying at what Carole considered an astonishing rate. She herself had refused, but the young soldiers happily accepted.

"And where have you boys been serving?" the most garrulous of the women asked.

"Here and there, Grandma," one of the boys answered. "Here, there and everywhere."

"Not so much of the Grandma," the woman said. "I'm still young enough to take care of you two lads," and cackling she pulled open her cloth coat and pushed forward heavy breasts beneath a layer of woolen cardigans and a print dress.

The soldier blushed uncomfortably.

"So where have you been, my lads? Our taxes pay you, we've a right to know. Out east? Defending us against the little slant-eyed men?"

"South," the other soldier said.

"Oh, they don't like us there either, do they? My husband said years ago that the Georgian girls wouldn't look at a Russian soldier. And if they did, their elder brothers would give them a good beating for it."

"That's right," the first soldier grunted.

"Anyway, so now you're home to chase the girls for a week or two," and she burst into a bawdy village song, kicking her fat brown legs, bare above the cloth boots, out in front of the soldiers.

At the town of Podolsk, Carole left the train. She walked down the platform and out into the semicircular concrete entrance hall, decorated only by the town's crossed pickax coat of arms. Among crowds stumbling toward the Tula train with their roped-up cardboard suitcases, Letsukov was shouldering his way toward her.

With his arms round her she felt the ungainly bulk of her old coat and the three sweaters she wore underneath.

"What happened to my smart American girl friend?" he whispered in English in her ear.

They caught a bus in the station yard and trundled for half an hour through factory suburbs, past a nineteenth-century Singer sewing machine plant until the country suddenly stretched and rolled before them. The road now was straight and narrow, the cleared middle section running between great banks of snow. At small isolated crossroads the peasants descended lugging their inevitable heavy bags. Presumably from there they walked to their distant villages.

It was already late afternoon and on their left the sun was glowering fiercely below low purple cloud. Across the great snow-covered hillsides the last rays gilded the whiteness and threw into deep shadow the rare footprints of man or horse along the edges of the woods.

At a crossroad as deserted as the others they left the bus. The low green vehicle vomited diesel fumes and ice chips from under its wheel chains as it skidded away.

"Have you ever used Russian skis?" Letsukov asked her.

"No."

"Then you'll learn. Sit down there."

"In the snow?"

"In the snow."

He dug into the snowbank beside her and pulled out two pairs of short skis. While she lay back against the drift he fixed them to her boots.

"Try them," he said, beginning to tie on his own skis. "It's a walking movement, sliding each foot forward."

She tried a few cautious steps, lifting the ski from the snow each time. "Just how far do we have to go like this?"

He stood beside her. "You keep your ski flat on the snow," he instructed, "then slide it forward . . ."

"You still didn't say how far."

"Not more than three miles, I promise."

Night fell quickly. She found she soon got into the rhythm as she moved along beside him down the country track. No vehicle had passed this way since the last fall of snow. Perhaps not since the first fall in early November.

In the moonlight their breath steamed into the cold air and disappeared in the darkness. Once or twice on the way they saw a light glimmering up on the hillside from an isolated woodcutter's hut. And once they heard, in a leafless copse beside the track, the furious grunting of a wild boar. It was a Russia she had only seen from a warm car or through the misted glass of a train window. For the first time she smelled the intense cold cleanliness of the air and heard the cries of nameless predators in the night.

After about an hour, when her calf muscles were just beginning to signal defeat, they turned onto an even narrower track through mixed woods of pine and bleak oak. Here the snow was thicker and they struggled forward, hand in hand, climbing thick drifts in the middle of the forest track, sliding down the other side.

After perhaps another twenty minutes, he slowed down, breathing heavily from a particularly sharp climb. "All this and you haven't complained once."

She stopped, her skis crossed like a pigeon-toed teenager. "I've never felt less like complaining in my life," she said.

With his arm round her shoulder they turned a bend in the track and approached a clutch of wooden farm huts with lights shining brightly in the windows of the main *izba*.

Wood smoke poured down upon them as Letsukov hammered on the door.

"That you, Alexei?" a voice shouted from inside.

"It's me, Volodya," Letsukov said. The door was unlocked and Carole entered a long low room, its rafters and wall beams painted in gold-rimmed reds and blues, its floor of cracked flagstones, the walls a dull clay. Three lamps hung on chains above a long table. Six or seven men and women were seated round an equal number of vodka bottles. She saw beards, flushed faces, all welcoming.

The man at the door, Volodya, slammed it closed and began to unbutton Carole's coat. "Your own fingers won't do this," he said, "not until you've warmed up." He peeled the coat off her and propelled her toward the stove. "This is Kitty," he said, tapping a dark-haired girl on the head, "and that's Lavrenty, Clara, Peter, Lev, Maria and Simochka."

Kitty got up and crossed to the stove carrying a glass of vodka. "What a walk you've had," she said, handing Carole the glass. "But dinner won't be long. Alexei," she shouted over her shoulder, "if you prefer plum brandy there's some in the cupboard."

"Does he prefer plum brandy?" Carole asked.

"Well, you know Alexei . . ." She laughed. But of course Carole didn't.

No special attention beyond the initial politeness was paid to Carole as they all sat round the table. Kitty and Volodya had put out some slices of garlic sausage and small bowls of onion rings and pickled gherkins. Dinner it seemed was forgotten in an exchange of argument, laughter, more discussion and jokes, some in Western terms amazingly crude and personal.

She was quickly aware that totally Russian as they were, none of them had a high regard for Soviet power.

"Are we then to live with it forever, Alexei?" Kitty asked vehemently.

"We'll have to live with it. At least until we learn how to overthrow it," Letsukov said.

Carole, sitting next to him, turned and stared at him in astonishment. He reached under the table and squeezed her hand.

"Would Americans be so supine?" Lev asked Carole, his black beard jerking toward her.

She shrugged, slightly intimidated. "How can I answer that?" she said. "If such things were imposed upon them today they'd strike, demonstrate. At least I hope they would. But all this began in Russia yesterday, when perhaps the world seemed more full of hope."

Simochka, big as many men, clapped her on the shoulder and poured her more vodka.

"But Alexei says we must wait," Lev persisted. "Why?"

"Because Alexei has seen the results of local efforts, of attempts to demonstrate in one city only. He's the only one of us, furthermore, who has actually met Joseph Densky."

"Who is Joseph Densky?" Carole asked Simochka next to her. But Letsukov touched her arm.

"Densky is a leader. *The* leader of the Free Trade Union Movement," Letsukov said. "That is what first brought us together. We are all members."

"And Joseph Densky?"

"He's in prison in Leningrad. Or perhaps now in a camp somewhere."

"An hour ago," she said, "I didn't know you belonged to an underground organization."

He put his arm round her and pulled her toward him to roars of approval from Lev and Volodya. "It's not too late to learn," he said.

After they had eaten, Letsukov announced that it was time to work. Leaving dishes on the table, they rose. Volodya had gone to the corner of the room and, removing the straw mat, he pulled up a trap door. One by one they descended the narrow stairway.

Carole clambered down into the cellar, her hand on the shoulder of Letsukov, a step or two below her. At the bottom of the stairs she stopped. Before her was a large, earth-walled room. Three printing presses occupied most of the floor space. Rolls of newsprint were stacked in rough wooden shelving.

"It's here that *Iskra* is produced," Simochka said proudly. "Your Alexei is our new editor—and sometimes printer's devil, too, it has to be admitted."

Carole turned to Letsukov. "It's you? *Iskra* is you?"

"And many others, darling," he said, using the English word. "Thousands now who risk everything to distribute it throughout the Soviet Union."

She held him tight. "I want to help," she said.

"You will," he smiled. "You can start by loading this machine."

They worked among the clattering machines until well past midnight. And when the roughly printed single-sheet newspapers were stacked all round the walls, they climbed the stairs again and the vodka bottles were brought out.

Much later they lay on a thick straw mattress on top of the brick stove. They were both wildly drunk, exhausted after a night of work, drinking and singing.

That night a blizzard blew that slashed snow across the windows and tore at the tiled roof. The wind, howling like wolves, blasted snow through cracks in the doorframe and billowed smoke from the stove into the moonlit room.

They made love too drunk to be inhibited by the presence of the other pairs in the hut, laughing sometimes at the shouted encouragements from Lev and Simochka or at the rustling straw and the groans from other corners of the room.

In the morning they awoke, friends and lovers. Maria, in a blue track suit, was frying bacon. Plates rattled at the table as Simochka threw them carelessly down. Volodya, stripped to the waist, was washing in a bucket of boiled snow. Lev still lay in bed, smoking and jocularly complaining about being disturbed all night by the noise from above the stove.

Kitty came in carrying wood as Carole and Letsukov descended from their sleeping place over the stove. She dropped the logs in a corner and turned back to Carole. "Good," she said, having completed her examination of Carole's face. "Where I come from they'd say you're glowing red as a well-poked stove."

Carole found she could laugh with the others. She slipped her arm round Letsukov's waist. "Good," she mimicked Kitty. "And why not? I've every reason to be."

It was a journey back heavily tinged with sadness. The wind had dropped very little and the snow, driving in their faces, made talking difficult. It had been already decided that they should part at the crossroad so that she could take the first bus into Podolsk, and he would wait the two hours for the next one. They had thought to have a little while together before the bus came. But the strength of the wind and their own misery had slowed their pace and when they arrived at the main road, the bus was already approaching.

They stood together struggling to ignore the lights of the bus piercing the driving snow.

"That word, 'good-bye,'" she said haltingly, "how can I say it to you now, Alex? How can I say it when I'm more in love than I ever imagined possible?"

She saw the pain tighten the muscles around his mouth.

On the road behind them the bus had slithered to a halt.

"You remember in Gorky Park, Carole? You remember we agreed to take this risk? I never guessed . . ."

She was shaking from cold and misery. The bus driver's horn blasted through the snow.

He ran his fingers across her lips. "Remember Russia," he said.

"I'll remember you," her voice was a whisper. "All my life." She turned away and stumbled toward the bus.

The last she saw of him was through the rear window as he stood at the empty crossroad, gradually fading from sight like a footprint in the still falling snow.

Chapter Thirty-eight

A GLANCE AT the rail map of the Soviet Union makes the situation clear. Moscow is the point through which almost all east-west rail lines pass. It is also for most north-south movements the *only* connecting point. The transport of nearly 300,000 penals from the north and northeast would inevitably bring the majority to Moscow.

As estimates of the number of penals arriving began pouring in from towns all over western Siberia, the lights began to burn late in the Lubyanka. Reports arrived of 20,000 penals awaiting transport to Moscow in Vologda; 35,000 marching to the railhead from Syktykar; 60,000 and no available rations at Perm; over 100,000 scattered throughout the Tomsk *oblast* looting their way west. What should have been a controlled flow had become a flood as camp commandants hastily turned over their responsibilities to railway officials and the local KGB.

From Gulag main headquarters in Moscow urgent messages were sent to camps all over Siberia instructing commandants to retain their prisoners until further orders. In practice the orders frequently arrived at empty camps, some like Panaka, where the bodies of the guards lay stiff-frozen in the snow.

Other rumors, too, reached the Lubyanka. It was reported that in some areas the penals had attacked civilian labor camps and released the *zeks*. From these distant snow-covered regions, Moscow Gulag was suddenly unable to gain confirmation.

Inevitably word reached the Moscow citizen, rumors spreading in the shopping queues throughout the city. But because no one had any real knowledge of the numbers originally sent to the penal camps, even the babushkas in the bread queues now talked only of hundreds, and infrequently thousands, of penals descending on the Moscow main stations.

On the night of December 5th, the first arrivals were seen at the Kazan Station. The militia were present in overwhelming force. Those Moscow travelers who had seen the penals, 500 cowed, half-starved men, reported to their families that the fears of the babushkas were grandmothers' fears.

The situation changed again the next morning. A long line of cattle cars arrived from the northeast, sixty men or more to a truck. Before the militia were able to issue orders, the penals had leaped from the cars and were running across the lines, leaping barriers and shouting and dancing through the main hall of the station. From a camp where perhaps the rations had been more adequate, they resembled only slightly the "poor devils" of the night before. Three thousand men flowed out into the area around the Kazan Station. Every man carried some item of value—a pair of good boots, a peasant coverlet for the wedding bed, curtains, books, even small pieces of furniture. All was quickly bartered for vodka.

As the area militia strove to bring the penals back into the station district a second, unscheduled train arrived from Perm. There was no possibility now of containing the penals in the area of the marshaling yards where lines of smoking soup kitchens had been set up. The penals had had enough cabbage soup.

Sophia B., who prefers to be known as Madame Sophie de Nerval, lived in a crumbling apartment close to the station:

Of course, I'm French. I was born in Paris in 1910, the daughter of a French member of the pre-Revolutionary (French Revolutionary, I mean) nobility. His name was Philippe de Nerval. The fact that my mother was a servant girl from the old Russo-Polish border areas, admittedly of humbler origins than my father, makes no difference. *I am French.* I've spent a lifetime trying to prove my case to the *vlasti* here, but they won't listen. To have an aristocratic lineage is a crime. To wish to leave Russia compounds the crime fourfold. Still I live in hope. Sadly I have no son to give the de Nerval name. But I have relatives in the West. One day, one day, my dears, I hope to join them.

Of course you'll say I'm a testy old woman and a snob. And you'd be right. But who wouldn't be a snob in this land of squalid tower blocks and shock-workers and political education, which of course means none whatsoever. My mother told me that in France my father's estate had a thousand serfs. "Immoral" I said when I was young. But at least *their* labors released *him* for civilized conversation.

I'm not the fool perhaps I seem to you. Cross me in argument, my dear, and I will worst you. Those poor men stumbling laughing from the station, well, my old aristocratic heart went out to them. Peasants they were. But like me, prisoners of this beautiful country, this awful State. I threw them flowers down from my window, and a bottle and a loaf.

So strange they looked with their shaven heads or (some of them) with those thin black, tight-fitting cloth helmets which were supposed to

protect their shaven skulls from the Siberian mosquitoes. How they
rioted! Milling around, shouting and laughing and drinking, shoving their
hands up the skirts of any little Russian office girl they cornered. Lord! If
the militia couldn't get them back into the station by nightfall I could see
trouble coming . . .

Sophie de Nerval (why not call her by the name she claimed) was right.
In the early afternoon a train approached the Yaroslavl Station which is
sited across Krasnoprudnaya Street from the Kazan Station. Militia
officers held it up not far away at the Tikhvin Virgin signal box while they
moved men into position to receive it. But hardly had it stopped when
small groups of penals from the earlier train, staggering drunkenly across
the lines, were thundering with their fists on the wooden slatted doors.
"Girls and vodka, this way, Brothers. Soup and a lonely bed of straw if
you stay in there!"

From outside the penals hammered the locks off the doors and men
jumped down, seizing pieces of stone, wooden spars, anything to release
their comrades.

In this way another 3,000 penals were added to the problems of the
militia in the Kazan-Yaroslavl station area.

Depend on it, most Muscovites did not take the arrival of the penals
with the same insouciance as Madame de Nerval. They were, first of all,
deeply shocked by the numbers involved, by the physical condition of
many of the men and by the air of wild-eyed violence they carried with
them. As evening fell not only the inhabitants of the Kazan Station district
locked themselves in their apartments. Word had spread that at other
Moscow main stations, too, drunken Asiatics were arriving by the
trainload.

But for Moscow these were early days. From small towns along the rail
route from the north and east, reports were reaching *oblast* militia
headquarters of a situation descending rapidly into chaos.

The town of Rostov-Yaroslavsky (population 35,000) can serve as an
example for many others.

The following is the report of a Western journalist, an American, on a
visit to Rostov to do a twin-town story with a "similar" township in
Minnesota:

Even in Russian terms Rostov-Yaroslavsky on Lake Nero is an old
settlement. Founded even before the days of King Rurik, it gets its first
mention in the chronicles of A.D. 892. It was a trading town dealing in
honey, silver, amber, grain and furs. In 989 it became officially Christian

when the inhabitants were divided into groups of ten and forcibly baptized in the lake.

Rostov has had its good times as the number of ornate churches testifies. "The Devil," it is said, "went to Rostov, but the churches sent him packing."

Last night the Devil came to Rostov again in the shape of four or five thousand released Army prisoners. But even the abundance of Rostov churches, even the great Uspensky Cathedral, was not enough to send him packing this time.

Most days Rostov-Yaroslavsky is a quiet town nestling round the earth wall which still surrounds its ancient kremlin. The people here work mainly in the food processing and linen industry but a strong craft tradition still produces beautiful enamel work in nineteenth-century styles.

Rostov, of course, like almost all Russian cities, has had its times of trouble. Back in the seventeenth century it was sacked by invading Poles and Lithuanians. As late as the 1950s it was struck by a fierce hurricane which damaged some of the onion domes of the kremlin.

And I suspect today will remain in the folk memory of inhabitants of Rostov for many, many generations.

Nobody seems to know how or why the so-called penals arrived at Rostov Station just north of the big Sverdlov Street. The men, several thousand half-starved ex-labor camp prisoners, arrived by cattle car the evening before. Why they were all taken off the cars remains a mystery.

The whole center of Rostov was filled with penals. Near the Church of Our Savior in the market I saw them beating down house doors with hammers and dragging out the women to dance with them. Blazing automobiles dotted the square. Groups of militiamen, fifty or a hundred strong, were trying to pen the ex-prisoners into side streets and among the flashing batons small arms' fire was to be heard too.

The sidewalk was literally heaving with groaning men, inhabitants of Rostov who'd been set upon and beaten up by the penals. On Karl Marx Street there was not one shop window intact.

The fighting continued all night with bursts of shooting to be heard every ten or fifteen minutes.

When dawn broke the militia had gained control. The penals had been forced back into the railway station and Lunacharskogo Street was a mass of militia vehicles and grim-faced young men with tired eyes and itchy fingers on the triggers of their automatic weapons.

The town itself will take some time to recover. At dawn the dead were still on the streets—both men and women. The bodies of four penals, obviously cut down by rifle-fire, were draped in ornate gold-embroidered materials looted from a church. Other penals, wounded and near death, lay still unattended on the sidewalks or in the gutters. Broken glass was everywhere and shop goods, which are not in any case that plentiful in the Soviet Union, were strewn across the streets. Wrecked and burned out cars were everywhere.

I had been out in the town for less than fifteen minutes when I was picked up by a militia car and driven back to my hotel and told that's where I would remain. In Rostov-Yaroslavsky that morning there was no arguing with the militia.

Throughout the Soviet Union now the forces of the militia, the Ministry of the Interior and the KGB were stretched to the breaking point.

In western towns of the Ukraine and Belorussia and in the rebellious Baltic republics of Latvia, Lithuania and Estonia, food riots and demonstrations occupied such numbers of militiamen that calls for reinforcement to the central authority became more common every day. Yet such calls often fell on deaf ears.

The KGB border guards, a 400,000 strong paramilitary force, had already been thinned by internal security requirements along the Trans-Siberian Railway, and refugees attempting the once hazardous crossing of the Soviet borders into Finland or Turkey or Iran now began to appear regularly on Western television news programs with horrendous tales of shortage, famine even, and a spreading anarchy throughout the Soviet Union.

The tales, like all such, were frequently highly exaggerated, self-justifying, émigré versions of a past they had put behind them. But the West received them and beamed them back into the Soviet Union via Russian-language radio broadcasts.

But KGB *oblast* generals and republic commanders, attempting to deploy their stretched forces, were now faced with yet another, and much more menacing, internal security problem.

The mobilization of A and B Class reservists was going badly. In a number of the republics, notably Armenia, where Mikoyan strove to ride the nationalist tiger, huge demonstrations began to take place and for the first time the familiar draft-card burning of America's Vietnam era was seen in the Soviet Union.

In Erevan and Leninakan in Armenia on December 14th, in Baku, Kirovabad and Sumgait in Azerbaijan during the following week, in Georgia's Tbilisi and Kirghizia's Frunze, reservists' negotiating committees were formed and Party Secretaries were presented with a list of demands. The first demand in every case was that no reservist should be called upon to serve outside the frontiers of his own national republic. The second was that every reservist should have the right to join one of the

national divisions rather than a regular Russian-speaking Soviet Army
unit. The third demand was that the national divisions now serving in the
north should be brought back home.

The first dribble of returning penals fanned the flames. Their stories of
captivity at the hands of the Slavs spread like wild-fire across the southern
nation-republics, sometimes now in the form of underground newspapers
like *Sakartvelo* (the name of the national language) in Georgia or *Pishpek*
(the former name of Frunze) in Kirghizia.

In republics which had never liked the Russian elder brother Rus-
sophobia spread. Russians were attacked on the streets or ejected from
their smart city center apartments. There were assassinations of Russian
experts in the country areas and it was an unwise man who now tried to
address a market trader in anything but the national language.

The virtual failure of the Class A and B mobilization in six southern
republics caused alarm in the Soviet military command.

In the third week of December, Marshal Kolotkin asked for a meeting
with General Secretary Kuba.

The request was the result of at least five turbulent conferences in which
dissension among Soviet military leaders had risen to the surface.

The older generals and marshals gathered around the now non-
agenarian figure of Marshal Kolotkin had fought a fierce rear-guard
action. The shortage of manpower, they claimed, was exactly what *they*
had predicted and feared while they were pressing for a muzhik army, an
army traditionally based on the unlimited reserves of the Soviet population.

Younger senior officers argued equally fiercely that the attempt to
maintain just such an army had resulted in half a million men in penal
battalions, unrest among the national units and the present chaos of the
General Amnesty.

Worse, at a time when China was maneuvering in the Amur border
areas and the Soviet Union was faced with an internecine war on the
Hungarian-Rumanian border, KGB commands were asking the military
to assume internal security roles. The intense dislike of any trained soldier
to perform this function supplied the Army's answer. Its responsibility
was not in education (Russification) nor in internal security. The Army's
responsibility was to protect the borders of the Soviet Union against
foreign adventurism. This must be the limit of the military's role.

The old marshal and his colleagues saw disaster staring them in the
face. They could not dispute the disastrous response to the mobilization
order. And where was a mass infantry-based army to come from today if
not from the republics?

At the end of the last of the conferences Marshal Kolotkin called for
vodka to toast the healing of what he called a former schism in Soviet

military thinking. Nobody was sure whether he was surrendering his position or claiming victory in debate over the younger generals.

In fact, Kolotkin himself was no longer sure. He made a speech referring to the dire warnings he had given the Party over the last forty years. Halfway through it seemed possible that he had confused Hitler's Germany with the United States. He agreed fiercely that the Party should be informed of the realities of the situation but revealed to no one what he considered those realities to be.

A committee was appointed at the end of Kolotkin's speech to draft a report to Comrade Kuba and the Politburo. It was significant that General Rossasky, one of the foremost figures among the younger leadership, was appointed Secretary-Chairman. The marshals had lost the day.

On December 19th the requested meeting took place at Arch-angelskoye with General Kuba, Prime Minister Bukin and the new Defense Minister, General Dora of the KGB. It was later to become known in the history of these times as the Second Archangelskoye Conference.

A last-minute decision by Kuba had brought Mikoyan, the Armenian Party Secretary, by special jet from the south. For the moment he was left waiting in the forehall while the conference opened in the galleried Oval Hall.

On Kuba's invitation old Marshal Kolotkin opened the session. For long seconds he shuffled the papers in front of him, looked up glaring fiercely round the table, then reapplied himself to his documents.

"In the old days," he said at last, his voice rumbling from his bemedaled chest, "we revolutionaries fought for the future of Soviet power. Enemies abounded! So do they still!" He snarled down at his papers and everyone present realized for the first time how drunk he was.

"Yes, they do still," he hammered the table.

Again the 90-year-old Marshal fell silent. "I've made my report," he said at length. "I've nothing more to say. Young General Rossasky here will present it for me. It's detail . . . detail . . . but Comrades, don't lose heart. We have gripped the old world by the throat and shaken it as a bear shakes a wolf. The other wolves gather and snap, but what can they do? What can they do against a Russian bear?"

He raised his old head, his rheumy eyes peering from one to another round the table. "What *can* the wolves do? Rossasky, read the report. Read the detail . . ."

Briskly General Rossasky began. He described the deployment and the state of readiness of Soviet forces throughout the U.S.S.R. In the west he said, the armored divisions facing the NATO alliance had been and must continue to be maintained at full strength. Any reduction in forces here would invite Western adventurism.

On the Hungarian and Rumanian borders ten divisions awaited the Politburo's decision. And on the Chinese border in Amur IV, V and VI areas where there were further reports of large adventurist Chinese troop movements, forty reserve divisions of the Soviet Army were now moving into position. With the current chaos in Trans-Siberian rail transport, air-bridge units of the Soviet Air Force were critically stretched. The National Divisions were inadequately equipped for a front-line reinforcement role. It was therefore possible that, on a strictly temporary basis, the National Divisions might be used in an internal security role against the increasingly violent penals. But that, in the present crisis, was as far as it was conceivable to go.

General Rossasky continued:

Combined military command headquarters has received numerous requests for assistance with the amnestied penals. These have not been granted. Combined headquarters believes that this must remain a militia-KGB responsibility. Involvement of the military in internal security operations has proved counterproductive in the recent past.

Combined headquarters, however, notes with concern the formation of a number of organized units from the former penal brigades now operating north and east of Moscow. In isolated areas it agrees that an air strike against such units would be feasible if the leadership decided to request it. In other areas the Army repeats that the only forces available for use in a general containment role are the National Divisions.

When the meeting broke up at Archangelskoye Chairman Kuba called Mikoyan into the huge Oval Room. As the Armenian First Secretary later described the interview, Kuba was standing alone by one of the great windows overlooking the terrace. The room was full of smoke and heaped ashtrays stood next to the places the military had vacated.

I knew immediately that he was in a dangerous mood. His opening words were enough:

"Well, Mikoyan," he said. "Are your penals coming home to roost?"

I said we had received a few hundred in Erevan but not yet the numbers expected. He sat down at the end of the long table, leaving me standing in front of him.

"The Soviet Union has been good to Armenia," he said.

I didn't deny it. Before the coming of the Soviets the Armenian people had been under the Turkish boot. Five years before the coming of the Soviets the Armenians had suffered, in 1915, the full fury of the modern world's first genocide. By systematic shooting, starving and beating the Turkish "Special Organizations" had murdered almost a million Armenian civilians. The new Soviet government was spared the problem of following a success.

"What have you to complain of?" Kuba asked, soft-voiced. "Your Armenians are highly placed in the academic world. There are Armenians in the ministries of trade and industry . . . your church, which you hang on to, is left undisturbed . . ."

All this was true. Visitors from other autonomous republics would often remark enviously on the share of Soviet resources we Armenians were able to command, and in particular how free the Gregorian Church had been for the most part from persecution.

"And yet you still riot in the streets against the mobilization order. Your young men, Mikoyan, still refuse their sacred duty. Why?"

How could I tell him at this late stage. Nationalism was sweeping the republics. Most other men would have known already.

"I believe Armenia, small as it is, occupies an important part in influencing the attitudes of our Central Asian and Transcaucasian republics," Kuba said. "As we used to say, it's Armenia that greases the slope."

He stood up and waddled in his Joseph Stalin walk toward the great double door. Opening it for me, he said:

"Deliver to me an ordered, disciplined Armenia. You have days, rather than weeks."

Like his uncle Anastas, the man who had served all masters and still died in bed, Mikoyan was a survivor. He took his official car into Moscow center and changed to a taxi at the Rossiya Hotel. At Sheremetyevo Airport he took a flight not direct to Erevan, but first to Leningrad, and caught a connection to the Armenian capital. He later calculated he arrived there just steps ahead of Kuba's arresting officers.

Chapter Thirty-nine

AMONG THE MANY hundreds of senior officials who decided to leave Moscow for a week or two were Peter Rinsky and his friend. Fired by the talk in Mother Hubbard's they had come to the decision to take a short holiday in Georgia. The fact that it was to be at the port of Batumi along the coast from Turkey, Peter Rinsky told himself, was of no importance. But he now had a name in his pocket of someone who would sail them to Turkey.

So although they assured each other that they had every intention of returning to Moscow, they nevertheless packed the valuables from their shared apartment with care.

Their intention was to drive south in Peter Rinsky's Zhiguli-Fiat and he had already secured ample gasoline ration tickets (necessary under the new Fuel Economy Measures) for the long journey.

We set out on the morning after the first Penal Brigades arrived at the Kazan Station [Peter Rinsky recounted]. It was a fine clear morning as we started, although the weather at this time can change like two sides of a knife. Finding the ring-road after no more than a slight spat between us, we were out onto the road to Podolsk in no time. By lunch, we had already completed the first 125 miles of our journey, arriving in the quite dreadful industrial town of Tula just before midmorning.

If central Tula is uninviting, and it is, the awful monotony of its southern suburb, Nove-Tulsky, is enough to chill the heart. Yet men and women live here and sweat in the great iron-ore smelting works for the long ruble and attend political meetings and stand in queues and suffer shortages. Can it really be Russia's role to suffer *always?*

The convoy of Army trucks had struggled since nightfall toward the town of Vologda. On the snow-covered road the chained wheels skidded, gripped and skidded again as the convoy crawled forward at ten miles an hour. Twenty-five *zeks* and three guards to a truck, they had shivered together beneath the canvas coverings praying that the journey would soon end.

Only as the late dawn began to break could the drivers see the lights of Vologda ahead. Even so the trucks edged forward for another hour or more until, first, houses began to appear on either side of the road, then a small church and finally lines of apartment blocks. With the outskirts of the city came a miraculous drop in the wind's bite.

The convoy halted in a small square surrounded by low-built concrete offices. There was no sign of the inhabitants, and the guards, climbing down from the back of the trucks, conferred with the drivers. In the back the zeks, all from Leningrad prisons on their way north to Vorkuta, could hear the baffled exchanges of the soldiers on the road.

There was no one, it seemed, in the KGB headquarters to which they had been ordered to report. Did they now go on into the middle of the town? Or wait here?

The captain in command was hesitant. He had brought his charges by cattle car from Leningrad as far as Cherepovets on the edge of the great lake. There he had been ordered to transfer the 250 prisoners to motor transport. Why? The rail transport officer at Cherepovets declined to say. Someone else hinted at difficult conditions for rail traffic through Vologda to the north. Yet no one could possibly have imagined that the motor vehicles could make the journey along the frozen, barely visible track to the wilderness of Vorkuta. The captain begged to know what his instructions were on arriving at Vologda. The transportation officer told him that that depended entirely on the situation. In all this bureaucratic confusion nobody mentioned the returning penals and their disruption of the rail system. Nobody wished to be guilty of spreading malicious anti-Soviet rumor. However true.

At midmorning the suburban KGB office was still closed and the only people the convoy captain had seen on the streets hurried nervously along as if hugging the doorways for protection. He had allowed the prisoners down from the trucks to relieve themselves, but he had no rations to distribute and precious little petrol for the vehicles.

He had decided he would go on to the town center alone and inquire at the main KGB headquarters building when he first heard the approaching commotion. He was crossing the square to investigate when a shabby mob of men came drifting round the corner. There were probably twenty or thirty of them, mostly drunk, and he could tell immediately by their remnants of uniform (even though most of them wore nonregulation fur hats and sometimes coats) that they were, or had recently been, members of a Penal Brigade.

He flipped open the top of his pistol holster, a more or less automatic gesture, and stepped out toward them.

They stopped, as he expected. But their further reaction was less than expected. With all eyes on his approach they began to chant . . . left, right, left, right . . . !

Angrily he stopped in front of them to ragged cries of *halt!*

"Line up, you men," he shouted. "Get in line there."

They cheered.

From the trucks the soldiers watched. The prisoners peered through splits in the canvas and passed back information to the others.

More ragged men drifted into the square from other side streets. The guards drew closer to their vehicles.

Stubbornly the young captain stood his ground. His thumb was twitching on his pistol holster. "Get back . . ." he shouted above the jeers.

A stone the size of a fist hit him in the cheek. His head snapped to one side, his fur cap was knocked askew. As he reeled under the blow a man ran from the front of the crowd and kicked him violently in the legs. Another reached out and tore at the captain's leather cross-belt.

Two guards, not 50 yards away, watched in horror. One fired his rifle high above the crowd surrounding the fallen officer. A man from among the newcomers hurled a short ax at the guard who had fired the shot. The ax flashed past him and clattered against the metal side of the truck, but the young guard dropped his rifle and scrambled back behind the vehicle.

There were over 200 men in the square now, most ranged in a half circle round the parked convoy, shouting abuse at the white-faced guards. The captain had disappeared in a mass of shouting, kicking men.

From the back of the crowd came the sound of glass smashing. A moment or two later a chair sailed over the heads of the men and crashed down on the hood of one of the trucks. The guards, their rifles across their chests, not daring to point them for fear of further provoking the penals, flinched as a second chair flew across their heads and shattered a windscreen behind them.

"Release the *zeks,*" the crowd of men took up the chant. "Release the *zeks* . . ."

The guards were pressed tight against the sides of the vehicles now; the closest, unshaven, dark-eyed faces were not five yards away. Each side realized the guards' weapons were all but useless.

A shower of missiles struck the vehicles and fell or broke on the ground—books, table lamps, bottles, another chair. The guards, ducking, ran for the back of the trucks as the penals closed in. The soldiers' rifles were snatched from them, they were dragged by the collars of their overcoats away from the back of the trucks. A gauntlet opened toward the side streets across the square. The first guard stumbled forward, his arms shielding his bare head from the blows. The flat of a rifle butt wacked against the back of his neck. As he pitched forward two more guards ran past him, and others in threes and fours, arms protecting their heads, while the jeers and blows of the penals rained down upon them.

From the back of the leading truck, Joseph Densky was the first to jump down. He stood for a moment among the cheering penals, then, his round snub-nosed face turned up toward the other prisoners hesitating in the truck.

"You hang if you stay, Brothers, that's for certain."

Then he turned round and moved through the crowd of penals, shaking hands, slapping backs until he reached the edge of the square and disappeared from sight.

All that day Zoya and Laryssa continued along the railway track. By early afternoon they had finished the last of their bread, but both felt confident that they would soon reach some habitation. What story they would make up then they were still not sure. They were, after all, *zeks* and hundreds of miles from their Gulag area. Having come this far from Krasibirsk they found it impossible to decide whether to surrender to the nearest militia post or to make good their escape.

But in the meantime they were both driven by a similar urge to make progress down the track and that, they could see by the red-and-white ten-mile poles, they were certainly making.

It was another bright, cold day, the vast skies a hazy blue-gray and the wind hardly enough to shake the tops of the snow-covered pines.

The track itself was almost clear of snow, the plow on the front of the penal's train having cleared it to a few inches above the ties. It made for a strangely irregular step onto the timber and then down into the deeper snow but they both, that first full day, suffered no more discomfort than aching calf muscles.

Their second night was colder than the first. By agreement if either of them was unable to sleep she was to wake the other. Laryssa still had a half-pocketful of rough *mahorka* tobacco which she had stolen from the cattle car and a box of matches. With a twist of newspaper, which every *zek* carries in the small of his back for extra warmth, they could make cigarettes.

It was not long after midnight when Zoya was woken by Laryssa's hand shaking her shoulder. And as she opened her eyes she saw that Laryssa was sitting up. Her face was in darkness but something about her conveyed immediately tension and fear.

Zoya was about to speak when Laryssa put her hand over her mouth and with the other hand pulled her up into a sitting position. Closer to her face now Zoya could see that her eyes were wide with fear.

"Listen . . ." Laryssa whispered.

Zoya sat rigid, terror communicated by her friend's eyes and by the compulsive grip on her arm. Then she heard it. Incalculably distant or near, she had no way of telling, but the wolf's howl rose and fell on the wind.

It was taken up by others. Again it was impossible to tell how far away, or even for certain, from which direction.

"We must light a fire," Zoya said. "Quickly."

She got up and started snapping the young pine branches from the trees, shaking snow off and throwing them down in a heap. Laryssa had withdrawn one of the precious sheets of newspaper from inside her shirt, and lighting it, thrust it under the pile of pine fronds.

The resinous greenery caught almost immediately and flames leapt upward casting frightening shadows into the forest.

It was an unbearably long night. Throughout it they kept the fire burning, but each trip for new branches now meant straying a few steps further into the forest and away from the comforting light of the fire.

All night the wolves howled, mocking it seemed sometimes, threatening always. But as the first light began to reveal the shape of the trees, the howling died away leaving the two trembling, exhausted girls staring dark-eyed at each other over the embers of the fire.

They finished the little vodka they had left and each broke off a branch to use as a staff. As they scrambled down now onto the track, there was no remnant left of their confidence of yesterday. Before them stretched a wearying day's march and after that the terrors of another night.

The weather had changed, too. It was not as cold, but the light was strangely uncertain as if a full dawn was reluctant to break. The wind which had arisen in the night to carry the keening of the wolves now blew harder, but sporadically, gusting for a few moments and then dying away to little or nothing. Despite their time in a northern camp, neither girl recognized the telltale signs of a rising blizzard, the terrifying Siberian purga.

They were making much slower progress now as the red-and-white markers showed. Once, in midmorning, they both stopped in horror as the howling of the wolves was carried on a gust of wind. As they trudged on they watched the forested banks on either side of the track, both convinced, though neither prepared to say it, that the pack was following, waiting only for the night.

By midday there was some change in the terrain. No longer was it possible to see the line of a perfectly flat track or (when the banks on either side were low) across an infinity of snowfields and woods. The ground now rose and fell gently. On either side the forest seemed to close in on the railway, sometimes rising steeply, hemming in the narrow track, sometimes falling away below them.

It was early afternoon when they heard the wolves again and this time there was no doubt about the direction of the dreadful keening. The light was fading and the slight rise before them made it in any case impossible to see more than a few hundred yards. But the howling came from there, from between the banks of snow and rising forest, from somewhere on the track itself, directly ahead.

With that single-minded instinct for flight they both looked back along the track from where they had come. Two lines of footprints leading back into the gloom showed the melancholic hopelessness of retreat. Yet the answering howls as wolf called to wolf were a presage of the terrors ahead.

Then they heard the woman's scream. Carried on or away by the wind, it was faint, uncertain and charged with fear.

They stood together trembling in the middle of the track.

"We must go," Zoya said.

Laryssa nodded, unable to speak.

"We've got sticks. Wolves can be frightened, too."

Again the woman's scream, nearer it seemed now and harsh with blind panic. The two girls began to stumble forward toward the rise in the track ahead.

The top of the slope was no more than a hundred yards away, but by the time they reached it the woman's screams were shrill in their ears. Their hearts were beating wildly and a fearful excitement knotted their legs.

At the top of the rise they stopped. Below them, not 20 yards away, Anna Maccari flailed her arms against the surrounding wolves. One, two, three at a time they leapt forward, snarling and snapping, tearing at her long coat, dragging her to her knees, before she stumbled up again screaming wildly, running, stopping, staggering forward as a lean gray shape hurled itself at her back.

The two women had no thoughts and perhaps no fear. Running forward they shouted and screamed, waving the sticks in the air.

The wolves pulled back, hesitant. The nearest to the approaching girls snarled and retreated and turned again. The whole pack of perhaps fifteen wolves stood for a moment, stock still, the breath pluming from their nostrils. Then they turned, as if directed, and raced silently across the snowbank for the forest beyond.

Anna fell to her knees, her head hanging. As they ran forward they could see the shuddering movements of her body. But the sobbing gave off no sound.

She was bleeding from a dozen places. Below her knees her work trousers hung in strips of bloody cloth, her shin bones visible through the torn flesh. Worst was the gash in her neck where the blood pumped into her matted hair and soaked the shoulder of her quilted coat.

Zoya had seen enough accidents at Panaka to know that there was little to be done out there in the wilds. She bound the wounds as well as she could, tearing strips from her shirt, but at Anna's neck the blood continued to pump through.

They laid her down beside the track on a bed of fir branches and lit a fire beside her. It was dark now but neither Zoya nor Laryssa gave any thoughts to the wolves. It was a fear they had conquered, a fear replaced by another, that Anna Maccari would not survive the night.

At first she did little more than mumble and sometimes pray. Then as she grew weaker she became strangely more coherent. She knew she was dying.

"In the cattle car," she murmured, "I lost my reason. I screamed and shouted and bit at each of the men that came down on me. When I was no more use to them they threw me out into the snow . . ." For a few minutes she was silent, breathing heavily and occasionally smiling vacantly up at them. Then she began to speak. "I walked . . . I walked all night away from the train. And in the early morning the wolves came. I could see them sometimes, waiting up on the hillside. I climbed up away from them on the other side of the banking. That's when I saw lights, I think I saw lights, a cottage, a house . . ." Her head turned toward the east. "Not far . . ."

Energized by hope they tore branches from the fir trees and laced and wove them into a rough stretcher. Placing Anna upon it they started off at midnight dragging the stretcher through the trackless forest in the direction of lights that may have only existed in Anna's imagination.

At about two o'clock the purga struck. It came at first with a gentle snowfall, heavy flakes drifting down as they emerged from a wooded hill. Anna was unconscious now, the snow behind them spotted by the continuous dripping of her blood. But the light was there. One solitary firefly glowing distantly through the falling snow.

As the wind rose they struggled forward. The snow, driving now, battered their faces and tore the stretcher from their hands. As they fumbled wildly to recover their grip the howling wind propelled the icy whiteness like a streaming curtain across their path. They could see neither the light ahead nor the shape of the ground below their feet.

Their only instinct now was to fall and roll into a ball and hide beneath the snow from the battering of this terrible wind.

They found themselves among trees again, tearing and scratching at them in alliance with the wind. In the white darkness the ground gave under them. Their screams, torn from their mouths, were lost as they tumbled forward, the stretcher rolling and crashing down with them.

Even then they made efforts to climb from the gulley, to drag the stretcher up with them until finally, without a word spoken or even attempted, they fell back into the shelter of the overhanging bank and surrendered to fatigue and hopelessness and the numbing cold,

Long before dawn the fierce wind began to abate, the snow thinned and stopped. By first light the purga had moved on.

Zoya woke with the desperate fear that she was alone. The stretcher was a hump of snow, a grave. Laryssa was curled beneath the ice overhang of the bank, her body no more than dusted with snow. She stirred and sat up facing Zoya, wild-eyed. Her lips were cracked and swollen, her eyes puffy with bruises.

Anna was dead. Perhaps she had been dead long before they reached the wood. They had no way of knowing.

They smoked a cigarette between torn lips, looking from time to time toward the white mound and Anna's face from which they had brushed the snow. They had no words for each other.

When the cigarette was finished they climbed the bank to the top of the gulley. They were in a thin wood of leafless oak and lime trees. Behind them, less than 500 yards away, smoke rose from the chimney of a wooden hut. At the height of the purga they had dragged the stretcher past the hut, past Anna's only hope of survival.

Chapter Forty

IT WAS NOT incompetence on the part of the Investigating Officer Gregory Platonov which caused the delay. The same morning on which he completed his preliminary investigation of the fire at Razina Street he had been instructed by his superiors to concentrate all efforts on a series of new fire-bomb attacks on Asiatic workers' hostels in the New Districts.

Had he been a less conscientious officer, Platonov would have signed the Razina Street Fire Report as he had several times been requested to do by the Senior Fire Officer. But Platonov was acutely conscious that he had still not interviewed the one surviving guard. After a further call from his Fire Service colleague, Platonov decided on the evening of December 17th to visit the guard on his own time.

Wheezing heavily at the end of each sentence the guard invited Platonov into a small flat crammed with plastic items of furniture and decoration.

The guard was under some misapprehension about the purpose of Platonov's visit. "As you can guess," he said, "I'm not the man I was. After an experience like that who would be? But if you're investigating my disability pension claim, then what you see before you is a seriously sick man."

Platonov's eyes alighted on the full ashtray on the table.

"And Comrade, if you're looking at the ashtray, assure yourself that it is not me that smokes, not anymore . . ."

"I'm not here to investigate your pension claim," Platonov told him. "I'm here, Comrade, to establish culpability, you understand me?"

"You want to blame someone for the fire?"

"It didn't start itself."

"An electrical fault?"

"Very doubtful."

The guard wheezed angrily. "You say you're not here on the subject of my pension but if any blame comes to rest on me, would I still get a pension?"

"A jail sentence more like," Platonov said laconically.

"Ah . . . I've got it," the guard said, his triumph momentarily obscuring his anger. "This is the way it's worked, is it? I've applied three weeks running for this pension and still not even received the forms."

A plastic bird on a shelf at Platonov's eye level swung downward, dipped its beak into a tray of water and swung upright again. Platonov had long learned that an investigation can often profit from a subject's anger.

"You look fit enough to me," he said.

"Fit," the guard spluttered. "I'm not fit, any doctor can tell you I'm not fit. But when it comes to stopping a man's disability pension, it's my pittance you're after. Nobody else is going to suffer."

"The other guards died in the fire, remember."

"Will I ever forget? But we weren't the only ones on the sixth floor. What about Comrade Letsukov?"

"What about him?" Platonov asked, his interest quickening.

"I know for a fact he was working late that day. I spoke to him in the office. But you can depend upon it, *he* won't lose his pension when the time comes."

Before he left, Platonov took a full statement from the guard. He had no need to look up his copy of Letsukov's statement. He remembered clearly that he had said that he had left at the normal time. Strangely Letuskov's secretary had corroborated his evidence.

Back in his own apartment Platonov considered the possibility of an office romance. But the statement he had just taken from the guard made it clear the girl had left alone—and that Letsukov's departure was more than half an hour later.

The Investigating Officer sat with his pipe empty, staring at the television set with the sound turned down. He could well understand Letsukov not admitting that he had worked late once he'd heard about the fire. But the girl . . . why had the girl risked backing him up?

Platonov went back to the possibility of a romance. But the girl was married and as ugly as sin and Letsukov was a good-looking young bachelor. No, that equation did not work.

On the silent television screen the picture showed the Moscow Dynamo Stadium. Conscientious as Platonov was, he turned up the volume as the two soccer teams lined up for the kickoff.

From some Gulag areas the amnesty evacuation was proceeding in a more or less orderly manner. Along the Trans-Siberian Railway where rolling stock was more readily available, almost 200,000 penals were transported west in the first two weeks of the amnesty operation. Some of these were routed through Moscow with very much the results that Sophie de Nerval recorded. But in mid-December, militia protests to the Gulag headquarters at the Lubyanka to slow down the rate of penals passing through the capital led to the fatal decision to create staging posts some 30 miles from Moscow at Noginsk and Pavlovsky Posad. At Noginsk four new factory buildings were taken over, the area hastily enclosed in a barbed wire fence and soup kitchens erected in each of the buildings. At Pavlovsky a long line of railway warehouses were emptied and the existing chain-link fencing supplemented with a series of rapidly improvised watchtowers.

Within a week 80,000 men had been herded into the Noginsk complex and a further 60,000 into the Pavlovsky warehouses. For the moment the exhausted men in these areas were acquiescent, but nobody in Gulag authority thought it necessary to tell them why exactly they were being held where they were. For the moment, with adequate food and straw Army mattresses, the penals ate and slept. The questions would come later.

On the northern approaches to Moscow no such order prevailed. The scarcity of rolling stock and the incompetence of the railway authorities were important factors. After the first days when possibly 10,000 reached Moscow's northern stations (where Sophie de Nerval had recorded their arrival) another factor entered the equation. Along the single-track approach to Moscow, across the northern Urals from Krasibirsk and down through Pechora, Ukhta, Kotlas, Velsk and Vologda, rumor spread like fire through straw.

Six long freight trains loaded with men had already passed through Pechora, but in each case during the night and without incident. But that morning the town committee had received messages from Vologda (to the south of Pechora) where Moscow orders to delay a penal train had caused a serious riot, bloodily suppressed by the local KGB forces. A second telephone call from Krasibirsk warned of a trainload of mutinous armed penals shortly to approach Pechora.

The committee now panicked and urgently contacted the *oblast* chairman, who in turn demanded from Moscow the deployment of the brigade of the Uzbek National Division at Pechora. With extreme reluctance Sovcom, the Combined Command Headquarters, ordered the Uzbek brigade to place itself under strictly temporary command of KGB headquarters, Pechora.

The senior officer there was an ageing KGB major who had never before commanded a unit of more than a hundred men. Now, under command, he found himself with an Uzbek junior general and nearly 3,000 troops.

His orders were to stop the approaching train at all costs and to arrest those of the penals prepared to surrender. These orders were transmitted to the Uzbek unit and a position was chosen for the operation some six miles beyond Pechora outside the township of Velinsky where the track passed through a deep wooded cutting.

Across the track a barricade of rock and felled trees was built (the major considered ripping up a section of line but decided that would be to exceed his orders) and the Uzbek troops were deployed in the woods on both sides of the cutting.

The Uzbeks' armament was of the oldest type. Their heavy weapons in fact consisted of Oerlikon guns captured from the German Army in the Hitler War. Against even light modern artillery they were totally ineffective.

Dragged by horses or manhandled into place, the Oerlikons were now ranged along both sides of the hill overlooking the railway track.

With some confidence the KGB major sat with the Uzbek general in the command vehicle awaiting the coming of the train.

At this point a duplication of orders came into play.

At No. 17 Air Training School outside Vologda, orders had been received from an entirely different channel from the one which had resulted in the deployment of the Pechora Uzbek brigade.

After the debacle at Krasibirsk the KGB commander had radioed a highly colored description of events direct to the Lubyanka. The new Defense Minister, General Dora, informed Semyon Kuba that in the absence of adequate KGB forces, he proposed to invoke the agreement at the Second Archangelskoye Conference to call in a limited air strike against the mutinous penals. Their train was now somewhere north of Pechora in an uninhabited area. The operation could remain entirely secret.

In Stalin's former apartments at the Kremlin's Poteshny Palace Semyon Kuba voiced his doubts: drawing on his pipe he told General Dora that he was concerned at the lack of political will in the higher echelons of the Armed Forces. "We, in the Party," he said, "have allowed ourselves to be overwhelmed by the new military sciences. We have retreated before these young generals with their incomprehensible jargon and their ever-increasing demands on the budget. Most seriously we have ignored their political education."

"I am in full agreement," Dora said.

"The military leadership has become an anti-Party force. Even old Kolnikov has been persuaded to offer his support."

"As Defense Minister, I intend to make it my early task to improve political control at all military levels."

Kuba nodded airily and walked across to the window which looked down onto a small courtyard. He was conscious of Stalin's shadow on his shoulder. He knew what he had to do but the precise timing still eluded him.

He turned back to Dora. "At a most crucial point in our Soviet history," he said, "Joseph Stalin faced this same problem. Two years before the Hitlerites launched their attack he, too, was faced with an anti-Party clique in the officer corps."

Even Dora swallowed hard. When Stalin had struck at the Red Army in 1938 he had executed half of all officers over the rank of colonel. In the first year of the war the great purge had left the Red Army virtually leaderless.

"When the moment comes, when these temporary crises have been settled, I will know how to act," Kuba pointed his pipe. "As he did." The pipe indicated somewhere near the middle of the room, as if Joseph Stalin himself were standing with his quiet merciless smile, there in the middle of the red Turkey carpet.

"And in the meantime?"

"In the meantime, I agree to your proposal. When invoking the Archangelskoye Agreements, emphasize that this is one single request and highly unlikely to be repeated. Stress that there is no breakdown in Security Forces' capability but that the distances involved require a Soviet Air Force intervention to protect a Soviet town."

Dora left immediately to transmit his request. Through the Air Defense Force chain of command the order was relayed within an hour to No. 17 Air Training School, Vologda.

The briefing was precise. Instructors from the school were to fly a sortie against the train approaching Pechora with MIG-19 training aircraft, armed with underwing rocket missiles. The slow speed of the training aircraft was intended to increase accuracy in an operation where no retaliation was possible.

A flight of six aircraft took off from Vologda at 12:30 that day, each MIG-19 flown by an experienced instructor pilot. Three-quarters of an hour later the aircraft passed over Pechora and picked up the railway line north.

They sighted the train immediately. It was stationary in a narrow cutting, not ideal for air attack. From their height at the first pass they were unable to see that a great barricade of stone blocked the train's progress.

It had arrived at the cutting less than fifteen minutes earlier. Its driver, an ex-engineer sergeant, had applied the brakes when he saw the huge stone pile on the track. As the train halted the Uzbeks in the hillsides had watched armed men jump down and take up positions along the banking.

For a minute or two the KGB major had waited. When his powerful loudspeaker equipment echoed his voice through the cutting he announced that the hills were full of regular soldiers with heavy weapons. He gave them five minutes to surrender.

In the hills the Uzbek gunners sat behind their Oerlikons. Along the snowbanks down in the cutting the penals began to shout up to the unseen men in the hills. And many of the voices calling on the troops not to fire on old soldiers were calling in Uzbek!

In the hills Uzbek voices shouted back. Some, hidden only 20 yards away among the snow-covered rocks, half stood, their rifles pointing in the air. The penals responded, climbing head and shoulders above the bank. The major roared instructions over the loudspeaker for all troops to retain cover. The penals jeered and invited their Uzbek brothers out in the open as they themselves now were. Rifles were thrown aside. Troops came streaming out of the hills until penals and regular troops were now hopelessly intermixed.

It was at this moment that the flight of MIG-19s passed overhead. For a few moments the roar of their engines faded as the aircraft disappeared, then the MIGs burst into sight along the narrow cutting, in line ahead not more than 50 yards above the top of the train.

It was a maneuver worthy of the instructors' skill. The rockets exploded with a terrifying crackle of flame-tinged black smoke, shattering the cattle cars crammed with men. Beside the track soldiers and penals were torn to pieces. Burning bodies were hurled across the snowbanks.

When the slow-flying MIGs came in for the second pass, the Uzbek gunners swung the barrels of their Oerlikons. Streams of cannon shells poured into the air. While the first and second aircraft emerged safely at the far end of the cutting, the third, fourth and fifth each exploded in turn and the last somersaulted dramatically onto its back, hurtling tail first into the hillside with a shattering impact.

Soldiers and penals cheered together. The KGB major reversed the command vehicle and drove wildly down the narrow hillside track. Beside him the Uzbek general sat white-faced, without speaking.

The disaster at Velinsky was the first occasion on which troops of a National Division were used against the penal threat. On later occasions some, even the majority of the National Divisions, obeyed their orders and suppressed the Penal Brigades they had been ranged against. But from Velinsky onward no local KGB commander or area military commander completely trusted a National Division. Since just these divisions constituted by now a large part of the Soviet Army's third-line reserve in the northern regions of Moscow, the options of military planners were severely limited in their handling of the Penal Brigades.

*   *   *

Investigating Officer Platonov reexamined Letsukov's secretary the evening after the Moscow Dynamo soccer match.

"You knew Comrade Letsukov had already left because his jacket was no longer there?"

"That is correct."

"You then locked the inner door, the door to his office?"

"Yes, Comrade."

"Does Comrade Letsukov often work late?"

"I am invariably the last to leave the office," the girl said. "None of the men have ever seen the lights turned out to my knowledge."

No, there was no office romance here, Platonov realized, not even a little illicit passion for Letsukov on his secretary's part.

So Letsukov *had* taken his coat. And *had,* it seemed, allowed himself to be locked in his office (he of course had a key, too) by the departing secretary. And all this strange behavior was *before* the fire.

The dogged Platonov worked late into that night. At the Examination Sheds where the burned and broken contents of the sixth-floor offices were kept until Platonov's signature on the Fire Report allowed them to be disposed of, he examined minutely every item. The fireproof filing cabinets interested him most. They had been crushed under tons of falling concrete. Locks had burst open and in some cases the side wall of the cabinets had been pierced.

Platonov knew the key system in use in the office so he concentrated on those filing cabinets which Letsukov's keys would not open. Each cabinet whose lock had burst carried at least one enormous dent in the side where falling concrete had caved in the metal. It was possible to relate, in almost every case, an impact to a burst lock or collapsed file drawer. Where there was no evidence of the impact, the drawer locks held. Except in the case of the Estonian file. And when he examined that drawer more closely he could see that the brass edging to the lock was misshapen, on one side bent inward and on the other side of the keyhole, bent *outward.*

No conceivable impact from the falling concrete could have bent that half-inch brass strip outward. But leverage could.

Platonov proceeded carefully. The next day was Saturday, which enabled him to interview the Department Head at his home.

Zelmetsky was a very worried man. "The Estonian file did contain one critical piece of information," he said, and told Platonov about General Avgust Pork's prisoner who had revealed the names of other so-called Free Trade Unionists.

"Were the three men arrested?"

Zelmetsky sat silent. "No," he said after a moment or two. "All three men had left their work hostel before the officers arrived. None of them have been seen since."

Platonov nodded. "In your opinion, Comrade Zelmetsky," he said, "is it conceivable that Letsukov might have illegal contacts with this movement?"

"It's his function to investigate these movements."

"Could there be a better cover for a man who was sympathetic to their cause?"

Zelmetsky shook his head slowly. "No, there could not." He paused, "What will you do now, Comrade?"

Platonov began to fill his pipe. "I am an investigating officer with the Arson Squad. If I am right, Letsukov is guilty of an act of arson which falls within my compass. But if I am right, then an altogether more serious question is also involved. The Lubyanka must be informed. From now on the investigation must be turned over to them."

Chapter Forty-one

To ANYONE OLD enough to have remembered the early days of the Revolution, the scenes in the camps of Noginsk and Pavlovsky would have been entirely familiar. Under the perimeter guard system, the penals were free to drift about within the huge compound as they chose. In the first days it was possible to see men standing on piles of crates haranguing great crowds of penals. Shortly afterward committees were formed and, for the distribution of food and what little information was available, the penals divided themselves into national groups of a thousand men. Nobody knows quite when it began but within a week or two the groups were referring to themselves ironically as Gulag Regiments. Soon the titles became accepted—the 1st (Vorkuta) Gulag Regiment, the 10th (Kolyma) Gulag Regiment. . . .

Perhaps the guards or the ration delivery troops carried the terminology from Pavlovsky to Noginsk, but within that first fortnight, in both camps, anarchic in some cases, ordered in others, the Gulag Regiment became the basic unit of the penals' own administration.

One of the penals at Pavlovsky at this time was to become in later years the distinguished historian of the Georgian nation, C. G. Kodadze. Years later he wrote this description:

I find what happened at Pavlovsky and indeed at Noginsk, too, at that time can only be understood by reference to the way medieval European men sought to organize themselves. I am not, of course, talking of Marxist views of feudalism. I mean associations more like the English inns of court or the old European universities and in particular the free companies of brigands—ex-soldiers who roamed France in the fourteenth century with cheerfully self-mocking names like the Society for Profit or the Society for Acquisition. There are many other examples in medieval times, the Teutonic Knights, for example, the Crusaders themselves . . .

In the same way that the Knights Templars of medieval universities would have an English Hall or a French Hall, we divided in a remarkably short time into national units of Armenians or Kirghizians or Uzbeks, and like medieval freebooters self-mockingly adopted the title of Gulag Regiments.

Powerful personalities arose among us. I remember the soldier-orator Oblinsky in particular. He was a Slav, a Belorussian I believe, and he spent his days in Pavlovsky haranguing the penals, ramming home the questions that were troubling all of us: Has the General Amnesty been revoked? Why are we back behind barbed wire and watchtowers? Are we prisoners or are we free?

And the greatest question of all was whether we would ever consent to return to Siberia, would we ever go back without fighting for our lives?

The earliest arrivals had been at Noginsk and Pavlovsky for almost a month now and suspicion of the authorities' intentions had hardened into the conviction that we were to be sent back. Every night in that last week at Pavlovsky, committees went from each Gulag Regiment to the central warehouse where they and figures like Oblinsky debated our uncertain future.

Sometime in mid-December it was decided that Oblinsky would carry a demand to the camp commandant (whom we had never seen) requiring an answer to the question: Are we prisoners or free?

To this day I do not know the name of the commandant of our camp. I do not know whether Oblinsky was ever able to present our petition in full. I don't know if he sat in a warm office discussing our concerns over a bottle of vodka or if he was forced to speak standing in the snow on some office steps.

I only know, as we all know, the result. On the morning after Oblinsky had left the Gulag committees with their commission to discover the truth about our position, his body was found, as dawn broke, hanging from the wooden bar of the main gate.

Ralph Merton of the London *Times* returned home that week (expelled for writing consistent anti-Soviet propaganda) and wrote the following piece for the December 14 issue:

The General Amnesty, a concession to the Party Chairmen in the autonomous republics of the Soviet Union, must now be seen as a disaster. Nobody (except the KGB and presumably the Army) knows the full numbers of penals involved, but reports from towns to the north and east of Moscow are that one, perhaps two hundred thousand men are being held in camps outside the capital while improvised arrangements are being made to return them to their homes. These homes, in almost every case, are in the national republics of Transcaucasia and Soviet Central Asia.

Those penals already seen in the areas of the Moscow stations in no sense appear to be possessed with patience and their unruliness, at best, and riotous indiscipline at other times is barely controllable by the Moscow militia.

The atmosphere in Moscow is beginning to be one of a town under siege. During the morning a large student Rodinist mob from the University fought a pitched battle with returning penals at the Pavelets Station. Shots were fired and there were large numbers of casualties on both sides.

The mobilization crisis in the republics (which everybody in Moscow now seems to know about) has created an even more intense bitterness among Russians toward what they call the "Asiatics."

Queues are everywhere in the capital and power failures, unannounced and often lengthy, add to the tense edginess which pervades the atmosphere.

But behind all this, another crisis is looming. Sources in the Soviet Army claim they are expecting another purge of Stalinist proportions. Semyon Kuba is undoubtedly unhappy about what is believed to be the Army's virtual refusal to accept an internal security role, i.e., to back the Party all the way. But the Army is not yet convinced that Semyon Kuba is the leader of the future. Still the question of Natalya Roginova remains unresolved. It is certain that Kuba has engaged in intense bargaining within the Party and the Politburo itself to get himself named Party Chairman and President. It is equally certain that until he achieves this he lacks the authority to force the Army to perform as he wishes. But until the question of Natalya Roginova is disposed of, perhaps by a massive show trial, the Army remains on the fence. And why Roginova's trial has not yet taken place is still anybody's guess.

Chapter Forty-two

"OUT HERE," THE old trapper said, "we build a fire, a big, blazing fire."
Laryssa shook her head in horror.

I put my arm around her, Zoya's account continues. "The ground's frozen hard," I said, "we could not get over a foot down."

Still she shook her head. The old man shrugged, raising his eyes toward me.

I could find no other way to persuade her. "The wolves, Laryssa," I said urgently, "she has to be protected from the wolves."

Perhaps I'd said too much, or just said what we all three knew. Laryssa went outside and I could hear her being sick in the snow. When she came back she looked from the old trapper to myself and nodded, bursting into tears.

That afternoon we built the pyre. The old man lifted Anna's body onto it while Laryssa sat in the hut, her hands over her ears to keep out the crackling of the fire. I sat with my arm around her, trying in vain to stifle my imagination.

As the smoke from the fire drifted down the chimney or through the cracks around the door, Laryssa fell to her knees and began to pray.

I, sad heathen, sat watching her and listening to the trapper's boots in the snow as he came to the wood stack for more wood.

We knew him as Zityakin. He never offered us another name, and it soon became easy enough to call him that. He was a true Siberian born far east of here in a town he described as if it were a capital city with streetlights and concrete buildings. I still can't remember the name.

He had been a *zek*. He had no need to admit that. His vocabulary and his kindness to us were admission enough.

He had thought when we first knocked on his door after the night of the purga that we were escapees from one of the many camps in the area of Pechora, which, he told us, was the town about 30 miles away. Had we been from one of the local camps he claimed he would have turned us away to protect himself from the inevitable searches. But I didn't believe him even so.

He was one of the most gentle men I have met in my life. I even include Anton. Although he trapped and shot wild animals for his living, Zityakin could spend the whole day gaining the confidence of a bird with a broken wing. Hypocrisy? It never seemed so in Zityakin.

He was, I suppose, in his sixties, a small grizzled man who had lived all his free life in this climate, and probably his life as a *zek,* too. Over dinner which was the same meal, twice a day, a great boiling pot of vegetable and meat soup and a few hard biscuits, we would ask him about his life. He was openly astonished by most of our questions.

"Tell me, Zityakin," I said one night, emboldened by a bottle of his berry vodka, "do you never miss women in your life out here?"

"Of course," he leaned his elbows on the table and clutched his large jug-ears. "But in the spring," he said, "when I take my furs to the collective. . . . !"

Laryssa broke into peals of laughter. Perhaps she suspected the truth more quickly than I did. But I was still, I suppose in some ways, ignorant of the ways of the world. What happened each year apparently was this: All the hunters and trappers in the area took their furs into the collective at the little town of Velinsky just outside Pechora. It appears Velinsky is a true Siberian town, although we were just east of the Ural Mountains. From Zityakin's account it is one long main street through which the branchline railway runs with clapboard houses on either side. Behind the houses are a few other streets, a Lenin Square and a blue-and-gold domed church of St. Gregory-by-the-Bridge. There is no bridge but the church is full each morning.

Somewhere behind Lenin Square is the building of the Hunters' and Trappers' Collective. There every spring men like Zityakin drive by sleigh two weeks before the snow melts (it seems they can tell without difficulty) and exchange their furs for money and food.

In his description of the town Zityakin had failed to mention the marketplace, and if a grizzled old man can blush, he did when we, mostly Laryssa, pressed him about his spring outing. In the market you could buy, any morning in spring, a live suckling pig or a plump chicken. But you could also buy, with your pocketful of rubles, any of the market women standing behind the stalls.

It had been a way of life since long before the coming of the railway, Zityakin insisted. In the old days perhaps the menfolk were away doing serf-service for the landowner, but now the railway employed almost every able-bodied man in the little community, and whether the men arranged it themselves or the spring schedule demanded it, there were precious few married men in Velinsky when the hunters came to town.

You bought, it appeared, a woman (how he complained at the rising prices) for a week. She took you to her izba, cooked and cleaned for you, and you both shared the bed over the stove at night, children in the room as well, like as not. If you stayed two weeks, it was acceptable to take another woman after the first Sunday. If not, your first choice should be stood by, or the good woman of Velinsky would lose face before her neighbors.

Laryssa of course loved it. As Zityakin told the spring story she would burst into incredulous laughter, but I could see that it appealed to some deep convictions in her nature.

Zityakin wanted us to stay until his spring visit but we had decided that we should make for Velinsky and Pechora beyond in the next few days. We had already been with the old hunter for almost two weeks.

We were, neither Laryssa nor myself, clear about our intentions. We seemed now to have been free so long that we could not really believe that we were still *zeks*. Somehow the fact that we had not escaped from Panaka of our own free will was important. Neither of us really worked it out. But we were both of the same mind as far as our men were concerned. Wherever they were, we wanted to be. For hours we would discuss with Zityakin what might have happened to them and always Laryssa and myself rejected the gloomy conclusion that they had been rounded up after the Panaka mutiny and transported east to follow all our old friends and enemies from Panaka One. Whenever we talked about it I thought of the doctor and that last dreadful plea, and guilt would rise in my throat, but I would turn my mind back to Anton, and that wasn't hard.

There seemed to be, rational or not, no conclusion other than that we should make for Moscow. I knew where Anton's mother lived on a collective farm outside the capital and we had somehow fixed on this as our one hope for information about Bubo and Anton. It was a slender, perhaps stupid hope, but what else did we have? It meant also that we would now become real escapees, and we shuddered to think of how many extra years that could gain us.

One day, after we had been with him for about a month, and this was long, long before spring, Zityakin harnessed up the horse to his sleigh and casually announced as we were washing the last night's stew plates that he would take us into Velinsky. We knew how much he wanted us to stay.

That day we coursed across the snowfields and through the woods, the old horse sure-footed as a goat, or perhaps it was Zityakin's steering that avoided the drifts and took us on long, curving detours to follow hillsides where the wind had swept the snow to a depth of an inch or two.

Most of the journey Zityakin sang, whether or not in the expectation of a village woman that night I have no idea. We didn't ask him about his chances on an unscheduled visit.

We approached Velinsky in the early afternoon while it was still light. As we breasted the brow of the hill we stopped, and Zityakin reined the horse. The little town of Velinsky was below us, straddling the railway track. It was exactly as Zityakin had described it with the church and houses on either side of the track. Except that every building had been reduced to a foursquare of charred wooden posts with thick gray ash heaped inside. Nothing stirred, not a windborne scrap of paper or a wisp of smoke.

We drove down to the town and Zityakin hitched the horse to one of the burned house posts. He told us he was going to the Hunters' Collective Building to see if anything remained. We felt he wanted to be once again alone.

For half an hour we kicked among the frozen ash. There were no bodies, nothing to suggest a battle, except, of course, the burned-out ghost town around us. We walked up to what must have been Lenin Square and an open space beside that was surely Zityakin's market. And we walked to the charred ruin of St. Gregory-by-the-Bridge. We were staring up at the remains of the church when an old woman emerged from a blackened doorway.

We greeted her uncertainly and she us, but as if it were an ordinary day in an ordinary Russian town. She carried a dented tin pail in which there were half a dozen small potatoes rattling in the bottom as she moved her arms to make a point.

She was not mad, as we first thought, or perhaps she was, because she had refused, she told us, to be evacuated after the penals and Uzbeks had burned the town. The story was obviously totally confused in her mind, but I think at last we understood what had happened when the fighter planes attacked the penal train.

We wondered briefly, Laryssa and I, if it was our train. And both, I must admit, fervently hoped it was. We plied the old lady with questions. But she could tell us very little. After setting fire to the town, the Uzbeks and the *zeks* (as she called them) had left in the Uzbek soldiers' motor vehicles, heading south to pick up the big road to Moscow where it begins at Ukhta.

"They'll suffer there, too," the old lady said with some satisfaction.

Zityakin asked us to return with him and stay until spring. By then he believed the townsfolk would have returned and rebuilt Velinsky. We could have told him that if it were to be rebuilt it would be done in concrete and tarpaper roofing. And there would be no room in the planner's dream for a marketplace of women.

It was a sad parting because we had both become deeply attached to him, but as the old horse hauled the sleigh over the hillside, we turned back to the remains of the railway station and the problems of surviving until the next train came in a town of charred corner-posts and frozen ash.

Laryssa and I walked through the square looking for a place to spend the night. On this side of the town there were one or two concrete buildings and they had naturally suffered less than the wooden izbas. We chose in the end the Hunters' Collective Building which had been burned out like the others but at least retained four walls and part of a roof. Laryssa soon had the stove going and a stew cooking from the food Zityakin had left us. I walked across to the church to ask the old lady to join us.

It was dusk and the snow was falling through the fire-ravaged roof. Inside great beams had collapsed as they burned through and now leaned crisscrossed against the charred, painted walls. I had been in churches before certainly, but not often and only with a touring group of Young Pioneers. In Leningrad the churches are mostly there to look at and wonder at the ignorance of the past. So, was it the fact that I was alone here (except for the old woman whose voice I could hear mumbling somewhere near the ikonastasis) that had such a powerful effect on me? Or was it the snow falling through the roof, the strange angles of the dark beams and my own desperate wish to see Anton again?

The old lady had heard me. She picked her way toward me through the rubble and I asked her if she would eat with us tonight.

"No, little daughter," she said, "you'll need your food if you're staying here. And I have plenty."

I was about to go but I suddenly turned back to her. "Let me ask," I said, "have you always believed in God?"

She looked at me with surprise. "Believed in God? Of course. Any sensible person must."

In the half-dark she must have seen my frown.

"Ah," she said, "without God how can you explain our sufferings?"

"Surely, it's the work of men."

She half turned toward the west. "My husband and two sons died at the front," she said as if it had happened only yesterday. "The work of men, but inspired by God."

I thought again that she must be a little mad. I found it impossible to follow her meaning.

"Russia has suffered too much for us not to believe in God," the old woman said, almost to herself. "It must be that we are a chosen people."

"Chosen? For what?"

"Chosen to absorb the sins of the world," she intoned crazily. "To redeem the world with our suffering. We, the Russian people."

I said good-night to her and began to find my way back to the doorway.

"The people," she called after me, "not the *vlasti*, not our rulers sitting in their heated train among the bodies of those poor men."

Was she completely mad? I stopped. I was hungry and anxious to get back to Laryssa but it was the word "train" that made me turn back toward the old woman.

"Which train is this?" I asked her.

She pointed behind her, north. "Along the line," she said. "I've been there and seen it. Two days they've been clearing the track. And the bodies of those poor souls left unburied."

I hurried back to Laryssa and told her what the old woman had said. "A train, full of what she calls the *vlasti,* is held up a few miles along the track."

"You want to go tonight?" Laryssa asked fearfully. She was thinking of the wolves.

But since they'd run from us I no longer feared them. "Let's eat, and get ourselves some sticks, an ax maybe, it's not far."

We finished our dinner and washed in a bucket of boiled snow. In an apartment above the Collective's offices Laryssa had found some clothes not more than badly seared by the heat. We made our selection, Laryssa laughing and pirouetting in the first skirt she had worn since her sentence. Then with knives tucked in our belts, a lantern with a little oil still in it and two pitchforks recovered from what had been a haybarn next door, we set off along the track.

It was an easy journey compared to our last. We were stronger now after a month of Zityakin's food and our lantern and pitchforks gave us confidence. But we heard no wolves.

We saw the lights while we were still several hundred yards away. The *vlasti,* if such they were, seemed to have come prepared. Bright blue arc lights illuminated a deep cuting. As we approached we saw a long line of shattered cattle trucks which had been tipped off the track. A modern diesel locomotive was hauling the ruined cattle trucks back over wooden ramps which had been constructed to raise one set of wheels to the point where the truck would unbalance and crash over its side clear of the track. It was a laborious process which I could well imagine had already taken two days or more.

We approached cautiously, throwing away our pitchforks and extinguishing the lantern. The bright lights which had been set up around the train cast us in darkness. We could see groups of men in uniform and fur-clad women eating and drinking as they stood among those little mounds of snow that could only have been the bodies of the penals.

We joined them. It was, as Laryssa would have said, as easy as that. Within minutes we were the center of a small group munching chicken wings and drinking wine and telling our story of two girls from Velinsky just along the track who had hid in the woods when the penals and Uzbeks fired the town.

The *vlasti* took us to their bosoms.

With the birth of Bukansky's son, Lydia Petrovna had emerged from her crisis.

It was not, by any means, that she had given up hope of seeing Bukansky again. But she had given up immediate hope. When she came out of the hospital she had found an apartment to share with an eccentric lady who insisted on being known as Sophie de Nerval. Despite the differences in their ages they had become close friends and Madame de Nerval now spent her days looking after the child while Lydia worked as a secretary for a local factory manager.

Her evenings she passed, without the aid of vodka, listening to the stories of Madame de Nerval's French noble ancestry and of her plans to emigrate to the West. Sometimes they thought of going together, taking the child with them to a new life. She sold what remained of her Western clothes and was now content to wear the same skirts and dresses as her fellow secretaries on the morning Metro.

Each week she wrote to Bukansky and told him how their child was progressing. She had no way of knowing whether he received the letters.

Sometime in December Igor Bukansky succeeded in bribing an orderly with one of his gold rings to take a message to Kuletsyn. On a scrap of paper he wrote:

"They have me in the *fiksatiya,* the chemical straitjacket, sodium amytal I think. I need above all some statement from you, some word."

But from Barskoye no word came.

In his office in the Lubyanka Colonel Y's preparations for the trial of Natalya Roginova continued. He had not, despite the initial setback, amended his plan to use Igor Bukansky as the chief witness. He could, he knew now, no longer hope that even the course of drugs which Bukansky had undergone would persuade him to hold the interview with the Western press. But he had not, by any means, given up hope.

In the third week of December Bukansky had stood with the doctor in the interview room waiting for the colonel to arrive.

The doctor had paced the small room, swinging round anxiously as footsteps approached along the corridor, drawing breath through his teeth as they passed on.

"Why so nervous, Doctor?" Bukansky asked, sitting on the edge of the table.

The doctor stopped pacing and faced him petulantly. "I could tell by the colonel's voice on the telephone that he was displeased by our result," the doctor said. "Your unrepentant attitudes are extremely distressing."

Bukansky eyed him silently.

"Extremely distressing," the doctor shuffled his feet in his agitation.

"Yes," Bukansky said reflectively. "I understand the colonel reports directly to Semyon Trofimovich himself."

"I believe that's so," the doctor said. "In the circumstances I would have thought even you were capable of seeing reason."

Footsteps sounded along the corridor and stopped at the door to the interview room. Bukansky stood up, laughing. "Are you asking for my help, Doctor? Are you really asking for my help!"

The colonel entered and coolly dismissed the doctor. As he took off his coat and hat he could see that Bukansky had emerged from the period of the *fiksatiya*, weakened physically but with his spirit undimmed.

"You look well, Bukansky." He sat down, placing his cigarettes and lighter on the table in front of him.

"Should I not, Colonel? Am I not in the care of some of the Soviet Union's foremost medical specialists?" He sat down opposite the colonel.

"Yet the doctors tell me the treatment has not been successful."

"I'm surprised to hear it. For my part," Bukansky reached out and took one of the colonel's cigarettes, "I seem to see things clearer than ever."

The colonel flicked his lighter across the table to Bukansky. "We're men of the system, you and me. Keep your games for that poor mouse of a doctor. I want something from you and I'm prepared to pay in return."

"You want me as chief prosecuting witness at the trial of Natalya Roginova."

"Yes."

"And you want me to stand up and tell a pack of lies."

"Not lies, Bukansky. What have lies to do with it?"

"Lies, Colonel."

The colonel laughed.

"It's true of course," Bukansky said, "that in our system, of which as you say we are both men, we live with mendacity. But what you're asking me to do is to set some seal on Natalya Roginova's fate. I will have no part in making things easier for you."

The colonel pursed his lips. "You realize the trial will go ahead anyway."

"Perhaps."

"And your evidence will be read into the record."

"Not by me."

"No. But it's a footling difference, Bukansky," the colonel urged. "Do it yourself and take your freedom. We'll take you to court anyway. You'll be seen to be taken *into* the trial, you will be seen *leaving*. It's enough."

"It's far too much," Bukansky said. "When will this trial take place?"

"You will be informed later," the colonel rose and circled the table. "I would like to believe," he said slowly, "that in your circumstances, I, too, would have behaved the same way. So far."

Bukansky was immediately alert to the menace of that final qualification.

"So far?"

"Yes. Because if we go a step further I would not find it admirable if you continued to refuse your cooperation."

Bukansky placed two large hands flat on the table and stared directly at the colonel. He knew he was no longer dealing with a man like the doctor.

"One thinks of exile for instance," the colonel said, "to remote regions of Siberia. A life among the stinking Yakuts. Admirable people, but try as we might to change their ways, they still stink."

Bukansky laughed shortly. "You don't expect to frighten me with that prospect, Colonel. Not after my stay here."

"No, no," the colonel sat down again. "Why should exile frighten you?"

"Come to the point then."

"I will. But first consider the disadvantaged life, even in our society which stresses equality, for let's say a child brought up out in the east. And for a mother, too." He paused. "Especially one accustomed to the best the Western world can produce."

It was as if an icicle had pierced his chest. He sat staring down at the patterned plastic of the table.

"Yes, Bukansky, Lydia Petrovna has borne you a son. Despite persuasion from many sources, she refused an abortion. Strange she should love you, given the considerable difference in your ages."

Bukansky's hands covered his face.

"Now," the colonel said, "control yourself, my dear man. And ask yourself this question—can you now reasonably refuse your cooperation?"

Bukansky reached slowly for another of the colonel's cigarettes. "All this may be lies," he said.

The colonel unbuttoned the flap of his sidepocket and took out a bundle of letters. He passed them across the table. "A quick glance, that's all we've time for."

He waited while Bukansky desperately leafed through the letters reading a sentence here, another there. Then he leaned over and took the bundle back.

"Am I not to be able to read them in peace?" Bukansky asked, swallowing hard.

"You are an unrepentant, Bukansky," the colonel said harshly. "When you decide to cooperate, the letters are yours. And so for that matter is Lydia Petrovna and your son."

He took his cigarettes and buttoned them into his pocket. "I can give you until tomorrow. After that you'll be of no use to us."

"This system of which we've been speaking," Bukansky said, "tell me why it should keep its promise. Why, after I'm no more use to it, should it release me?"

"It will." He threw his coat over one arm and picked up his hat.

"Will it, Colonel? Will our system release *me*, Bukansky, someone who knows the West, knows how to smuggle a *samizdat* memoir to London or New York? Will it, Colonel?"

"Your only hope is to believe it will," the colonel said, and pausing at the door to nod confirmation of his own words, he left.

That night Bukansky sat writing at a table among the shuffling figures in long gray dressing gowns. When he had finished he took his remaining gold ring and went in search of the orderly.

At three o'clock that morning a patrolling guard discovered the body of a man on the snow-covered path below an open seventh-floor window. No one, in the subsequent inquiry, was able to establish how Patient Igor Alexandrovich Bukansky acquired a key to unlock the normally secure armor-plate window.

Chapter Forty-three

DURING THE EARLY hours of December 20th, the penals in the great Pavlovsky compound tore down the chain-link fence and marched out. Before this vast assemblage of men, the guards on the improvised machine-gun platforms fearfully held their fire. In the intense cold, the Gulag Regiments, each flying a rough-sewn national flag of one of the autonomous republics, formed up on the Moscow highway and set out for the capital. They were going home.

Perhaps messengers were dispatched to Noginsk, or perhaps an independent decision had been taken there, but however it happened, the men in the smaller camp broke out of their compound at just after dawn. In long ragged columns they, too, set off on the 25-mile march to the city. Like the Pavlovsky Gulag Regiments they were unarmed.

In the early dawn the two columns marched roughly parallel routes for the first hours. The Noginsk column, with the more direct route to Moscow's eastern suburbs, found itself only a half-mile behind the Pavlovsky Gulags where the two roads joined at the M8 highway. The commissary of each Gulag Regiment was adequately stocked. The dawn was cold but not intolerable. As they marched the regiments sang the sad convict songs of Siberia.

The train journey [wrote Zoya], for all its comfort and good food, was a nightmare. Every town along the way seemed crowded with penals. We passed through stations where hundreds of men were sleeping on the platforms, others where militiamen were struggling to control them, yet others where the penals themselves seemed to be in control. Then bricks and iron bars would be hurled at the windows as our train sped through.

At night, as we got closer to Moscow, we could see the fires blazing in towns on either side of the railway line. From the train, at least, our impression was that the whole area north of the capital was in the grip of anarchy.

I remember the blue-and-white station boards announcing our arrival in Vologda. It was early morning and we could see a pall of smoke drifting across the town. The outskirts seemed empty of people and vehicles except for a few trucks abandoned in the middle of the street or a burned-out trolleybus turned on its side.

Then to our alarm we heard the train's brakes squealing, jerking us forward violently onto the official and his wife and daughter in the seats opposite.

As the train crept forward slowly through the marshaling yards we could see that Vologda Station was a burned-out skeleton of iron work.

We stopped. Hanging out of our broken window (we had received a brick through it at the last station) I saw that the men on the locomotive had jumped down and were trying to swing the canvas water funnel across the top of the engine. I also saw through the fretwork of black metal, a group of perhaps fifty horsemen galloping down the street toward the station.

Within moments the whole train was an uproar of screaming women and frightened men. The horsemen galloped through the wrecked station, swerving round obstacles and leaping fallen iron girders with incredible skill. There was no need to see their faces to know that they were Asiatics from one of the horse-worshipping Central Asian Republics. Or to know that they were penals.

We were dragged from the train and lined up along the platform. Any man carrying a gun was taken off and shot before our eyes. These men, these penals, brutalized by years in the northeast camps, had no pity for the *vlasti* when they found them trembling and begging before them.

Other horsemen arrived as I stood shivering in the dawn cold, huddled next to Laryssa. One or two of the women, especially the middle-aged ones in silk dresses and furs, were hauled away and we heard their screams of panic from behind the station a few moments later. But Laryssa and I were left untouched. The penals (we hadn't yet learned to call them Gulag Regiments) were more interested in dragging the *vlasti's* possessions from the cattle trucks at the back of the train.

We were still awaiting our fate when one of the horsemen, galloping along the line of trembling *vlasti,* reined his horse violently and turned back toward *me.*

I looked up terrified into the Asiatic face that smiled toothlessly down at me. "It's the doctor," he said. He swung off his horse and came over and clasped me in his arms. "It's the doctor from Panaka Five," he repeated, stepping back. "What are you doing with this trainload of rubbish, Comrade Doctor?"

Laryssa giggled near hysterically. The man turned. "I remember you, too," he said, shaking her hand.

"I was the doctor's assistant," Laryssa said hurriedly. "Look, we just fell in with this lot for the ride back to Moscow. Tell us what's happening, friend."

One or two of the officials and their wives gathered round us, but the Asiatic gave them such a menacing hiss of hate that they quickly fell back.

"We're taking the train," he said. He gestured to the officials. "The ordure here will be lucky to get away with their lives."

"You're going to Moscow?"

"Moscow first, then home."

"Take us to Moscow," Laryssa said. "Can you do that?"

He shrugged. "That depends on the cripple," he said doubtfully.

"The cripple?" I could see something light up in Laryssa's face.

"The cripple's our leader now. He gives the orders."

We were taken before Bubo in the headquarters he had set up in Lenin Square.

I had never seen Laryssa so happy. After the tears and kisses she kept circling him, prodding at his chest or arm with her finger as if in need of further confirmation that it was really her man.

And Anton was with him. Not in the office when we arrived. In fact he was down at the station supervising the loading of their horses into the cattle cars. Bubo sent a messenger down straight away but simply to tell Anton that he was wanted in Lenin Square immediately. No mention was to be made of me.

Then he poured vodka.

I can remember the nervous excitement of that short wait, even to this day. I think Bubo must have been telling Laryssa what had happened since we were separated at Panaka. Then I hardly absorbed a single sentence. Only later the pieces came together.

When I heard his step outside and his voice shouting to Bubo I ran toward the door and literally exploded into his arms as the brute walked in.

He was no more coherent than I was. "Holy Jesus," he kept saying, "Holy Mother of God" and all sorts of other strange incantations from his village past. And then I was just like Laryssa. I could not stop touching his hand or edging close to him as we four drank our way through a bottle.

The first toast, I'm glad to say we remembered, was to Anna.

Walking hand in hand through the town we selected a house. The door was open, the rooms richly furnished. What did we care that afternoon about the fate of the *vlasti* who had lived here? We wandered from floor to floor. In the kitchen we collected glasses and a bottle of vodka, in the vaulted bedroom we lit a huge fire and threw ourselves upon the wide oak bed.

I undressed him. Undressing myself I nestled between his legs.

He reached down touching my hair as my tongue ran over him. "If we'd met somewhere else, other than in Panaka," he said, "would we still feel like this about each other?"

I looked up. "We did," I reminded him. "We met in Leningrad."

"Ah, but you were a child then. Sixteen."

"Seventeen. And desperately in love with you from our first meeting."

He pulled me up toward him. "How can a man without words say what he feels about you, Zoyushka?"

We lay silent together.

"In the West," he said, "lovers swear some sort of oath. 'For richer, for poorer, in sickness and in health . . .'" he rolled on top of me, parting my legs . . . "with my body I thee worship."

When Bubo and Anton had recovered consciousness that last night in Panaka, not all of the penals had marched away with Barkut Khan.

Many who hated and feared the Khans had hidden in the forest. Others simply slept through the departure. On the appel-square that day they had gathered under the only leader they knew, Bubo, whom some of them had worked with in the woods.

Since that day they had battled their way out of the far north. In Krasibirsk they had found an old locomotive in a siding and succeeded in hitching a string of cattle trucks to it. After a journey of nearly 250 miles they had been attacked by a militia unit and scattered in the snow forests. When the survivors re-formed they had marched on the next town and fought a pitched battle with staves and flying rocks against other penals. Somewhere outside the town they had found buses and trucks and in them completed another vast section of the journey. Then they had found the horses. In an abandoned cavalry stable outside Vologda where they were intending to sleep the night they had found stall upon stall, in five great stable blocks, of shaggy cossack ponies. Their former riders, a Kirghiz National Division, had deserted with an earlier trainload of penals, one of the many units on the penals' route home which simply joined them in those wild times.

The old Russian grooms had handed the horses over without complaint and Bubo's ragbag army had become a mounted unit.

Our gentle friend Bubo kept discipline with a ferocity which shocked Laryssa and me. He would have a man flogged or even shot for failure to carry out an order. And yet, at any time, a man could announce that he no longer intended to ride with Bubo and would then be free to leave unmolested. As a system it seemed to work. These strange men, changed in God knows what fashion by their experiences, worshiped their limping leader.

In the station the cattle trucks had been loaded with horses, the boiler filled with water and the tender piled high with coal. A messenger came up to find Anton and myself to say that food and ammunition were being loaded now. The train would be ready to leave at any time Bubo ordered.

Until this point I had not even thought about what happened next. I was with Anton again; Laryssa was with Bubo. After the nights at Krasibirsk and the nights of horror with the wolves, it was enough to be here.

But more serious decisions were afoot. Sadder ones, too.

Bubo, I think must have read my thoughts when we returned to Lenin Square.

"Some things have changed, Zoyenka," he said gently. "We should talk now."

His tone was enough. I nodded although not understanding. Anton's face was suddenly set and troubled. Laryssa became silent.

"Great things are about to happen in Moscow," Bubo began. "Or at least we believe and hope so. There are tens of thousands of penals there already. Thousands more are coming in from the north every day. According to the telex upstairs, in the eastern suburbs there's already fighting. Over a hundred thousand men, some with weapons, have organized themselves into Gulag Regiments. It could be that just one more push is needed."

I told him I didn't understand. I looked at Anton but he was biting his lip, looking down at the carpet.

"This whole area north of Moscow is already out of control," Bubo said urgently. "Not only the penals but some of the regular Army divisions have broken loose. Asiatic units here in Vologda have refused to attack us and have turned over their arms instead . . ."

"You want to overthrow the government?" Laryssa said in an awed voice. "Overthrow the Party?"

"I want to string up every corrupt judge and every camp guard. I want to burn every Security Board record, I want to catch the *vlasti* in their big apartments and turn them out into the snow to work. I want to tear down this whole stinking pigsty that they've built on Lenin's Revolution. And if I can't," he said, "I want to tear down Moscow with my bare hands."

I looked at him in amazement.

"I'm not mad, Zoyenka," he said quietly. "Or not more mad than I have every right to be, or any of us has. But by God what it's done to us, that city!" His voice rose again. "If ever there was a Babylon, Moscow it *must* be. Not a city of harmless lust and drink and idleness, but a true Babylonian seat of power, greed and cruelty, from Ivan the Terrible to Stalin the Cruel, from Leonid Brezhnev to Semyon Trofimovich Kuba. Moscow must be destroyed!"

Moscovia delenda est ran like a scarlet ribbon through my mind. Bubo was from Bratsk, I myself from Leningrad, others among Bubo's penal followers were from the far corners of Moscow's old empire. In those few moments I believed like Bubo that if Babylon was destroyed its empire of misery must crumble with it.

"No," said Anton, his hand coming down flat on the table. "Our duty is to save ourselves. To take advantage of the anarchy and go south to a Black Sea port. We're a few thousand men, perhaps tens of thousands, but what can we do against tanks and aircraft?"

"If we get into the city they'll have to destroy Moscow to destroy us," Bubo said.

"Then they'll destroy Moscow, you know that," Anton said.

"So be it," Bubo grunted. "So be it."

I of course knew where I stood, although much of what Bubo said appealed to my vengeful imagination. But for Laryssa it was different. Bubo put no weight on her. Far from it. "You have to decide, little one," he said. "But I think you would be mad to come with me. Go south with Anton and Zoya. Find some fishing village with a boat to hire."

He pulled out of his pocket a canvas bag and spilled coins on the table. They were English sovereigns, gold francs, silver dollars and a few heavy gold rubles. He reached down and took the gold rubles from the scatter of coins. "Take them, Anton," he said. "Let them remind you of your mother's gold ruble."

The rest of the money he pushed back in the bag and handed it to Laryssa. She took it silently.

I ran round the desk to hug Bubo. Like Anton I had no wish to be there when Laryssa said good-bye.

She came stumbling out into the cold five minutes later. As we crunched across the frozen snow down to the station she was shaken by bouts of sobbing.

"We'll take the last coach," Anton said, as we picked our way through the burned-out station. "He'll let us off in the outskirts of the city."

That evening the train stopped in some Moscow suburb and Anton, Laryssa and myself climbed down onto the track.

As the train lumbered slowly away, the old-fashioned whistle blew twice, then twice again. Anton and I put our arms round Laryssa as we watched the last red light fade. I never saw Bubo again. And neither, of course, did Laryssa . . .

In the huge courtyard of the new American Embassy the green bus rolled forward and stopped under the eyes of the Marine guards.

As the American, British and German embassy staffs crossed toward it, David Butler ticked them off on his pad. Jack Bennerman, the American evacuation officer, waved to the driver as the door closed and the bus moved slowly away. The journey to Sheremetyevo Airport on the northwest of the city would take about forty minutes. There a Finnair 747 was waiting within the heavily guarded perimeter.

From beyond the embassy walls the Englishman and American could see the dawn light rising above the city. As the last bus drove into the courtyard the senior embassy staff from half a dozen Western embassies, including two ambassadors, straggled across the courtyard while Jack Bennerman checked off names.

Near the end of the line Tom Yates was walking with Harriet, both hauling heavy leather suitcases.

"Where's Carole?" David Butler asked, looking quickly down the line.

Tom Yates' face was set. "She's not coming."

"What the hell do you mean, she's not coming?" Bennerman said.

"She's not coming, that's what he means. She's staying in Russia with her Russian," Harriet snapped nervously. "Now for God's sake, let's get aboard." She hurried forward.

Yates watched the other two men hesitate. "What is it?" he said bitterly. "Are you both in love with her too?"

Past the Pavelets Station Carole took the Varshovskoye Shosse, then drove south on Highway 5 toward Podolsk.

She was still shaking from what she had heard at Letsukov's apartment. While she was hammering on the door a stranger had wrenched it open angrily. He had stood barefoot in an unbuttoned lumberjack shirt and baggy gray trousers staring at the obviously distraught Westerner opposite him.

When she asked for Letsukov the man had snorted angrily, "It's we who live here now," and he gestured to an unseen family behind him. "The old occupant's gone."

"Where, do you know where?"

Behind the man's head she saw a militia uniform hanging on the cupboard door.

"Where he ought to have been a long time ago is my guess," the man said and closed the door in her face.

There was no traffic on the southern road but the snow was thick and uncleared and she felt she was making agonizingly slow progress. Yet during the afternoon she had reached Podolsk and followed the railway track to the station where Letsukov had met her. For an hour after that in the almost deserted town she had driven through the suburbs looking for the old nineteenth-century Singer Sewing Machine Company building and only as the factory's English sign stood out against the last pink streaks of daylight did she know she was on the right road.

Yet there were still another two hours of false turnings before she found the crossroads where she had last seen Letsukov, and another three or four miles along the lane she had finally abandoned the car.

Without snowshoes, sinking in the deep drifts almost to her waist, Carole had been in a state of collapse when Kitty and Volodya pulled her into the hut.

While Volodya took off her coat, Kitty wrapped her in a blanket and dragged her chair closer to the stove.

"He was arrested last week," Kitty said. "Just after you were here." She brought a glass of tea and placed it carefully between Carole's hands.

"As far as we can understand," Volodya said, "he was arrested for something to do with a fire at his office."

"Do they know about the newspaper?"

"It won't take them long to make the connection. We're moving the presses tonight," Kitty said.

The hot tea burned her fingers. "Do you know where he's being held?" Carole asked.

"At the Lubyanka," Volodya said shortly.

"He's being questioned?"

They both nodded.

"Tortured you mean?" Carole said. She was shivering too much to hold the tea and Kitty stepped forward and took it from her.

Kitty placed the glass of tea on the stove-top and looked up at her husband. "You can tell her," she said. "There can be no harm now. Not now that we're just leaving ourselves."

Volodya hesitated. "Do you remember us talking of a man named Joseph Densky?"

"Yes. He's in prison in Leningrad."

"No longer. Joseph Densky is now in Moscow. He has called on every Moscow worker to demonstrate tomorrow night. 'Have courage,' he said. 'No one can guess what Moscow or even Russia will be the next morning.'"

Chapter Forty-four

THE MORNING WORE on and the Gulag Regiments marched and sang through the thickening eastern suburbs of Moscow. Women hung from their tower-block windows and men on the street watched silently. But all through that long morning there were no incidents as nearly 150,000 men passed through the first suburban villages of the capital.

At Balashika they stopped. In the drab factory suburb the field kitchens were set up along the highway.

Before this day the Balashika suburb had little claim to fame. Its industries were electrical and railway engineering. The new soap factory infused the area with an uncertain, sweet-putrid odor and the workers lived in concrete apartments among graffiti, peeling paint and abandoned, rusting junk. It was no worse than Glasgow, South Chicago or Nanterre, but it fell far short of a brave new world.

Still the Gulag Regiments might have passed peacefully through Balashika if one of the Tajik regiments had not seen signs in their national language over a gateway in a long anonymous brick wall in the back streets behind the main highway.

A few of the more energetic spirits had rattled the gates and pressed their faces between the bars and yelled "Salom . . . Salom."

At first the low barrack-like blocks had remained silent, apparently empty, then a window had opened and a smiling face appeared shouting "Salom" in response.

"Hasan Rudaki!" the penals had called. Other windows opened. "Hasan Rudaki!" men shouted down in reply.

As the tenth-century founder of Tajik national literature Rudaki's name had become a battle cry for Tajik independence.

A great crowd of penals was now gathering round the barrack gates. One man clambered up the ironwork and dropped down the other side.

Others followed. Soon there were fifty or sixty in the courtyard, dancing and singing Tajik songs.

"Come and join us, Brothers," they invited the conscripts. "We're on our way home, Brothers, come home with us!"

In the headquarter block the Russian colonel and staff of the newly formed Tajik Artillery Training Regiment phoned the militia post at Balashika center. He described the situation at the barracks and requested aid before it got out of hand.

The local militia officer ordered his full force of forty men into their personnel carriers. He knew no way to avoid the request. Yet he could guess what effect militia armored vehicles would have on the penals. With their 30-millimeter guns loaded with riot control gas shells and the men in plastic visors beneath their steel helmets the five vehicles drove by side streets to the barracks.

There is no available account of the next hour. The only thing certain is the outcome. By midday when the Gulag Regimental commanders managed to restore order among their men, the armored vehicles of the militia were burning in the courtyard, the Russian staff had been stripped to their underpants and now huddled fearfully in the snow, and the armory had been broken open and looted. Rifles, light machine guns and ammunition were seized by the Gulag penals. More significantly, three batteries of old German 88 guns, the deadly infantry support artillery of Hitler's Wehrmacht, were hauled out and linked up to tow trucks.

It was early afternoon when the ragged army got onto the road again and the mood had changed. The Baltic formations—Latvians, Estonians and Lithuanians—took the lead. Of all the Gulag Regiments they were the most fiercely anti-Russian. Among them there was no laughter and no songs. Six miles ahead, on the road to the city, a screen of armed militia lay in wait.

The great Trinity Monastery of Saint Sergei dominates the town of Zagorsk, 45 miles north of Moscow. Three hundred yards long and over half as wide, its walls contain two cathedrals and half a dozen churches and chapels. Founded by Saint Sergei in 1345, the monastery was besieged in the Tatar invasions of the next century. It was now a quiet lamp-lit precinct in the middle of Zagorsk, its painted churches and domed cathedrals a secure enclave of old Russia within its walls.

Since March it had been even more secure, guarded by a battalion of uniformed KGB troops, its great seventeenth-century refectory building guarded by armed plainclothesmen who sat outside during their long shifts shivering on wooden benches, running unappreciative eyes over its brightly painted checkerboard exterior.

Inside, above the richly decorated refectory hall were the apartmentsthat Natalya Roginova had occupied since her arrest.

During the afternoon of December 20th, when the chanting of the seminarists in the north section of the monastery murmured through a light snowfall, a green-painted military car drove through the Uspensky Gate. At the checkpoint it stopped and General Rossasky climbed from the back. The KGB guard-lieutenant saluted and followed the young general into the guard post, baffled that no explanation for the visit had yet been offered.

Rossasky, in long gray greatcoat but bareheaded, offered the lieutenant a handful of papers to examine.

"You will see from those, Lieutenant, that I have authority from Army Command to remove Natalya Roginova to a safer region."

The lieutenant had no understanding of the overlapping areas of authority of the Army and Security Forces. But he did know that he would be unwise to agree to anything unless his captain were first informed.

"One moment, Comrade General," he said lifting the phone and cranking the handle.

Rossasky waited, his lower lip pushed out to caress gently his rich black mustache.

The lieutenant frowned and cranked the handle again. "I can't hear it ringing," he said. "Will the Comrade General excuse me while I speak to the guard-commander?"

"No," Rossasky said. "You stay here."

Uncertainly the lieutenant stood his ground. "It is my duty, Comrade General, to report all visitors to the monastery."

The general went to the door and opened it. Three sergeants wearing parachutist insignia on their uniform topcoats entered the post. Each man was armed. Without another glance at the guard-lieutenant Rossasky left the post and got back into his car.

The whole operation was concluded without bloodshed. Within fifteen minutes of the general's arrival at the Uspensky Gate nearly 200 soldiers were moving through the gardens beyond the Gate Church, fanning out to face the seminary and to occupy the watchtowers along the south wall. Individual security men protested but were silenced by the impressive array of generals and colonels arriving at the Refectory Building. Those who seized an opportunity to telephone for instructions from higher KGB authority discovered that the lines had been severed.

After half an hour Natalya Roginova came through the Refectory from her apartment above. Oil lamps burned in iron brackets round the richly painted room. In the lamplight the deep-hued crimson and blue and gold beloved of Old Russia merged in a warmth of color. The officers around her stopped respectfully.

She turned to face them. "You are aware, Comrades," she said quietly, "that this is the great refectory of the monastery of Saint Sergei. On this site six hundred years ago a Russian Army was blessed before marching to victory at Kulikove against the Golden Horde."

She turned again, her eyes slowly traveling round the room. It was as close as she would allow herself to come to a genuflection to Russia's distant past.

In his dacha at Zhukova, Semyon Trofimovich Kuba did not respond to the anxieties of Prime Minister Bukin. If suffering were to be inflicted upon the city of Moscow it would serve to justify the harsh measures necessary to face the future. Moscow could burn. If he had learned one lesson from Joseph Stalin it was that Russians were capable of absorbing an infinitude of suffering.

Of much greater concern to Kuba was the timing of the purge of the Army which he realized, since Bukansky's suicide, was now vitally necessary.

But when Defense Minister Dora arrived with the news of the Army's release of Natalya Roginova, Semyon Kuba knew that a subtle time schedule for the purge was no longer among his options.

While the two others watched him, he sat down at his desk and drafted a telex to all military, militia and KGB units throughout the Soviet Union:

> At a recent conference at Archangelskoye, State Security Minister Kuba and Marshal Kolotkin, in concert, agreed that in these times of international crisis only the closest cooperation between the Soviet Armed Forces and the forces of State Security can liquidate the present threat to the Soviet system. This threat has now revealed itself as an anti-Party movement in sections of the Armed Forces of the Soviet Union. This order, until rescinded, places all Soviet military formations under the direct command of equivalent local KGB and militia commands. Resistance to this order by local military headquarters must be interpreted as evidence of anti-Party activity. Such anti-Soviet elements must be resisted wherever they raise their heads. Only the fullest mobilization of the armed forces of the Bureau of State Security can ensure the defeat of anti-Party elements. All orders which do not come through strict Party and KGB Command channels must be resisted by force if necessary.
>
> The signatories of this order require it to be carried out with the utmost ruthlessness and determination.
>
> Signed: Kuba, Chairman, KGB
> Kolotkin, Marshal of the Soviet Army

Kuba waved the two men over. "Read that."

He stood up from the table while they leaned forward to read what he had written. Bukin nodded at each paragraph. Dora read through to the end and straightened.

"Well?"

"It's a mobilization order for civil war," Dora said.

Chairman Kuba nodded, then turned to Bukin. "Telex this signal to all State Security Bureau Commands. And all military formations."

Bukin took the signal and hurried out.

"I want you to move tonight," Kuba said, turning back to General Dora. "You've got your list. I want every senior officer on it arrested at the first possible moment. It's Katyn forest, Dora," he said grimly. "It's our only chance to save the Revolution."

The door opened and Bukin reentered, his normally flushed face drained white. Behind him six officers came into the room. The leading major general was carrying the signal.

"Semyon Trofimovich," the major general said. "I am instructed to inform you that at an emergency meeting of the Politburo this evening you were removed from all offices of State. Former Chairman of the Party of the Russian Federated Republic Roginova was restored to all her previous offices in the government and the State. I must also inform you that by the same authority of the Politburo, I am instructed to place you in protective custody. Former Prime Minister Bukin and former Defense Minister Dora are also to be placed in protective custody," he ended curtly.

From outside in the extensive grounds of the dacha came the thin clatter of automatic fire. The major general consulted his watch. "We will wait until all opposition has been disposed of," he said.

Semyon Trofimovich Kuba sat down at his desk and took out his pipe. Not looking toward the center of the room, he sucked on the pipestem, one elbow on the desk which Stalin had once used. Try as he might, he could not imagine where he had gone wrong, or how Joseph Vissarionovich might have done better.

Chapter Forty-five

DURING THE NIGHT of December 20th–21st Moscow waited in darkness. Throughout the city, responding to a call in *Iskra* signed by Joseph

Densky, power workers had failed to come in to the night shift, as had transportation workers and snow-plow operators. The only lights on the streets around the city center were now from the slowly moving patrol vehicles of the militia. A few candles glimmered feebly behind apartment windows but the great wedding-cake skyscrapers and hotels of Moscow disappeared now into the darkness of a starless sky.

The only exception was the Kremlin. Operated by their own generators, searchlights, pointing down from the crenellated wall, isolated bright pools of light in the darkness of Red Square. Above the ancient towers of the Kremlin, spotlights hit great rectangles of red cloth writhing slowly in the freezing wind. Perhaps most bizarre of all was the brightly lit multicolored onion domes of St. Basil's against the pitch-black background of the city.

From apartment blocks on the eastern side of the capital a steady trickle of people left to cross to relatives in what were believed to be the safer, southern suburbs. As ever in the land of the Soviets, it was information above all else which was lacking. Rumors of the anarchy in towns north of Moscow had circulated for some days, but while those few Penal Brigades reaching the city rail stations had been more or less contained by the militia, there had been no panic. Then the news began to filter through of a vast ragged army marching through Balashiki and of the failure of the militia to turn them back. And for the first time, too, Muscovites heard the term the Gulag Regiments.

During the night all foreign airlines canceled or diverted their flights to and from Moscow's Sheremetyevo Airport. Long before morning Aeroflot operations had ceased too. While broadcasting continued no mention was made of the crisis and all news items were replaced with programs of patriotic music.

In thousands of apartment blocks throughout the city people speculated on whether or not the *vlasti* had already fled to safety. Some claimed to have seen limousines racing south or west down the privileged center lanes throughout the afternoon. Others said that militia units had been withdrawn from the menaced eastern suburbs to protect just those *vlasti* who were supposed by others to have left. Of certainty there was very little, and more than anything the darkness overhanging the city added to their fears.

Before first light people living in the area of workers' flats around the Kursk Station began to hear scattered rifle-fire and the thud of heavier armament. Coming out onto the balconies they could see, far across the city ring road, points of leaping light as fires started in the Reutov District.

Every apartment now had an appointed watcher at the window whose task it was to report on the advance of the Gulag Regiments. By three or four in the morning the early confidence that the armed militia would turn them back had dissipated. The approaching rifle-fire and buildings burning ever closer were evidence enough of a steady advance by the Gulags. Now the first families of refugees, those without relatives in other parts of the city, began to leave their homes and trudge through the snow-covered streets toward the city center. Soon, from the area of the Aviamotor Metro Station the Shosse Entusiastov was thick with people carrying suitcases and children wrapped in blankets. And for these refugees already moving toward the center of the city, the clatter of militia helicopters and the beams of their headlights shining down from among the dark tower blocks added a new dimension of eeriness to their fears.

At first light it was evident that the city was in chaos. Thousands of refugees tramped westward along Kirov Street past the Lubyanka in Dzerzhinsky Square and on down Marx Prospekt. Thousands more exhausted people huddled for protection in Red Square, along the Kremlin Wall and around the GUM department store. Some lay in the snow, wrapped in sleeping bags or blankets. Others produced small stoves or even lit wood fires to boil kettles for their tea. Like some huge marketplace, which once it had in fact been, Red Square steadily filled with people.

Then the first two shells exploded among them. In indescribable panic the vast crowd scrambled across the snow. The point of impact of each shell was marked by mangled bodies hurled in a bloody ray-like pattern across the trampled snow.

The next two shells struck the GUM department store showering glass over the fleeing crowd. As four more shells were fired in quick succession, women screamed wildly, men cried for help and children lost their parents and scattered for the safety of the side streets.

The Georgian historian, C.G. Kodadze, described that first morning from the point of view of the Gulag Regiments.

In my regiment, and I imagine in most others, too, we had experienced several distinct changes in mood since setting off from the camp at Pavlovsky. To this day I believe that the original intentions of the men were simply to return home. There was this fierce underlying suspicion of the authorities' intentions, and there is no doubt that the regiments were prepared to fight rather than return to Siberia.

But until that first attack upon us by the militia unit at Balashiki I don't believe any of the regiments, except perhaps the Latvians and Estonians, whose bitterness exceeded all others, in any way intended what followed.

During that first night, from Balashiki to the Moscow Ring Road, we were attacked incessantly by militia units using gas and even mortars. And all the rage and desperation of the last years of camp life exploded within us. The Baltic Regiments, as so often, acted first. It was they who set up the first battery of German 88 guns in Ismaylovsky Park and began to shell the city. After that battery was attacked and destroyed by Soviet fighter planes, the Balts located the other guns among apartment blocks and warehouses, where it was impossible to strike at them from the air. In their furious determination to inflict as much damage on the Russian capital as possible the Baltic gunners fired throughout the next morning and early afternoon until the last shell was spent.

But by then the armament of the other Gulag Regiments had received the addition of captured militia mortars and gun-carrying personnel vehicles, and in every street in the Reutov District where my unit, the 5th (Georgian) Gulag Regiment was fighting, you could see a mortar team shelling the militia units to our front.

Probably very few among us stopped to ask ourselves why regular Soviet Army units were not being used by the authorities, but at that time we had no knowledge of the Armed Forces' reinforcement problems nor indeed of the widespread rebellion against the mobilization order in our hometowns. We did know, however, that a unit of an Azerbaijanian National Division had been marched up from south Moscow but had refused to join the battle when it saw that it was expected to fight other Azerbaijanians.

We had no commander, or command organization. But there is no doubt that the ferocious hatred of the Balts spearheaded the attack on the capital, and in that sense most of the Gulag Regiments were indeed following a single objective . . .

And now a new element began to enter the situation. In the eastern suburbs through which the Gulag Regiments had already passed, those people who had remained in their homes began to emerge. At Balashiki, which had seen the first clash, the streets were littered with smoking hulks of vehicles, shop windows were shattered, warehouses burning. Most important of all, there was no visible authority, no militia. At first the people of the district drifted through the streets. Some, furtively, began to rob the bodies of militiamen shot down in the alleys. Then bolder spirits entered wrecked Party offices and began carrying out television sets and the contents of well-stocked canteen refrigerators. The Balashiki Party special store, unknown all these years to the people in the district, was discovered and looted before being burned. It was here in Balashiki that the first Party members were hanged.

Kuntsevo, in the so far unaffected west of the city, the scene of the disturbances on the day of President Romanovsky's funeral, woke that morning to find that the local militia had been drafted into the clashes in the east suburbs. Within hours the old pattern reasserted itself. Street fires were built and food and vodka brought out. Pianos were carried into the cold morning air and dancing began beneath the squalid stilted blocks of flats. Arguments and fights became frequent as the vodka flowed. By midmorning the first Party offices had been ransacked. By the afternoon the militia headquarters was on fire and fuel tanks were exploding in the blazing bus station.

In others of the new districts, too, the smoke pall which hung over the center of the city, the rolling sound of heavy gunfire and the virtual absence of militia forces began to infect the populace. Urban peasants that many of them still were, they began to march on Party offices to drag out filing cases and hack them open and burn their contents. Like the peasantry of the French Revolution they had an atavistic dread of the contractual power of the written word.

By now the ferment in the Soviet Union was matched by a ferment in the West. To accounts of the international crises of the Soviet Union in Transylvania and the Chinese border were added press stories of rioting around the Moscow main stations and the towns of the north. Reports now flowing in from the capitals of the Central Asian and Transcaucasian autonomous republics described massive demonstrations to welcome home returning members of the Penal Brigades. In some cases unconfirmed reports from the southern autonomous republics spoke of fighting breaking out between Russian regular Army units and formations of the National Divisions.

Great shuddering shocks were passing through the Soviet Union. The world looked on in trepidation. There were even rumors that Semyon Kuba had been arrested by the Army.

Then on the morning of December 21st, in a special appeal to the United Nations, Mikoyan's Armenia declared its independence. Former First Secretary Mikoyan announced that he had agreed to a request to form a provisional government.

Within three hours a similar announcement was made from Tbilisi, the capital of the Georgian S.S.R. During the day, Azerbaijan and all four Central Asian Republics east of the Caspian followed suit. Only Kazakhstan, with its nearly fifty percent Russian population and its huge common border with the Russian Federal Republic, remained silent.

The Ukrainian delegate to the United Nations in his first act independent of the Soviet Union called for an emergency session. From governments throughout the world came floods of condemnation or approval. Cuban and Vietnamese radio stations ran hours of confused abuse of the declarations of independence. Chile recognized all new states immediately, as did much of South America. The United States consulted with its European allies and announced that no decisions had been taken in view of the uncertainties in the southern autonomous republics of the

Soviet Union. The very use of the old title implied a cautious refusal to recognize the new Transcaucasian and Central Asian Federations formed within nine hours of Mikoyan's first announcement.

Chapter Forty-six

IN THE LATE afternoon Bubo's mounted units fell upon the northern suburbs of Moscow with the fury of the Tatar horde. They had no plan, no object but to loot and pillage and destroy. Throughout the afternoon around the Kazan Station and across the Sardovoye Koltso clattering hooves pursued screaming citizens. Men were torn from official buildings and shot in lines on the sidewalk; vehicles were burned; no one in uniform escaped the noose hanging from a lamp-bracket or a street sign.

Beyond revenge, Bubo saw a massive act of provocation, an invitation to the workers of Moscow to rise against his own Huns and against the system which had first created them and then failed to protect Moscow from their vengeance.

His hatred was no longer containable. It was a hatred of the Soviets, of the Russians and of all those who had remained silent while the prison trains rattled through their lives, and, once safely out of sight, began again to excuse the failings and praise the achievements of a system which had brought unequaled misery to mankind.

All afternoon he fought, urged his horsemen on. Joined by great mobs of unarmed penals they burned this northeast corner of the hated city into an inferno of collapsing buildings.

Only toward the evening was their fury spent and then, in small groups of six or seven mounted men, they were themselves hunted down by militia units in armored patrol cars. Bubo, the tailor from Bratsk, died trapped in an alleyway, his horse bucking wildly and squealing in pain as the militia bullets ricocheted off the narrow walls. A Tatar death.

From the back of the wood truck Zoya, Anton and Laryssa could see the burning city receding in the distance.

Since dawn they had fought and punched their way through panicked crowds of refugees:

When I had time to draw breath, when I had time to look around me at the burning buildings and the fleeing people, at the frightened, white-faced militiamen and the shells exploding in the streets behind us, I found myself crying with strange exultation. At one moment I recognized Razina Street where I had stood, clasping my pathetic percussion grenade on the morning of Romanovsky's funeral. When I looked up now and saw that the twenty stories of the Rossiya Hotel were on fire above my head I wanted to go into Red Square and stand in the middle of a blazing Kremlin and gloat. I had not, you will see, after the months in Panaka, escaped my own share of madness.

Before midmorning Anton had found an abandoned car with a few centimeters of gasoline still in the tank. It had not taken us far, but driving straight down the Ordynka Boulevard we seemed to bypass the worst of the fighting. By afternoon we were out of the city. There was a lot of luck involved.

After the gasoline ran out we walked. Or rather stumbled in the thick snow on the uncleared highway south of Pavelets Station trying to wave down a passing truck. We never discovered what our crazy woodcutter was doing in his lone ancient truck plowing through the snow toward Podolsk, but then we didn't ask. All that was important was that he stopped and let us climb on the back.

South of Tula things seemed more normal. The snowplows had been out and there was more traffic on the road. Without too much difficulty we got another lift taking us almost 120 miles south to Orel. There, on the Moscow Road, just outside the city, the driver dropped us off at a gasoline point.

It was a fairly new concrete structure built, we heard later, for the 1980 Olympic Games. It had a shabby new hotel attached to it and Anton left with one of Laryssa's silver pieces to see if he could buy us food.

I suppose it was a few minutes later that Laryssa and I heard the raised voices in the filling-station office. We could see the outline of two men and another sitting behind a desk. But what amused us most I suppose was the extraordinary inflections of the two men's voices. They weren't so much rising in anger as high-pitched in sheer fury.

I think Laryssa laughed for the first time that day. "Golden boys," she said.

The problem, as we had no difficulty in overhearing, was their Zhiguli-Fiat, which we now saw was standing in a repair bay beside the pumps. From their exaggerated protests they might have been waiting years for the repair (whatever it was) to be completed.

Then suddenly within the office voices dropped. Perhaps you have to have grown up as a Soviet citizen to know by instinct that money was changing hands.

The two men came out of the office a few minutes later. They were both in their fifties, both exquisitely dressed with graying wings of hair brushed back from their temples. Laryssa immediately put on a remarkable performance. She glanced, apparently casually at the two men, then recoiled in affected surprise.

The two men looked at her in bewilderment.

"Leningrad," she said. "The Saint-Tropez Club."

They looked at each other in alarm. How were they to know that Laryssa knew every illicit drinking club, straight or homosexual, in Leningrad. And there was nothing straight, as she told me afterward, about the Saint-Tropez Club.

"You must have been there, gentlemen," Laryssa said amiably. "It couldn't have been anywhere else."

Naturally they admitted nothing, although when Laryssa said she had worked in the kitchens of the club (quite untrue) for over two years, they relaxed a little. But perhaps it was only when my blond Anton came back that they really became friendly.

And so that was how we got a lift, the three of us crammed in the back of their repaired Zhiguli-Fiat, all the way to Batumi on the coast a few miles along from Turkey. And how the two golden boys, Peter Rinsky and his friend, in that turbulent Georgian port where Russian troops were still fighting a rearguard action against the independence forces, shared with us the precious name of a boatman.

Chapter Forty-seven

IN RED SQUARE the GUM department store, looted of its tawdry stock, was blazing. On the corner of 50th Anniversary of the Revolution Square, fire had gutted both the Intourist and the National Hotels. Along the northeast wall of the Kremlin, across the Alexandrovsky Gardens, the whole of the Prospekt Marksa seemed to be alight. Flames pouring from the huge Rossiya Hotel cast a leaden orange glow over the waters of the Moskva River.

The random shelling had taken a terrible toll of the refugees. Along every sidewalk in the center of the city dark crumpled figures lay in the snow. Some still moved. At the great Botkin Hospital, where Lenin himself had been treated for a gunshot wound, at the ancient Burdenko and the Filatov Children's Hospital, surgeons operated throughout the day and long into the night.

Deep in the Lubyanka Letsukov had heard the shelling. Throughout the day no guard had visited his box cell. No one had slopped soup into the wooden bowl chained to the back of the door. No one had brought a chair and a table and a man to stand behind you when the questions were asked. His neck was swollen out below the skull. His ribs were punched and kicked to a dropsical blue-blackness. If he moved it was to feel the pain in every bone and muscle in his legs and body.

Yet he had told them nothing. From that fact alone he derived a sense of pride that no beating could erase. He knew with certainty that he could hold out against them.

They had used all their resources of terror. In the night men in hoods had flayed him with chains. At dawn he had been menaced with unspeakable suggestions. He held before him the example of Joseph Densky even while he recognized that he would never possess that man's capacity to influence evil. Sometimes he sang through cracked lips. Sometimes he shouted cheerful abuse at the guards. He had learned that above all he must not fear provoking them. Above all he must not be respectful.

Where it began nobody could say. Perhaps before the smoking wreck of the GUM department store, perhaps on the Marx Prospekt or in the gardens of the shell-shattered Polytechnical Museum. Or perhaps in all these places at once. But while the Gulag Regiments slept or rested, while the men from the camps wrapped themselves in the cotton blankets of the shops along Kuybysheva Street, in some unspoken alliance of the dispossessed, the *Iskra* march on the Lubyanka began.

They carried flaring torches even though the buildings still burned around them. They assembled in small groups and joined with other groups. They came together in hundreds and joined with other hundreds. While the Gulag conquerors of the city looked on in bleary approbation they marched toward the Lubyanka.

In Dzerzhinsky Square they gathered in their thousands, the handheld torches umbring the faces of Joseph Densky's Russia.

They faced the gray stone building which had once been the home of the All-Russia Insurance Company and through whose dark Victorian basements, since the Revolution, the prisoners of Dzerzhinsky, Yezhov, Beria, Andropov and Kuba had passed to the hutted camps of Soviet correction.

And now the servants of the system began to melt away. Through side entrances and alleys the secret policemen began to scuttle out. When the great crowd surged forward, those few caught in the courtyards of the prison were trampled underfoot.

Carole Yates found herself swept down one of the green-painted corridors. All around her men tore filing cabinets from the walls and emptied their contents through shattered windows. Thick wads of ribbon-tied records were seized by the crowd below and thrown onto blazing fires in exultant contravention of their red stamp: *To Be Preserved Forever.*

She fought her way through the mass of men at the entrance to the basement rooms as prisoners were handed up across the heads of the crowd, shaven, gray-clad figures, some still trailing chains.

Punching, scratching, fighting with her elbows, she followed him as he was passed across the heads of the crowded men. Only in the courtyard could she reach him, lead him to a corner, lower him down into the oil-stained snow and hold him in her arms.

In the courtyard of the most dreaded prison in the world she rocked him slowly in her arms. "You're safe, darling," she whispered. "The Kremlin's burning. The people of Moscow have risen."

She stroked his torn mouth and bruised cheeks. "I will never part from you again, Alexei," she said, using the Russian form of his name for the first time. "Wherever we go, we go together."

"And wherever we stay?" he forced the words through swollen lips.

"And wherever we stay," she said turning, on her knees in the snow, her arm cradling his head, as the exultant crowds roared and chanted around them and the first flames illuminated the dark, dark passages of Stalin's Lubyanka.

A Far Longer Travail

Chapter Forty-eight

LIKE SOME FOUL cloud the smoke hung above the rooftops. In the dawn, flames and the energy of hate and fear had burned out. From every mound of rubble wisps of smoke rose and faltered. Exhausted men slept beside the dead as the snow fell in some soft pacification of the fury that had been visited upon Moscow.

Encircling the city eight regular Russian divisions, withdrawn from the Transylvania border, awaited the order of Natalya Roginova to advance.

In her speech to the great assemblage in the Oval Room at Archangelskoye, President of the Russian Republic Roginova referred, for the first time, to "the former Soviet Union." While leaders of the one-time vassal states of the Russian Empire applauded, she revealed to the world the new political shape of one-sixth of the earth's surface. The newly constituted Republic of Russia was to stretch, as it had for 200 years, from Leningrad to the Pacific Ocean. The new Republic actively rejected political, military or economic responsibility for any of the autonomous republics of the former Soviet Union. It proposed, however, the closest possible links with the Slav nations of the Ukraine and Belorussia. It specifically renounced *any* military interest in the states of Eastern Europe. The enormous military power of the Russian Republic was, however, available to provide military advice to those nations which requested it.

Then, to a stunned Western world, she announced the new Russian-Japanese State Treaty. In return for the vast resources of Japanese technology and capital, the Russian Republic was to supply energy, raw materials and military assistance in the most far-reaching program ever agreed between two nations on earth.

"What power on earth," she asked, "can menace our *Rodina,* united in this new commonwealth of nations, our great resources linked to the capital and talent of our Japanese neighbor?"

At a simple ceremony on the eve of the first Christmas to be publicly celebrated in Russia since 1917, Natalya Roginova laid a wreath on the grave of Igor Alexandrovich Bukansky. Her efforts to trace Lydia Petrovna and Bukansky's child had been unsuccessful. Rumor reported that they had fled to the West.

Surrounded by her ministers and a group of senior Army officers she had stood in the biting wind while a single trumpeter played a lament. Before the party filed away, the snow was already re-covering the grave.

Perhaps the wheel of fortune is too naturally warped to run true. But I am completing the last pages of this book, where I first conceived it, in the de Nerval château in central France. My mother's blue-leather traveling trunk lies before me. She had carried it and her child, myself (with old Sophie de Nerval's help) hundreds upon hundreds of miles across Russia, to the refugee camps which were set up on Russia's borders during the last agony of the Soviet Union. In one of these camps she died, still a young woman, but not before she had collected accounts, memoirs, copies of diaries from others who had fled and survived the Sovietschina.

I owe to the obsessions of a snobbish old woman my de Nerval name. But I owe, too, to that same Sophie de Nerval, my discovery of the papers my mother had collected. Where else would the old lady will the trunk but to that château in France where she imagined, rightly or not, she had been conceived?

I close the tattered leather trunk before me. In my hand I hold one last scrap of paper. I will include this, too.

The night before she had begun her long journey to the West, my mother received a package from a hospital orderly. The last memoir written by my father, Igor Bukansky, was placed in the trunk. The contents of the letter accompanying the memoir, she never revealed. Only the words on a separate scrap of paper:

For sure. No nightingale inhabits this dark wood,
And yet the trilling comes from there.
These chains are mine, I swear.
As is the gibbet squeak that follows
Such as me.
I ask,
Is it eternity I seek?
Or dreamless sleep beneath my hessian hood?

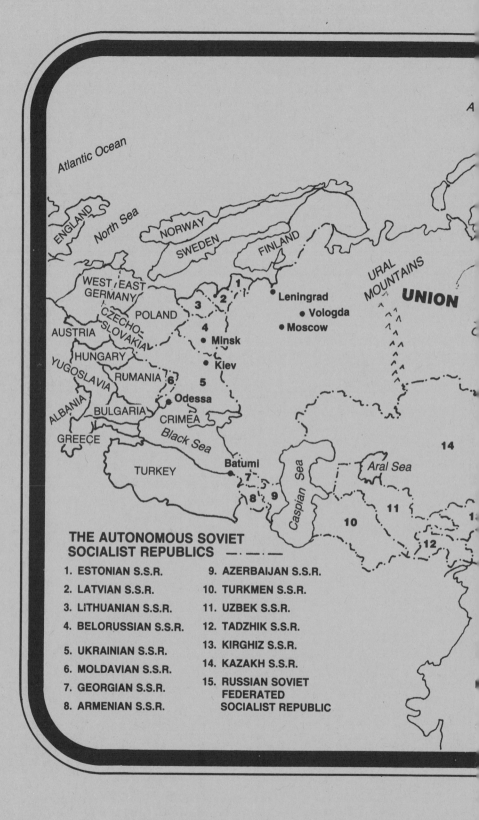

A

Atlantic Ocean

ENGLAND

North Sea

NORWAY

SWEDEN

FINLAND

WEST/EAST
GERMANY

POLAND

CZECHO-
SLOVAKIA

AUSTRIA

HUNGARY

YUGOSLAVIA

RUMANIA

ALBANIA

BULGARIA

GREECE

TURKEY

CRIMEA

Black Sea

1

2

3

4 • Minsk

• Kiev

6 5

• Odessa

• Leningrad

• Vologda

• Moscow

URAL
MOUNTAINS

UNION

Batumi

7

8 9

Caspian Sea

Aral Sea

14

10

11

12

13

THE AUTONOMOUS SOVIET
SOCIALIST REPUBLICS — · — · —

1. ESTONIAN S.S.R.

2. LATVIAN S.S.R.

3. LITHUANIAN S.S.R.

4. BELORUSSIAN S.S.R.

5. UKRAINIAN S.S.R.

6. MOLDAVIAN S.S.R.

7. GEORGIAN S.S.R.

8. ARMENIAN S.S.R.

9. AZERBAIJAN S.S.R.

10. TURKMEN S.S.R.

11. UZBEK S.S.R.

12. TADZHIK S.S.R.

13. KIRGHIZ S.S.R.

14. KAZAKH S.S.R.

15. RUSSIAN SOVIET
    FEDERATED
    SOCIALIST REPUBLIC